The Music of the
STANLEY BROTHERS

MUSIC IN AMERICAN LIFE

*A list of books in the series
appears at the end of this book.*

The Music of the
STANLEY BROTHERS

GARY B. REID

Foreword by Neil V. Rosenberg

UNIVERSITY OF ILLINOIS PRESS
URBANA, CHICAGO, AND SPRINGFIELD

Library of Congress Control Number 2014956949
ISBN 978-0-252-08033-3 (pbk.)
ISBN 978-0-252-09672-3 (e-book)

CONTENTS

ACKNOWLEDGMENTS

In many respects, compiling a history on the recordings of the Stanley Brothers has been a collaborative effort. The first person to attempt to do this was Pete Kuykendall, who conducted interviews with Carter and Ralph Stanley and published his research in a 1961 issue of *Disc Collector* magazine (issue no. 16). A revised version was printed several years later. The Stanley Brothers Fan Club, under the leadership of Fay McGinnis and Norma Fannin, issued a 1966 publication called *Meet the Stanley Brothers: Introductory Book, Biography, Discography, Club Staff.* The discography was "Reprinted from Disc Collector Publications: with thanks to Pete Kuykendall, Lou Denumoustier [*sic*] & Jerry Mills, foreign releases credit of Dave Crisp, Charles Benson, Charles Newman & Rodney McElrea." From 1967 until 1970, a group of dedicated researchers—Walter V. Saunders, Norm Carlson, Robert Ronald, and Nick Barr—under the banner of the Ralph Stanley Fan Club, worked tirelessly to further refine the discography. Their efforts appeared in several Fan Club journals during this time period. It was a circa 1973 *Ralph Stanley International Fan Club Journal*, which I received in 1975, that sparked my interest in the recorded legacy of the Stanley Brothers.

As I began to study the material presented in the *Journal*, I started making notes in the margins . . . tidbits of information I came across that I didn't see listed in the discography. On Thanksgiving Day in 1975, I decided to become proactive about my research. The December issue of *Bluegrass Unlimited* arrived a few days ahead of its issue date, and an article by Frank and Marty Godbey about fiddler and disc jockey Paul Mullins whetted my appetite. The article briefly touched on the tours of duty that Mullins pulled with the Stanley Brothers. But I had to know more. So, I dashed off a letter to Paul, hoping he would reply with a more in-depth description of his time as a Clinch Mountain Boy. I never heard back from him . . . not from this letter anyway. But the process had begun.

Over the years, I have contacted numerous individuals in an attempt to compile a concise as possible Stanley Brothers discography. These have included Ralph Stanley, former Clinch Mountain Boys and guests who appeared on the recordings, label owners and session producers, songwriters, and bluegrass historians. I've also made use of research materials at various libraries, museums, and universities.

From the beginning, Neil Rosenberg has been a supporter, enthusiast, and role model for my endeavors. His 1974 book, *Bill Monroe and his Blue Grass Boys: An Illustrated Discography*, served as a template for much of my research, as did his later collaboration with Charles Wolfe, *The Music of Bill Monroe*. Other scholars and writers have provided much useful information: Mary Katherine Aldin, Bob Artis, Fred Bartenstein, Roy Burke III, Bob Carlin, Eddie Dean, Wayne Erbsen, Nate Gibson, Douglas Gordon, Clarence Green, Scott Hambly, Lance Leroy, Penny Parsons, Dave Samuelson, Ivan Tribe, Bill Vernon, Joe Wilson, Charles Wolfe, and John Wright, as well as the Country Music Foundation's Danny Hatcher, Robert K. Oermann, Ronnie Pugh, and John Rumble, and the staff of the Roanoke, Virginia, Public Library.

This story would not be complete without the remembrances of the Clinch Mountain Boys and guest artists who performed on the various recordings: Chubby Anthony, Johnnie Bonds, Roger Bush, Charlie Cline, Jack Cooke, Vernon Derrick, Henry Dockery, Al Elliott, Howdy Forrester, Barry Glickman, Melvin Goins, Jay Hughes, Curley Lambert, Hazel (Mrs. Pee Wee) Lambert, Bill Lowe, Vernon McIntyre Jr., Red Malone, Benny Martin, Ralph Mayo, Gene Meadows, Joe Meadows, Sonny Miller, Doug Morris, Paul Mullins, Bill Napier, Bobby Osborne, James Shelton, George Shuffler, John Shuffler, Charlie Sizemore, William "Bill" Slaughter, Larry Sparks, Art Stamper, Harold "Red" Stanley, Ray Tate, Earl Taylor, Little Roy Wiggins, Benny Williams, Jim Williams, Lester Woodie, and Art Wooten.

Songwriters likewise added their own insights with commentary about how their songs came to be written or passed to the Stanley Brothers. Among those who shared their recollections with me were Jim Eanes, Cuddles Newsome, Mac Odell, Lance Spencer, Buddy Starcher, and E. P. Williams.

People from the recording industry—label owners, producers, recording engineers, production staff, and Musicians' Union representatives—provided a lot technical information such as recording dates and session locations as well as personal insights. These included Rich-R-Tone's Jim Stanton; Mercury's D. Kilpatrick and Tom Pile; Starday's Martin Haerle; King's Ron Lenhoff and Chuck Seitz; Magnum Recording Studio's Tom Markham and Tom Rose; Gusto/IMG's Moe Lytle, Lawrence Bailey, Virginia Biggs, Amy Brakefield, Judy Larson, Randall Merryman, Dorothy McCormick, and Chuck Young; Wango's Ray Davis; *The World of Folk Music's* Oscar Brand; Cabin Creek's Ola Belle Reed; Rimrock's Wayne and Loys Raney; Rebel/County Records owner David Freeman; and Bonita Maynard of the Musicians' Union Pension Fund.

Tapes of live concert performances provided source material that was issued on albums and CDs. The documentation of these releases added significantly to the discography. The live tapes also provided information about a number of the songs that were recorded in studio settings. In his introductions to these and other songs during live performances, Carter Stanley was fond of offering background information about the selections. In numerous instances, this commentary served as the basis for the song histories that appear throughout the discography. Among those who recorded live shows or made material available were

Benny and Vallie Cain, Larry Ehrlich, Alice Gerrard, Lamar Grier, Don Hoos, Pete Kuykendall, Bill Offenbacher, Mike Seeger, and Peter K. Siegel.

Musicians (in addition to the Clinch Mountain Boys), associates, and friends helped to shade and color the discography. Some were contemporaries of the Stanley Brothers and offered personal recollections. Others were young devotees of the Stanley Sound who provided perspectives, enthusiasm, moral support, and—in some instances—companionship on research road trips. These include Johnnie Bailes, Stephen Brandt, Bill Breazeale, Bill Clifton, John Cohen, Dudley Connell, Lars Deijfen, Bob Ensign, Tom Gray, Gary Henderson, James Leva, David McLaughlin, Frankie Moore, Tracy Schwarz, Mike Seeger, James Stiltner, Eddie Stubbs, Dick Spottswood, and Roland White.

I have been privileged to have a variety of experts serve as readers of the manuscript. Each was invaluable in pointing out errors, suggesting form and substance, and asking probing questions about topics I had overlooked. Grateful appreciation to Heather Brush, Hank Edenborn, Kerry Hay, Johnny Martin, Neil Rosenberg, Peter Thompson, and Richard F. Thompson.

Members of the Stanley families have been very supportive of my efforts over the years to document the music of the Stanley Brothers. Special thanks to Carter and Ralph Stanley for making the music, and to Jeanie Stanley Allinder, Doris Bradley, Bill Stanley, Carter Lee Stanley, and Mary Stanley.

The Stanley Brothers' years in Florida are a separate subset of their overall career. A lot of their recording activities during the late 1950s and early '60s took place there. Helping to put this era in perspective were Charles R. Bisbee Jr. of Jim Walter Homes, Aubrey Fowler, Red and Murphy Henry, Clarence "Cousin Clare" Parker, and Bill Savitz.

Last, and by no means least, as I have navigated through life, my family has been very gracious in affording me time and space in my pursuit of the Stanley Sound. Special thanks to Susan Jordan, Bonnie Leder, Brice Reid, Corey Reid, and Maureen "Mosie" Welch.

GETTING TO KNOW GARY REID

In the summer of 1976 I received a letter from Gary Reid, a man I had never met. By way of introduction, he wrote: "For the past several years now I have been trying to compile a combination biography/discography on the Stanley Brothers and the Clinch Mountain Boys."

He'd sent his letter to me in care of the Country Music Foundation in Nashville, Tennessee, which two years earlier had published my first book, *Bill Monroe and his Blue Grass Boys: An Illustrated Discography*. I'd been writing about bluegrass music since the late 1960s. My first academic article argued that bluegrass became a style in the late 1940s when the Stanley Brothers began copying the sound of Bill Monroe's band.

Gary had read both of these. He asked about several interviews of the Stanley Brothers I'd mentioned in footnotes. "Do published copies of these interviews exist?"

His letter, neatly and politely typewritten on his own letterhead, was the start of a year of intense and frequent correspondence. Nineteen years old and two years out of high school, Gary still lived in the Maryland suburbs north of Washington, DC, where he was born and raised.

His family enjoyed camping. In the early 1970s, at a KOA campground in nearby Indian Springs, his parents noticed a flyer for a bluegrass festival that was going to be held there. Curious, they attended and, in Gary's words, "become converts." Bluegrass was popular in the region, and the most popular local bands were "progressive bluegrass" pioneers—the Country Gentlemen and the Seldom Scene, best sellers and award winners at bluegrass festivals everywhere. But Gary—then a teenager listening to Top 40 radio—wasn't that interested and didn't go with them. In 1973 a family vacation trip included a visit to the *Grand Ole Opry*. "Interesting but not life-changing," he recalled recently.

That fall his high school political science teacher won a police auction in downtown DC. His winnings included "stacks and stacks of then current country music albums," which he offered to sell to Gary at thirty-three cents each. Borrowing a school-owned record player, he listened to the first track of each LP and ended up buying five bluegrass albums—two by Bill Monroe, two by Flatt & Scruggs, and one by the Stanley Brothers.

"I wasn't searching for bluegrass," he recalled. But "something emanating from those grooves completely captivated my attention." The music on the five albums Gary bought that fall came from the early days of bluegrass.

In 1973 the musical genre called "bluegrass" wasn't very old. It's generally accepted that it began with the 1945–48 version of Bill Monroe's Blue Grass Boys, which included Flatt & Scruggs. They were part of the postwar country and western music boom. By 1947 other musicians—like the Stanley Brothers—were basing their music on the sound of that Monroe band. Within a few years, fans were speaking of it as "bluegrass music," though that phrase didn't enter print until 1956, the year Gary was born.

Of the five albums, the Stanley Brothers' in particular moved him. Their band had lasted just two decades, ending with the 1966 death of the older brother, Carter Stanley. Gary began collecting their recordings.

Gary comes from a generation born after bluegrass was established. It was an establishment celebrated in the bluegrass festivals that began in 1965 with reunions of Monroe's early bands to re-create the sounds they'd made on now famous recordings during the preceding two decades.

In the early years of bluegrass, recordings were valued for the favorite songs and tunes they carried and as souvenirs of familiar bands from live performances. By the time Gary came along, recordings had taken on new value as historical documents that showed how the music sounded at the start.

He was interested in what lay behind the recordings: What were the names of the musicians? When and where did they record? He soon discovered that one of the Stanley Brothers, Ralph, was an active solo artist, but he found that while Ralph was willing to help answer such questions, he didn't always recall the details. Gary's search for Carter's answers led him to write me.

Alas, those two "interviews" with Carter I'd footnoted were brief backstage conversations, unrecorded, documented only in notes made soon after. So I was of little assistance there. But I had been working on the Stanley Brothers discography almost as long as I'd been working on the Monroe one, so I was in a position to help. I was pleased to know of a researcher who shared my interest in the history of early bluegrass.

So at the end of August 1976, I sent Gary forty pages of photocopied manuscript—all my Stanley Brothers discographical notes. He wrote back gratefully, "This really put me over the hump." But he was really just getting started. During the next year, Gary wrote me regularly, describing his adventures in learning about the Stanley Brothers. He'd met tape and record collectors, and began traveling to interview people connected with the band—family, friends, and sidemen.

When asked how he found the time to do this research, he told me, "I've been a bank teller for about three years now. They are very good about letting me off for my Stanley trips. Usually I take two weeks with pay and then two weeks without pay." Gary's growing knowledge about the Stanleys was his entrée into the music business. In 1977 he wrote his first album liner notes for a County Records reissue of an obscure out-of-print Stanley Brothers album on the Wango label.

The following year he formed a record company, Copper Creek. "The Best in Traditional Bluegrass Music," its letterhead read. "Traditional Bluegrass"? That was new to me in the mid-1970s. The greater DC area had become a national bluegrass music center through its well-known "progressive" groups like the Seldom Scene. Yet at the height of this popularity a new traditional bluegrass movement was underway in the Washington suburbs. Gary was part of this musical youth movement. His desire to hear and learn about the pioneers of bluegrass was fueled by reissue albums and historical interviews in fan magazines.

It's not surprising that when Copper Creek's first record came out in 1979, it was a 45 single by the Johnson Mountain Boys, local teenagers who had become deeply involved in playing traditional bluegrass. They became one of the stellar bluegrass bands of the 1980s.

Copper Creek's first LP album was a collection of live recordings by the Stanley Brothers, *Shadows of the Past*. Reflecting Gary's research into the Stanley Sound, it was the start of a series of projects that published live Stanley Brothers performances. In 1983 Gary went to work at Rebel Records, the company for which Ralph Stanley recorded. These and other music business connections enabled him to further his research. In 1984 he published a preliminary edition of the Stanley Brothers discography.

In the decades that followed, Gary continued to do research while building Copper Creek into a successful old-time and bluegrass music recording company. His many Stanley Brothers projects—over a hundred at last count—have made him the leading authority on their music.

All of this energy and knowledge has culminated in the book you're reading. Thanks, Gary, for your work—it's much appreciated.

Neil V. Rosenberg
Professor Emeritus of Folklore
Memorial University
St. John's, Newfoundland, Canada

FORMAT OF THE DISCOGRAPHIES

Neil Rosenberg, with additions by Gary Reid

The discographies that follow each chapter are organized chronologically to present the details of the Stanley Brothers' commercial recording career from their first recording session in 1947 to their final session in October of 1966. Here, "commercial recording" is defined as any recording, audio or video or film, that was made available to the general public. The principle unit of organization is the session, which is understood to mean a single period of time at the recording venue on a specific day. Each session unit is arranged as follows:

I. **Session Data**
   A. The number of the session is at the left-hand margin of the first line of the unit. This is a number that was created for this book. Session numbers are based on the date of the session. The first two digits represent the year; the next two, the month; and the final two, the day.
   B. On the same line, to right of the session number, is the name of the company associated with that session, followed by the names, where known, of the individuals associated with the session: producer(s), artists and repertoire (A & R) personnel, session leaders, and so forth.
   C. On the line below is the recording venue and the names of the city and state in which that venue is located. Most often, the venue is a recording studio, but it can also be a radio station, a festival, or some other performance location. The city and state in which the venue is located follow the name of the venue.
   D. On the next and final line is the date of the session.

Within each session is a list of songs or tunes. Here, the fundamental descriptive unit is the master, which is a recording of a single musical performance. Historically, a master number is the number assigned by the recording company to a song or instrumental for their own internal filing systems.

II. Master Data, Line One

A. The master number is at the left-hand margin. Master numbers enable record companies to identify individual recorded performances in their files. The master is, in most cases, the same as one side of a "single," one band on an LP "album," or one track on a CD. Most of the companies with which the Stanley Brothers were under contract assigned master numbers that are combinations of numbers and letters.

B. Following the master number is the title of the song as given on the record label or album container.

C. Directly after the title, and in parentheses, is the composer credit as published on the record label or album container or, in the case of unreleased masters, as listed in company files. Occasionally, this information may be incomplete or erroneous, but for bibliographical accuracy, it is presented exactly as it appears on the original issue. In many cases, the legal copyright owner of a song was not necessarily its composer, but someone who purchased the song outright from a songwriter or attached his or her name to a song from traditional sources. In other cases, the artist may have followed a standard practice of asking to be listed as a song's co-composer before agreeing to record it. The Stanley Brothers did this themselves a few times. They also recorded other songs—especially gospel songs—that had already been "branded" by someone other than the composer. Where such songs have a traceable history, it is discussed in the text, but the credits in the discography continue to stand as they were on the original record.

D. Next comes the listing of single record catalog descriptors (a set of symbols, either numbers or a combination of letters and numbers, used by the recording company to identify the published recording in their catalog). The term "single" means any publication released in a 7" (usually 45 rpm) or 10" (usually 78 rpm) format and sometimes including EPs, discs with two or three songs per side. If there are more than two single record numbers for a master, the list continues immediately below, indented by one space, in the same column. Releases outside of the United States are not included.

E. Finally comes the listing of album catalog descriptors. The term "album" means any publication, either on vinyl or compact disc, that includes more than two masters. If there are more than three album catalog descriptors for a master, the list continues immediately below, indented one space, in the same column. Releases outside the United States are not included except for those on the Bear Family, which are, or were, widely available to US consumers.

F. A lack of catalog descriptors in both the singles and albums listing spaces indicates that the master has not been published. Some masters have been simply shelved because they were considered flawed. Others have been lost.

III. Master Data, Line Two

On the second line, directly below the title, are vocal part identifications or an indication that the master is an instrumental. Here, abbreviations are used that follow standard bluegrass terminology for harmony parts.

    A. First comes the last name of the singer. The full name is given only when the singer does not play an instrument. Otherwise, it is given in the personnel data (IV), along with instrument identification.

    B. Separated from the name by a hyphen is a capital letter or letters indicating the part sung: L, the lead vocal part (the melody line); T, the tenor vocal part (that part sung in harmony above the lead part or melody line); B, baritone vocal part (that part sung in harmony below the lead part or melody line); and BS, the bass vocal part (the lowest harmony part in vocal quartets).

        A slightly more complicated set of abbreviations is necessitated by Ralph Stanley's occasional practice of singing lead on the verse of a song and tenor on the chorus, whereupon the lead part is sung by another singer. LV/TC indicates the lead vocal part on the verse, tenor vocal part on the chorus, while LC indicates the lead vocal part on the chorus.

A number of guidelines were used to determine vocal part identifications, including aural recognition based on an awareness of the sounds of various singers' voices, statements by musicians, and educated guesses based on the fact that certain vocal roles in the Clinch Mountain Boys were usually taken by certain instrumentalists. Carter Stanley predominately sang lead, Ralph Stanley sang tenor (and sometimes lead), and mandolinists and fiddlers usually sang baritone.

IV. Personnel and Instruments

    A. The first time a musician's name appears, his or her full name is listed, along with a nick-name if widely used. Subsequent listings of that individual use a standard name.

    B. Separated from the name by a colon is a lowercase letter or letters indicating the standard bluegrass instruments played: m, mandolin; g, guitar; f, fiddle; b, banjo; sb, string bass; and bs, bass. All other instruments are identified in full. These names are placed in a standard arrangement that generally takes up two lines. On the first, the rhythm guitarist (Carter Stanley) is at the left, the banjoist (Ralph Stanley) in the center, and the mandolinist on the right. On the second line, the fiddler is at the left, the bassist in the center, and additional instruments on the right. Where there are variations in who plays what from one master to the next in a session, that information is either noted in parentheses that include the master number of the applicable title or, where master numbers are not available, with asterisks and daggers.

1

DEATH IS ONLY A DREAM

1947–1948

The Stanley Brothers are recognized today as members of a trio of bands that helped define and popularize the style of music that came to be known as bluegrass. Along with Bill Monroe, the acknowledged "Father of Bluegrass Music," and the duo of Lester Flatt and Earl Scruggs, Carter and Ralph Stanley were instrumental in shaping the destiny of the music, imprinting it with a soulful tinge culled from the mountainous region of their native southwest Virginia. They added a distinctive array of excellently crafted original material and delivered it in a highly emotive manner that remains unequaled to this day.

The duo traveled and recorded together for twenty years, from 1946 to 1966, until the untimely passing of Carter Stanley. In their two decades of performing, they recorded nearly 350 songs for a variety of labels including Columbia, Mercury, Starday, and King. They appeared in forty-three states and seven foreign countries.

After the death of Carter Stanley, esteem for the duo continued to rise, and their music is more popular today than it was during their brief time together. They have been the subject of several comprehensive boxed-set reissue projects, and the Barter Theatre, the State Theatre of Virginia, presented a well-received theatrical portrayal of their lives in a play called *Man of Constant Sorrow*. Carter and Ralph Stanley are members of the International Bluegrass Music Association's Hall of Honor (renamed Hall of Fame in 2007). The duo's popularity received its biggest boost with the inclusion of their music in the soundtrack of the runaway movie success *O Brother, Where Art Thou?* Ralph Stanley has maintained a successful forty-plus-year solo career that includes multiple Grammy awards, congressional and presidential honors, the erection of a state-of-the-art museum in his hometown of Clintwood, Virginia, and countless awards from music and civic organizations.

Oft My Thoughts Drift Back to Childhood

Carter and Ralph, the Stanley Brothers, were born in Dickenson County in rural southwestern Virginia, near a small community known as Big Spraddle Creek. Their mother, Lucy Smith Stanley, was one of twelve children—all of whom played five-string banjo. Their father, Lee Stanley, a logger by trade, was a gifted singer who enjoyed old mountain ballads. Both Lucy and Lee Stanley had been married previously and had lost their first spouses to death. Both had children from their prior marriages.[1] Carter and Ralph were the only two children the couple had together. Carter Glen Stanley was born on August 27, 1925, and Ralph Edmond Stanley followed on February 25, 1927.

In addition to musical parents, Carter and Ralph had an extended family that influenced them. Their uncle, Jim Henry Stanley, would sometimes join their father in leading hymns such as "Village Church Yard." Their half-sisters on their father's side of the family were acquainted with ballads such as "Omie Wise," "The Brown Girl," and "Ellen Smith." The McClure Church, a Primitive Baptist church, exposed the young Stanleys to the "lined out" style of hymn singing, a method in which a song leader chants a line of a song and the congregation then sings the line.

Music started to make an impression on the young Stanley boys as they neared their teen years. In addition to the music of their parents, aunts, and uncles, they began to hear music from across the mountains when the family acquired a radio in 1936. Among the programs they heard was the *Grand Ole Opry*, a live Saturday evening show that aired over WSM from Nashville, Tennessee. Started in 1927, the show was, by the late 1930s, home to a number of popular personalities, including Roy Acuff, Ernest Tubb, and Bill Monroe. Also popular in the Stanley household were programs from stations located just south of the Texas-Mexican border. Free from the constraints of the US Federal Communications Commission, these border stations broadcast at very high levels of wattage that allowed them to blanket much of the United States. They used singing cowboys and hillbilly acts such as the Carter Family and Mainer's Mountaineers to help sell a plethora of products aimed at rural audiences. As Carter and Ralph went about their morning chores before school, they would imagine that sticks of kindling wood were instruments and pretend to replicate on them the sounds heard over the airwaves.[2]

Traveling musicians would also contribute to the Stanleys' musical development. A local appearance of Clayton McMichen and the Delmore Brothers made a significant impact on Carter Stanley. He related in later years that it was McMichen's showmanship that inspired him to pursue a career in music. It wasn't long afterward that the boys got to see an early incarnation of Bill Monroe's Blue Grass Boys when it featured vocalist Clyde Moody, who worked with Monroe from the latter part of 1940 through 1944. Monroe would be an inspiration to the Stanley Brothers throughout their career.

Carter Stanley ordered a guitar from a mail-order catalog some time in 1938 or '39. The local mailman, who made his rounds on horseback, showed Carter how to make his first chords on the guitar.[3] Ralph purchased a banjo from one of his aunts not long afterward; he had the choice of a pig or banjo and opted for the musical instrument. His mother showed him his first tunes, which he played in the old clawhammer style.[4] When performing "Shout Little Lulie," a regionally popular tune that was commonly used to teach beginning musicians, Ralph invariably informed his audience, "this is the first tune I learned to play from my mother."

Carter and Ralph honed their skills by performing with other musicians. A 1939 photograph shows them in the company of a young teenage fiddler named Bernard Nunley.[5] Another friend, Jewel Martin, recalled being in a band with Carter and Ralph called the Lazy Ramblers. He noted, "We were all just learning to play. If one of us learned a new chord or run, we couldn't wait until we showed the others."[6]

Performance opportunities were usually limited to their home, but the brothers occasionally provided music for school plays and the like. Their first radio exposure occurred—most likely in the early 1940s—when they appeared on the *Barrel of Fun* program, a Saturday morning show that was broadcast over WJHL from the Bonnie Kate Theater in Elizabethton, Tennessee. The show served as a proving ground for other aspiring entertainers, notably fiddler Clarence "Tater" Tate.

World War II interrupted any thoughts the brothers might have had about a career in music. Upon graduation from high school in 1943, Carter entered the army.[7] During part of his hitch, he was stationed at Kingman Army Air Field, where he worked, according to one of the brothers' songbooks, as "an armourer."[8] A similar fate awaited Ralph in May of 1945. Although hostilities had officially ended, Ralph still did a tour of duty in Germany, serving in General George Patton's Third Army.

Carter Stanley was discharged at Fort George G. Meade in Maryland in late February of 1946.[9] At the time of his discharge, he made the acquaintance of another musician from southwestern Virginia, Roy Sykes. Sykes had had a band before the war, and he was intent on organizing a new one. It wasn't long until he made good on his goal. In April advertisements, articles, and daily radio listings began appearing in the Norton, Virginia, newspaper showing that Sykes and his Blue Ridge Mountain Boys—a group that included the recently discharged Carter Stanley—had a daily radio show and were performing at theaters, land auctions, park openings, and even a Kiwanis club meeting. No doubt Carter was getting a good education in the mechanics of operating a band.

Ralph's discharge came in the middle of October 1946. Carter and their father met him at the bus station in St. Paul, Virginia. Before he had a chance to make it home, they took a detour to radio station WNVA in Norton, where Ralph sang a song on the air with the Sykes band.

Ralph continued to work with Sykes for a few weeks but grew dissatisfied with the situation. He quickly came to the conclusion that life in the Roy Sykes band wasn't for him and thought of using his GI benefits to go to school to become a veterinarian. Finally, he told Carter that he'd be willing to start a new band, as the Stanley Brothers; otherwise, he was going to explore other opportunities.[10]

Consequently, Carter and Ralph organized their own group in November of 1946. They took with them the mandolin player from Sykes's band, Darrell "Pee Wee" Lambert. They found a fiddler, Bobby Sumner, from a town not far away in eastern Kentucky. The group did some radio work on WNVA in Norton and made at least one personal appearance, near Big Stone Gap, Virginia. Carter noted, "We was sponsored by a company called Clinch Valley

Insurance Company, and we had originally planned to name the group the Clinch Valley Boys, and as a result of their name they suggested we call it the Clinch Mountain Boys."[11]

The area takes its name from the Clinch Mountain range, which lies slightly to the east of Carter and Ralph's home in Dickenson County and runs approximately 150 miles, from near Blaine, Tennessee, in the south to near Burke's Garden, Virginia, in the north. The first recorded reference to the area's name was made on April 9, 1750, when Dr. Thomas Walker, a physician and explorer for the Loyal Land Company, wrote in his journal that his expedition came to a river, "which I suppose to be the one the hunters call Clinch's river, a hunter who first found it."[12]

Rolling Along, Singing a Song

The Tennessee-Virginia border town of Bristol has been witness to two monumental events in country music history. The first took place in July and August of 1927 when Victor talent scout Ralph Peer set up shop in a building on State Street for the purpose of recording songs to release on phonograph records. The recordings that were made in Bristol resulted in what has often been referred to as the "Big Bang of Country Music." These sessions weren't the first to record country music; Peer had recorded the first country music session four years earlier when he cut two sides by a Georgia musician, Fiddlin' John Carson. But the Bristol sessions, as they have come to be known, were influential in that they launched the careers of two of country music's early stars: the Carter Family and Jimmie Rodgers.

Much attention, both locally and nationally, has been paid to the Bristol sessions. The Country Music Foundation issued a splendid two-CD set highlighting thirty-five of the seventy-six recordings made at the sessions; a collection of articles about the sessions has been assembled in a book called *The Bristol Sessions: Writings About the Big Bang of Country Music*; the city of Bristol's Rhythm and Roots Festival draws tens of thousands of attendees annually; and the Birthplace of Country Music Alliance (BCMA) recently opened the 24,000-square-foot Birthplace of Country Music Museum that documents the region's musical legacy that began with the Bristol sessions.

The other big event is less well known. It had its start in December of 1946. Like many communities throughout the United States, people in Bristol were adjusting to a new prosperity that was ushered in with the close of World War II. Innovative ventures were springing up everywhere, and one that energized people locally was the birth of a radio station. The station in Bristol was part of a wave of broadcasting facilities that were opening up across the nation, many of which were located in rural municipalities. Local radio offered a decidedly hometown flavor. This contrasted with the programming of the more established urban stations and struck a responsive chord with country audiences, many of which were recently electrified and proud radio owners. WCYB took its name from <u>C</u>it<u>Y</u> of <u>B</u>ristol. Its premier transmission took place, in a snub to superstition, on Friday, December 13, 1946.[13]

The first day of broadcasting at WCYB contained a mixture of programs, including "music and news from leased wires of the Associated Press."[14] Other items of interest included local tobacco market reports, sports events, and a story hour for children. One program that made its debut in the 12:50 to 1:30 p.m. time slot, with a five-minute break for news at the top of the hour, would ensure the station's musical legacy: *Farm & Fun Time*.[15]

The program got off to a rather inauspicious start with music being performed by two local musicians, Roy Webb and Therl E. "Cousin Zeke" Leonard.[16] But in time, *Farm & Fun Time* was host to virtually all of the seminal first-generation bluegrass performers: the Stanley Brothers, Flatt & Scruggs, Mac Wiseman, Jim & Jesse, Jimmy Martin and Bob Osborne, and the Sauceman Brothers. Traditional country performers such as the Blue Sky Boys and Charlie Monroe also worked the program.

Soon, *Farm & Fun Time* occupied the popular 12:05 to 1:00 spot. It reached a five-state area that included Virginia, West Virginia, Kentucky, Tennessee, and North Carolina, and quickly became a regional institution. Prior to WCYB's debut, noontime country music programs had been a feature of many radio stations, especially in the South, for well over a decade.

In December 1946, the Stanleys learned of the new station going on the air in Bristol. Lee Stanley spoke to WCYB management on his sons' behalf and secured an audition for them.[17] They were one of thirty-five bands the station previewed. The Stanley Brothers and Curly King and the Tennessee Hilltoppers were the two bands chosen to appear on the station.[18] Carter related once that station vice president and general manager Fey Rogers told them that he wouldn't "promise you a dose of medicine" but that they were welcome to appear on the show. The program didn't pay a salary to any of the performers, but it did provide an outlet for advertising their show dates.

It's hard to say whether the Stanley Brothers made *Farm & Fun Time*, or *Farm & Fun Time* made the Stanley Brothers. Perhaps it was a little of both. Lee Stanley had posters and window cards made up advertising Carter and Ralph's spot on *Farm & Fun Time*. Their performances on WCYB garnered fairly immediate results as far as obtaining personal appearance dates. Speaking with Mike Seeger in 1966, Ralph Stanley recalled:

> And then we started on Bristol on this *Farm & Fun Time*, and like I say, the first show, I think we made two dollars and forty-eight cents apiece and the next show we played we had two full houses . . . from then on we couldn't find a house big enough to hold the people for the next two or three year.[19]

Also speaking with Mike Seeger about requests for personal appearance dates, Carter Stanley remembered that in the early days, "We used to get anywhere, I think . . . twelve or fourteen is about the highest we ever got in one day."

For farm families gathering for dinner, live hillbilly music was a regular fixture of the meal. Mac Wiseman related, "I've had hundreds—maybe thousands—of people tell me over the years how they'd get up early and work late out in the fields just so they could come in the house at noon and hear the program."[20] Speaking of the early appeal of *Farm & Fun Time*, Ralph Stanley noted, "We got a big pile of mail every day. We got so many job offers from the program, at times we couldn't meet the demand. When the show was one hour long, there was a waiting line for sponsors trying to advertise on it. They went to two hours and there was still a waiting line!"[21]

Tennessee's Tri-Cities area of Bristol, Kingsport, and Johnson City had more than a popular radio program going for it. Johnson City was home to an upstart independent record label that specialized in hillbilly music. Rich-R-Tone Records later touted itself as the first indie label dedicated exclusively to bluegrass music. James Hobart Stanton, who went by Jim or "Hobe," organized the company. Eventually, the label would put out releases by a host of artists, including Wilma Lee and Stoney Cooper, the Stanley Brothers, the Bailey Brothers, the Sauceman Brothers, Jim Eanes, and the Church Brothers, as well as regional favorites such as Curly King, the Mullins Family, and Buster Pack.[22]

Rich-R-Tone Records: First Recordings

With their popularity growing, the Stanleys soon had an opportunity to make recordings. There are two conflicting stories as to how the Stanleys arrived at Rich-R-Tone Records. Jim Stanton stated that it was the Stanley Brothers who sought him out:

> First time I ever met 'em they came to Johnson City to see me, and honestly I wasn't all that impressed because I was looking for something tight like Lester and Earl. [It should be noted that at this time Flatt & Scruggs were still working with Bill Monroe as members of the Blue Grass Boys and had not yet formed their own group, the Foggy Mountain Boys.] Then they made a return trip in their big '46 model Packard I think it was, and they had a mail sack in the trunk of the car. I checked the post dates and it was every bit current mail for "Little Glass of Wine." I said, "Man, you mean you're getting that many requests to sing that?!" They said, "You can check 'em." And they were legit. I said, "Well, by all means, man, let's get together on something." So, really, like all artists, they pursued me to impress me to record them.[23]

In an interview conducted by Ralph Rinzler in 1974, Ralph Stanley recalled:

> This fellow by the name of Hobart Stanton had this company in Johnson City. We didn't know him. I guess he heard us on the radio station, and he contacted us, and we made some records for him. At that time we didn't know A from B. We didn't know about things like that . . . The first time we recorded, I guess two songs: "Mother No Longer Awaits Me at Home" and "The Girl Behind the Bar."[24]

Carter Stanley gave pretty much the same story:

> Well, actually, the first records we ever made was for a small label I believe back about 1947 called Rich-R-Tone. That was out of Johnson City, Tennessee, and we was working a town called Bristol at that time. And they came over there and told us they'd like to record us and they did. We made a few numbers for them, I don't know, fourteen I guess . . . fifteen, something like that.[25]

The Stanley Brothers cut four sessions for Rich-R-Tone: one in the middle part of 1947 (session #470200), one in late 1947 or early 1948 (session #471200), one in the middle of

1948 (session #480700), and one in mid-1952 (session #520600). The first two were recorded at radio station WOPI in Bristol, the third at WCYB, and the last one at radio station WLSI in Pikeville, Kentucky. Jim Stanton recalled:

> We sort of called WOPI our home base for recording because Russ [Robinson, the engineer at the station], we liked Russ, and they had a right good facility there. That was before tape was invented or anything, and they had a good disc cutter, and it was handy for the Stanley Brothers 'cause they were living in a rooming house there and working on WCYB and *Farm & Fun Time*.[26]

The early Rich-R-Tone recordings of the Stanley Brothers are important and valuable in that they show the growth and development of not only the Stanley sound but bluegrass music as well. By examining this group of recordings by the Stanleys, it is possible to see the transition from old-time mountain music to Bill Monroe–style bluegrass.

When the Stanley Brothers first began their professional career, they were very much in the old-time camp. Bill Malone, author of *Country Music, U.S.A.*, noted that "the Stanley Brothers possessed the most tradition oriented repertory in country music and a vocal style that was heavily influenced by the Monroe Brothers and Mainer's Mountaineers."[27] Ralph Stanley has said of his banjo style, "I was playing with one finger and thumb when we started working professionally. Very soon after I started playing banjo, I started with finger and thumb . . . a little of the other [clawhammer] too."[28] This two-finger style of banjo playing was used and popularized by Wade Mainer during the 1930s and '40s.

Carter Stanley reflected, "In the beginning, yeah, we used to try to copy the Monroe Brothers, you know, and of course the Carter Family. We learned a lot from the old records of people like the Monroe Brothers, the Carter Family, Clayton McMichen and the Georgia Wildcats, people like that a good many years ago."[29] Songs from the early Rich-R-Tone sessions such as "Little Maggie" and "The Jealous Lover" demonstrate Ralph's use of the two-finger banjo and the traditional, old-time nature of their duet singing.

Rich-R-Tone #1 (Session 470600)

Exact dates for any of the Rich-R-Tone sessions are not known, but it appears likely that the Stanley Brothers' first session for Rich-R-Tone took place in the middle part of 1947. The band at the time consisted of mandolin player Pee Wee Lambert, fiddler Leslie Keith, and bass player Ray Lambert.

Pee Wee Lambert was a charter member of the Clinch Mountain Boys. He and Carter Stanley had met in 1946 when they were both members of the Roy Sykes group. A native of Thacker, West Virginia, he was born on August 5, 1924. He made music with Sykes briefly prior to World War II and did so again when the war ended. Like a number of rural mountain musicians in the 1940s, he fell under the spell of the music of Bill Monroe. He fashioned his mandolin playing after Monroe's and, like Monroe, sang solos and harmonies in very high registers. This created a bond between him and Carter Stanley, who was also

This mid-1960s album served as a vehicle to make available the early Rich-R-Tone recordings of the Stanley Brothers. The photo on the cover features four of the five musicians who were present on the very first session. From left to right are Pee Wee Lambert, Leslie Keith, and Carter and Ralph Stanley. Absent from the photo is bass player Ray Lambert.

a budding disciple of Monroe's music. In Sykes's group, Pee Wee and Carter performed duets with mandolin and guitar accompaniment in a manner that recalled Monroe's work of the 1930s when he recorded with his brother Charlie as the Monroe Brothers.

Not much is known of Ray Lambert. He and Pee Wee shared the same last name but were not related. A brief song and picture folio that Ray and Pee Wee issued in 1947 listed a short biography for Ray:

> As you listen to me on Farm and Fun Time everyday, I decided to introduce to you this folder. I was born two miles from Haysi, Virginia, September 25, 1924 and have been in music for about 10 years. I have been on several radio stations including WNOX, Knoxville, Tennessee, with Charlie Monroe and His Kentucky Partners. I think WCYB has the nicest people to work for, of all the stations I have been on. I sure thank you for all the mail and will look forward to more of it.[30]

He was also a member of the Roy Sykes group at the same time as Carter and Pee Wee. He doesn't appear to have left that group with the others, but came to the Stanley Brothers later, in the early part of 1947.

Leslie Keith was an old-time fiddler from Pulaski County, Virginia. He was considerably older than the Stanley boys, having been born on March 30, 1906. His chief claim to fame, aside from his work with the Stanley Brothers, was his creation of the popular fiddle tune "Black Mountain Blues." During the depression days of the 1930s, Keith did a lot of hoboing, honing his talents as a fiddler and entertainer. One of his exploits was the staging of a fiddle contest near Bluefield, West Virginia, that pitted him against Arthur Smith, a *Grand Ole Opry* star and one of the most influential fiddlers of the day. The event was witnessed by over nine thousand paying spectators and ended in a draw. Following service in World War II, Leslie continued his musical travels. While in Norton, Virginia, in 1946, he met members of the Roy Sykes band, including Carter Stanley. The early part of 1947 found Leslie in Newport News, Virginia, where he received a call from Lee Stanley, who asked him to "play fiddle and teach the business to his two boys."[31] It wasn't long afterward that Leslie was on a bus bound for Bristol; he arrived shortly before noon on a Saturday morning—just in time to take part in the Stanley Brothers' noontime appearance on *Farm & Fun Time*. The older and experienced Leslie Keith is credited with "showing the ropes" to the young Stanley brothers. The liner notes to Leslie's lone fiddle album, *Black Mountain Blues*, tells how "he handled most of the MC work and business side of the show, teaching every bit to Carter and Ralph."[32]

Carter and Ralph's first session for Rich-R-Tone features two religious quartets and two Stanley originals. Of the two gospel selections, Ralph recalled, "We got them two tunes, 'I Can Tell You the Time' and 'Death Is Only a Dream,' we got 'em from old songbooks that we found somewhere."[33] "Death Is Only a Dream" is a hymn that dates to the late 1800s. A half dozen or so old-time recordings of it were made in the 1920s and '30s. The song gained in popularity when, starting in 1939, it began appearing in various shape-note hymnals issued by music publishers such as Stamps-Baxter. "I Can Tell You the Time" was another hymn that received exposure in shape-note hymnals. It made its first appearance in the 1939 James D. Vaughan publication *Heaven's Hallelujahs*. Additional exposure to the hymn may have come from Wade Mainer, who recorded a version for Bluebird on September 29, 1941.

The Stanleys' performance of these two hymns shows the influence of Bill Monroe. Monroe's religious quartets at that time spotlighted the voices, with instrumental accompaniment from the guitar and mandolin only. The two Stanley numbers here follow the same pattern. Monroe had featured this type of quartet singing on his first records in 1940 and '41 and continued to feature it in his *Grand Ole Opry* broadcasts and personal appearances throughout the 1940s. On these Stanley quartets, mandolin player Pee Wee Lambert, like Monroe, sings tenor. Ralph—who would come to be known for his distinctive tenor harmonies—sings baritone, Carter handles the lead vocals, and Ray Lambert supplies the bass vocals.

The final two selections recorded at the session are duets by Carter and Ralph, "Mother No Longer Awaits Me at Home" and "The Girl Behind the Bar." "Mother No Longer Awaits Me at Home" represents one of Carter Stanley's first attempts at songwriting. A copyright filed on December 4, 1946—before the band's move to Bristol—shows that Carter and Ralph were interested in protecting their work from the very start. "The Girl Behind the Bar," also a Carter Stanley composition, is set to the melody of another tune they had yet to record, "The Little Glass of Wine," which in turn borrows melodically from a recently released recording by Charlie Monroe called "No Depression in Heaven."

The very first record release of the Stanley Brothers' career appeared on Rich-R-Tone Records of John-son City, Tennessee. Shown here are the labels from each side of the 78 rpm disc, #420. Side A contained "Mother No Longer Awaits Me at Home" while side B consisted of "The Girl Behind the Bar." Carter Stanley was credited with writing both songs.

Farm & Fun Time (Session 470700)

The year 1947 was a euphoric one for the Stanley Brothers. They were gaining mass re-gional acceptance for their brand of old-time mountain music. Carter Stanley recalled that a review of their personal appearance schedule showed they had worked ninety days in a row without a break. They performed six days a week on the noontime *Farm & Fun Time* program and then ventured out to surrounding communities to present evening concerts. Most of the shows were sufficiently close to Bristol that the band could be back in time for the next day's radio broadcast. Many groups, the Stanleys included, made provisions for the times when they would be away by creating transcriptions that could be played in their absence; magnetic recording tape was not yet commonplace. To facilitate their recording needs, bands recorded their programs on 16" blank discs. Most radio stations had disc cut-ters that etched the grooves of music onto the blank discs. Usually, the programs were used several times and then discarded. One of the DJs at WCYB, "Cousin Zeke" Leonard, saved several of the Stanley Brothers transcriptions. Some forty years later, the discs made their way to Rebel Records, which made the music commercially available for the first time.[34]

Two complete programs were saved; they provide an excellent representation of what the Stanleys' music was like in 1947, much more so than what is portrayed by the group's Rich-R-Tone recordings.

The shows start with a buoyant introductory theme song:

> Rolling along, singing a song,
>> Singing a song of home sweet home,

The Stanley Brothers gained wide-spread regional fame through daily radio broadcasts on WCYB's *Farm & Fun Time* program from Bristol, Virginia/Tennessee. Most of the shows were performed live, but when distant personal appearances made it difficult for the group to be back at the station on time, programs were recorded onto 16" transcription discs that could be played in their absence. In 1988 two surviving transcribed programs from 1947 were discovered and issued on Rebel Records as *The Stanley Brothers on WCYB Bristol*. The photo on the cover of the album jacket shows Ralph and Carter Stanley as they appeared at about the time the shows were recorded.

> Come on along, join in our song,
>   Singing our troubles away.

Carter Stanley welcomes the listeners to the broadcast with an upbeat "Hello, everybody everywhere." Leslie Keith keeps the momentum rolling by launching into an up-tempo fiddle number such as "Cotton-Eyed Joe" or "Old Joe Clark."

A duet by Carter and Ralph follows. "Our Darling's Gone" was a song the duo would soon record for Rich-R-Tone. Carter presents it on the program as one that he and Ralph had recently introduced on *Farm & Fun Time*. "They're at Rest Together" was a song they never recorded commercially, although their debut songbook featured its lyrics. The song originated with the Callahan Brothers, a duo originally from western North Carolina, who recorded it for Decca Records on April 27, 1941. How the song came to the Stanley Brothers is not known, but other duos such as the West Virginia–based Lilly Brothers were making use of it. Both of these songs are of a tragic nature and among the first of many in this genre that the Stanleys would feature throughout their career. "Our Darling's Gone" deals with death in the coal mines, while "They're at Rest Together" tells the sorrowful plight of young lovers separated by death as a result of tuberculosis.

After a duet by Carter and Ralph, it's time for a solo by Pee Wee Lambert. In most cases, this takes the form of a selection popularized by Bill Monroe, such as "Molly and Tenbrooks" or "White House Blues." Monroe had yet to record either of these tunes, and Lambert's adaptations of them in all likelihood came from listening to Monroe's performances on the

Grand Ole Opry. "White House Blues," which chronicles the 1901 assassination of President William McKinley, appeared earlier in old-time music and was performed by players such as banjoist Charlie Poole. The Stanleys added contemporary elements to it with lines such as "Roosevelt's in the graveyard" (a reference to recently deceased Franklin D. Roosevelt) and "Truman's in the White House."

Other songs featured on the remainder of the programs include fiddle tunes ("Cacklin' Hen" and "Orange Blossom Special") by Leslie Keith, more duets ("Little Glass of Wine" and "The Jealous Lover") by Carter and Ralph, and sacred songs ("Standing in the Need of Prayer," "Lonely Tombs," and "Just One Way to the Pearly Gate").

Although Bill Monroe had recorded "Orange Blossom Special" a few years earlier, it's difficult to say if that recording directly influenced Keith's rendition. It's possible the tune had by this time entered popular music vernacular. "Little Glass of Wine" was quickly developing into Carter and Ralph's first, albeit minor, hit, while "The Jealous Lover" was their reworking of a traditional ballad; both of these tunes would soon be recorded for Rich-R-Tone.

Carter characterizes "Standing in the Need of Prayer" as a spiritual, and he and Ralph would record it in 1964 for Ray Davis's Wango label. The original radio transcription received broad exposure in 1991 when it was used as background music for the movie *Doc Hollywood*. Carter offers "Lonely Tombs" as a song of encouragement to the band's sick and shut-in listeners. The song dates from 1918, when William M. Golden introduced it, and it subsequently appeared in numerous shape-note hymnals that were issued and sold throughout the South. Another tip of the hat to Bill Monroe is the quartet's rendering of "Just One Way to the Pearly Gate," which the Monroe Brothers had recorded in the 1930s. Even more telling of Monroe's influence is Carter's introduction of Ralph and his "fancy banjo" on several selections; it is an obvious reference to how Judge Hay, the *Grand Ole Opry*'s master of ceremonies, was then introducing Monroe's banjo player, Earl Scruggs.

Pee Wee Lambert is featured on several additional selections: "Blue Moon of Kentucky" and "Goodbye Old Pal." Like his other solos, these are also from the repertoire of Bill Monroe. Both appeared on a Monroe 78rpm disc that was released on Columbia on September 20, 1947. Lyrically, the versions of "Blue Moon of Kentucky" by Lambert and Monroe are pretty similar, but the arrangements are slightly different. For example, both versions are fairly driven by the fiddle, but whereas Monroe does take a mandolin break on his recording, Lambert does not. On "Goodbye Old Pal," there are quite a few textual differences between the Monroe and Lambert renditions, indicating that Pee Wee most likely learned the lyrics from a radio performance by Monroe; the Stanley Brothers are known to have learned several of Monroe's songs by listening to them on the radio and writing down the lyrics. This method, as evidenced by Pee Wee's singing on "Goodbye Old Pal," did not always yield perfect results. Whatever the case, Monroe—a top star on the *Grand Ole Opry* with a distinctive individual style and repertoire—was not happy that the Stanleys and Pee Wee Lambert were making use of his sound and material.[35] Mac Wiseman noted, "When the Stanley Brothers first started, whatever Bill did Saturday night on the *Opry*, they did next on the Bristol program that they were on . . . Well, Bill used to see red. He used to hate the word Stanley Brothers."[36]

Lastly, a band performance of an old-time tune known by several titles, including "Whoa, Mule, Whoa" and "Riding the Humpbacked Mule," gives Leslie Keith, Carter Stanley, and Pee Wee Lambert a chance to intersperse some comedic verses between Keith's fiddle breaks.

Rich-R-Tone #2 (Session 471200)

The Stanley Brothers' second recording session for Rich-R-Tone took place in the latter part of 1947 or the early part of 1948. The personnel for the session included the same core group of Carter and Ralph Stanley, Pee Wee Lambert, and Leslie Keith. Ray Lambert was absent from this session, and as such, no bass was present on these recordings. The Stanley Brothers at times performed without a bass, and the omission of the instrument from this session indicates that at this time they were between players.

One of Ralph's signature songs, "Little Maggie," was recorded at this session. On it, Ralph plays two-finger banjo in the style made popular by Wade Mainer, and it was from the Mainer band that Ralph learned the song. "I heard Steve Ledford do that. He used to be with Mainer's Mountaineers, Wade and J. E. [Mainer]. He was the fiddle player."[37] Ledford recorded this song for Bluebird Records in 1937 as part of Mainer's Mountaineers; the earliest recording of this song, by the duo of G. B. Grayson & Henry Whitter, dates from 1928.

The remaining three selections in the Stanley Brothers' session are all duets by Carter and Ralph. "The Jealous Lover" is an old ballad that is quite well-known in North America. Ralph recalled, "We got that from an old man, Johnny Baker I believe was his name. [He was] a neighbor of ours. He knew a lot of the old songs, but I think that was the only one we ever used."[38] "The Little Glass of Wine" is one of the songs that helped popularize the Stanley Brothers. They first heard it when they were young boys, learning it from Otto Taylor, who worked for the Ritter Lumber Company. Ralph remembered, "He had some

One of the most popular songs from the early days of the Stanley Brothers' career was a piece called "Little Glass of Wine." Recrafted from a tune the boys heard in their youth, this version was recorded at their second session for Rich-R-Tone in the waning days of 1947 or the very early part of 1948.

words to it and we took it and finished it out and put the melody to it and so forth. That was a long time before we ever started in the music business; we were little boys. We finished it out after we started in the music business."[39] The final selection in the session is "Our Darling's Gone," whose lyrics were written by a woman whose husband had been killed in a mining accident. She wrote a poem about her family's life since her husband's death and sent it to the Stanley Brothers, who composed a melody for it.

Rich-R-Tone #3 (Session 480700)

By the time of the band's third session, in the middle part of 1948, Leslie Keith had left to form his own group, the Lonesome Valley Boys, and Art Wooten, a former member of Bill Monroe's Blue Grass Boys, took his place. The addition of Wooten to the band brought a different sound to the Stanley Brothers' music. Where Keith's fiddle had an old-time quality to it, Wooten's work reflected a quicker pace and drive that he had picked up while working with Monroe.

Born on February 4, 1906, in Sparta, North Carolina, Wooten, like Keith, was considerably older than the rest of the Stanley band members. His early professional work included performances on live radio in Asheville with another North Carolinian, Clyde Moody. It is interesting that both Wooten and Moody had associations with Bill Monroe in the late 1930s and early '40s; it was shortly after Moody joined the Blue Grass Boys, on September

In the spring and summer of 1948, the Stanley Brothers underwent a transition from being a basically old-time mountain string band to one that emulated the sounds of *Grand Ole Opry* star Bill Monroe and the Blue Grass Boys. A defining characteristic of this sound—which in later years came to be known as bluegrass—is Ralph Stanley's revolutionary three-finger style of banjo playing. The first Stanley disc to feature the new sound, "Molly and Tenbrook," was recorded in the summer of 1948 and appeared on the market not long afterwards. The different appearances of the two labels pictured here show that the disc was popular enough to be pressed, or manufactured, on more than one occasion by Rich-R-Tone. Monroe was not happy with the band at the time, feeling that the Stanley Brothers were trading on his sound and style.

6, 1940, that Carter and Ralph saw him in concert with Monroe. It was during the middle 1930s that Monroe first took note of Wooten's fiddling. In 1939, Wooten joined Monroe and accompanied him on his first *Grand Ole Opry* appearance. He was also featured on one of Monroe's sessions for Bluebird Records, on October 2, 1941. Selections from that session featuring Art's fiddling include "Orange Blossom Special" and "Back Up and Push." In addition to fiddling with Monroe, Wooten was also featured on Monroe's shows with a one-man-band contraption he built that allowed him to play organ, banjo, guitar, and mouth harp all at the same time. Following service in the navy during World War II, Art found musical employment with several bluegrass bands, including the Stanley Brothers and Flatt & Scruggs. In addition to his professional work, Art was a frequent competitor at the annual fiddlers convention in Galax, Virginia, and had the distinction of winning the contest for seven consecutive years. Art died on October 6, 1986.

In addition to Wooten's fiddling, another stylistic innovation appeared in the Stanley band at this time: Ralph's three-finger style banjo playing. As noted earlier, Ralph had been using the two-finger style of Wade Mainer. Some uncertainty exists as to how Ralph came to learn the three-finger method. In the spring of 1948, Flatt & Scruggs began broadcasting at WCYB. In his article on the development of bluegrass, "From Sound to Style," Neil Rosenberg stated:

> Some musicians assert that he [Stanley] learned directly from Scruggs during their joint tenure at WCYB. Ralph Stanley, however, insists that he learned directly from the playing of Snuffy Jenkins, the North Carolina banjoist who was responsible for much of Scruggs' style.[40]

Ralph states, "Snuffy Jenkins was actually the first fellow I heard use the three-finger. There was a fellow by the name of Hoke Jenkins I heard in Knoxville, Tennessee, and there was a fellow down in North Carolina, Jes Fulbright, he played some on the radio there. But I was trying to play that [three-finger style] before Earl and Lester came to *Farm & Fun Time*."[41]

Only two numbers were recorded at the Stanley Brothers' third Rich-R-Tone session. Leslie Keith wrote one selection, "The Rambler's Blues." He recalled:

> Pee Wee wanted to do a song and he didn't have one of his own that he could sing without doing somebody else's stuff. So, I just gave him that one. I was coming home from a show date one night and everybody's asleep and I decided to write a song driving along.[42]

The other tune recorded at the session is a Bill Monroe selection called "Molly and Tenbrooks." The song celebrates a race between two horses, Mollie McCarty and Ten Broeck, before a crowd of thirty thousand spectators at the Louisville Jockey Club on July 4, 1878. Although printed copies of the song are known to exist from the 1880s, Monroe's performances and recordings of it, starting in the mid-1940s, account for its popularity today. Monroe recorded the tune on Columbia on October 28, 1947, but at the time the Stanley Brothers recorded it, his version had yet to be released. Monroe's version would not hit the market until February 9, 1949, almost a whole year after the Stanley Brothers' record was released. Since Monroe's version was unreleased at that time, the Stanleys obviously learned the tune from one of Monroe's personal appearances or *Opry* broadcasts. The Stanleys' version is a close, bluegrass-style copy of Monroe's. This was the first time that any group, other than Monroe, had recorded Monroe's style of music. Mandolin player Pee Wee Lambert, as opposed to Carter or Ralph, sings lead on the record. His lead is crisp and clear and is pitched just as high as Monroe's. Pee Wee also plays mandolin on the song but, as Monroe had done, plays a backup rhythm only. The instrumental leads are handled by fiddler Art Wooten and Ralph on banjo. For the first time on record, Ralph plays banjo in the three-finger style that had been featured in Monroe's band by Earl Scruggs. The entire group produces an incredible drive, and their rendition of the song definitely demonstrates the effect that Monroe's music was having on the Stanley band.[43]

The Stanleys' new fusion of old-time and bluegrass caused quite a stir among fans and industry alike. Speaking of the Stanleys' early popularity, bluegrass pioneer Carl Sauceman noted,

> About this time Hobe Stanton started recording the Stanley Brothers and they were hot! I know because I went on the road part-time, selling records for Hobe, who also had a distributorship for Mercury. So I was a salesman for both labels. Every time I walked into a record store and they found out I was selling Rich-R-Tone, they'd holler for me to bring them a load of Stanley Brothers records. Hobe would know that if I hadn't been to a place for a week that they'd be out of Stanley Brothers. So I'd take a carload with me, deliver them and bring the money back to him. It was kind of embarrassing when they'd order 500 Stanley Brothers and maybe three of yours, which may be why Hobe got the idea for us to record that "corn." One day a salesman for RCA walked into a record store in Harlan, Kentucky, with his supervisor. The salesman asked who the biggest selling artist was, thinking the answer would be Eddy Arnold. When the dealer said it was the Stanley Brothers, the supervisor reared back like a judge and said, "Who are the Stanley Brothers?" The reply was that they were the hottest thing in the country. So RCA negotiated with the Stanley Brothers to try to sign them, but Carter Stanley was a very independent individual. RCA wanted them to come to Nashville, but Carter told them he didn't have time and if they wanted to talk to him they could come to Bristol.[44]

Clearly, the early days of recording for the Stanley Brothers were ones of youthful exuberance. With immediate regional fame garnered from frequent and widespread radio exposure, the duo was on the fast track to establishing themselves as popular practitioners of the newly emerging art form of bluegrass music. Their early Rich-R-Tone recordings and radio broadcasts caught Carter and Ralph in a state of transition and hinted strongly at new musical adventures looming on the horizon.

DISCOGRAPHY, 1947–1948

470600   Rich-R-Tone session; producer: Hobart Stanton
Radio Station WOPI, Bristol, Virginia
Middle 1947
Carter Glen Stanley: g | Ralph Edmond Stanley: b | Darrell "Pee Wee" Lambert: m
Leslie Clayborne Keith: f | Ray Lambert: sb

2324	**Death Is Only a Dream** (Stanley)	RRT-466	MLP-7322, REV-203, ROU-1110
	C. Stanley–L, PW Lambert–T, R. Stanley–B, R. Lambert–BS		
2326	**I Can Tell You the Time** (Stanley)	RRT-466	MLP-7322, REV-203, ROU-1110
	C. Stanley–L, PW Lambert–T, R. Stanley–B, R. Lambert–BS		
2328	**Mother No Longer Awaits Me at Home** (Carter Stanley)	RRT-420	MLP-7322, REV-203, ROU-1110, B0007883-02
	C. Stanley–L, R. Stanley–T		
2330	**The Girl Behind the Bar** (Carter Stanley)	RRT-420	MLP-7322, REV-203, ROU-1110, B0007883-02
	C. Stanley–L, R. Stanley–T		

470700   Rebel reissues of *Farm & Fun Time* Transcriptions
Radio Station WCYB, Bristol, Virginia
ca. 1947
Carter Stanley: g | Ralph Stanley: b | Pee Wee Lambert: m
Leslie Keith: f | Ray Lambert: sb

Theme and Introduction	REB-855, REB-2003, B0007883-02
C. Stanley–L, R. Stanley–T	
Cotton-Eyed Joe (Traditional)	REB-855, REB-2003, B0007883-02
Keith–L	
Our Darling's Gone (Carter Stanley)	REB-855, REB-2003
C. Stanley–L, R. Stanley–T	
Molly and Tenbrook (Traditional)	REB-855, REB-2003
PW Lambert–L	
Cacklin' Hen (Traditional)	REB-855, REB-2003
Instrumental	
Little Glass of Wine (Carter Stanley)	REB-855, REB-2003
C. Stanley–L, R. Stanley–T	
Blue Moon of Kentucky (Bill Monroe)	REB-855, REB-2003
PW Lambert–L	
Lonely Tombs (Traditional)	REB-855, REB-2003
C. Stanley–L, PW Lambert–T, R. Stanley–B, R. Lambert–BS	

Orange Blossom Special (Rouse-Rouse) Keith–L		REB-855, REB-2003
Theme and Introduction C. Stanley–L, R. Stanley–T		REB-855, REB-2003
Old Joe Clark (Traditional) Keith–L		REB-855, REB-2003
They're at Rest Together (Callahan Bros.) C. Stanley–L, R. Stanley–T		REB-855, REB-2003
White House Blues (Traditional) PW Lambert–L		REB-855, REB-2003
Standing in the Need of Prayer (Traditional) C. Stanley–L, PW Lambert–T, R. Stanley–B, R. Lambert–BS		REB-855, REB-2003
Riding the Humpbacked Mule (Traditional) Keith–L (1st & 4th verses), Lambert–L (2nd verse)/TC, C. Stanley–L (3rd verse and choruses)		REB-855, REB-2003
The Jealous Lover (Traditional) C. Stanley–L, R. Stanley–T		REB-855, REB-2003
Goodbye Old Pal (Bill Monroe) PW Lambert–L		REB-855, REB-2003
Just One Way to the Pearly Gate C. Stanley–L, PW Lambert–T, R. Stanley–B, R. Lambert–BS		REB-855, REB-2003

471200 Rich-R-Tone session; producer: Hobart Stanton
Radio Station WOPI, Bristol, Virginia
Late 1947 or early 1948
Carter Stanley: g | Ralph Stanley: b | Pee Wee Lambert: m
Leslie Keith: f

3108	**Little Maggie** (Traditional–P. D.) R. Stanley–L	RRT-423	MLP-7322, REV-203, ROU-1110
3117	**The Jealous Lover** (Carter Stanley) C. Stanley–L, R. Stanley–T	RRT-435	MLP-7322, REV-203, ROU-1110
4102	**The Little Glass of Wine** (Carter Stanley) C. Stanley–L, R. Stanley–T	RRT-423	MLP-7322, REV-203, ROU-1110
4114	**Our Darling's Gone** (Carter Stanley) C. Stanley–L, R. Stanley–T	RRT-435	MLP-7322, REV-203, ROU-1110

480700	Rich-R-Tone session; producer: Hobart Stanton		
	Radio Station WCYB, Bristol, Virginia		
	Mid-1948		
	Carter Stanley: g | Ralph Stanley: b | Pee Wee Lambert: m		
	Arthur James "Art" Wooten: f		
9633	**The Rambler's Blues** (Pee Wee Lambert)	RRT-418	MLP-7322, REV-203, ROU-1110
	Lambert—L		
9754	**Molly and Tenbrook** (Bill Monroe)	RRT-418	MLP-7322, REV-203, ROU-1110, B0007883-02
	Lambert—L		

2

TO US, THAT WOULD HAVE BEEN THE IMPOSSIBLE

Columbia Records, 1949–1952

In July of 1948, the Stanley Brothers relocated from Bristol, Virginia, to Raleigh, North Carolina.[1] They had been in Bristol for a year and a half and had pretty much "played out" the area, saturating the market with repeated performances. They secured another radio program on WPTF, a station that would be home to numerous bluegrass performers in the late 1940s and early '50s.

The Blue Sky Boys, an old-time duo that supplied several songs to the Stanley repertoire over the years, were in Raleigh at the same time, on a competing station. It wouldn't be the last time that the two groups would work in the same city together.

Carter and Ralph might have missed their earlier opportunity for affiliation with a major label when they didn't connect with RCA, but talent scout "Uncle Art" Satherley made sure they wouldn't be missed by Columbia, a label that, at the time, was one of the largest recording companies in the United States. His official title was vice president in charge of country, dance, and folk music. He wore his title well. By his own admission, Satherley traveled more than 1,000,000 miles in search of talent to record, and in his twenty-five years at Columbia, he recorded 80,000 songs.

A native of Bristol, England, Satherley came to the United States in 1913. Among his early jobs was assisting Thomas Edison, who was then in the business of making phonograph records. Although Satherley scored major successes at Columbia in the 1940s with artists such as Roy Acuff and Bill Monroe, his interests lay in the types of music being created on the back roads and byways of America, not in the big cities. Consequently, it came as no surprise that Carter and Ralph Stanley appealed to Satherley's sense of authenticity. According to Ralph Stanley,

> Mr. Satherley had taken a personal interest in us . . . [he] was firm on letting us record in our natural style. He said there was already plenty of slick commercial country. He loved old-time music and he'd spent his career chasing it down . . . We were back-

In October 1948, the Stanley Brothers were courted by Columbia Records. The label's artist and repertoire man (or producer, in today's terms), Art Satherley, was enthusiastic about Carter and Ralph's brand of mountain music and was anxious to add the team to Columbia's roster of talent. The group went on to record four sessions for Columbia from 1949 to 1952. In 1980 Rounder Records reissued all twenty-two songs on two albums. The first volume, shown here, features a photo showing the composition of the group when they signed the contract with Columbia. From left to right are Pee Wee Lambert, Ralph Stanley, Art Wooten, and Carter Stanley. By the time of the first session, Art Wooten had moved on.

woods even compared with Acuff, and Mr. Satherley wanted to get as much of that on record as possible.[2]

The group performed several instrumentals as an audition for Mr. Satherley, but this was in many respects a triviality. He already knew he wanted the band. Ralph Stanley recalled the events leading up to the contract signing:

> Six months after we'd been in Bristol [Virginia], why we got a call from Art Satherley of Columbia and he wanted us to record. A little time elapsed, and I believe the next radio station we went to was Raleigh, North Carolina, and that was about 1948. Art Satherley flew down to Raleigh and signed us up. At the time we had Pee Wee Lambert, Art Wooten, Carter, and myself, and he rented a room or two in the hotel. We went to see him there and we signed the contract. I think he pulled out of his coat pocket a couple of hundred dollars and said, "You might need a little money, I'm gonna give you this."[3]

The contract with Columbia was signed on October 14, 1948. Satherley's trip to Raleigh coincided with a visit to the city by President Harry Truman, who was then running for reelection. A number of Raleigh residents mistook Satherley, a distinguished-looking elderly gentleman who had several facial features that resembled Truman's, for the president.[4] Although the contract was signed in October, it would be six months before the band could record. James C. Petrillo, the head of the American Federation of Musicians, had imposed a ban on recording that lasted from January 1 through December 14, 1948. Described once as one of the most colorful, powerful, and controversial labor leaders of the twentieth century, Petrillo's recording strike of 1948 was brought on by replacement of union musicians at radio stations across the country with recorded music. The settlement of the strike resulted in the formation of the Music Performance Trust Fund, an entity that pays musicians who perform at free public concerts.[5]

In January of 1949, the group moved back to Bristol and WCYB. Their return to the station was noted with the release of a new song and picture book, their second to date. The sale of songbooks was an important income generator for the band. Carter Stanley noted, "We sold books about three or four different times there at Bristol on this *Farm & Fun Time* program. We'd average selling about eleven or twelve thousand books every six weeks. They let us sell six weeks and then knock off."[6] This particular publication highlighted several new and returning band members, most notably bass player Jay Hughes and fiddler Bobby Sumner.

Unfortunately, little is known of either of these musicians. The songbook offers brief bios of each:

> Bobby Sumner was born at Vicco, Kentucky, March 6, 1924, and has been playing the fiddle ever since he can remember. Bobby has been doing radio work four years. He is married to the former Jamoe Dixon of Vicco. They have two children, Sandra Joan, three years, and Michael, 6 months.[7]

> Jay Hughes was born at St. Paul, Virginia, December 16, 1923, and has played the Bass Fiddle for the past two years. He sings bass in the CLINCH MOUNTAIN Quartet. He is unmarried.[8]

Jay related once,

> I worked with them thru '49 and some of 1950 and Carter and them decided to carry a four-piece band for a short while and then I just dropped out . . . I played a year with them, something like that, over a five-state area. Shortly after that I went to work in the coal mines and then I got married.[9]

His prior work included a stint with Jim & Jesse.

Finding Their Voice

Even though the Stanleys were taking their musical cues from Bill Monroe, Carter and Ralph were determined to develop a separate identity. Starting in 1949, they featured an innovative vocal trio that is considered by many to be a hallmark of their Columbia sound. Conventional trios of the day were composed of a regular lead vocal, with a tenor harmony above it, and baritone harmony below it. The Stanleys rewrote the structure of the trio into a stunning new form. In addition to the regular lead and tenor, an even higher third part, called a high baritone, was added. It gave a lovely effect to songs such as "The White Dove," "The Fields Have Turned Brown," and "The Lonesome River." Carter Stanley recounted,

I never heard that sound before, and I don't mind to tell you who suggested it and helped us do it. It was a boy by the name of Art Wooten playing the fiddle with us. He said he felt that that would be a good sound for us if we could work it out, the parts, the harmony. So, as the records will tell, we worked some out but we didn't perfect it, of course. It's been done much better since then by others. But anyway, that was the sound of "Lonesome River," "The Fields Have Turned Brown," and some of them numbers.[10]

Another striking development in the Stanley Brothers' music of the late 1940s was their new material. For the most part, it was fresh and original. Of the twenty-two songs they recorded for Columbia, all but five were originals. Carter had an interest in writing songs before the band started, but it became a necessity afterwards. Ralph Stanley related how the arrival of Flatt & Scruggs in Bristol in 1948 affected Carter's songwriting:

> Flatt and Scruggs come to Bristol, and about all we was doing then was Bill Monroe tunes. Well Lester, he didn't like that, so he tried to ground us, he tried to stop us from doing any of Monroe's tunes. That didn't do much good. There were some words over it, you know, and, I don't know . . . Carter stepped out more [i.e., was more outgoing] than I did, and he just decided . . . and he started writing. I'd say in the next year's time he had fifty or sixty songs wrote and that's when we began singing Stanley Brothers. So, I guess it was a help after all.[11]

In the Deep Rolling Hills of Old Virginia: Columbia #1 (Session 490301)

On March 1, 1949, the Stanley Brothers recorded their first session for Columbia Records, at Castle Studio, located in the Tulane Hotel in Nashville. A young Carter Stanley was proud and amazed: "To us, that would have been the impossible."[12] The band that recorded that day included Pee Wee Lambert, fiddler Bobby Sumner, and bassist Jay Hughes. It was Pee Wee who added the essential high baritone part to the new trio sound. Three trios were recorded that day, and all of them were Carter Stanley originals. The first is a lovely sentimental piece reflecting on the joys of childhood called "A Vision of Mother." One of the most memorable Stanley songs is featured next, "The White Dove." Carter described how this song came to be written:

> That was one of the first that I ever tried to write. I do . . . or have done the most songs that I have written at night. A lot of times traveling, you know, nobody saying much, your mind wanders, one thing to another. I guess you'd call it imagination. I remember very well when I wrote "The White Dove." We was coming home from Asheville, North Carolina, to Bristol, Tennessee, and I had the light on because I wanted to write it down and Ralph was fussing at me for having the light on. He was driving and he said the light bothered him, but he hasn't fussed anymore about that.[13]

Ralph gave pretty much the same account:

One of the most enduring songs from the Stanley repertoire is "The White Dove." Credited to Carter Stanley, it was one side of the group's first release for Columbia, #20577. The song features the stunning trio harmonies, of Carter and Ralph Stanley and Pee Wee Lambert, that were a hallmark of the band's best Columbia recordings.

> Carter wrote that song one night . . . we had been to a personal appearance somewhere . . . it was one of his first songs. He was in the back seat of the car writing that and by the time we got to the radio station near home we had a verse and a chorus worked out. I don't know what caused him to think of the white dove except that he was studying on it, how it could affect you . . .[14]

In later years, Ralph reflected on the enduring nature of the song:

> A song like "The White Dove" is the backbone of the Stanley Brothers. If you were ever to go to the place where we was raised, and look around, and study the words to "The White Dove," you could just see it in your mind. Carter really loved our parents, our mother and daddy, and he dreaded the day when, according to nature, we'd have to give them up. In "The White Dove" he visioned that he—he always visioned going back home, and they wouldn't be there.[15]

The remaining trio from the March 1 session is a song concerned with the loss of a deceased loved one, "The Angels Are Singing in Heaven Tonight." The other songs from that session are duets. Only one is not an original, the sacred song "Gathering Flowers for the Master's Bouquet." According to Ralph, "We heard the Maddox Brothers and Rose do that."[16] Cut next is another of the Stanleys' most popular tunes—their signature song of the late 1940s—"The Little Glass of Wine." They had recorded this song two years earlier on Rich-R-Tone, but must have felt that the song would benefit from the better distribution that Columbia offered.

The last song recorded at the session, "Let Me Be Your Friend," is a duet by Carter and Pee Wee Lambert. The tune borrows heavily from the Bill Monroe composition "It's Mighty Dark to Travel." As demonstrated on the 1947 WCYB transcriptions, Pee Wee often dupli-

Although the Stanley Brothers had recorded "Little Glass of Wine" earlier for Rich-R-Tone, they felt the song would benefit from the wider distribution that Columbia offered. The new remake was their second release for their new label.

cated Monroe's style on the mandolin and sang many of his songs. Consequently, it seems only natural that Pee Wee would supply the vocal harmony on this Monroesque selection.

Farm & Fun Time, Once Again (Session 490600)

From Nashville, the Stanley Brothers returned to WCYB in Bristol. They continued to transcribe selections for use at the radio station when they were on the road making personal appearances. A 1988 album on Rebel Records entitled *Live Again! WCYB Bristol Farm and Fun Time* features five tracks by the Stanleys—plus Pee Wee Lambert and Bobby Sumner—that were recorded shortly after their Columbia session: their opening theme song (the same one they used on their 1947 broadcasts, " . . . Rolling along, singing a song . . ."), "Let Me Be Your Friend," "Short Life of Trouble," "Blackberry Blossom," and "Rose of Old Kentucky."

Carter introduces the first song as follows:

> Friends, a duet number coming up right now. Here's a number you're gonna hear on a Columbia record some of these days. It's one of our own, entitled "Let Me Be Your Friend."

The studio recording was made on March 1, 1949, and was issued by Columbia on June 20, 1949, indicating that these radio transcriptions were made within the four-month window between March and June of 1949.

Ralph is featured in a solo version of "Short Life of Trouble." A tune quite popular in old-time music, it was recorded numerous times in the 1920s and '30s by performers such Grayson & Whitter, Tom Ashley, and the Blue Sky Boys. "Blackberry Blossom," a tune written and recorded in the 1930s by legendary country fiddler Arthur Smith, showcases

Bobby Sumner's talents. In his notes to the *Live Again!* recording, Jack Tottle observes that Sumner's rendition is "closer to Fiddlin' Arthur Smith's than to the chord-changin'-every-two-beats version prevalent today."[17] Lastly, "Rose of Old Kentucky" highlights Pee Wee Lambert on a selection written and recorded by Bill Monroe.

By the summer of 1949, Bobby Sumner had moved on and a North Carolina fiddler by the name of Lester Woodie replaced him. Jim Shumate, a Hickory, North Carolina, fiddler and a former member of both Bill Monroe's Blue Grass Boys and Flatt & Scruggs' Foggy Mountain Boys, suggested him to the Stanleys. Woodie gained much of his early performance experience by playing with Valdese, North Carolina, musicians George and John Shuffler. He well remembered joining the Stanley Brothers:

> In June of 1949 I graduated from high school, and went to work in a bakery. I was working the night shift there one night when about 10 o'clock they called me up front. Somebody was there to see me. I came out and introduced myself to the two strangers standing there in the front of the bakery. It was Ralph Stanley and Pee Wee Lambert . . . So there they were, asking me to join them. I didn't debate about it too long, because I wanted to get out of that bakery. I was to meet Carter Stanley the next day. They had reserved a room in the Hickory Hotel for me to get together with them to try me out.[18]

Lester stayed with Carter and Ralph for nearly two years, recording two sessions with them for Columbia. Around May of 1951, as hostilities were raging in Korea, Woodie received his draft notice. After his discharge, he found musical employment for several years with the Lynchburg, Virginia, band of Bill & Mary Reid. Eventually, he wound up at radio station WKDE in Altavista, Virginia, working as a disc jockey and later as the station manager. He continues to make select local appearances as well as annual pilgrimages to Ralph Stanley's Memorial Day Festival.

For a period of time, the Stanley band included two fiddlers, Lester Woodie and Leslie Keith. Woodie acted as the band's fiddler and Keith was an added showman. Lester recalled,

> He and I had an act together on stage. About half way during the show Ralph and Carter would do some duets, and I would go back and get on a Raggedy Ann outfit, with old clothes and wide tie. I played the comedian. Leslie was a real hand with a black snake or bull snake whip. I would come out in my comedy outfit, and would hold papers for Leslie between my legs, and light it on fire. I'd even put cigarettes in my mouth, and Leslie would cut the fire out of it. We had a real circus act.[19]

The Fields Have Turned Brown: Columbia #2 (Session 491120)

In November of 1949, the Stanley Brothers relocated to Winston-Salem, North Carolina, and radio station WTOB. On November 20, approximately three weeks after their arrival at the station, they journeyed to Nashville for their second recording session with Columbia Records. The band included Carter and Ralph Stanley, Pee Wee Lambert, and Lester Woodie. For the first time on record, the Stanleys made use of a studio bass player—Ernie Newton.

From 1946 until the 1960s, Ernest "Ernie" Newton (November 7, 1909–October 17, 1976) was among the busiest session acoustic bass players in Nashville. His early pre-Nashville days included work with minstrel shows, Chicago's WLS with Bob Gardner (of Mac & Bob fame), and the Les Paul Trio. He came to the *Grand Ole Opry* in 1946 as a member of Red Foley's band. His playing was somewhat unique in that he mounted on his bass a drum head that, between beats, gave a percussive sound to his music. Among the early hit recordings from Nashville that he participated on are Red Foley's "Chattanooga Shoe Shine Boy," Hank Snow's "I'm Movin' On," and Johnnie & Jack's "Poison Love."[20]

The first three songs recorded during the Stanleys' November session are duets by Carter and Ralph: "We'll Be Sweethearts in Heaven," "I Love No One but You," and "Too Late to Cry." "The Old Home" is also a vocal duet, but by Carter and Pee Wee Lambert. The composition of all four of these selections is credited to Carter Stanley.

Closing out the session are two trios, both of which feature high baritone harmonies by Pee Wee Lambert. The Stanleys learned "The Drunkard's Hell" from their father. Ralph recalled, "Our Daddy, we heard him do that. He knew some words to that, and I think maybe we put some to it."[21] Old-time music has three recorded versions of the song, by Vernon Dalhart, Maynard Britton, and Wade Mainer & the Sons of the Mountaineers; these all date from between 1925 and 1939.[22] Perhaps most significant is the fact that the song was collected by E. J. Sutherland of Clintwood, Virginia, on December 20, 1928, from Claude A. Sutherland of Dickenson County.[23] This gives a good indication that the song was in circulation in and around the Stanley homestead. The last song from the session is another Carter Stanley original called "The Fields Have Turned Brown." Regarded as an early classic of the Stanleys' career, the song describes a wayward son's lament after learning of his parents' passing while pursuing a wanderlust life.

Lester Woodie recounted some of his impressions of his recording sessions with the Stanleys:

> That was quite a big thing for me. It was the first time that I'd made any records and I was quite young at the time and amazed by it all. One thing that impressed me, on the sessions we did for Columbia, Art Satherley and Don Law, they, for some reason or another, took the time to fly in from New York to those sessions and they sat right in there. For some reason they liked the Stanleys and the old-time music and I guess that's why they did it. Don was quite active in the sessions and making suggestions and so forth. They took a big interest in it. As far as I can recall they would suggest a mandolin break would be good here or doing a certain type of arrangement on it. They would help in the arranging of it. They went to great lengths to talk it out. They were fascinated evidently with the country style of living the Stanleys were used to. The sessions were cut in November and I remember Carter took Art a country ham one time.[24]

In the late 1940s, there were few studios operating in Nashville and the bulk of all recording activities took place at Castle Studios. Lester Woodie remembered it as follows:

[It was] like your back room, compared to today's studios. It wasn't elaborate. They, I'm
sure, had good equipment, but it wouldn't be compared to the equipment today. About
all I remember about the studio is just there wasn't much there except the mic and the
guy with the controls behind the glass. We used three mics. I know the fiddle had a mic
and Pee Wee had a mic.[75]

George Shuffler, who later recorded on Columbia with the Stanleys, had the same impression of Castle Studios.

It was what we'd call now about a second-rate hotel. It wasn't plush. The studios were
just dim and dingy and dusty and smoky. They wasn't elaborate at all.[26]

After the November 20th session, the group returned to WTOB in Winston-Salem. They
remained at the station until early January of 1950. Lester Woodie recalled that the group
took some time off not long afterwards:

They took a little hiatus. Now I don't know how that came about, but there at one time
they came off the road for like, maybe a couple of months. They didn't do anything, you
know. Ralph went back to the farm and he stayed there a while, and within a couple
of months, why, Carter called me, and I went back with 'em.[27]

The most likely reason for the time-out was the seasonal nature of the music business;
bookings were harder to come by in the dead of winter.

In July of 1950, the group began a three-month stay in Huntington, West Virginia.[28]
They appeared on WSAZ radio and also did some work on WSAZ-TV, becoming one of
the first bluegrass-styled groups to ever appear on television.

Following their stay in West Virginia, Carter and Ralph relocated south to Shreveport,
Louisiana, and radio station KWKH. At the time, this station was considered a close second
to Nashville's WSM and its flagship program, the *Grand Ole Opry*. Many artists used the
Shreveport station as a springboard to Nashville. In Shreveport the Stanley Brothers had
an early morning program[29] and also starred on the popular Saturday evening show, the
Louisiana Hayride. Lester Woodie recalled that the band worked several dates in Texas with
country music singer Slim Whitman. The Stanleys' stay at KWKH was rather brief, lasting
only two weeks, from October 9 until October 25, 1950.[30] Several factors contributed to
their departure. Ralph noted, " . . . we wanted to get back close [to] home." He continued,
" . . . we got a call there from Lexington, Kentucky. They had a Saturday night jamboree in
Lexington and they offered us a good thing."[31]

The Lonesome River: Columbia #3 (Session 501103)

Soon the group was headed north to Lexington and radio station WLEX.[32] As they had done
in Shreveport, they appeared on another Saturday evening jamboree, the *Kentucky Mountain
Barn Dance*.[33] It was at this time, November 3, 1950, that the Stanleys were in Nashville for
their third Columbia session. It had been a full year since their previous session. The band

Carter and Ralph's third session for Columbia took place in November of 1950. Only four songs were recorded, but two of them would come to be regarded as classics. This promotional disc featured both of them back to back. "The Lonesome River" was perhaps one of the most chillingly mournful recordings of the Stanleys' career, while Ralph's rendering of "I'm a Man of Constant Sorrow" would have big pay-offs a half century later.

continued to consist of Carter and Ralph, Pee Wee Lambert, and Lester Woodie, as well as the guest bass player on the session, Ernie Newton.

Only four selections were recorded this time. Curiously, there are no duets by Carter and Ralph. The first song recorded is a duet by Carter Stanley and Pee Wee Lambert called "Hey! Hey! Hey!" Lester Woodie had a clear recollection of Carter writing the song:

> I remember very definitely when he wrote "Hey! Hey! Hey!" At the time it struck me that he was fishing for some words, so in fact I kidded him about that, that he couldn't get any good words, so he said "hey, hey, hey."[34]

Only one trio, with high baritone harmonies by Pee Wee Lambert, was recorded: the now classic "The Lonesome River." Carter's delivery of the song is chillingly mournful and echoes the heartbreaking words of loss and despondency that he wrote. The climax comes with the blending of voices on the choruses, when the stacked harmonies cast an eerie pallor over the entire song. It is one of Carter's most poignant compositions and a masterpiece of early recorded bluegrass.

The remaining two songs, "I'm a Man of Constant Sorrow" and "Pretty Polly," are both solos of old mountain ballads by Ralph. Carter said,

> Dad knew some of 'em. He couldn't play a thing as far as an instrument, but his voice was just the same as ours is. He sang "Pretty Polly" and "Man of Constant Sorrow," "Little Bessie," I believe. So, I guess that's where we got what little singing we know.[35]

By February of 1951, the Stanley Brothers were back in Bristol. They worked for several months with Pee Wee Lambert, Lester Woodie, and bass player John Shuffler. An occasional guest on live shows was a comedian known as Smokey Davis. An item from the May 12, 1951, edition of *Billboard* magazine mentioned that the Stanley Brothers had returned to WSAZ in Huntington. However, the daily radio listings from the local newspaper show no record of any programming for the Stanleys. It was about this time that Lester Woodie and John Shuffler received their draft notices for military service. With a turnover of band members and the draft making the prospects for replacements somewhat tenuous, things must have seemed uncertain at best for the Clinch Mountain Boys.

Bill Monroe A-Callin'

On June 20, 1951, Bill Monroe and the Blue Grass Boys appeared on stage at the American Theatre in Roanoke, Virginia. Playing guitar and singing lead that day was Carter Stanley. It's uncertain when Carter joined the group, but this was undoubtedly among his first appearances with Bill. For the young Stanley, playing in Monroe's band was the culmination of a lifelong dream.

Rotation Blues: Decca #1 (Session 510701)

Monroe wasted no time getting into the recording studio while he had Carter in the band. On July 1, 1951, Monroe recorded two songs that feature himself on solo vocals: "Rotation Blues" and "Lonesome Truck Driver Blues." Monroe played mandolin and sang lead vocals for the session, while also on hand were Carter Stanley on rhythm guitar, Gordon Terry on fiddle, Rudy Lyle on banjo, and Ernie Newton on bass.[36] It's quite probable that, as Carter was still under contract to Columbia, he was unable to sing any solos on Monroe's recordings that were made for the competing Decca label.

Life with Monroe was busy, but Carter seemed intent on sticking around. The day after the session, on July 2, he was issued a Tennessee driver's license.[37] On July 5, the Blue Grass Boys appeared in Fayetteville, Arkansas, for a show at the 71 Drive-In.[38] On July 6, they were back in Nashville for another recording session. Then on July 7 they performed on the 10:00 p.m. portion of the *Grand Ole Opry*[39] before heading out the next day for a Sunday appearance at New River Ranch in Rising Sun, Maryland.[40] Baltimore disc jockey Ray Davis, who would cross paths often with the Stanleys during their career, met Carter Stanley for the first time at this show. He noted that Carter emceed the show that day for Monroe, and he was very impressed with his showmanship.[41]

Sugar Coated Love: Decca #2 (Session 510706)

The recording session for July 6 contains four songs and displays considerably greater participation by Carter. The personnel remains the same except that Howard Watts replaces Ernie Newton on bass. The first tune recorded is a duet by Monroe and Stanley called "Sugar Coated Love."[42] Ray Davis took credit for adding that song to Monroe's repertoire. He gave Bill a copy of the 78 rpm record, most likely by Red Kirk or Tex Williams, as well as a small kid's record player, which he paid thirteen dollars for at Reed's Record Store in Baltimore, for Monroe to listen to it on.[43] The song later entered the Stanley Brothers' repertoire and was performed by them throughout the balance of their career.

Recorded next is a gospel quartet written by Monroe called "You're Drifting Away." The hymn features Carter Stanley singing lead, Monroe singing tenor, banjoist Rudy Lyle on baritone, and fiddler Gordon Terry singing bass. As was typical of bluegrass quartets, the only instrumentation featured on this track is Monroe's mandolin, Carter Stanley's guitar, and Howard Watts's bass.[44]

Another Monroe-Stanley duet follows in the form of "Cabin of Love," a selection credited to Monroe's brother, Birch Monroe. Closing out the session is another gospel quartet, the haunting "Get Down on Your Knees and Pray."[45] Of all the songs Carter Stanley recorded with Monroe, this one seems to have elicited the most attention and has been reissued more often than the other tracks. Decca sensed the quality of the song as well, and rushed it out as the first release from the session, getting it on the market less than four weeks after it was recorded. The song's sparse instrumentation, just mandolin and guitar, make a perfect backdrop for the searing vocals. Monroe's crisp high vocals implore sinners to heed the word of God, to "get down on your knees and pray," while each of the quartet members separately reinforce the command with "get down" (by bass singer Gordon Terry), "get down" (by baritone singer Rudy Lyle), "get down" (by lead singer Carter Stanley), and "get down" (by tenor singer Bill Monroe). The quartet then comes together with an authoritative "Get down on your knees and pray." Added to the mix are Monroe's masterful mandolin solos. It all makes for a stunning performance.

As it did the Stanley band earlier in the year, the draft was tapping musicians from Monroe's Blue Grass Boys. In the summer of 1951, Rudy Lyle was called into military service. For a brief period of time, Ralph Stanley filled in on banjo.[46] Monroe liked the sound and offered to change the name of his band to Bill Monroe & the Stanley Brothers if the duo would agree to stay on with him. Ralph reflected that Carter never considered his tenure with Monroe permanent, that the main focus was—and would continue to be—the Stanley Brothers. For his part, while flattered by the offer, Ralph was not keen on joining the Blue Grass Boys. Other factors soon complicated matters. On August 17, while returning from one of his appearances with Monroe, Ralph Stanley (along with Pee Wee Lambert) was involved in a serious automobile accident near Mountain City, Tennessee.[47] He spent the next four weeks recuperating. By the end of this time, Carter Stanley turned in his notice to Monroe and played his last date as a Blue Grass Boy on September 13, 1951, in Roxboro, North Carolina, at the Pioneer Warehouse.

Together Again

After being separated musically for four months, Carter and Ralph reorganized the Clinch Mountain Boys and started up again at WCYB. The new version of the band included fiddler Bobby Sumner, mandolin player Bobby Osborne (who later gained fame as one half of the Osborne Brothers), and bass player Charlie Cline, a former member of the West Virginia–

based Lonesome Pine Fiddlers.[48] Osborne's stay was rather brief—about six weeks—and his induction into the Marines soon took him overseas to Korea.[49]

In December Curly Seckler, a veteran of the Charlie Monroe and Flatt & Scruggs bands, signed up on mandolin. He arranged for the Clinch Mountain Boys to move to Lexington, Kentucky, where they had a daily radio show on WVLK and Saturday evening appearances on the *Kentucky Mountain Barn Dance*.[50]

Seckler's stay in the band was likewise rather brief. Pee Wee Lambert replaced him for a short time, and other changes took place in the band. Bass player George Shuffler started with the band on their arrival in Lexington, and Art Stamper soon appeared on fiddle.

At the conclusion of their stay in Lexington, on April 5, 1952,[51] the Stanley Brothers recorded their last session with Columbia. They recorded as a foursome with George Shuffler on bass and Art Wooten on fiddle.

Although Shuffler was new to the band, he had been connected with the Stanleys for several years. A group he had with his brother John served as a proving ground for Lester Woodie, and John played bass for Carter and Ralph during the first half of 1951.

George was born in Valdese, North Carolina, on April 11, 1925. His early professional work included a stint at the *Grand Ole Opry* with the Bailey Brothers in the mid-1940s, work with his brother John and Lester Woodie, and a stay with the up-and-coming bluegrass duo Jim & Jesse. A phone call from Carter Stanley at Christmastime in 1951 led to George's longtime affiliation with the Stanley Brothers. He worked off and on with them for the next sixteen years and is perhaps the most celebrated of all the Clinch Mountain Boys. He also worked briefly with Ralph at the start of the younger Stanley's solo career in 1967. He is known for his distinctive walking style of bass playing as well as his cross-picking method of lead guitar playing. In the late 1960s, he toured with the duo of Don Reno & Bill Harrell. In the 1970s and '80s, he performed with his family gospel group, the Shuffler Family. He is a recipient of the North Carolina Arts Council's Folk Heritage Award and is an inductee to the International Bluegrass Music Association's Hall of Fame. He died on April 7, 2014.

A Life of Sorrow: Columbia #4 (Session 520411)

Four tunes were recorded in a session for Columbia on April 11, 1952, which was George Shuffler's twenty-seventh birthday. The first is a song called "A Life of Sorrow." Carter and Ralph Stanley wrote it, with an assist from George Shuffler. The melody is strikingly similar to a tune the Stanley Brothers had recorded earlier on Columbia, "I'm a Man of Constant Sorrow," and is a good example of how the Stanleys recycled old tunes to create "new" material. The song is sung as a trio, though with Pee Wee Lambert absent from the group, the high baritone harmonies that were prevalent on the earlier Columbia sides are gone. Instead, "A Life of Sorrow" features a conventional three-part harmony of lead (Carter Stanley), tenor (Ralph Stanley), and baritone (George Shuffler).

Another Carter and Ralph Stanley composition, "Sweetest Love," follows next. It is a duet featuring the two brothers, which seems to be their preferred vocal pattern for much of the rest of their career. Ralph Stanley noted, "After Pee Wee left, we got down to doing the Stanley style."[52]

A rare vocal solo from Carter Stanley is featured at this session, a rendering of a Carter Family favorite called "The Wandering Boy." The song dates from 1894, when it appeared as "Somebody's Boy Is Homeless Tonight," with words and music by R. S. Hanna. The Carters recorded it during their second day of recording at the famed Bristol sessions, on August 2, 1927. The Stanleys' release of this song is credited to A. P. Carter, thus reflecting the brothers' awareness of the Carters' connection to the song. However, Carter Stanley's lyrics differ quite a bit from those of the original Carter Family recording and are closer to a version performed by Bill Monroe in the mid-1940s, as evidenced by a recently discovered privately made Monroe recording from this period.[53]

Closing out the session is another duet, credited to Carter and sung by Carter and Ralph, called "Let's Part the Best of Friends." Curiously, this song was held back for release by Columbia. Since the Stanley Brothers' contract with the label expired after this session, it's likely that the label didn't see the point in promoting material by a group it was no longer associated with. The recording made its first appearance on vinyl in the mid-1970s when it was issued on a Japanese collection of Stanley Brothers recordings.[54]

Rich-R-Tone #4 (Session 520600)

After the session for Columbia, the band headed to Pikeville, Kentucky, and radio station WLSI. Like their stay in Shreveport, their time in Pikeville was brief. They were on the air for just two weeks, from April 15 to April 30, 1952.[55] Their next move was to WOAY in Oak Hill, West Virginia.[56] The band consisted of Carter and Ralph Stanley, Art Stamper, and George Shuffler. While in Oak Hill, they picked up mandolin player Jim Williams.

Born in Wythe County, Virginia, on February 29, 1932, Jim Williams came from a musical family. His father was an old-time fiddler, and his mother played Jew's harp, harmonica, and organ. In his teen years, he performed often with his cousin, Paul Humphrey (later known as Paul Williams). The duo worked with groups like the Lonesome Pine Fiddlers. In the early 1950s, Jim recorded and performed with Mac Wiseman, appearing on a number of his now classic Dot recordings. It was while working with Mac that Jim received word that the Stanley Brothers were interested in him. He noted that "a long, black Packard Limousine"[57] with Carter Stanley at the wheel and passengers Ralph Stanley, Art Stamper, and old-time fiddler Cam Powers met him at the Williamses' family farm. He joined them and headed to Oak Hill.

Jim Williams recorded on a number of sessions with the Stanley Brothers during the early and mid-1950s. He left the band several times, alternating back and forth between the Stanleys and Mac Wiseman. His final tenure with Carter and Ralph ended in 1955. He did some local work in the Bristol area and not long afterwards dedicated his life to Christ. He teamed up for several years with a disc jockey by the name of Red Ellis, and together they recorded some memorable sides for Starday in the early 1960s. Jim kept a hand in music over the years, but his main area of interest was his work as an evangelist.[58] He died on September 9, 2012.

The exact date of the Stanley Brothers' final Rich-R-Tone session is not known, but it appears likely that the recordings were made in the summer of 1952. Label owner Jim Stanton was doing some booking work for the group at the time, and was with them when they happened to be near Pikeville for a show date.

> (We) got in a hotel room there one night and started knocking these songs around and they got anxious to cut 'em. WLSI was real strong on giving 'em good radio plugs and their facilities were decent. So we decided to cut the session there to stimulate more interest in the area. Man, that studio . . . that radio was [full], there was people waiting out in the yard to see 'em. You know, it was a big thing then to have a record session in your community. We started one morning, seemed to me like around nine o'clock 'cause they had a show date that night in a little place called Betsy Layne. About noon we had the yard full, the station full, and people trying to do the newscast aggravated at us and all that type of thing.[59]

The session produced a variety of material. Three songs are duets by Carter and Ralph, and another is a solo that highlights Ralph's singing and old-time banjo work. The first song is "The Little Girl and the Dreadful Snake," which Carter learned from Bill Monroe when he was working as a Blue Grass Boy. Apparently, Monroe composed the song shortly before Carter joined the band. Carter once mentioned Monroe on a show date when he helped to introduce the song in Nashville.[60] The Stanleys recorded their version about the same time as Monroe, who cut it for Decca Records on July 18, 1952.

While the Stanley Brothers were at Columbia, they re-recorded their early hit, "The Little Glass of Wine." Curiously, for this Rich-R-Tone session they recorded it yet a third time. It is interesting to listen to the three cuts back to back. The first Rich-R-Tone version is rather archaic and old-time sounding; the Columbia version is very smooth, with all of the rough edges gone; the final version on Rich-R-Tone shows much of the drive and punch that the group was developing. This drive, in fact, is displayed on the whole session. "Are You Waiting Just for Me" is an Ernest Tubb song that he featured on the *Grand Ole Opry* in the mid-1940s. Ralph remembered that, in sharp contrast to the Stanley Brothers' version, Tubb performed the song in a really slow style.[61] The Stanleys featured the song on many of their show dates well into the mid- and late 1950s. Bill Monroe featured it on numerous occasions, in bluegrass style, on the *Opry* in the mid- and late 1940s. Surviving private recordings of Monroe's *Opry* performances from this period reveal striking similarities between the Monroe and Stanley Brothers renditions of the song. Although the Stanleys probably did hear Tubb's version of "Are You Waiting Just For Me" on the radio, it appears that Bill Monroe heavily influenced their rendition.

The remaining selection from the session, "Little Birdie," is a solo number by Ralph in which he plays clawhammer banjo for the first time on a recording. Ralph couldn't remember exactly where he learned the song:

It probably come from Steve Ledford, Wade Mainer, somewhere in there, I guess. I could have heard the Coon Creek Girls, Cousin Emmy, or somebody. I don't remember on that exactly . . . I think they all sung it.[62]

Carter and Ralph experienced a lot of career changes in the period spanning 1948 to 1952. They signed with a major label, Columbia Records; developed a striking substyle— complete with a radically new vocal structure—within the emerging bluegrass genre; created a unique canon of quality original material; took their music to six major markets (Bristol, Raleigh, Winston-Salem, Huntington, Shreveport, and Lexington); and became one of the first bluegrass-styled bands to appear on television. And, no less important, Carter Stanley apprenticed in Bill Monroe's Blue Grass Boys. The brothers were leaving an indelible mark on the formative days of bluegrass music.

DISCOGRAPHY, 1949–1952

490301   Columbia session; producers: Art Satherley and Don Law
Castle Studio, Tulane Hotel, 206 8th Ave., Nashville, Tennessee
March 1, 1949
Carter Stanley: g | Ralph Stanley: b | Pee Wee Lambert: m
Robert Franks "Bobby" Sumner: f | James "Jay" Hughes: sb

CO-40506	**A Vision of Mother** (Carter Stanley) C. Stanley–L, R. Stanley–T, Lambert–HB	20647	HL-7291, ROU-SS-09, BCD-15564, CK-53798
CO-40507	**The White Dove** (Carter Stanley) C. Stanley–L, R. Stanley–T, Lambert–HB	20577, 54008, 2833	HL-7291, ROU-SS-09, BCD-15564, CK-53798, B0007883-02
CO-40508	**Gathering Flowers for the Master's Bouquet** (M. D. Baumgardner) C. Stanley–L, R. Stanley–T	20577, 54008, 2833	HL-7291, ROU-SS-09, BCD-15564, CK-53798
CO-40509	**The Angels Are Singing** (Carter Stanley) C. Stanley–L, R. Stanley–T, Lambert–HB	20617	HL-7377, HS-11177, ROU-SS-09, BCD-15564, CK-53798
CO-40510	**It's Never Too Late** (Carter Stanley) C. Stanley–L, R. Stanley–T	20617	HL-7377, HS-11177, ROU-SS-09, BCD-15564, CK-53798
CO-40511	**Have You Someone** (Carter Stanley) C. Stanley–L, R. Stanley–T	20647	HL-7377, HS-11177, ROU-SS-09, BCD-15564, CK-53798
CO-40512	**Little Glass of Wine** (Carter Stanley) C. Stanley–L, R. Stanley–T	20590	HL-7377, HS-11177, ROU-SS-09, BCD-15564, CK-53798, B0007883-02
CO-40512	**Little Glass of Wine** (alternate take) C. Stanley–L, R. Stanley–T		BCD-15564
CO-40513	**Let Me Be Your Friend** (Carter Stanley) C. Stanley–L, Lambert–T	20590	HL-7377, HS-11177, ROU-SS-09, BCD-15564, CK-53798

490600   Rebel Records reissue of *Farm & Fun Time* transcriptions
WCYB, Bristol, Virginia
ca. June 1949
Carter Stanley: g | Ralph Stanley: b | Pee Wee Lambert: m
Bobby Sumner: f

Introduction C. Stanley–Spoken intro	REB-854, REB-2003
Let Me Be Your Friend (Stanley) C. Stanley–L, Lambert–T	REB-854, REB-2003
Short Life of Trouble (Traditional) R. Stanley–L	REB-854, REB-2003

Blackberry Blossom (Traditional)   REB-854, REB-2003
Instrumental

Rose of Old Kentucky (Monroe)   REB-854, REB-2003
Lambert–L

| 491120 | Columbia session; producers: Art Satherley and Don Law
Castle Studio, Tulane Hotel, 206 8th Ave., Nashville, Tennessee
November 20, 1949
Carter Stanley: g \| Ralph Stanley: b \| Pee Wee Lambert: m
Lester Woodie: f \| Ernest "Ernie" Newton: sb | | |

CO-41936	**We'll Be Sweethearts in Heaven** (Carter Stanley) C. Stanley–L, R. Stanley–T	20735	HL-7291, ROU-SS-09, BCD-15564, CK-53798
CO-41937	**I Love No One but You** (Carter Stanley) C. Stanley–L, R. Stanley–T	20697	HL-7291, ROU-SS-09, BCD-15564, CK-53798
CO-41938	**Too Late to Cry** (Carter Stanley) C. Stanley–L, R. Stanley–T	20697	HL-7377, HS-11177, ROU-SS-09, BCD-15564
CO-41938	**Too Late to Cry** (alternate take) C. Stanley–L, R. Stanley–T		CK-53798
CO-41939	**The Old Home** (Carter Stanley) C. Stanley–L, Lambert–T	20667, 2833	HL-7377, HS-11177, ROU-SS-10, BCD-15564, CK-53798, B0007883-02
CO-41940	**The Drunkard's Hell** (Arr. Carter Stanley) C. Stanley–L, R. Stanley–T, Lambert–HB	20735	HL-7291, ROU-SS-10, BCD-15564, CK-53798
CO-41941	**The Fields Have Turned Brown** (Carter Stanley) C. Stanley–L, R. Stanley–T, Lambert–HB	20667 2833	HL-7377, HS-11177, ROU-SS-10, BCD-15564, CK-53798, B0007883-02
CD-41941	**The Fields Have Turned Brown** (alternate take) C. Stanley–L, R. Stanley–T, Lambert–HB		BCD-15564

| 501103 | Columbia session; producers: Art Satherley and Don Law
Castle Studio, Tulane Hotel, 206 8th Ave., Nashville, Tennessee
November 3, 1950
Carter Stanley: g \| Ralph Stanley: b \| Pee Wee Lambert: m
Lester Woodie: f \| Ernie Newton: sb | | |

4310	**Hey! Hey! Hey!** (Carter Stanley) C. Stanley–L, Lambert–T	20770	ROU-SS-10, BCD-15564, CK-53798
4311	**The Lonesome River** (Carter Stanley) C. Stanley–L, R. Stanley–T, PW Lambert–HB	20816	HL-7291, ROU-SS-10, BCD-15564, CK-53798, B0007883-02
4312	**I'm a Man of Constant Sorrow** (Carter Stanley) R. Stanley–L	20816	HL-7377, HS-11177, ROU-SS-10, BCD-15564, CK-53798
4313	**Pretty Polly** (B. F. Shelton) R. Stanley–L	20770	HL-7291, ROU-SS-10, BCD-15564, CK-53798

510701   Decca session; producer: Paul Cohen
Castle Studio, Tulane Hotel, 206 8th Ave., Nashville, Tennessee
July 1, 1951, 2–5 P.M.
Carter Stanley: g | Rudy R. Lyle: b | Bill Monroe: m | Gordon H. Terry: f | Ernest Newton: sb

NA 2420 81249	**Rotation Blues** (Lt. Stewart Powell) Monroe–L	46344	BS 1, BCD-15423
NA 2421 81250	**Lonesome Truck Driver's Blues** (Lee Roberts) Monroe–L	46344	BS 1, BCD-15423

510706   Decca session; producer: Paul Cohen
Castle Studio, Tulane Hotel, 206 8th Ave., Nashville, Tennessee
July 6, 1951, 8:30 A.M.–12 noon
Carter Stanley: g | Rudy Lyle (-22, -24): b | Bill Monroe: m | Gordon Terry: f (2422, 2424) | Howard Staton Watts: sb

NA 2422 81272	**Sugar Coated Love** (Audrey Butler) Stanley–L, Monroe–T	46369	DL 4780, MCAD 4-11048, BCD 15423
NA 2423 81273	**You're Drifting Away** (Bill Monroe) Stanley–L, Monroe–T, Lyle–B, Terry–BS	28608	DL 7-5066, BCD 15423
NA 2424 81274	**Cabin of Love** (Burch [sic] Monroe) Stanley–L, Monroe–T	28749	BS 1, CCS-114, BCD 15423
NA 2425 81275	**Get Down on Your Knees and Pray** (Bill Monroe) Stanley–L, Monroe–T, Lyle–B, Terry–BS	46351	ED 3254, DL 7-5135, BCD 15423, MCA 088 113 207-2, MCA B0002907-2

520411   Columbia session; producer: Don Law
Castle Studio, Tulane Hotel, 206 8th Ave., Nashville, Tennessee
April 11, 1952
Carter Stanley: g | Ralph Stanley: b
Art Wooten: f | George Saunders Shuffler: sb

CO-47811	**A Life of Sorrow** (Carter & Ralph Stanley) C. Stanley–L, R. Stanley–T, Shuffler–B		HL-7291, ROU-SS-10, BCD-15564, CK-53798
CO-47812	**Sweetest Love** (Carter & Ralph Stanley) C. Stanley–L, R. Stanley–T	20953	HL-7291, ROU-SS-10, BCD-15564, CK-53798
CO-47813	**The Wandering Boy** (A. P. Carter) C. Stanley–L	20953	HL-7377, HS-11177, ROU-SS-10, BCD-15564, CK-53798
CO-47814	**Let's Part the Best of Friends** (Carter Stanley) C. Stanley–L, R. Stanley–T		ROU-SS-10, BCD-15564, CK-53798

520600   Rich-R-Tone: producer: Jim Stanton
          Radio Station WLSI, Pikeville, Kentucky
          ca. June 1952
          Carter Stanley: g | Ralph Stanley: b | James Lee "Jim" Williams: m
          Arthur Sturgil "Art" Stamper: f

1347   **The Little Girl and the Dreadful Snake** (Bill Monroe)   RRT-1055   MLP-7322, REV-203, ROU-1110
        C. Stanley–L, R. Stanley–T

1348   **Little Glass of Wine** (Carter Stanley)   RRT-1056   MLP-7322, REV-203, ROU-1110
        C. Stanley–L, R. Stanley–T

1446   **Are You Waiting Just for Me** (Ernest Tubb)   RRT-1055   MLP-7322, REV-203, ROU-1110
        C. Stanley–L, R. Stanley–T   B0007883-02

1447   **Little Birdie** (Traditional–P. D.)   RRT-1056   MLP-7322, REV-203, ROU-1110
        R. Stanley–L

3

SOME OF OUR BEST RECORDINGS
WERE THE MERCURYS

1953–1958

The early 1950s continued to be a time of nomadic activity for the Stanley Brothers. In September of 1952, following their final session for Rich-R-Tone, they finished up their stay at WOAY in Oak Hill, West Virginia. From there, they journeyed to North Wilkesboro, North Carolina, and then back to Bristol. The onset of winter and the scarcity of show dates brought about another temporary break-up of the Clinch Mountain Boys. According to Ralph,

> [In 1952] we went to Detroit and we worked at the Ford factory. I worked ten weeks and Carter worked about between three and four months. I went home before he did. Spring of the year come around, and I went back to start farming some. At the time I got all my crops out on the farm, why, I called him [Carter] and told him I was ready to go. So he quit and come in, and we started back and we've been playing ever since.[1]

By July of 1953, they were back in their old routine at WCYB, with Art Stamper and Jim Williams rounding out the group. The next month, they began a five-year association with yet another label, Mercury Records. It would be a time of their career noted for its high level of creativity and musicianship. Ralph stated simply, "Some of our best recordings were some of the Mercurys,"[2] while Carter acknowledged, "I always liked the first sound that we got there the best."[3] Their recordings were, in many respects, high-water marks for not only their career, but recorded bluegrass as well.

Mercury Records was formed in 1945 by Irving Green, a veteran manufacturer of plastic and resin manufacturing equipment; Berle Adams; and Arthur Talmadge. Under Green's leadership as label head, the firm set up two pressing plants, one in Chicago and one in St. Louis. Green set an ambitious goal of pressing 700,000 discs per week. In less than a decade, Mercury had established itself as one of the top five or six players in the record industry, going head-to-head with heavyweight rivals including RCA Victor, Columbia, Decca, and Capitol.

The label had a major presence with pop (Frankie Laine, Vic Damone, Tony Fontane, and Patti Page) and jazz (Charlie Parker and Billie Holiday) and developed a decent country catalog as well. Some of Mercury's better-known country artists of the late 1940s included Flatt & Scruggs, Carl Story, Rex Allen, Eddie Dean, and Archie Campbell.

In 1951 Mercury hired Walter David "D." Kilpatrick to take over its country division and establish a foothold in Nashville. No stranger to the music business, Kilpatrick got his start in the industry shortly after the end of World War II when he went to work for Capitol Records, then one of the rising new independent labels. He worked for a year and a half in the Charlotte, North Carolina, office before heading to Atlanta to serve as a branch manager. When he switched to Mercury, he recorded performers such as the Carlisles (one of the top acts on the *Grand Ole Opry*), Johnny Horton, and Carl Story. In 1956 he left Mercury to become the general manager of the WSM *Grand Ole Opry* as well as the head of their Artist Service Bureau. In 1958 he was voted by disc jockeys as the country and western "man of the year." He was a founding member of the Country Music Association and a frequent organizer of WSM's annual disk jockey convention.[4] In his capacity as a producer at Mercury, he supervised the various recording sessions that Carter and Ralph held for the label between 1953 and 1956.

Mercury #1: August 1953 (Session 530809)

The Stanley Brothers' first session for the label, held on August 9, 1953, was recorded at Bradley Studios in Nashville, Tennessee. The facility was the creation of Owen and Harold Bradley, two brothers who figured prominently in the development of the Nashville sound in the 1950s and '60s. Owen was a producer for Decca Records who recorded artists as diverse as Bill Monroe and Patsy Cline, and Harold was a guitarist who became a member of the "A team" of session musicians. The Bradleys became the first to give competition to Nashville's first and only serious recording studio, Castle, when they opened Bradley Film and Recording Studio, located at the corner of 2nd Avenue South and Lindsley Avenue, in 1951. The next year, they relocated to the Hillsboro Village of Nashville, not far from Vanderbilt University. It was here that Carter and Ralph recorded all of their sessions for Mercury in 1953 and 1954.

The group displayed a marked advancement in their musical development. Bob Artis, in his book *Bluegrass*, accurately describes the spirit of the first session.

> To say that the first Mercury session was hot would be a woeful understatement. Carter's lead singing was strong and self-assured, and Ralph was sending his hard, mountain tenor right up through the rafters. The younger Stanley was playing his banjo hard and loud, establishing once and for all the Stanley-style of bluegrass banjo. [Jim] Williams played some inspired Monroe-style mandolin, and [Art] Stamper played breaks and fiddle backup that are still talked about. Giving the session an almost unbelievable forward thrust was bassist [George] Shuffler, playing some of the most complicated bluegrass bass ever recorded. Only four numbers were recorded: "(Say) Won't You Be Mine," "The [*sic*] Weary Heart You Stole Away," "I'm Lonesome Without You," and "Our Last Goodbye." All became standards against which the group would be judged.[5]

In August of 1953, the Stanley Brothers signed a recording contract with Chicago-based Mercury Records, one of the leading independent labels of the day. Their first session is regarded by many as a high water mark of not only their career, but also early recorded bluegrass. One side of their first Mercury release was a Carter Stanley composition called "This Weary Heart You Stole Away."

Stamper and Williams were the only full-time members of the band then; George Shuffler appeared as a guest at the request of Carter Stanley. While the majority of the recordings the Stanleys made for Mercury did feature their regular touring bands, it was not uncommon for substitutes to be called in from time to time. In a number of instances, as was the case here with George Shuffler, those asked to participate had a history with or connection to the Stanley Brothers.

All four of the tunes recorded at the August session were Stanley originals, three by Carter and one by Ralph. Though not officially credited as such, "(Say) Won't You Be Mine" was a collaboration between Bill Monroe and Carter. The two had started the song when Carter worked for Monroe in the summer of 1951. Carter finished the song after his departure from the Blue Grass Boys and added it to the Stanley Brothers' repertoire.[6] Monroe also used the song but saved it for twenty-five years, recording it for MCA in the mid-1970s as "Mary Jane, Won't You Be Mine." The lone trio from the session, as well as Ralph's only composition to be featured, was "I'm Lonesome Without You." Art Stamper was originally slated to sing the baritone part, but on the way to the session, the Stanleys and George Shuffler worked out the arrangement that was recorded.[7]

The band personnel changed shortly after the session. In September, Art Stamper was called into military service. The group apparently went without a fiddle for several weeks, but by November, Don "Chubby" Anthony filled the spot. John Shuffler, George's younger brother, played bass and Jim Williams continued in fine style with his Monroe-inspired mandolin work. Rounding out the group was comedian Smokey Davis.

Mercury #2: November 1953 (Session 531125)

The Stanleys' next session for Mercury was on November 25, 1953, and it offered another set of four songs that rivaled those of their classic debut session for the label. The only band member present from the previous session was Jim Williams. John Shuffler played bass. Appearing on fiddle was Ralph Mayo, an excellent musician from Kingsport, Tennessee. At the time of the session, Chubby Anthony was the regular fiddle player for the band, but Carter Stanley felt that Chubby's playing was not fully developed. Consequently, he asked veteran fiddler Mayo to substitute for the session.

John Shuffler worked with the Stanley Brothers on two separate occasions, first in 1950-51 and again in 1953. He was born on January 16, 1931, in Valdese, North Carolina, and began playing the guitar while in the first grade. At age twelve, he joined George's group, the Melody Mountain Boys. He played a plywood bass for four years, and when he was sixteen, his mother ordered a Kay bass for him from Sears Roebuck. John made monthly payments of $10.00 each until he repaid the purchase price of $129.00. His first stint with the Stanleys found the group working at WCYB in Bristol; Lester Woodie and Pee Wee Lambert were also in the band at the time. He stayed until the middle of 1951, at which time he was called into military service. He served twenty-two months and was stationed in Korea. Upon his discharge in 1953, he again played with the Stanley Brothers and recorded his only session with the duo. Finding that life on the road didn't agree with him, John left the Stanleys right around Christmastime of 1953. He worked in a furniture store for twenty-six years, but continued to play music off and on, including an eight year stretch with L. W. Lambert and the Blue River Boys. He also played with fiddler Jim Shumate, and in 1989 helped banjoist Eric Ellis with several recording projects. In 2003, he organized his own John Shuffler Band.[8] He died on December 21, 2012.

Ralph Eugene Mayo was born on January 4, 1930, near Surgeonsville, Tennessee. His first professional work was at age seventeen, when he appeared with the Bailey Brothers in Rome, Georgia. A year later, he signed on with Carl Sauceman in Knoxville. Around 1950, he went to work with Mac Wiseman and shortly thereafter moved with him to Shreveport to appear on the *Louisiana Hayride*. While there, Mayo made his first recordings, on Mac Wiseman's first session for Dot Records. By 1952 Mayo was back in east Tennessee and coleading a band called the Southern Mountain Boys. The group appeared on *Farm & Fun Time* and made appearances throughout the area. It was around this time that Carter Stanley asked Mayo to appear on the Stanleys' second session for Mercury Records. Mayo did several tours of duty with the Stanleys, including the summer of 1955 and various parts of 1960, 1962, and 1965. In the 1960s, he worked with the Webster Brothers, two brothers from Knoxville who set up shop in Alabama, and the duo of Charlie Moore & Bill Napier. Mayo was out of the public eye for most of the '70s, '80s, and early '90s, although he did make a few guest appearances at Ralph Stanley's festival. He died on September 20, 1992.[9]

The November session introduced some firsts for the Stanleys. It features their first

The Stanleys' early recordings for Mercury appeared on the market as the music industry was transitioning from the 78 rpm format to 45s. Consequently, the duo's releases were issued in both formats, as evidenced by this 1954 release of a song they learned from Bill Monroe, "A Voice from On High."

recording of an instrumental, a banjo tune called "Dickenson County Breakdown," which was named in honor of the brothers' native county in Virginia. Mercury mistakenly titled the track "Dickson County Breakdown" when it was first released. It was the first of many instrumentals that Ralph wrote. Throughout the 1950s, this was the familiar theme song that opened all of their personal appearances.

The other significant first from this session is the Stanley Brothers' introduction of a unique vocal styling that gives a lovely effect to the Bill Monroe–Bessie Lee Mauldin hymn, "A Voice from On High." Instead of featuring a conventional trio with lead, tenor, and baritone parts, the group opts for a different treatment with a high lead part by Ralph, a low tenor part by John Shuffler, and a baritone part by Carter. It is a novel arrangement with extraordinary results, but one that the group used sparingly. This is the same vocal structure that later established the Osborne Brothers as a major force in bluegrass.

Two duets were also recorded at the session, both of which are Carter Stanley originals. "I Long to See the Old Folks" displays a theme that is common to many of his songs, a longing for family and home. "Poison Lies" recounts a lover's refusal to face the hard facts in a relationship gone wrong, dismissing bad news as "poison lies."

The months shortly after the session, starting in April of 1954, saw a steady stream of work for Carter and Ralph in local movie theaters. They worked a series of dates in Tazewell and Norton, Virginia, in conjunction with another WCYB talent, Cuzzin' Don McGraw. Together, they conducted talent contests at the theaters. Drive-in theater appearances in Abingdon, Vansant, and Galax, Virginia, accounted for show dates in May. Although Mercury was distributing the group nationally, a large percentage of their work was still very regional.

Mercury #3: May 1954 (Session 540530)

May 30, 1954, was the date of the Stanleys' third session for Mercury. All four of the tunes recorded at this session were Carter Stanley original duets. Jim Williams continued on the mandolin, and Nashville studio musician Lightnin' Chance appeared on bass. Making his debut with the Stanley Brothers was Joe Meadows on fiddle. He had recently started with the Stanleys, having replaced Chubby Anthony, and played some very intense fiddle on the session. According to Carter Stanley,

> The first professional work he ever done was with us. Frankly, I was ashamed for Joe to play with us on stage. I told him to stand way back where people couldn't hear him. I had Chubby Anthony at the time, too. Chubby was getting ready to leave and I broke Joe in that way. And every spare minute that boy had he would work on that fiddle and he didn't work on somebody else's songs all the time, he worked on the songs that he felt we'd be doing. As a result, Joe Meadows made us one of the best fiddlers we ever had. He was young and he was willing to learn and he did. I've always admired Joe Meadows for that.[10]

Joe Meadows was born on December 31, 1934, in Basin, West Virginia. In his youth, he was exposed to various live country music programs such as the *Grand Ole Opry* and *Farm & Fun Time*. His first professional work came in 1950 with the West Virginia duo the Goins Brothers. His next move was to the Stanley Brothers, in late 1953 or early 1954. He stayed with Carter and Ralph until the middle of 1955 and helped record twenty selections for Mercury Records, including their signature rendition of "Orange Blossom Special." After leaving the Stanleys, Joe logged time with the Lilly Brothers, Jim & Jesse, and Bill Monroe. He then worked with several regional bands, such as Bill & Mary Reid and Buddy Starcher. Joe's last stints of professional touring occurred between 1974 and 1980 when he traveled with the Goins Brothers and, later, Jim & Jesse. Starting in 1983, he lived in the Washington, DC, area and performed locally. His day job consisted of working on the staff of Senator Robert Byrd, also a fine West Virginia fiddle player.[11] He died on February 8, 2003.

Session bass player Floyd T. "Lightnin'" Chance was born in Como, Mississippi, on December 21, 1925. He earned the nickname "Lightnin'" as a football player in high school. After World War II, he moved to Memphis and worked for Smilin' Eddie Hill. He joined the *Grand Ole Opry* in 1952 and toured with various acts, playing bass. About the same time, he began working as a studio musician. Along with Bob Moore and Ernie Newton, he became one of Nashville's most sought after session bass players. His 1960s activities included work at WLAC-TV in Nashville, the opening of the Chappell Music office in Nashville, and work on popular media personality Ralph Emery's early morning program on WSM-TV, a position he held until his retirement in 1988. He died on April 11, 2005.[12]

Again, the months after the session found the Stanleys working a number of drive-in theater engagements, with appearances in Floyd, Virginia; Knoxville, Tennessee; Middlesboro, Kentucky; and Glen Jean, West Virginia. A few far-reaching outdoor park and jamboree dates also dotted their appointment calendar, with shows being performed at the Brown County Jamboree in Bean Blossom, Indiana; Estel Lee's Barn in Felicity, Ohio; and New River Ranch in Rising Sun, Maryland.

Mercury #4: August 1954 (Session 540829)

The Stanleys' August 29, 1954, session for Mercury introduced two more Clinch Mountain Boys on record, mandolin player Bill Lowe and multi-instrumentalist Charlie Cline. At the time of the session Charlie was playing fiddle for Bill Monroe, and he appeared on these recordings as a guest.

William Harold "Bill" Lowe (not to be confused with the Bill Lowe from eastern Kentucky who recorded with Ron Thomason and Suzanne Thomas) was born on April 5, 1930, and was raised in Nebo, Virginia, near Marion. Some of his first professional work was with Curly King and the Tennessee Hilltoppers, which included Roy Russell on fiddle. Other bands that Bill worked with in the Bristol area included Doug Ham & the Cedar Boys and Art Wooten & the Sunny Mountain Boys. He was called into military service in 1951 and saw action in Korea. After his discharge in 1953, he went to work for the Stanley Brothers, playing mandolin and singing baritone. He stayed with the Stanleys for two years. As Jim Williams would come and go from the band, Bill sometimes switched to bass. He later served a brief stint with Charlie Monroe when he was working out of Mt. Airy, North Carolina. In 1965 Bill organized his own band, the Sons of the Blue Ridge. For a period of time, he relocated to Maryland and worked as a painter. He returned to the Marion area and died on November 12, 1988.[13]

Charles "Charlie" Cline was born on June 6, 1931, in Baisden, West Virginia. His exposure to rural music came early in life as older brothers Curly Ray and Ned as well as an uncle, Ezra, had a band known as the Lonesome Pine Fiddlers. He joined that band in the late 1940s. By 1951 he was part of a group with Curly Ray that was headed by Jimmy Martin and Bob Osborne and known as the Sunny Mountain Boys; this group made four recordings for King Records in the summer of 1951. Charlie worked for the Stanley Brothers for several months in the fall of 1951, playing bass. The balance of the early '50s found him alternating between the Lonesome Pine Fiddlers and Bill Monroe; he participated in classic recording sessions for both groups. By the 1960s he had left music and was devoting his life to evangelistic work with his wife. The mid-1970s found him combining music and preaching, and he eventually returned to bluegrass with the Alabama-based band the Warrior River Boys. He died on November 19, 2004.[14]

The August recording session heralded some notable changes to the Stanley sound that came from an unlikely source. The evening before the session, Carter Stanley met with Bill Monroe at the *Grand Ole Opry*. According to Carter,

> [Bill had] "something I want you to hear." He had the record with him . . . "Blue Moon of Kentucky" by Elvis Presley. We had to go up where there was a machine, you know. So he said, "I want you to hear something" and he had never said anything like that to

In July of 1954, Elvis Presley caused a minor stir with his recording of Bill Monroe's "Blue Moon of Kentucky." At Monroe's urging, the Stanley Brothers recorded their own version of the song that clearly bore the imprint of the Presley disc. It was one of two times on Mercury that Carter and Ralph flirted with rockabilly.

me before. So we went up there and that's what we heard, "Blue Moon of Kentucky" by Elvis Presley. I laughed a little bit and looked around and everybody else was laughing except Bill. He said, "You better do that number tomorrow if you want to sell some records, it'd be a good idea for you to do that number tomorrow" and we did it on Sunday. He was scheduled to record the next week and he said, "I'm gonna do it next Sunday." So, I guess he had some vision there that I didn't have. Of course, I probably had vision, too, and then never recorded that. Boy, it was a different sound, there's no doubt.[15]

Monroe appeared at the session along with his companion at the time, bass player Bessie Lee Mauldin, and Charlie Cline. Although Monroe was not officially credited as a producer on this session, he left an undeniable imprint on the proceedings: he suggested material, arrangements, and even supplied one of his musicians. The Stanley Brothers' version of "Blue Moon of Kentucky" bears a definite resemblance to the then recent Presley version in terms of rhythm and the overall approach to the song—it certainly is not patterned after the Bill Monroe Columbia recording of the mid-1940s, a "lilting 3/4 waltz"[16] with solo vocals. The Stanleys open their track, an up-tempo 4/4 piece, with a boogie woogie vocal intro that features several repeats of "blue moon," which is echoed by a quartet of singers. Carter and Ralph then launch into a soaring vocal duet that is interspersed with very nontraditional instrumental breaks. It is the first of the Stanleys' two attempts on Mercury to achieve a rockabilly sound.

Monroe also persuaded the group to record "Close By," a tune that was written by Little Robert Van Winkle of Knoxville, Tennessee. Monroe had recently recorded the song in

The "Blue Moon of Kentucky" session also produced one of Ralph Stanley's most memorable banjo instrumentals, "Hard Times." Its release in the very early part of 1955 figured prominently in the Stanley Brothers being named as the Best New Instrumental Group in a survey of readers of *Country and Western Jamboree* magazine.

June, but it had yet to be released. The Monroe version of "Close By" appeared in October of 1954, while the Stanleys' version remained unissued until it appeared in an early 1970s Japanese compilation of Stanley Brothers' Mercury material. While there are several stylistic differences between the Stanley and Monroe versions (Carter and Ralph sang it as a duet all the way through, while Monroe offered it up as a solo that was bolstered with triple fiddles, the first recording of his career to make use of the arrangement), the overall feel of the two tracks is not that different.

This session marks the Stanleys' first use of lead guitar, played by Charlie Cline. On these recordings, Cline plays some adventuresome Merle Travis–style guitar leads. On the two gospel quartets, "Calling from Heaven" and "Harbor of Love," the Stanleys' first for Mercury, the guitar and mandolin share some of the breaks together, with the guitar playing harmony to the mandolin. Gospel quartets had always been an important part of Carter and Ralph's radio programs and personal appearances, but, curiously, they had not featured them on record since their very first recording session in 1947.

The final selection recorded at the session is the classic banjo instrumental "Hard Times." Bluegrass scholar Neil Rosenberg notes that this tune is a "structurally complex (three parts with a minor bridge) piece that was a big hit with the young folk music revival banjo players who were just discovering bluegrass."[17] The tune came to the Stanleys by way of banjoist Wiley Birchfield. In 1950, during an informal picking session at WCYB with the Stanleys' fiddler, Les Woodie, he played as much of the tune as he had written up to that point. Woodie added an additional part to help complete the composition. Les previewed it for the band, and it was added to the group's repertoire.[18]

While "Hard Times" has gone on to enjoy status as one of *the* classic early bluegrass instrumentals, there is little indication that the tune made much of an impact on the industry at the time. Reviews were favorable, but not glowing. *Billboard* said, "Good string band instrumental here which should do nicely in country juke locations. It's good pickin' and bowin'."[19] The fan magazine *Country & Western Jamboree* observed, "Brother Ralph gets in some real fancy pickin' on the top side of the record."[20]

Indeed, the Stanley Brothers' entire Mercury output is today held in such high esteem, it seems incomprehensible that reviewers of the day glossed over it so casually: "The brothers have an authentic country sound on this ditty,"[21] "Excellent twangy harmony group,"[22] ". . . flavorsome brother singing on a mournful mountain song,"[23] "Sincere warbling on a sentimental tune with a happy country styled beat,"[24] and "Again, we have another mountain country group, of which there are too many."[25]

Mercury #5: November 1954 (Session 541128)

Recorded on November 28, 1954, Carter and Ralph's fifth session for Mercury features four more Stanley originals. The personnel, with the exception of the absent Charlie Cline, remains the same as before, with Joe Meadows, Bill Lowe, and Lightnin' Chance. They recorded only one duet, "You're Still on My Mind," and the rest are trios. Two of the trios, "Baby Girl" and "I Worship You," are conventional, with lead, tenor, and baritone. The remaining trio, "Say You'll Take Me Back," features the same arrangement (high lead, low tenor, baritone) that was used earlier on "A Voice from On High." Ralph carries the high lead, Bill Lowe takes the low tenor, and Carter sings baritone. This is the last time that the Stanleys used this type of vocal arrangement on Mercury.

Carter wrote "Baby Girl" in honor of his daughter, Doris, who was born the previous year. It was published by Acuff-Rose, the prestigious Nashville-based firm with whom he had been under contract as a songwriter since the Stanleys began their association with Mercury. The other three songs from the session bear Ralph's name as the composer and were published through Cedarwood Publishing. In the mid-1950s, Cedarwood Publishing was owned in part by *Grand Ole Opry* house manager Jim Denny. He was also the director of the Grand Ole Opry Artists Service Bureau, an agency that controlled the personal appearance bookings that came in through the *Opry*. It is believed that artists who recorded songs from the Cedarwood catalog received a larger share of the better paying jobs that came in through the Artists Service Bureau. It's possible that the Stanleys' publication of these songs through Cedarwood was an attempt to garner some of the work Denny had to offer.

The Stanley Brothers debuted as cast members of the *Old Dominion Barn Dance* in Richmond, Virginia, on March 12, 1955.[26] The popular Saturday evening program originated from the WRVA Theater and had been on the air for nine years at the time of the Stanleys' arrival. The station had a powerful signal that reached up and down the East Coast, and once a month the show was heard nationally through syndication. The Stanleys' stay was short-lived; they seem to have left by mid-April.[27] They hooked up with another weekend jamboree type of program in August when they appeared on WDVA's *Virginia Barn Dance* in Danville.[28] The show was hosted by Blue Grass Boy alumni Clyde Moody. Their stay lasted until the middle of November.[29] Their time between the two programs found the Stanleys working at a variety of venues, including New River Ranch in Rising Sun, Maryland; the Summit Drive-In Theater in Glade Spring, Virginia; the Brown County Jamboree in Bean Blossom, Indiana; the Fox Theater in Kingsport, Tennessee; a package show at the Emery Theater in Cincinnati, Ohio; and the *Carolina Jamboree* at the Broadway Theater in Reidsville, North Carolina.

Mercury #6: April 1955 (Session 550405)

During their next visit to the recording studio—on April 5, 1955—the Stanleys recorded a marathon session, cutting seven songs. The group recorded at a different facility for the session, the RCA studio at 1525 McGavock Street in Nashville. The studio was opened in 1954 under the direction of Steve Shoals, the RCA producer who oversaw earlier sessions by groups such as the Blue Sky Boys, Eddy Arnold, Johnnie & Jack, and the Lonesome Pine Fiddlers; he was later in charge of Elvis Presley's debut recordings on RCA. Guitarist Chet Atkins was hired to handle the day-to-day operations of the studio. Veteran Nashville bass player Bob Moore, who recorded on numerous occasions at the studio, recalled that the curved ceiling of the room "created low frequency problems causing bass notes to be boomy and roll around for a long time."[30] Large curtains hung on the wall to help absorb some of the sound.

For the session, Joe Meadows remained on fiddle, Jim Williams returned to the band to play mandolin, and Bill Lowe switched to bass.

Two of the selections were authored or coauthored by Bill Monroe. "I Hear My Savior Calling" is a sacred quartet, written by Monroe. "You'd Better Get Right" is credited to Monroe, although it was a collaboration between him and Carter Stanley. According to Carter,

> All I knew of that song was the chorus and after I left Bill we wanted to record it. I didn't know the verses that he used, and I just kindly took a word here and there from what I'd heard him do and added a few words to 'em and done our version. Of course I give him credit for the writer of the song because I think that was right. It was his idea, it was his tune and everything. We're always kidding each other about things like that.[31]

"Just a Little Talk with Jesus" is performed as a sacred quartet; Cleavant Derricks, a black songwriter who was born in Chattanooga, Tennessee, in 1910, copyrighted the song in 1937 when it was included in a Stamps-Baxter songbook called *Harbor Bells No. 6*. The hymn appeared in several songbooks in the 1930s and '40s and became a favorite among white audiences as well. Though never recorded by Monroe, the Blue Grass Quartet featured the song quite often on the *Opry* in the late 1940s. Ralph related that it was a song that "we'd

Although "Orange Blossom Special" had been recorded earlier by artists such as Bill Monroe, the Stanley Brothers' 1955 rendition was the first to feature it in a modern bluegrass setting. It was also the first recording of the tune to feature a driving three-finger-style banjo. At some point in the mid-1950s, Mercury changed the color of their single release labels. The green label at left was found on the earlier discs, while the black one at right was used on the records that issued from about 1955 onward.

heard all our life, that's an old standby. Probably got it from Bill Monroe, heard him do it. Charlie Monroe done it, too."[32]

Ralph contributed one song to the session in the form of "So Blue," a selection that repeats their arrangement of "Blue Moon of Kentucky." The song displays the same kind of boogie-woogie call-repeat intro of "Blue Moon of Kentucky" and features acoustic lead guitar work, played by fiddler Joe Meadows. When asked if Mercury was responsible for this updated style, Ralph replied, "No, they never did do that, they liked the old original stuff. [D. Kilpatrick, our producer] really loved bluegrass music."[33] Although credited to Ralph, the song is reported to have actually been composed by his first wife, Peggy.[34]

The Stanleys' recording of "Tragic Love" marks the first time they recorded traditional material on Mercury. Carter and Ralph used it as an opportunity to recycle the melody to one of their earlier recordings, "Little Glass of Wine." Known by a number of titles, "Tragic Love" is most commonly called "The Silver Dagger."[35] It was collected from a variety of people in Dickenson County in the early 1930s, one of whom learned it in the county in the 1890s.[36] The song was copyrighted for the session but was done so under the name of Buddy Dee, a pseudonym of D. Kilpatrick's. The Stanleys included the lyrics in a 1951 songbook, which titled the song "True Lover's Warning."[37]

Also appearing in that same songbook is "Lonesome and Blue," a Carter Stanley original and the only song of his to be featured on this session. Whether by accident or design, its fiddle kickoff is very similar to the intro of a 1950 Bill Monroe release called "When the Golden Leaves Begin to Fall." (*Continued on page 56*)

FAN TAPING

The invention of the magnetic tape recorder fostered what would become a whole new dynamic in the story of the Stanley Brothers' music. The device was invented in Germany in the 1930s, and was refined there during the early and mid-1940s. At the end of World War II, Jack Mullin, an American serviceman, happened upon two recording machines in Germany and had them shipped back to the States. Mullin worked for two years to develop the machines for commercial production. He attracted the attention of Bing Crosby, who invested in the idea and helped make Ampex the first company to manufacture and distribute tape recorders in the United States. The first recorders were geared toward professional uses, but by the early and mid-1950s, they were affordable enough that nonprofessional audiophiles could buy them.

One of the first people to develop an interest in using tape recorders to document live folk and bluegrass performances was Mike Seeger (1933–2009), a native of the Washington, DC, area. His father, musicologist Charles Seeger, brought a tape recorder into their home in 1952. Among Mike's first projects was recording Elizabeth Cotten, who became famous for her composition "Freight Train." By 1955 Mike had acquired a Magnecord M 33 recorder with an Electrovoice 635 omnidirectional microphone. Mike traveled to regional country music parks, such as New River Ranch and Sunset Park. He noted,

> I would come in with my heavy tape recorder, ask permission to record from Alec [sic] Campbell and the artists who were there, and I would set up my one microphone on a tripod near as possible to the PA microphone with the recorder on one side of the stage and I would string an AC cord to the nearest plug which was often back stage. I would usually listen over the earphones since the quality was so much better. There was much curiosity about what I was doing as tape recorders were a new thing then, and I would often let people listen over the earphones to what I was recording. In the beginning I was real selective, taking only what I considered the most important, and then I would take the tape home and listen to it over and over, and of course, I soon realized that I had been raised too Scotch. I missed some real good music and talk on those first shows, and with later shows I took most everything and more often than not recorded on a fast speed for better quality.[1]

Mike was the first person to tape record a live concert by the Stanley Brothers, having caught their appearance at New River Ranch on July 3, 1955. He was most active the following year, but continued to record Carter and Ralph at various venues over the next several years. His last recordings of them were made in March of 1966 during a tour of Europe.

Another enthusiast who also recorded the Stanley Brothers in 1955 was Marvin Hedrick (1925–1973). A native of Brown County, Indiana—the home of Bill

Monroe's music park the Brown County Jamboree (later the site of Monroe's long-running Bean Blossom festival)—he operated a radio and electronics shop. In fact, he installed the sound system that was used at the Brown County Jamboree and also put in a series of output devices that people with tape recorders could patch into to record the shows. Hedrick was an amateur musician and a regular attendee at Jamboree shows. He made numerous requests of park manager, Birch Monroe, Bill's brother, to bring in shows by his favorite entertainers. These included the Stanley Brothers, the Lonesome Pine Fiddlers, and Mac Wiseman.

With a few exceptions, most of the taping of Stanley Brothers concerts took place in the Washington–Baltimore area, mainly because this was where most of the tapers lived. Most, if not all, of the initial interest in taping live concerts in this area started with Mike Seeger. Others who were most active were Jeremy Foster, Lamar Grier, Bill Offenbacher, and, later, Leon Kagarise.

William "Bill" L. Offenbacher (1935–1987) was a fixture of the Washington, DC, bluegrass scene in the 1950s and '60s. He was proficient on guitar and bass and also played mandolin. He went by the stage name of Bill Bailey. A close friend of mandolin virtuoso Buzz Busby, Bill appeared on four recording sessions with him in the late 1950s and mid-'60s. He also recorded an album with Leon Morris—along with Buzz Busby—in 1970. Other band associations included the National Troubadours (a group that included banjoist Gene Cox—who was then married to Roni Stoneman—Scott Stoneman on fiddle, Pee Wee Fadre on dobro, and Al Jones on bass) and the Melody Mountain Boys (with Jack Tottle on mandolin, Lamar Grier on banjo, and Tracy Schwarz on fiddle). Bill began his recording activities in the mid-1950s and traveled to New River Ranch and Sunset Park. Like a number of his fellow recording enthusiasts, his activity level waned by the early 1960s. A number of songs from his collection form the nucleus of the 1981 Stanley Brothers album, *Shadows of the Past.* By trade, Bill worked for the Teamsters Union as a mimeograph operator and later worked in their reproduction department. As a sideline during the 1970s and '80s, he had a mail-order business that specialized in selling blank recording tape. In his later years, he took pleasure in sharing his live recordings with young bluegrass performers who were coming of age in the 1970s and '80s.

Jeremy Foster was born in Washington, DC, on November 20, 1933. He was a high school friend of Mike Seeger's. He attended Antioch College in Yellow Springs, Ohio, where he met his future wife, Alice Gerrard. They relocated to the DC area in 1955 or 1956, and were married there in October of 1956. Music was a driving force in their lives, and spare time was spent attending or hosting picking parties and traveling to nearby country music parks to see Bill Monroe, the Stanley Brothers, Reno & Smiley, Flatt & Scruggs, and others. Trips were usually made with friends, including Mike Seeger and Hazel Dickens. It was during this time that Jeremy became active in tape recording concerts; he and Mike would often be at shows together, simultaneously recording the same events. Rather than cluttering the stage with excess microphones, the duo would run a patch cord from the output of one recorder to the input of the other. Jeremy was drafted into the military in the late 1950s. Sometime after his discharge, he returned to Antioch College, and there he and Alice persuaded the school to sponsor concerts by the Osborne Brothers (February 1960) and the Stanley Brothers (May 14, 1960). These events are generally regarded as the first college concerts to feature bluegrass music. In 1962 Jeremy and Alice returned to the DC area, where music continued to be a significant part of their lives. This included more picking parties and budding record producer Peter Siegel's chance discovery of Alice and Hazel Dickens's singing. In September of 1964, as plans were underway to produce Alice and Hazel's first duet recording, which would include—at Jeremy's suggestion—the fiddling of legendary bluegrass musician Chubby Wise, Jeremy was killed in an automobile accident while en route to work at the Quantico Marine Base. He was thirty-one.[2]

Lamar Grier was born on April 15, 1938, and lived in the Maryland suburbs of Washington, DC. His interest in taping sprang from a dilemma he had concerning the radio. He heard a lot of exciting things on the air, but was unable to locate recordings of them locally. So he went to a shop in Washington, DC, that sold tape recorders and bought a top of the line Wilcox for $145. Among his first projects was taping some Bill Monroe 78s on Columbia that were in the possession of Bill Harrell. Lamar became friends with Bill Offenbacher, and it wasn't long before the two of them were taking their recorders to concerts. Lamar noted,

> You had to have that tape recorder going all the time to catch any extra, different note that they'd never done before and then come rushing home and even stay up late that night after coming home from the day's performance and listen to that tape . . . one particular spot over and over, trying to understand what they were doing.[3]

Lamar credits Mike Seeger for a lot of his enthusiasm for making live recordings. "Mike was always there, he was taping, too. Talking with Mike, getting revved up to Mike's enthusiasm towards the music . . . it rubbed off. I don't think he got me there initially but once I was there, yeah."[4] Mike encouraged Lamar to record at a faster speed, thus ensuring better sound quality, and Bill persuaded him to upgrade to a high-end recorder, a Tandberg. As far as his tapes of the Stanley Brothers were concerned, Lamar had an affinity for the earlier ones he made:

> I like the older ones better than the new ones. It seemed like as time went on, Carter seemed to play more songs out of a guitar E. When he played earlier, playing in an open G chord, he would just rock that 6th and 4th and I liked that. When he did that just sort of raking across the strings, I sure noticed a change and I didn't care for that. The older stuff was more simple . . . but it seemed like his guitar had more tone.[5]

Lamar's interest in making live recordings decreased by the early 1960s. In 1965, he went to work for Bill Monroe, playing banjo as a Blue Grass Boy for two years. After that, the constraints of a nonmusical career did much to curb Lamar's picking and taping activities. He is retired and lives in Maryland. His son, David, is a renowned bluegrass guitarist.

While most of the DC-based tapers were easing out of their enthusiasm for making live tapes by 1960, a Baltimore audiophile, Leon Kagarise, was just gearing up. Born on June 7, 1937, in Pennsylvania, Leon was still in his youth when his family moved to Baltimore, where his father took a job working for Bendix Radio. His father's occupation in electronics rubbed off on Leon, and soon he was building crystal radios and hi-fi record players. In 1958, upon graduation from high school, he got a job with High Fidelity House in Baltimore, working in their installer and service departments. His fascination with electronics, including radios, eventually led to his discovery and appreciation of country music. As soon as he was old enough to do so, he began attending country music shows at New River Ranch and Sunset Park. He acquired an Ampex 960 stereophonic recorder and an omnidirectional ElectroVoice 654 microphone and began taking the machines with him to shows. His first recording of this type was of a Flatt & Scruggs show in 1960. He had a passion for bluegrass, but also recorded a lot of the country music acts, including Johnny Cash, Ernest Tubb, Roy Acuff, the Louvin Brothers, and countless others. In addition to taping live shows, he discovered how to directly hook his recorder to his television and was able to make pristine audio recordings of country music shows, such as the locally produced *Don Owens Show*, the *Jimmy Dean Show*, and the *Porter Wagoner Show*. Leon also had a zeal for photography and took nearly seven hundred color slides of the artists he saw at New River Ranch and Sunset Park. These have been chronicled in a book called *Pure Country: The Leon Kagarise Archives, 1961–1971*. Leon had occasion to record the Stanley Brothers at New River Ranch, on August 27, 1961. He died on January 26, 2008.

Notes

1. Mike Seeger, as quoted in liner notes to Stanley Brothers, *Stanley Series*, vol. 1, no. 3, Copper Creek CCLP-V1N3, 1982, 4.

2. Basic biographical information about Jeremy Foster can be found in Alice Gerrard, "Remembering These Recordings," *Hazel Dickens & Alice Gerrard—Pioneering Women of Bluegrass*, Smithsonian Folkways SF CD 40065, 1996. See also "Man Killed in Crash on Shirley Hwy.," *Washington Post*, September 25, 1964, C1.

3. Lamar Grier, as quoted in liner notes to Stanley Brothers, *Stanley Series*, vol. 1, no. 1, Copper Creek CCLP-V1N1, 1982, 3.

4. Ibid.

5. Lamar Grier, as quoted in liner notes to Stanley Brothers, *Stanley Series*, vol. 1, no. 2, Copper Creek CCLP-V1N2, 1982, 6–7.

The remaining selection, "Orange Blossom Special," is a tune from the early 1940s that was recorded by Bill Monroe for Bluebird. The Stanleys recorded it as an afterthought when they still had studio time left after finishing the other six songs. To fill the remaining time, they decided to rip off a fast version of this old standard. Ironically, it was their recording of this tune that helped earn them an award from *Country & Western Jamboree* magazine for Best New Instrumental Group for 1955.[38] Although the tune had been recorded several times previously in country music, the Stanleys' recording was the first to feature it with driving three-finger style banjo.

Independence Day at New River Ranch 1955 (Session 550703)

On July 3, 1955, the Stanley Brothers performed at the outdoor park New River Ranch. Carter Stanley first performed there in 1951 as a member of Bill Monroe's Blue Grass Boys.[39] The Stanley Brothers returned there later that fall and again in 1952 and 1954 as well as several times in 1955. This particular two-day engagement included Independence Day. The event provided a full day's worth of entertainment, all for a one dollar admission. According to an advertisement in the local newspaper, appearing throughout the day were

> The Stanley Brothers and the Clinch Mountain Boys, Bill Dudley—Capitol Recording Star, Joseph Smiley—Magician—Saws a Lady in Half, DAVY CROCKETT DAY—Free gifts for all the kiddies, RAY DAVIS—WBMD, Baltimore, Md., Melvin Price and his Santa Fe Rangers, Cactus Bill, Deacon The Steel Driving Man—from WORK, York, Pa., Patty and Kenny Cummings, Ola Belle and Alex and the New River Boys—from WASA, Havre de Grace, Md., and the New River Ranch Square Dancers.[40]

Significantly, folk enthusiast Mike Seeger tape-recorded much of the Stanley Brothers' show in the earliest known field recording of Carter and Ralph. The contents of the tape were issued on LP in 1982 by Copper Creek Records as part of their *Stanley Series*, a subscription service that made live recordings of the Stanley Brothers available to followers of their music.

Appearing in the band with Carter and Ralph that day were Jim Williams on mandolin, Doug Morris on bass, and Lindy Clear, performing imitations. The tape contains selections that were recorded at the discretion of Mike Seeger. He later admitted that with his first efforts at field recording, he was "raised too Scotch. I missed some real good music and talk on those first shows . . . I didn't keep the machine running long enough."[41] Renditions of the Stanleys' current record releases are glossed over in favor of performance tunes that the band had no intention of recording ("That's Alright, Mama," "Poor Ellen Smith," "Rabbit in a Log," "White House Blues," and "Wait a Little Longer, Please Jesus") or recent compositions that the band had yet to record ("Big Tilda" and "Will He Wait a Little Longer"). Also captured were comedic routines by Lindy Clear.

Lawrence Douglas "Doug" Morris was born in Abingdon, Virginia, on September 1, 1934. He learned to play guitar in his youth when a cousin showed him several chords. Doug's first professional work was with Ralph Mayo and the Southern Mountain Boys. This led to his meeting other groups and musicians at WCYB, including the Stanley Brothers, whom he played bass with for several years in the mid-1950s. He helped out with their daily broadcasts on *Farm & Fun Time*, personal appearance dates, and one recording session, and accompanied the band on a tour of Canada. His later work included a stint with another *Farm & Fun Time* band, Red Malone and the Smoky Mountain Boys. Doug passed away on July 8, 2010.[42]

Lindbergh Hugh "Lindy" Clear was born on August 31, 1930, in Holston, Virginia, near Abingdon. He worked with the Stanley Brothers off and on throughout the 1950s and into 1960. He played bass with the group and delighted audiences with his imitations of nature and machine sounds. He attended one year of high school, in 1945–46, but did not graduate. By the early 1950s, he was appearing at WCYB with various groups, including the Stanley Brothers. He was with the Stanleys at several notable events, including their first appearance at the Newport Folk Festival in 1959 and their first college performance, at Antioch College in Yellow Springs, Ohio, in 1960. He sometimes played bass with the Stanleys, but his real talent was as a master of impersonation. His routines included sounds of old-time steam locomotives, Model T cars, dog fights, ringing hogs, old women singing in church, babies crying, and more. Following his last stint with the Stanley Brothers, he worked and recorded with Charlie Moore and Bill Napier. He eventually returned to the Abingdon area, where he worked as an evangelist and performed for school and church groups. He died on June 23, 1971; Ralph Stanley served as an honorary pallbearer.[43]

Bean Blossom 1955 (Session 550800)

The Stanley Brothers were taped again at another live performance in the summer of 1955 when they appeared at Bill Monroe's Brown County Jamboree in Bean Blossom, Indiana. Marvin Hedrick recorded the event. Only one song from this show was released commercially; "Will You Be Loving Another Man" appears in a Time Life collection, *The Definitive Stanley Brothers 1947—1966*. It was a song Bill Monroe recorded in 1946 when Flatt & Scruggs were in his band. Carter and Ralph enjoyed performing Monroe's classic material on personal appearances and occasionally made use of them in the recording studio. This is one selection they never put out on record. Appearing with them on this performance are George Shuffler on bass and Ralph Mayo on fiddle.

Mercury #7: December 1955 (Session 551219)

The Stanleys' seventh session for Mercury was held on December 19, 1955. They again recorded at a different facility; earlier in the year, Bradley Studio had moved from Hillsboro Village to a house located at 1804 16th Avenue South in Nashville. It was the first studio on what is now known as Music Row. Initially, the studio was set up in the basement, but when that proved too small, it was moved to a Quonset hut located directly behind the house. Harold Bradley noted, "When we started recording back there, the studio had a tile floor and it had a 'ping' in it, a bad echo bounce off of the tile floor, and we didn't know exactly what to do with that. Then Al Gannaway rented out the studio for some programming he was filming . . . so he put up wood along each side . . . And what that wood did, it evened out the sound and made it a fantastic studio."[44] It became a major center for recording in Nashville. The Bradleys operated the studio until 1962, when they sold it to Columbia Records.

For their session, the Stanley Brothers were reunited with former Clinch Mountain Boy Art Stamper, who was recently discharged from the military. Stamper's stay in the group was short-lived and he left in January of 1956 to play with the Osborne Brothers and Red Allen. Also helping out was Bill Lowe, who played and sang bass on the session. Making his first appearance on record with the Clinch Mountain Boys was Curley Lambert, an impressive mandolin player and baritone singer who joined the band in October of 1955.

Richard Edward "Curley" Lambert was born in Brodnax, Virginia, on June 13, 1930. His first professional work was in 1946, when he provided music for cowboy film star Fuzzy St. John. In 1949 and '50, he worked in the Lynchburg, Virginia, area with the husband and wife duo of Bill & Mary Reid. A stint in the military interrupted his time with the Reids, but Curley still found time for music with his fellow soldiers. After his discharge, he resumed work with Bill & Mary, helping them record sessions for Columbia and Starday. During this time, he also assisted Bill Clifton with several recording sessions. He worked with the Stanley Brothers on two separate occasions in the 1950s, a year-long stint in 1955-56, and another in 1958. At the end of his second stay, he went to work briefly with Flatt & Scruggs. In May of 1960, he returned to the Stanleys for another tour of duty. The early '60s found Curley working briefly for Charlie Moore & Bill Napier as well as the country gospel group the Masters Family. Curley was with the Stanleys one last time in the mid-'60s and then left music for several years. He resurfaced in the early 1970s, performing with Richmond-based Chief Powhatan. Other work during the decade included travels with Charlie Moore & the Dixie Partners and the Goins Brothers.[45] He died on October 22, 1982.

This session offers an odd mix of material in that it features two instrumentals and two sacred quartets. Only one song from the session, "Big Tilda," was issued on a single. Two other tunes, "Clinch Mountain Blues" and "Angel Band," lay dormant for several years until they appeared on the Stanleys' *Country Pickin' and Singin'* and *Hard Times* albums.

Though credited to Ralph Stanley, "Angel Band" is an old hymn that dates back to 1862, when William B. Bradbury copyrighted it under the title "Land of Beulah." The remaining song, "Will He Wait a Little Longer," was never commercially released on vinyl in the United States. Its first issue was in 1974, when it appeared in Japan on a collection of the Stanley Brothers' Mercury recordings.[46] Ralph wrote the tune, and as the song remained unissued for many years, he re-recorded it on his first album for Rebel Records in 1971.

Leslie Keith, author of the famous "Black Mountain Blues," composed the session's first instrumental, "Clinch Mountain Blues." Leslie taught the tune to Art Stamper especially for this session.[47] Ralph and Jim Williams put the other instrumental, "Big Tilda," together in the summer of 1955. It is a variant of the traditional tune "Big Ball in Brooklyn."

The Ehrlich Session: March 1956 (Session 560324)

The year of 1956 was a busy one for folk enthusiasts making live recordings of the Stanley Brothers. The first, by Larry Ehrlich, a Chicago-based attorney who befriended the

Stanley Brothers in the mid-1950s, took place on March 24, 1956. On this particular day, he traveled with Carter and Ralph, attending their noontime *Farm & Fun Time* broadcast, a livestock auction, and an evening concert performance. At the conclusion of the day, he persuaded the Stanley Brothers to return to the WCYB studio in Bristol, where he set up a recorder and captured eighteen songs and tunes on tape.[48] Although the group eventually commercially recorded several of the selections, they are, for the most part, traditional songs that were used as performance pieces. Curley Lambert and Ralph Mayo play mandolin and fiddle, respectively, although Lambert, tired out, is absent from the end of the session.[49] Also absent from the session is a bass player; it was not uncommon for the group to travel as a four-piece band. This tape was for years a favorite among Stanley enthusiasts for trading on reel-to-reel tapes and, later, cassettes. The session was formally issued on CD in 1999 when it appeared on Ralph Stanley's StanleyTone label as *Old-Time Songs*. It was subsequently sold to Columbia/DMZ/Legacy which re-released it in 2004 as *An Evening Long Ago*.

Shenandoah Valley Bowl 1956 (Session 560603)

June 3, 1956, found the Stanley Brothers making their first concert appearance in the Shenandoah Valley. They appeared at the Shenandoah Valley Bowl in Edinburg, Virginia, for a show that was promoted by Benny and Vallie Cain. Natives of the eastern panhandle of West Virginia, the Cains had relocated to Falls Church, Virginia, where Benny was employed as an Alcohol, Tobacco, and Firearms agent. From the 1950s through the 1980s, Benny and Vallie were fixtures of the bluegrass music scene in the Washington, DC, Maryland, and Virginia area. Among their early endeavors was leasing the Shenandoah Valley Bowl for promoting country music concerts. One of their first shows featured the Stanley Brothers.[50] Appearing at the event with Carter and Ralph were Curley Lambert, Chubby Anthony, and Doug Morris.

Donald Lee "Chubby" Anthony was born on December 20, 1935, and grew up near Cherryville, North Carolina, an area that was actively involved in textile manufacturing. Chubby learned the art of fiddling from his father, who started teaching him when he was five or six. By age thirteen, he was participating in area fiddling competitions and had won the North Carolina State Fiddling Contest. His exposure to rural music included radio broadcasts by Bill Monroe on the *Opry*, the Stanley Brothers on *Farm & Fun Time*, and Flatt & Scruggs from Raleigh, North Carolina, and Bristol. Chubby's first professional work came at age sixteen when he went to work for the Stanley Brothers. His stay lasted only a few months, and he returned home to improve his skills. He auditioned again in 1955 and was rehired. An announcer at WCYB gave Chubby his nickname when his given name proved too hard to pronounce on the radio. Chubby appeared on recordings with the Stanleys on Mercury, Starday, and King Records. He was most active with the group between 1956 and 1961. Other work included stints with the Lilly Brothers and Don Stover and also Charlie Moore. By the end of the '60s, Chubby had left music; he drove a laundry truck for several years, but the mid-'70s found him back in music with his own band, Big Timber.[51] He died on February 5, 1980, of complications from diabetes.

In addition to highlighting fine live renditions of the band's current records, the Shenandoah Valley Bowl recording shows the Clinch Mountain Boys featuring several surprises: Curley Lambert's version of a song popularized by Gene Autry called "I'll Be True While You're Gone"; Carter and Ralph's adaptations of Bill Monroe's latest release, "I Believed in You, Darling," and the Carter Family's "Meet Me by the Moonlight"; and Chubby Anthony's excellent version of the fiddle tune "Leather Britches."

Several people recorded the show, including Jeremy Foster, Benny Cain, and Pete Kuykendall. The concert is included in Copper Creek's Stanley Series, and it first appeared on LP in 1984. Foster's tapes were used for the Copper Creek issue. Two tunes, "I Believed in You, Darling" and "Meet Be by the Moonlight," were earlier used on an album of live Stanley Brothers recordings on the Joy and Rebel labels called *Together for the Last Time*. "Moonlight" is also featured in the soundtrack of the 1994 film *High Lonesome: The Story of Bluegrass Music*.

Shipps Park 1956 (Session 560708)

On July 8, 1956, a month after the show in Edinburg, the Stanley Brothers were again back in the northern Virginia area for a show at Shipps Park in Morrisville. The band remained the same for the most part, the only change being that Lindy Clear replaced Doug Morris on bass.

The complete show was issued on Copper Creek's Stanley Series in 1986, but several songs from it were used earlier in Rebel Records' *The Legendary Stanley Brothers* albums. Volume one was issued in 1969 and contained "Roving Gambler"; volume two appeared in 1970 and contained "Are You Waiting Just for Me," a tune the Stanleys had waxed for Rich-R-Tone in 1952. *Together for the Last Time* made use of "I Just Got Wise" and "Who'll Call You Sweetheart."

Mercury #8: July 1956 (Session 560716)

The Stanley Brothers recorded their first session with twin fiddles, played by veteran musicians Chubby Anthony and Ralph Mayo, on July 16, 1956. It was a sound Carter Stanley had wanted to feature on record for some time.[52] Anthony had become the band's regular fiddle player by then, but this was the first time he recorded with the group. Mayo appeared as a guest at the request of Carter Stanley. This session also features bass player Doug Morris's only recorded studio work with the Stanleys.

The first selection recorded is "The Cry from the Cross," a hymn written by Johnnie Masters of the Masters Family, which recorded it for Columbia Records in 1951. This was a popular tune for the Stanleys throughout the late 1950s and remained so with Ralph during his solo career. It was the title cut for Ralph's first album with Rebel Records in 1971. "Who Will Call You Sweetheart" is another Carter Stanley–Bill Monroe composition. Ralph believed Monroe wrote the chorus and that Carter finished out the song later with the verses.[53] The July recording features the same high baritone trio arrangement the band had used several years earlier on Columbia. Carter sings lead, Curley Lambert tenor, and Ralph the even higher high baritone. Another sacred selection is a quartet by Carter called "Let Me Walk, Lord, by Your Side." Both Ralph Stanley and George Shuffler had recollections of Carter composing this song while on tour in Idaho.[54] However, the tour took place in August of 1956, after this session supposedly took place. Either both musicians have faulty memories (not likely), or the date supplied for this session is incorrect. The final song recorded at the session is "A Lonesome Night." Mercury never issued this song on album. It appears in a Stanley Brothers songbook from the mid-1950s and was featured on their live shows during this time. The song even escaped the comprehensive series of reissues that appeared in Japan in 1974. It made its first appearance on a 1993 two-CD set that was issued in Germany by Bear Family Records.

New River Ranch Again 1956 (Session 560729)

On July 29, 1956, the Stanley Brothers appeared at New River Ranch, with Curley Lambert on mandolin, Chubby Anthony on fiddle, and Lindy Clear on bass. Twenty-five songs and tunes were recorded by Mike Seeger and Jeremy Foster, and the show appears on CD as part of Copper Creek's *Stanley Series*. Notable exceptions to their standard repertoire include "Crazy Arms," a hit for country singer Ray Price and sung by Curley Lambert; "Black Mountain Blues" and "Carroll County Blues," played by Chubby Anthony; and several songs by Carter and Ralph in tribute to the Monroe Brothers, "Drifting Too Far from the Shore" and "Rabbit in a Log."

Silver Creek Ranch 1956 (Session 560805)

The last live recording of 1956 to be issued commercially is a show from August 5 at the Silver Creek Ranch in Paris, Virginia. Recorded by Jeremy Foster, the show was issued on LP as part of Copper Creek's *Stanley Series*. One track, "Going to Georgia," appears on the 1981 album *Shadows of the Past*, a Copper Creek collection of live recordings that features songs never commercially recorded by the Stanley Brothers.

By the end of August, the Stanley Brothers had embarked on their farthest road trip away from home. For several weeks, they were headquartered in Idaho Falls, Idaho, and played dates throughout several Pacific Northwest states.[55] A number of photos from a 1957 songbook show the band in a television station in Idaho Falls as well as at border crossings into Oregon and Washington. The band that made the tour consisted of Carter and Ralph, George Shuffler, Chubby Anthony, and Curley Lambert.[56] Other dates closer to home included shows in St. Paul, Virginia, as part of a Wise County centennial celebration; a street dance in Bristol, Virginia, as part of a city centennial; and a school date at an elementary school in Oak Hill, West Virginia.

Bill Clifton #1: November 1956 (Session 561100)

In November of 1956, Ralph Stanley flew to Nashville—his first time to travel by plane—to participate in a recording session with Bill Clifton, a guitarist and singer from Maryland who had previously released a few songs on the Blue Ridge label. At Carter Stanley's urging, Bill went to see the Stanleys' producer at Mercury, D. Kilpatrick, who was impressed with Bill's talents and recommended him to Don Pierce of Starday Records. A session was arranged and four songs were recorded at the RCA studios on McGavock Street. These include "Gathering Flowers from the Hillside," "Little White Washed Chimney," "Railroading on the Great Divide," and "Take Back the Heart." Also appearing on the session are several Stanley-related sidemen, Curley Lambert on mandolin and George Shuffler on bass. Rounding out the session are fiddlers Sonny Mead and Bill Wiltshire. As Ralph Stanley was under contract to Mercury, he confined his participation in the session to being an instrumentalist. His appearance on the session came about matter-of-factly: Bill Clifton was lamenting that his regular banjo player, Johnny Clark, was unable to make the session. So Carter volunteered, "Well, just take Ralph."[57] This was the first time Ralph appeared as a guest artist on a recording.

Don Pierce, Pappy Daily, and Mercury-Starday

As 1956 drew to a close, changes were taking place at Mercury. Carter and Ralph's producer of the last four years, D. Kilpatrick, departed the label to take over as head of the WSM Artist Bureau and the *Grand Ole Opry*. The void he left opened the way for a partnership between Mercury and Starday Records. Starday label heads Harold W. "Pappy" Daily and Don Pierce inked a five-year deal under which they would supervise Mercury's country and western division in Nashville. Daily would oversee recording sessions, while Pierce would concentrate on sales. Record releases would receive a Mercury-Starday imprint. The agreement was to take effect on January 1, 1957.

Don Pierce's career would be intertwined with that of the Stanley Brothers above and beyond the Mercury-Starday merger. He was born on October 10, 1915, in Ballard, Washington. He served a four-year stint in the army after graduating from the University of Washington. Upon his discharge, he settled in Los Angeles and took a job as a salesman for Four Star Records. His stay with that label was rather brief, and he left to form Starday with Pappy Daily. After the termination of the Mercury-Starday alliance, Pierce bought out Daily's interest in Starday and successfully ran the company for a decade or so. He sold the business for $2 million in 1968. His later ventures included real estate development. He died on April 3, 2005, at the age of eighty-nine.

Mercury #9: February 1957 (Session 570201)

In January of 1957, raging floodwaters swept through much of southwestern Virginia and parts of eastern Kentucky and Tennessee. The Stanleys witnessed much of the destruction. In fact, they were stranded in the town of Haysi, Virginia, and forced to stay there until the waters receded. It was while returning to the family farm in Dickenson County that Carter Stanley put together "The Flood," a set of his original lyrics paired with the melody of a tune recorded by the Bailes Brothers in the mid-1940s, "Searching for a Soldier's Grave." Obviously inspired by the song and the events surrounding them, Carter made a call to Wesley Rose of Acuff-Rose Publications. Carter woke Wesley during the middle of the night and sang him the song over the phone. Upon hearing the song, Wesley advised

The Stanley Brothers' "The Flood" was the first of two topical songs they recorded chronicling real life events in the news. On January 29, 1957, newspapers of the area began covering the deluge of flood waters that would ravage portions of southwestern Virginia and eastern Kentucky and Tennessee. Carter Stanley wrote "The Flood" one evening as the group was sidelined by heavy rains. The printed paper sleeve shown in this photo calls attention to the diversity of music to be found on Mercury and features the Stanley Brothers in a listing of its artists.

the group to record it as soon as possible.[58] A quickie session was arranged at radio station WCYB in Bristol, Virginia, and the one song was recorded.

Several items of interest are connected with this session. First, George Shuffler, usually known for his keen bass work, plays mandolin on this recording, the only time he ever did so with the Stanley Brothers. Second, the high harmony vocals feature Chubby Anthony singing the high baritone part while Carter sings lead and Ralph sings tenor. In the mid- and late 1950s, Ralph usually handled the high baritone chores, and, as such, it is interesting that Chubby sang the part on the record. Lastly, playing bass on the session is local Bristol musician Red Malone.

Following the session, the master was rushed to Mercury for a quick release. The entire event was handled with the utmost speed and urgency. The first mention of the flood in the newspapers was January 29, 1957, and the recording was released on February 14, 1957, remarkably a little over two weeks later.

Mervin Haskell "Red" Malone was a musician who appeared on *Farm & Fun Time* in the mid-1950s. He was born on September 9, 1927, and was a World War II veteran. He started on *Farm & Fun Time* in 1955, fronting a band called the Smoky Mountain Boys. The group featured two acoustic guitars, an electric guitar, steel guitar, acoustic bass, and, at times, drums. They occasionally worked dates together with the Stanley Brothers as well as with Jimmy Martin, Mother Maybelle & the Carter Sisters, Doc Watson, and Little Jimmy Dickens. The group disbanded in 1957 or so. Red wrote two songs that the Stanley Brothers later recorded, "Love Me, Darling, Just Tonight" for King in 1958, and "A Little at a Time" for Starday in 1959. Red accepted Christ into his life in 1960 and was subsequently called to preach. He visited Carter Stanley in the hospital in November of 1966, about three weeks before his passing, and assisted in Carter's accepting Christ.[59] Red continued with his ministerial work until he passed away on March 1, 1993, at the age of sixty-five.

Mercury #10: February 1957 (570227)

Two weeks after the release of "The Flood," the Stanleys were in the studios again, this time at the RCA studio on McGavock Street in Nashville. Typically, a recording session in those days consisted of four songs, but as they had just sent one master, "The Flood," to Mercury, only three tunes were recorded at this session. George Shuffler returns to his usual spot on the bass, and Chubby Anthony continues to be featured on the fiddle. Making a special guest appearance is former Clinch Mountain Boy Pee Wee Lambert, the mandolin player and harmony singer who contributed so much to the Stanleys' sound on their late 1940s Columbia recordings. The circumstances surrounding his appearance on this session are unclear, but he was there at Carter Stanley's request. Curiously, there was no attempt to re-create the famous trio sound of years earlier. Only one trio was recorded, a Carter Stanley original called "I'll Never Grow Tired of You," and it is a conventional trio with George Shuffler singing the baritone. The first selection recorded at the session is an instrumental by Ralph called "Fling Ding," a reworking of the traditional fiddle tune "Sally Ann." The final selection recorded is another Carter Stanley original called "Loving You Too Well," and it is featured as a duet between him and Ralph.

Live Recordings: 1957 (Sessions 570148, 570512, 570601, 570711, 570831)

The spring and summer of 1957 saw the recording of a number of live concerts by enthusiasts such as Mike Seeger, Jeremy Foster, and Bill Offenbacher. A half dozen tracks from these 1957 shows from the Offenbacher collection are used as part of the *Shadows of the Past* album. These include "Lonesome Road Blues" (recorded on April 18, 1957, at the Melody Ranch in Glen Burnie, Maryland); "Here Today and Gone Tomorrow" and "Thinking of the Old Days" (both recorded on May 12, 1957, at Valley View Park in Hellam, Pennsylvania, an area the foreword from their 1957 songbook mentions: "The Stanleys enjoy an excellent business from the parks in Southern Pennsylvania"[60]); "I Hope You Have Learned" and "White House Blues" (recorded on June 1, 1957, at New River Ranch); "Just Another Broken Heart" (recorded on July 11, 1957, at the Melody Ranch); and "Going to the Races" (recorded on August 30, 1957, in Front Royal, Virginia).

Of the songs, "Lonesome Road Blues" is somewhat of a standard; how it came to the Stanley band is unknown. "Thinking of the Old Days" is a Carter Stanley composition the brothers never recorded. Carter gave the song to Bill Clifton, who recorded it for Starday a year later, in March of 1958, as "Are You Alone" with Ralph Stanley playing banjo. "I Hope You Have Learned" was recorded by Bill Monroe and released in March of 1954. "White House Blues" has a fairly wide circulation in traditional music circles, but it is worth noting that Bill Monroe recorded it earlier, releasing it in May of 1954. "Just Another

Broken Heart" is a song the Carter Family recorded for Decca Records twenty-one years earlier, on June 8, 1936. Lastly, "Going to the Races" is a Carter Stanley composition. The Country Gentlemen, with the permission of the Stanley Brothers, recorded it as one side of their very first 45 rpm release, for the Dixie label, in the latter part of 1957. The following summer, Carter and Ralph recorded another song that used the same melody and tempo, "Gonna Paint the Town."

These live recordings show the Stanley band in transition throughout the summer. The group started out with the personnel who had been with them the previous year: Curley Lambert, Chubby Anthony, and Lindy Clear. By the end of May, Frank Wakefield and Jack Cooke had replaced Lambert and Clear. Wakefield's stay was rather brief, and he had exited the band by the first of June, at which time the Clinch Mountain Boys consisted of Chubby Anthony and Jack Cooke. By the second week of June, Bill Napier had signed on to play mandolin and Chubby Anthony had departed. The band continued as a foursome for the balance of the summer.

Vernon Crawford "Jack" Cooke was born on December 6, 1936, in Norton, Virginia. He learned to make music at home in his youth. As a teen, he and his brothers came to the attention of the Stanley Brothers when they entered a talent contest. Jack's first professional work was with the Stanleys, starting in 1957. He stayed with them for a year or so before leaving to work for Bill Monroe, a job he held for several years. Following his tenure with Monroe, he worked in the Baltimore, Maryland, area and fronted his own band. By the end of the '60s, he had returned to Norton to care for his aging mother. After her passing, a chance encounter with Ralph Stanley led him to rejoin the Clinch Mountain Boys, a job he held for close to forty years. In 2006, he released his first solo recording, *Sittin' on Top of the World*. Due to health issues, Jack retired from the road in the early part of 2009.[61] He died later that year, on December 1.

Billy Edward "Bill" Napier was born on December 17, 1935, in Wise, Virginia, and grew up in nearby Grundy. Exposure to the music of Bill Monroe on the *Grand Ole Opry* as well the *Farm & Fun Time* program played a part in developing Bill's musical tastes. He learned to play on a mandolin that his father obtained from a coworker. When he was eighteen, his family moved to Michigan. Jim Williams recommended Bill to the Stanley Brothers, and he sent them a demo containing two songs, "Roanoke" and "Rawhide." In the early part of June 1957, Bill joined the Stanley Brothers at WCYB. He added a classic mandolin instrumental to their repertoire with "Daybreak in Dixie." He did much to establish the sound of the lead guitar in the Clinch Mountain Boys with recordings the group made for King and Starday in 1959. In the early part of 1960, he teamed up with Charlie Moore, a mellow-voiced guitarist from South Carolina, for a decade-long partnership. Although his primary instruments were the mandolin and guitar, Bill played banjo with Charlie. The duo worked a series of TV shows in the Deep South and, starting in 1962, recorded ten albums for King Records. Bill eventually returned to Michigan and performed in the Detroit area. By the 1990s, he had moved to east Tennessee.[62] He died on May 3, 2000.

Mercury #11: November 1957 (Session 571115)

In November of 1957, the Stanleys recorded their last formal session for Mercury. The session was held at the new RCA Studio at the corner of 17th Avenue and Hawkins (now Roy Acuff Place), just a few blocks from Bradley's Quonset hut studio. In fact, the new RCA facility was built to compete directly with Bradley. The studio had opened earlier in the month, and the Stanley Brothers were among the first groups to record there. The studio operated for twenty years and earned the nickname of "Home of 1,000 Hits." Today, the facility is maintained by the Country Music Hall of Fame and is open for tours.

For this Stanley session, Carter again wanted to feature the twin fiddle sound, and he summoned two of Nashville's best fiddlers: Benny Martin and Howdy Forrester. This session marked the only occasion on which this duo recorded together. This session marked the debut of Bill Napier.

Benjamin Edward "Benny" Martin was born on May 8, 1928, in Sparta, Tennessee. A superb fiddler, he is best known for the excellent recordings he made with Flatt & Scruggs in the early 1950s. He performed earlier with Bill Monroe, but didn't have the opportunity to record with him. His other work included stints with Johnnie & Jack, Kitty Wells, and Roy Acuff. For a period of time, he was an opening act for Elvis Presley. He recorded for Mercury, Decca, RCA, and Starday, and his best-known song is "Me and My Fiddle." In the mid-1960s, he teamed up briefly with bluegrass banjoist Don Reno. The balance of his career was spent as a solo artist. One of his career highlights is the 1973 album *Tennessee Jubilee*. He is a member of the International Bluegrass Music Association's Hall of Honor. He died on March 13, 2001.[63]

Howard Wilson "Howdy" Forrester was born on March 31, 1922, in Vernon, Kentucky. A bout with rheumatic fever at age eleven left Howdy with a long recuperation, during which time he learned to play the fiddle. He was soon playing local square dances with his brothers. In 1938, he was performing on the *Grand Ole Opry* as a member of Harold Goodman's Tennessee Valley Boys. One of Howdy's chief inspirations was *Opry* fiddler Arthur Smith. From 1940 to 1943, he was a member of Bill Monroe's Blue Grass Boys. His tenure with Monroe was interrupted by naval duties in World War II. He returned to Monroe briefly after the war then moved to Texas to perform with various groups. He returned to Nashville in 1949 and worked first with Cowboy Copas before beginning in 1951 a long-running association with Roy Acuff. His relationship with Acuff resulted in employment with Acuff-Rose Publications as a booking agent and staffer. Howdy remained with Acuff the rest of his life, passing on August 1, 1987.[64]

The first selection recorded at the session is a mandolin instrumental Bill Napier wrote called "Daybreak in Dixie." This is one of the first non-Monroe mandolin instrumentals to enter into mainstream bluegrass.

Featured next is the only song recorded by the Stanley Brothers to include electric steel guitar, "If That's the Way You Feel." Long-time Eddy Arnold veteran Little Roy Wiggins plays the steel on the song. Composer credits show that Ralph Stanley and his wife, Peggy,

In November of 1958, Carter and Ralph recorded the only song of their career to feature an electric steel guitar, "If That's the Way You Feel." It was intended to be released on Mercury single 71258, as shown in the photo above. The music actually on the disc, however, was another song from the same session called "A Life of Sorrow." The mistake was corrected by making a new label that matched the music. Consequently, "If That's the Way You Feel" lay dormant for nearly fifteen years, eventually seeing the light of day as part of a foreign reissue of Stanley Brothers' Mercury material.

wrote it. The song was never released in the United States, but it did appear in Japan in the early 1970s. As the song had never been released during the Stanley Brothers' career, they recorded the tune again in 1962 for King Records and featured it as a quartet. That version, too, remained unissued until it appeared as a bonus cut on a 1986 reissue of their King album *Country Folk Music Spotlight*.

Ivan Leroy "Little Roy" Wiggins was born on June 27, 1926, in Nashville, Tennessee. He developed an interest in steel guitar at an early age after hearing *Grand Ole Opry* performer Burt Hutcherson. At age thirteen, he joined Paul Howard's Arkansas Cotton Pickers and later Pee Wee King's Golden West Cowboys, a group that also included vocalist Eddy Arnold. When Arnold formed his own band, he took Wiggins with him. The sound of Wiggins's steel guitar was an essential component of Arnold's early sound of the 1940s and '50s. In the late '50s and into the '60s, Wiggins made a series of solo albums for Dot and Starday. He stayed with Arnold for twenty-five years and later worked for *Opry* acts such as the Willis Brothers, Ernie Ashworth, and George Morgan. For several years in the 1960s and '70s, he operated Little Roy Wiggins' Music City, a music store near the Ryman Auditorium in Nashville. He later relocated to Pigeon Forge, Tennessee. In 1985, he was inducted into the Steel Guitar Hall of Fame. He died on August 3, 1999.[65]

Also featured on the session is a remake of a song the Stanley Brothers had originally recorded for Columbia in 1952 called "A Life of Sorrow." Columbia had yet to release the cut at the time of the Mercury session, and not wishing to waste a good song, the Stanleys recut it then. The Columbia version finally appeared in the early 1960s on a Harmony compilation of Stanley Brothers material. The last selection recorded is the lone duet from the session, a song called "I'd Rather Be Forgotten." The Stanleys' long-time friend from the Bristol area E. P. Williams wrote the song. He surfaced again in Ralph's career in the early 1980s when he produced and recorded a gospel album by Ralph for his label, Blue Jay Records.

Bill Clifton #2: March 1958 (Session 580300)

In March of 1958, Ralph Stanley participated in another recording session for Bill Clifton. Bill recalled that he stopped in Bristol to pick up Ralph to take him to Nashville for the session, and that it was Ralph's first time flying. Recorded at the new RCA studio on Hawkins Street in Nashville were five songs, including "You Go to Your Church"; "Are You Alone"; "Another Broken Heart"; "When You Kneel at Mother's Grave"; and "Corey." Several of these songs have a Stanley tie-in. The song "You Go to Your Church" was featured in a Stanley Brothers songbook from the early 1950s and was evidently a favorite with the Clinch Mountain Boys Quartet. The Stanley Brothers were not, however, the source for this recording. Bill first started singing the song in about 1952 after being "completely enthralled"[66] by a release of it by Jim & Jesse McReynolds and Larry Roll, a group that was billed as the Virginia Trio. "Are You Alone" is a Carter Stanley composition. The Stanley Brothers performed this song in 1957 as "Thinking of the Old Days," and it was one of several songs Carter gave to Bill Clifton. Lastly, while best known as a Carter Family recording from the 1930s, Carter and Ralph featured "Another Broken Heart" on live performances in 1957. Bill noted that this song was "learned from the Carter Family—but I certainly recall Carter [Stanley] singing it, and that may well have been a 'prod' for me to record it."[67]

Musically, the Clifton session is very rich, especially in terms of talent. In addition to Clifton and Ralph Stanley, also present are fiddlers Benny Martin and Tommy Jackson, bass player Junior Huskey, and rhythm guitarist Jimmy Selph, all four highly respected Nashville session players. Completing the all-star line-up is DC area picker and Country Gentleman cofounder John Duffey on mandolin, dobro, and tenor vocals.

Mercury #12: March 1958 (Session 580310)

The Stanleys were to record one final song for Mercury that, like "The Flood," was made as a rush release to capitalize on a tragedy. The event was a school bus accident that occurred on February 29, 1958, in Floyd County, Kentucky, not far from Prestonsburg.[68] Twenty-three children as well as the driver drowned when the bus careened into the Big Sandy River; sixteen children escaped. Hobo Jack Adkins, a performer and songwriter from eastern Kentucky, wrote the song, which he called "Kentucky School Bus," and had his own quick release of the tune on Starday Records (45–363).[69] The Stanleys promptly sent their recording, titled "No School Bus in Heaven," to Mercury for a quick release. It's not certain exactly when their recording was made, but Mercury released it on April 30, 1958, two months after the event. As with "The Flood," a pick-up bass player was used, another Bristol musician, Curly

The last single to be released on Mercury by the Stanley Brothers was another topical tragedy song. On February 29, 1958, a school bus in Floyd County, Kentucky, plunged into the wintery waters of the Big Sandy River, killing twenty-three children as well as the driver of the bus. The event made headlines nationwide and was the inspiration for a song by local tunesmith Hobo Jack Adkins called "Kentucky School Bus." His song was adapted and covered by the Stanley Brothers as "No School Bus in Heaven."

King. No further recording sessions were scheduled during the year for the Stanleys with Mercury, and their contract was allowed to expire without being renewed.

Cecil Haynes Crusenberry, aka Curly King, was an entertainer who is best known for his work on WCYB's *Farm & Fun Time* program. Along with the Stanley Brothers, he and his group, the Tennessee Hilltoppers, were the first live entertainers to appear on the station. He was born in Bristol on August 20, 1921, and formed his first band in 1940. During the early and mid- '40s, King performed on WOPI in Bristol. He switched to WCYB in December of 1946. He remained at the station for at least a decade and is reported to have been on the roster when the *Farm & Fun Time* program was retired. Curly played guitar and sang lead. He featured a traditional country sound that borrowed elements from popular groups of the day, such as the Bailes Brothers and Eddy Arnold. He died on December 13, 1989.

Live Recordings: 1958 (Session 580504)

On May 4, 1958, the Stanley Brothers performed at Sunset Park in Oxford, Pennsylvania. For a number of years, Carter and Ralph were the act that kicked off the season at the park. The band on this occasion included Carter and Ralph, Bill Napier on mandolin, Ralph Mayo on fiddle, and Jack Cooke on bass. Bill Offenbacher recorded the program. While this set does have a number of live versions of their Mercury releases, there are quite a few musical treats as well. Ralph Mayo gets to solo on several fiddle tunes, most notably "Cacklin' Hen" and "Lee Highway Blues." Bill Napier sings solos of two fairly recent country songs; "Country Waltz" is a Bill Monroe release, while Bobby Helms, who is better known for his Christmas favorite "Jingle Bell Rock," popularized "Fraulein." Napier also offers up two mandolin instrumentals, "Rawhide" and "Daybreak in Dixie." Jack Cooke features a bit of comedy that is unfortunately cut off before its conclusion, and he sings a song made popular by the Louvin Brothers called "Cash on the Barrelhead." The Stanley Brothers

In the latter part of 1958, Mercury issued the first long play album of the Stanley Brothers' career. It was called *Country Pickin' and Singin'* and featured a country scene of fall foliage on the cover. It contained a mixture of instrumentals, hymns, and love songs. Significantly, it introduced a half dozen songs that had remained unissued up until that time. The album rates as one of the classic bluegrass releases of the 1950s.

pull out a few oddities as well. "The Hills of Roane County," "Mother's Not Dead," and "Can You Forgive" were all unrecorded by the Stanley Brothers at the time but eventually showed up on King Records several years later. The live recording also shows the Stanleys still performing "Going to the Races" even though the Country Gentlemen had already recorded it. Ralph is featured on "Tennessee Blues," a tune he reworked and recorded three weeks later as "Midnight Ramble." Lastly, the quartet features several gospel songs that they never commercially recorded, "Wait a Little Longer, Please Jesus" and "He'll Set Your Fields on Fire."

The Stanley Brothers covered a lot of ground during their association with Mercury Records. They recorded what many believe to be their best work. They maintained some sense of stability, having been headquartered at WCYB's *Farm & Fun Time* program during their entire tenure with Mercury. The group worked at expanding the scope of their performance activities with shows at popular outdoor parks in Ohio, Maryland, and Pennsylvania, as well as with several long-range tours of the Pacific Northwest and Canada. As stable and productive as the Mercury years were for the Stanley Brothers, 1958 would bring big changes.

DISCOGRAPHY, 1953–1958

530809 Mercury session; producer: Dee Kilpatrick
Bradley Studios, Nashville, Tennessee
August 9, 1953
Carter Stanley: g | Ralph Stanley: b | Jim Williams: m
Art Stamper: f | George Shuffler: sb

7845	**(Say) Won't You Be Mine** (Carter Stanley) C. Stanley–L, R. Stanley–T	70270	BCD-15681, MERC-314-528-191-2, MERC-088-170-222-2, MERC-B0000534-02, B0007883-02
7846	This Weary Heart You Stole Away (Carter Stanley) C. Stanley–L, R. Stanley–T	70217	BCD-15681, MERC-314-528-191-2, MERC-B0000534-02, B0007883-02
7847	**I'm Lonesome Without You** (Ralph Stanley) C. Stanley–L, R. Stanley–T, Shuffler–B	70217	BCD-15681, MERC-B0000534-02, B0007883-02
7848	**Our Last Goodbye** (Carter Stanley) C. Stanley–L, R. Stanley–T	70270	MG-20884, MGW-12327, BCD-15681, MERC-088-170-222-2, MERC-B0000534-02, B0007883-02

531125 Mercury session; producer: Dee Kilpatrick
Bradley Studios, Nashville, Tennessee
November 25, 1953
Carter Stanley: g | Ralph Stanley: b | Jim Williams: m
Ralph Eugene Mayo: f | John William Shuffler: sb

7520	**Poison Lies** (Carter Stanley) C. Stanley–L, R. Stanley–T	70437	MG-20349, BCD-15681, MERC-B0000534-02
7521	**Dickson County Breakdown** (Ralph Stanley) Instrumental	70437	BCD-15681, MERC-B0000534-02
7522	**I Long to See the Old Folks** (Carter Stanley) C. Stanley–L, R. Stanley–T	70340	MG-20884, MGW-12327, BCD-15681, MERC-314-528-191-2, MERC-088-170-222-2, MERC-B0000534-02
7523	**A Voice From On High** (Bill Monroe) R. Stanley–high lead, Shuffler–low tenor, C. Stanley–B	70340	MG-20349, BCD-15681, MERC-314-528-191-2, MERC-088-170-222-2, MERC-B0000534-02, B0007883-02

540530 Mercury session; producer: Dee Kilpatrick
Bradley Studios, Nashville, Tennessee
May 30, 1954
Carter Stanley: g | Ralph Stanley: b | Jim Williams: m
Ralph Joe Meadows: f | Floyd T. "Lightnin'" Chance: sb

7598	**Memories of Mother** (Carter Stanley) C. Stanley–L, R. Stanley–T	70400	BCD-15681, MERC-314-528-191-2, MERC-B0000534-02
7599	**Could You Love Me (One More Time)** (Carter Stanley) C. Stanley–L, R. Stanley–T	70400	BCD-15681, MERC-314-528-191-2, MERC-B0000534-02

7600	**Nobody's Love Is Like Mine** (Carter Stanley) C. Stanley—L, R. Stanley—T	70789	MG-20884, MGW-12327, BCD-15681, MERC-B0000534-02, B0007883-02
7601	**I Just Got Wise** (Carter Stanley) C. Stanley—L, R. Stanley—T	70453	BCD-15681, MERC-B0000534-02, B0007883-02

540829	Mercury session; producer: Dee Kilpatrick Bradley Studios, Nashville, Tennessee August 29, 1954 Carter Stanley: g | Ralph Stanley: b | William H. "Bill" Lowe: m Joe Meadows: f | Lightning Chance: sb | Charles "Charlie" Cline: lg		
7632	**Blue Moon of Kentucky** (Bill Monroe) C. Stanley—L, R. Stanley—T	70453	MG-20884, MG-20857, MG-12267, MGW-12327, BCD-15681, MERC-314-528-191-2, MERC-B0000534-02, B0007883-02
7633	**Close By** (B. Monroe—VanWinkle) C. Stanley—L, R. Stanley—T		BCD-15681, MERC-314-528-191-2, MERC-B0000534-02
7634	**Calling from Heaven** (Carter Stanley) C. Stanley—L, R. Stanley—T, Lowe—B, Meadows—BS	70483	BCD-15681, MERC-314-528-191-2 MERC-B0000534-02
7635	**Harbor of Love** (Carter Stanley) C. Stanley—L, R. Stanley—T, Lowe—B, Meadows—BS	70483	BCD-15681, MERC-B0000534-02
7636	**Hard Times** (Ralph Stanley) Instrumental	70546	MG-20884, SRW-16327, MGW-12327, BCD-15681, MERC-B0000534-02, B0007883-02

541128	Mercury session; producer: Dee Kilpatrick Bradley Studios, Nashville, Tennessee November 28, 1954 Carter Stanley: g | Ralph Stanley: b | Bill Lowe: m Joe Meadows: f | Lightning Chance: sb		
7659	**Baby Girl** (Carter Stanley) C. Stanley—L, R. Stanley—T, Lowe—B	70886	BCD-15681, MERC-314-528-191-2, MERC-088-170-222-2, MERC-B0000534-02
7660	**Say You'll Take Me Back** (Ralph Stanley) R. Stanley—high lead, Lowe—low tenor, C. Stanley—B	70886	BCD-15681, MERC-B0000534-02
7661	**I Worship You** (Ralph Stanley) C. Stanley—L, R. Stanley—T Lowe—B	70546	BCD-15681, MERC-314-528-191-2, MERC-088-170-222-2, MERC-B0000534-02
7662	**You're Still on My Mind** (Ralph Stanley) C. Stanley—L, R. Stanley—T		MG-20349, BCD-15681, MERC-B0000534-02

550405	Mercury session; producer: Dee Kilpatrick RCA Studios, Nashville, Tennessee April 5, 1955 Carter Stanley: g | Ralph Stanley: b | Jim Williams: m Joe Meadows: f (lg on 7716) | Bill Lowe: sb		
7714	**I Hear My Savior Calling** (Bill Monroe) C. Stanley—L, R. Stanley—T, Meadows—B, Lowe—BS	70718	BCD-15681, MERC-B0000534-02

7715	**Just a Little Talk with Jesus** (Derricks)	70718	MGW-12262, SRW-16262, BCD-15681, MERC-314-528-191-2,
	C. Stanley–L, R. Stanley–T, Meadows–B, Lowe–BS		MERC-088-170-222-2, MERC-B0000524-02
7716	**So Blue** (Ralph Stanley)	70612	MG-20884, BCD-15681, MERC-B0000534-02
	C. Stanley–L, R. Stanley–T		
7717	**You'd Better Get Right** (Bill Monroe)	70612	BCD-15681, MERC-B0000534-02
	C. Stanley–L, R. Stanley–T		
7718	**Tragic Love** (Buddy Dee)		MG-20349, MGW-12267, BCD-15681, MERC-314-528-191-2,
	C. Stanley–L, R. Stanley–T		MERC-B0000534-02
7719	**Lonesome and Blue** (Carter Stanley)	70663	BCD-15681, MERC-B0000534-02
	C. Stanley–L, R. Stanley–T		
7720	**Orange Blossom Special** (Rouse-Rouse)	70663	MG-20349, MG-20884, MGW-12327, BCD-15681,
	C. Stanley–L, R. Stanley–T		MERC-B0000534-02, B0007883-02

550703   Copper Creek reissue of show, recorded by Mike Seeger
New River Ranch, Rising Sun, Maryland
July 3, 1955
Carter Stanley: g | Ralph Stanley: b | Jim Williams: m
Lawrence Douglas "Doug" Morris: sb | Lindburgh Hugh "Lindy" Clear: imitations

Dickenson County Breakdown (Ralph Stanley) Instrumental	CCSS-V1N3
Big Tilda (Ralph Stanley) Instrumental	CCSS-V1N3
That's All Right Mama (Arthur Crudup) Morris–L	CCSS-V1N3
Poor Ellen Smith (Traditional) Williams–L	CCSS-V1N3
Turkey in the Straw (Traditional) Clear–L	CCSS-V1N3
So Blue (Ralph Stanley) C. Stanley–L, R. Stanley–T, Williams–B (tag line at end)	CCSS-V1N3
Will He Wait a Little Longer (Ralph Stanley) C. Stanley–L, R. Stanley–T, Williams–B	CCSS-V1N3
Rabbit in a Log (Traditional) C. Stanley–L, R. Stanley–T	CCSS-V1N3
Blue Moon of Kentucky (Bill Monroe) C. Stanley–L, R. Stanley–T	CCSS-V1N3
White House Blues (Traditional) C. Stanley–L	CCSS-V1N3
Dickenson County Breakdown (Ralph Stanley) Instrumental	CCSS-V1N3

You'd Better Get Right (Bill Monroe) C. Stanley–L, R. Stanley–T		CCSS-V1N3
Say You'll Take Me Back (Ralph Stanley) R. Stanley–high lead, C. Stanley–low tenor		CCSS-V1N3
A Voice from on High (Bill Monroe) R. Stanley–high lead, C. Stanley–low tenor, Williams–B		CCSS-V1N3
Angel Band (Traditional) C. Stanley–L, R. Stanley–T, Williams–B		CCSS-V1N3
Wait a Little Longer Please Jesus (Hazel Houser) C. Stanley–L, R. Stanley–T, Williams–B		CCSS-V1N3
Model T, Frogs, and Trains (Arr. Lindy Clear) Clear–L		CCSS-V1N3
Hard Times (Ralph Stanley) Instrumental		CCSS-V1N3

550800 Time Life reissue of show, recorded by Marvin Hedrick
Brown County Jamboree, Bean Blossom, Indiana
Summer 1955
Carter Stanley: g | Ralph Stanley: b | Ralph Mayo: f |
George Shuffler: sb

Will You Be Loving Another Man (L. Flatt–B. Monroe) C. Stanley–L, R. Stanley–T		B0007883-02

551219 Mercury session; producer: Dee Kilpatrick
Bradley Studios, Nashville, Tennessee
December 19, 1955
Carter Stanley: g | Ralph Stanley: b | Richard Edward "Curley" Lambert: m
Art Stamper: f | Bill Lowe: sb

7787	**Clinch Mountain Blues** (Leslie Keith) Instrumental		MG-20349, MG-20884, BCD-15681, MERC-B0000534-02
7788	**Big Tilda** (Ralph Stanley) Instrumental	70789	MG-20349, MG-20884, MGW-12327, BCD-15681, MERC-B0000534-02
7789	**Will He Wait a Little Longer** (Ralph Stanley) C. Stanley–L, R. Stanley–T, Lambert–B, Lowe–BS		BCD-15681, MERC-314-528-191-2, MERC-088-170-222-2, MERC-B0000534-02
7790	**Angel Band** (Ralph Stanley) C. Stanley–L, R. Stanley–T, Lambert–B, Lowe–BS		MG-20349, BCD-15681, MERC-314-528-191-2, MERC-088-170-222-2, MERC-B0000534-02, B0007883-02, M-19493,

560324   StanleyTone reissue of show, recorded by Larry Ehrlich
         Radio Station WCYB, Bristol, Virginia
         March 24, 1956
         Carter Stanley: g | Ralph Stanley: b (* m) | Curley Lambert: m
         Ralph Mayo: f

Handsome Molly   ST-5001, CK-86747
C. Stanley–L

East Virginia Blues *   ST-5001, CK-86747
C. Stanley–L, R. Stanley–T

The Story of the Lawson Family   ST-5001, CK-86747
C. Stanley–L, R. Stanley–T

Dream of a Miner's Child   ST-5001, CK-86747
C. Stanley–L

Come All You Tenderhearted   ST-5001, CK-86747
C. Stanley–L

Poor Ellen Smith   ST-5001, CK-86747
C. Stanley–L

Darling Do You Know Who Loves You   ST-5001, CK-86747
C. Stanley–L, R. Stanley–T

Shout Little Lulie   ST-5001, CK-86747
Instrumental

Bound to Ride   ST-5001, CK-86747
C. Stanley–L

Meet Me Tonight   ST-5001, CK-86747
C. Stanley–L, R. Stanley–T

My Long Skinny Lanky Sarah Jane   ST-5001, CK-86747
C. Stanley–L

Little Bessie   ST-5001, CK-86747
C. Stanley–L

Train 45   ST-5001, CK-86747
C. Stanley–Spoken intro and L

John Henry   ST-5001, CK-86747
Instrumental

Little Birdie   ST-5001, CK-86747
R. Stanley–L

Drifting Too Far from the Shore   ST-5001, CK-86747
C. Stanley–L, R. Stanley–T

Orange Blossom Special   ST-5001, CK-86747
C. Stanley–L, R. Stanley–T

Nine Pound Hammer	ST-5001, CK-86747
C. Stanley—L, R. Stanley—T	

Feast Here Tonight	ST-5001, CK-86747
C. Stanley—L, R. Stanley—T	

Tragic Love	ST-5001, CK-86747
C. Stanley—L, R. Stanley—T	

560603 Copper Creek reissue of show, recorded by Jeremy Foster
Shenandoah Valley Bowl, Edinburg, Virginia
June 3, 1956
Carter Stanley: g | Ralph Stanley: b | Curley Lambert: m
Donald Lee "Chubby" Anthony: f | Doug Morris: sb

Dickenson County Breakdown (Ralph Stanley)	CCSS-V2N1
Instrumental	

Orange Blossom Special (Rouse-Rouse)	CCSS-V2N1
C. Stanley—L, R. Stanley—T	

I'll Be True While You're Gone (G. Autry—F. Rose)	CCSS-V2N1
Lambert—L	

Hard Times (Ralph Stanley)	CCSS-V2N1
Instrumental	

A Voice from on High (Bill Monroe)	CCSS-V2N1
R. Stanley—high lead, C. Stanley—low tenor, Lambert—B	

Nobody's Love Is Like Mine (Carter Stanley)	CCSS-V2N1
C. Stanley—L, R. Stanley—T	

Say You'll Take Me Back (Ralph Stanley)	CCSS-V2N1
C. Stanley—L, R. Stanley—T, Lambert—B	

Baby Girl (Carter Stanley)	CCSS-V2N1
C. Stanley—L, R. Stanley—T, Lambert—B	

Big Tilda (Ralph Stanley)	CCSS-V2N1
Instrumental	

Little Glass of Wine (Carter Stanley)	CCSS-V2N1
C. Stanley—L, R. Stanley—T	

Man of Constant Sorrow (Traditional)	CCSS-V2N1
R. Stanley—L	

Rabbit in a Log (Traditional)	CCSS-V2N1
C. Stanley—L, R. Stanley—T	

I Believed in You, Darling (Bill Monroe)	Joy-10329, SLP-1512, CCSS-V2N1
C. Stanley—L, R. Stanley—T	

Little Birdie (Traditional)	CCSS-V2N1
R. Stanley—L	

Leather Britches (Traditional)
Instrumental

CCSS-V2N1

Meet Me by the Moonlight (Traditional)
C. Stanley–L, R. Stanley–T

Joy-10329, SLP-1512, CCSS-V2N1, SH-DV 604,
CMH-CD-8412

Molly and Tenbrooks (Traditional)
C. Stanley–L

CCSS-V2N1

560708   Copper Creek reissue of show, recorded by Jeremy Foster
         Shipps Park, Morrisville, Virginia
         July 8, 1956
         Carter Stanley: g | Ralph Stanley: b | Curley Lambert: m
         Chubby Anthony: f | Lindy Clear: sb

Dickenson County Breakdown (Ralph Stanley)
Instrumental

CCSS-V2N3

Roving Gambler (Traditional)
C. Stanley–L, R. Stanley–T

SLP-1487, Joy-10329, SLP-1512, CCSS-V2N3

Cry from the Cross (Johnnie Masters)
C. Stanley–L, R. Stanley–T, Lambert–B

CCSS-V2N3

Katy Hill (Traditional)
Instrumental

CCSS-V2N3

Boil Them Cabbage Down (Traditional)
C. Stanley–L, R. Stanley–T

CCSS-V2N3

Roll in my Sweet Baby's Arms (Traditional)
C. Stanley–L, R. Stanley–T

CCSS-V2N3

I Just Got Wise (Carter Stanley)
C. Stanley–L, R. Stanley–T

Joy-10329, SLP-1512, CCSS-V2N3

Little Maggie (Traditional)
R. Stanley–L

CCSS-V2N3

Little Glass of Wine (Carter Stanley)
C. Stanley–L, R. Stanley–L

CCSS-V2N3

Who'll Call You Sweetheart (Monroe-Stanley)
C. Stanley–L, Lambert–T, R. Stanley–HB

Joy-10329, SLP-1512, CCSS-V2N3

Drifting Too Far from the Shore (Charles E. Moody)
C. Stanley–L, R. Stanley–T

CCSS-V2N3

Wait a Little Longer Please Jesus (Hazel Houser)
C. Stanley–L, R. Stanley–T, Lambert–B

Joy-10329, SLP-1512, CCSS-V2N3

Just a Little Talk with Jesus (C. Derricks)
C. Stanley–L, R. Stanley–T, Lambert–B, Anthony–BS

CCSS-V2N3

Imitations (Traditional)
Clear–L

CCSS-V2N3

Lee Highway Blues (G. B. Grayson)
Instrumental

CCSS-V2N3

Are You Waiting Just for Me (Ernest Tubb)
C. Stanley—L, R. Stanley—T

SLP-1495, CCSS-V2N3

560716 Mercury session; producer: Dee Kilpatrick
Bradley Studios, Nashville, Tennessee
July 16, 1956
Carter Stanley: g | Ralph Stanley: b | Curley Lambert: m
Chubby Anthony: f | Ralph Mayo: f | Doug Morris: sb

12724 **The Cry From The Cross** (Johnnie Masters)   71135   MG-20349, BCD-15681, MERC-B0000534-02, B0007883-02
C. Stanley—L, R. Stanley—T, Lambert—B

12725 **Who Will Call You Sweetheart** (Carter Stanley—Bill Monroe)   MG-20349, BCD-15681, MERC-088-170-222-2,
C. Stanley—L, Lambert—T, R. Stanley—HB   MERC-B0000534-02, B0007883-02

12726 **I'm Lost, I'll Never Find the Way**   71064   BCD-15681, MERC-B0000534-02
  (Ralph Stanley)
C. Stanley—L, R. Stanley—T, Lambert—B

12727 **Let Me Walk, Lord, By Your Side** (Carter Stanley)71135   BCD-15681, MERC-314-528-191-2, MERC-B0000534-02
C. Stanley—L, R. Stanley—T, Lambert—B, Anthony (possibly)—BS

12728 **A Lonesome Night** (Carter Stanley)   BCD-15681, MERC-B0000534-02
C. Stanley—L, R. Stanley—T, Lambert—B

560729 Copper Creek reissue of show, recorded by Jeremy Foster
New River Ranch, Rising Sun, Maryland
July 29, 1956
Carter Stanley: g | Ralph Stanley: b | Curley Lambert: m
Chubby Anthony: f | Lindy Clear: sb

Dickenson County Breakdown
Instrumental

CCSS-5513

Orange Blossom Special
C. Stanley—L, R. Stanley—T

CCSS-5513

Crazy Arms
Lambert—L

CCSS-5513

Hard Times
Instrumental

CCSS-5513

Nobody's Love Is Like Mine
C. Stanley—L, R. Stanley—T

CCSS-5513

Cry from the Cross
C. Stanley—L, R. Stanley—T, Lambert—B

CCSS-5513

Fling Ding
Instrumental

CCSS-5513

Say You'll Take Me Back	CCSS-5513
C. Stanley=L, R. Stanley=T, Lambert=B	
Big Tilda	CCSS-5513
Instrumental	
Baby Girl	CCSS-5513
C. Stanley—L, R. Stanley—T, Lambert—B	
Little Glass of Wine	CCSS-5513
C. Stanley—L, R. Stanley—T	
Little Birdie	CCSS-5513
R. Stanley—L	
Black Mountain Rag* [actually "Blues Mountain Rag"]	CCSS-5513
Instrumental	
Just a Little Talk with Jesus	CCSS-5513
C. Stanley—L, R. Stanley—T, Lambert—B, Anthony—BS	
A Voice from on High	CCSS-5513
R. Stanley—high lead, C. Stanley—low tenor, Lambert—B	
Rawhide	CCSS-5513
Instrumental	
I Just Got Wise	CCSS-5513
C. Stanley—L, R. Stanley—T	
Hard Times	CCSS-5513
Instrumental	
Carroll County Blues	CCSS-5513
Instrumental	
White Dove	CCSS-5513
C. Stanley—L, R. Stanley—T, Lambert—B	
Could You Love Me One More Time	CCSS-5513
C. Stanley—L, R. Stanley—T	
Cry from the Cross	CCSS-5513
C. Stanley—L, R. Stanley—T, Lambert—B	
Drifting Too Far from the Shore	CCSS-5513
C. Stanley—L, R. Stanley—T	
Rabbit in the Log	CCSS-5513
C. Stanley—L, R. Stanley—T	
Boil Them Cabbage Down	CCSS-5513
C. Stanley—L, R. Stanley—T, Lambert—B	
A Parting Cry from Tennessee Mort	CCSS-5513
Clear—L	

560805   Copper Creek reissue of show, recorded by Jeremy Foster
Silver Creek Ranch, Paris, Virginia
August 5, 1956
Carter Stanley: g | Ralph Stanley: b | Curley Lambert: m
Chubby Anthony. f | Lindy Clear. sb

Dickenson County Breakdown (Ralph Stanley) Instrumental	CCSS-V3N1
Orange Blossom Special (Rouse-Rouse) C. Stanley—L, R. Stanley—T	CCSS-V3N1
Crazy Arms (R. Mooney—C. Seals) Lambert—L	CCSS-V3N1
Going to Georgia (Traditional) C. Stanley—L, R. Stanley—T	CCLP-0101, CCSS-V3N1
Little Maggie (Traditional) R. Stanley—L	CCSS-V3N1
I'm a Man of Constant Sorrow (Traditional) R. Stanley—L	CCSS-V3N1
Little Glass of Wine (Carter Stanley) C. Stanley—L, R. Stanley—T	CCSS-V3N1
Jealous Lover (Traditional) C. Stanley—L, R. Stanley—T	BRI-002, CCSS-V3N1
The Little Girl and the Dreadful Snake (Albert Price) C. Stanley—L, R. Stanley—T	CCSS-V3N1
The Cry from the Cross (Johnnie Masters) C. Stanley—L, R. Stanley—T, Lambert—B	CCSS-V3N1
Molly and Tenbrooks (Traditional) C. Stanley—L	CCSS-V3N1
Pretty Polly (Traditional) R. Stanley—L	CCSS-V3N1
Little Birdie (Traditional) R. Stanley—L	CCSS-V3N1
A Lonesome Night (Carter Stanley) C. Stanley—L, R. Stanley—T, Lambert—B	CCSS-V3N1

561100	Starday session; producer: Bill Clifton		
	RCA Victor Studio, Nashville, Tennessee		
	November 1956		
	Bill Clifton: g	Ralph Stanley: b	Curley Lambert: m		
	Sonny Mead: f	Bill Wiltshire: f	George Shuffler: sb		
2549	**Gathering Flowers from the Hillside** (Bill Clifton–Buddy Dee)	290	SLP-104, BCD-16425
	Clifton–L, Lambert–T		
	Little White Chimney (Bill Clifton)		BCD-16425
	Clifton–L, Lambert–T		
	Railroading on the Great Divide (Sara Carter)		BCD-16425
	Clifton–L, Lambert–T		
2550	**Take Back the Heart** (Bill Clifton)	290	SLP-104, BCD-16425
	Clifton–L, Lambert–T		

570201	Mercury session; producer: Stanley Brothers		
	Radio Station WCYB, Bristol, Virginia		
	ca. February 1, 1957		
	Carter Stanley: g	Ralph Stanley: b	George Shuffler: m		
	Chubby Anthony: f	Mervin Haskell "Red" Malone: sb		
14944	**The Flood** (Carter Stanley–Ralph Stanley)	71064	MG-20349, BCD-15681, MERC-B0000534-02
	C. Stanley–L, R. Stanley–T, Anthony–HB		

570227	Mercury session; producer: Pappy Dailey		
	RCA Studios, Nashville, Tennessee		
	February 27, 1957		
	Carter Stanley: g	Ralph Stanley: b	Pee Wee Lambert: m		
	Chubby Anthony: f	George Shuffler: sb		
14755	**Fling Ding** (Ralph Stanley)	71207	MG-20349, MG-20884, MGW-12327, BCD-15681,
	Instrumental		MERC-B0000534-02
14756	**I'll Never Grow Tired of You** (Carter Stanley)	71302	BCD-15681, MERC-B0000534-02
	C. Stanley–L, R. Stanley–T, Shuffler–B		
14757	**Loving You Too Well** (Carter Stanley)	71207	BCD-15681, MERC-088-170-222-2, MERC-B0000534-02
	C. Stanley–L, R. Stanley–T		

570418	Copper Creek reissue of show, recorded by Bill Offenbacher		
	Melody Ranch, Glen Burnie, Maryland		
	April 18, 1957		
	Carter Stanley: g	Ralph Stanley: b	Curley Lambert: m		
	Chubby Anthony: f	Lindy Clear: sb		
	Lonesome Road Blues (Traditional)		CCLP-0101
	C. Stanley–L, R. Stanley–T		

570512 Copper Creek reissue of show, recorded by Bill Offenbacher
Valley View Park, Hellam, Pennsylvania
May 12, 1957
Carter Stanley: g | Ralph Stanley: b | Curley Lambert: m
Chubby Anthony: f | Lindy Cloar: sb

    Here Today and Gone Tomorrow (Wally Fowler)   CCLP-0101
    C. Stanley—L, R. Stanley—T, Lambert—B

    Thinking of the Old Days (Bill Clifton)   CCLP-0101
    C. Stanley—L, R. Stanley—T

570601 Copper Creek reissue of show, recorded by Bill Offenbacher
New River Ranch, Rising Sun, Maryland
June 1, 1957
Carter Stanley: g | Ralph Stanley: b | Chubby Anthony: f
Vernon Crawford "Jack" Cooke: sb

    I Hope You Have Learned (Bill Carrigan—Eugene Butler)   CCLP-0101
    C. Stanley—L, R. Stanley—T

    White House Blues (Traditional)   CCLP-0101
    C. Stanley—L

570711 Copper Creek reissue of show, recorded by Bill Offenbacher
Melody Ranch, Glen Burnie, Maryland
July 11, 1957
Carter Stanley: g | Ralph Stanley: b | Billy Edward "Bill" Napier: m
Jack Cooke: sb

    Just Another Broken Heart (A. P. Carter)   CCLP-0101
    C. Stanley—L

570831 Copper Creek reissue of show, recorded by Bill Offenbacher
Front Royal, Virginia
August 30, 1957
Carter Stanley: g | Ralph Stanley: b | Bill Napier: m
Jack Cooke: sb

    Going to the Races (Carter Stanley)   CCLP-0101
    C. Stanley—L, R. Stanley—T

571115 Mercury session; producer: Pappy Dailey
RCA Studios, Nashville, Tennessee
November 15, 1957
Carter Stanley: g | Ralph Stanley: b | Bill Napier: m
Howard Wilson "Howdy" Forrester: f | Benjamin Edward "Benny" Martin: f | Curley Lambert: sb
Ivan Leroy "Little Roy" Wiggins: steel guitar (14801 only)

14800 **Daybreak in Dixie** (Carter Stanley)   MG-20884, MGW-12327, BCD-15681, MERC-314-528-191-2,
      Instrumental   MERC-088-170-222-2, MERC-B0000534-02

14801	**If That's the Way You Feel** (Ralph Stanley–Peggy Stanley)		BCD-15681,
	C. Stanley–L, R. Stanley–T, Lambert–B		MERC-B0000534-02, B0007883-02
14802	**Life of Sorrow** (Carter Stanley)	71258	BCD-15681, MERC-314-528-191-2, MERC-B0000534-02
	C. Stanley–L, R. Stanley–T, Lambert–B		
14803	**I'd Rather Be Forgotten** (E. P. Williams)	71258	BCD-15681, MERC-B0000534-02
	C. Stanley–L, R. Stanley–T		

580300	Mercury-Starday session; producer: Bill Clifton with Don Pierce
	RCA Victor Studio, Nashville, Tennessee
	March 1958
	Bill Clifton: g | James Edward "Jimmy" Selph: g | Ralph Stanley: b
	Curley Lambert: m | John Duffey: m (20, and 22) and dobro (18, 19, and 21)
	Thomas Lee "Tommy" Jackson: f | Benny Martin: f | Roy M. "Junior" Huskey: sb

16318	**You Go to Your Church** (Arr. Bill Clifton)	290	SLP-104, BCD-16425
	Clifton–L, Duffey–T, Lambert–HB		
16319	**Are You Alone** (Bill Clifton)		BCD-16425
	Clifton–L, Duffey–T, Lambert–B		
16320	**Another Broken Heart** (A. P. Carter)		BCD-16425
	Clifton–L, Duffey–T, Lambert–HB		
16321	**When You Kneel at Mother's Grave** (L. Lilley–Bill Clifton)	290	SLP-104, BCD-16425
	Clifton–L, Duffey–T, Lambert–B		
16322	**Corey** (B. Clifton–York)		
	Clifton–L, Duffey–T		

580310	Mercury session; producer: Stanley Brothers
	Radio Station WCYB, Bristol, Virginia
	ca. March 10, 1958
	Carter Stanley: g | Ralph Stanley: b | Bill Napier: m
	Ralph Mayo: f | Cecil Crusenberry, aka Curly King: sb

16342	**No School Bus in Heaven** (Jack Adkins–Buddy Dee)	71302	MG-20857, BCD-15681, MERC-B0000534-02
	C. Stanley–L, R. Stanley–T, Mayo–B (last line only)		

580504	Copper Creek reissue of show, recorded by Bill Offenbacher
	Sunset Park, West Grove, Pennsylvania
	May 4, 1958
	Carter Stanley: g | Ralph Stanley: b | Bill Napier: m
	Ralph Mayo: f | Jack Cooke: sb

	Dickenson County Breakdown		CCCD-5511
	Instrumental		
	Cacklin' Hen		CCCD-5511
	Instrumental		
	Country Waltz		CCCD-5511
	Napier–L		

I'm Lost, I'll Never Find the Way	CCCD-5511
C. Stanley—L, R. Stanley—T	
I'll Never Grow Tired of You	CCCD-5511
C. Stanley—L, R. Stanley—T, Napier—B	
Hard Times	CCCD-5511
Instrumental	
No School Bus in Heaven	CCCD-5511
C. Stanley—L, R. Stanley—T	
Orange Blossom Special	CCCD-5511
C. Stanley—L, R. Stanley—T	
Wait a Little Longer Please Jesus	CCCD-5511
C. Stanley—L, R. Stanley—T, Mayo (probably)—B	
I Just Got Wise	CCCD-5511
C. Stanley—L, R. Stanley—T	
Cash on the Barrelhead	CCCD-5511
Cooke—L	
Hills of Roan County	CCCD-5511
C. Stanley—L, R. Stanley—T	
Rawhide	CCCD-5511
Instrumental	
Little Birdie	CCCD-5511
R. Stanley—L	
Dickenson County Breakdown	CCCD-5511
Instrumental	
Dickenson County Breakdown	CCCD-5511
Instrumental	
Lee Highway Blues	CCCD-5511
Instrumental	
Fraulein	CCCD-5511
Napier—L	
I'd Rather Be Forgotten	CCCD-5511
C. Stanley—L, R. Stanley—T	
Going to the Races	CCCD-5511
C. Stanley—L, R. Stanley—T	
A Life of Sorrow	CCCD-5511
C. Stanley—L, R. Stanley—T, Napier—B	
Fling Ding	CCCD-5511
Instrumental	

He Will Set Your Fields on Fire   CCCD-5511
C. Stanley—L, R. Stanley—T, Mayo—B, Napier—BS

Daybreak in Dixie   CCCD-5511
Instrumental

Mother's Not Dead   CCCD-5511
C. Stanley—L, R. Stanley—T

Tennessee Blues   CCCD-5511
Instrumental

Can You Forgive   CCCD-5511
C. Stanley—L, R. Stanley—T

4

"HOW MOUNTAIN GIRLS CAN LOVE"

The Early King/Starday Years, 1958–1962

In 1958 Carter and Ralph Stanley were seasoned professionals with nearly twelve years of performing under their belts. They had recorded some classic music for Columbia Records in the late 1940s and early 1950s, and from 1953 to 1958 were under contract to Mercury Records, where what many fans consider the group's best recordings were made.

In spite of their past successes, though, things seemed shaky for the duo. In the early or middle part of the year, the Stanley Brothers' contract with Mercury was allowed to lapse, leaving the duo without a label home. And, with five years of uninterrupted broadcasting on WCYB's *Farm & Fun Time* program and repeated appearances within a 150-mile radius of the station, the group was starting to wear out their welcome.

Starday #1: August 1958 (Session 580815)

In August of 1958, the fifth anniversary of their first Mercury session, the Stanleys recorded four songs in a session held in the studios of WCYB. With the exception of the sessions for two songs that were rush released on Mercury, this session marked the first time in nearly a decade that the duo did not record in Nashville. The songs were intended for release on Starday Records, a label that specialized in the traditional styles of country music that were being ignored by the major labels. The five-year pact between Starday and Mercury that began in 1957 had evidently been scuttled by 1958. According to Shelby Singleton, a Nashville record producer who worked at Mercury in the latter part of 1957,

> . . . at the end of '57 or beginning of '58, Pappy was telling me [that] one of the top brass at Mercury [the curmudgeonly Art Talmadge] decided we didn't want that deal to carry on anymore, or something went wrong.[1]

Pappy Daily returned to Dallas and started his own D label, and Don Pierce was left at the helm of Starday.

Bill Clifton noted of the Mercury-Starday split,

... Mercury decided to keep George Jones who sold more records than all the other artists put together and drop everybody else . . . they dropped all of us like hot potatoes: Carl Story, the Stanley Brothers. Don Pierce said, "Well okay, if Mercury drops you, I'll take you." So he decided to have all of us on his Starday label. As a result, he became "the" bluegrass label as he had everybody. There was no place else for us to go.[2]

At the time, Pierce was quite energetic. He developed a mail-order service that sold directly to consumers, especially those who couldn't find "real" country music in conventional retail outlets. He was also very active in servicing disc jockeys with the latest releases by artists on Starday. Sensing that there was a market for country music beyond the borders of the United States, Pierce established a worldwide network for the distribution of his releases and made arrangements for sales in Japan, Germany, England, and South Africa. He was quick to embrace 33⅓ rpm LPs, the then emerging album format, believing that it appealed more to the adult audiences he was trying to reach; 45s—the dominant format for records of the previous decade—catered more, in Pierce's opinion, to teenage record buyers. The following year, 1959, Don Pierce was selected by *Billboard's* twelfth annual jockey poll as the C & W Man of the Year.[3]

Pierce was already familiar with the Stanley Brothers from the Mercury-Starday years, so it seemed natural to continue the relationship. When Carter and Ralph recorded their session for Starday, Bill Napier and Al Elliott were the only full-time members of the band, playing mandolin and bass, respectively. At Carter Stanley's request, Joe Meadows and his brother Gene appeared on fiddle and lead guitar. The lead guitar had been used sparingly on previous Stanley recordings, and this session marks the third time the brothers use the instrument this way. Gene Meadows was apparently not too familiar with the Stanleys' sound, as he showed up at the session with a "Gibson electric and Carter told me I couldn't use that thing . . . so, he had a Martin I used. It was a good sounding Martin, I thought."[4]

Lowell Eugene "Gene" Meadows was born on February 14, 1932, in Dunns, West Virginia, a small community located just south of Beckley. A Korean War veteran, he became acquainted with the Stanley Brothers in the mid-1950s, most likely through Joe's tenure with the group. He related,

> They tried to get me back in 1955; they tried to get me to go with 'em. They wanted me to go to Nashville . . . not really to play with them, but they told me if I would go down then they would get me a job with either the Carlisles or at that time Martha Carson, the Louvin Brothers or some of them. So, I didn't go. He said if he didn't get me a job, he said I could just play with them. So, I didn't. It hadn't been long since I come out of the service so I wanted to stay around home a little bit . . . they played out one time up in Blacksburg, Virginia [and] they had me to play with 'em you know. I happened to be there and I played on the show with them.[5]

He never pursued a career in music and settled in Amherst, Virginia, working at the Bailey Saw Mill and, later, the Driskill Funeral Chapel. He died on May 3, 2008.[6]

Of the session, Joe Meadows remembered,

> At the time we done that, I was living in Lynchburg, Virginia, and playing with Bill
> and Mary Reid. I lost my job over that session. I was working in a shoe factory and
> was playing with Bill and Mary on the side and Carter called me at the factory. So me
> and Curley Lambert . . . both of us was working there, both of us went down. When
> we got back Monday morning why they had our checks ready. We laid off a day to go
> down, but they heard the phone conversation. He fired both of us.[7]

The first track recorded is an instrumental by Ralph called "Holiday Pickin'." In a live
show recorded at Unity Hall on Dundalk Avenue in Baltimore on July 6, 1957, Ralph
Stanley performed the tune and called it "Wild Horse." It appears to be unrelated to an-
other old-time tune of the same name, "Wild Horse at Stony Point," as well as its variants,
"Stony Point" and "Buck Creek Gals." When the Stanley Brothers submitted their track to
Starday, they realized it would be the flip side of a seasonal song and changed the name to
"Reindeer." Starday changed the title yet again, to "Holiday Pickin'."

"That Happy Night" is credited to the Stanleys, but is patterned after a song composed
by the Callahan Brothers called "North Carolina Moon." Walter and Homer Callahan
recorded the tune on January 3, 1934. It's more likely that the recording that influenced
the Stanley Brothers was one made by Wade Mainer and the Sons of the Mountaineers, a
group that included fiddler Steve Ledford and guitarist Clyde Moody, on September 26,
1938. The lyrics to "That Happy Night" first appeared in a 1950 songbook that Carter and
Ralph issued; the song subsequently appeared in three additional songbooks the duo issued
throughout the 1950s.

"Gonna Paint the Town" is a then fairly recent Carter Stanley original based on several
other songs. The basic outline for the song originates from a piece that was popular in
the 1930s called "Let Her Go, God Bless Her," as recorded by J. E. Mainer's Mountaineers.
From this song, Carter wrote a song called "Going to the Races" that he then gave to the
Country Gentlemen to record as one side of their first single release. Not wishing to let
the tune go, Carter then wrote "Gonna Paint the Town" off of "Going to the Races."

The final tune recorded at the session is another Carter Stanley original, "Christmas Is
Near." The lyrics first appeared in a circa 1957 Stanley Brothers songbook entitled *Clinch
Mountain Song Review*.

Throughout the summer of 1958, the group kept busy with performance dates at a
variety of country music parks. Among the highlights were shows at Verona Lake Ranch,
in Kentucky, with George Jones (also in attendance was Don Pierce of Starday Records);
a June appearance at Hillbilly Park in Newark, Ohio; a guest spot on the WWVA *Jamboree*
in Wheeling, West Virginia; and a date at the Brown County Jamboree in Bean Blossom,
Indiana. The band, for most of the summer, included Bill Napier on mandolin, Benny
Williams on fiddle, and Al Elliott on bass.

After the Stanley Brothers' contract with Mercury was allowed to lapse, they hooked up with Don Pierce and Starday Records. Their first release, "Gonna Paint the Town," hit the streets not long after the August 1958 session at which it was recorded.

Live Recordings #1: September 1958 (Session 580907)

September 7 found the group back at one of their familiar haunts, New River Ranch. Napier and Elliott were there, but the band was without a regular fiddle player. Filling in for part of the day was Pete Kuykendall. He, along with Bill Offenbacher and Carl Chatzky, was responsible for tape recording the show.

Pete Kuykendall, who was born on January 15, 1938, and discovered bluegrass as a young teen in the early 1950s, was twenty years old at the time. A proficient picker on a variety of instruments, he was an early member of the Country Gentlemen. Among his favorite musicians were the Stanley Brothers. He researched the first of several discographies that appeared on Carter and Ralph, publishing it in an early 1960s issue of *Disc Collector* magazine. A poorly promoted Stanley Brothers concert in Waldorf, Maryland, prompted Pete, and others, to form a magazine he has edited and managed for many years, *Bluegrass Unlimited*. What started as a newsletter to let fans know of upcoming show dates has for years been viewed as *the* bluegrass publication. Pete has also been active as a recording engineer, music publisher, and record label owner, and is a driving force behind the success of the International Bluegrass Music Association.

Among the highlights of the 1958 New River Ranch show is a lightning quick version of "Boil Them Cabbage Down," which later appeared on the first volume of a Rebel Records album, *The Legendary Stanley Brothers*. The show, in its entirety, was issued on Copper Creek's *Stanley Series*. The group introduces three new songs, "How Mountain Girls Can

Love," "The Memory of Your Smile," and "Think of What You've Done." Of the last tune, Carter notes in the recording, "That's the first time we ever tried to do that, we wrote it yesterday on the way up to Washington."[8]

Later in the month, Carter vacationed in Florida. A postcard to Pee Wee Lambert announced that he was also combining some business with pleasure, namely looking for a new radio station to be affiliated with.

King Records

By the end of the month, the Stanley Brothers were affiliated with a new record label, King Records of Cincinnati. To finalize the deal, Carter and Ralph had to free themselves from their contract to Starday. Don Pierce gave them their freedom under the condition that they record twenty-four additional tracks for him, presumably over a two-year period. The move to King Records began a relationship that would last, off and on, until after Carter Stanley's passing in 1966; Ralph stayed with King Records until 1969. The liner notes to a 1963 album release on King called *Folk Concert* relate an amusing story of how the Stanley Brothers tried to get on King in the mid-1940s:

> It is interesting to note that the Stanley Brothers cut an audition tape in 1946 at Radio Station WCYB in Bristol, Virginia and forwarded this audition tape by mail to Mr. Sydney Nathan, president of King Records Inc. Carter still tells the story of getting a nice letter from Mr. Nathan telling the boys to practice harder, to learn more about their musical heritage and in a few years to come back and see him. In 1958 [they] signed an exclusive contract with King . . . where the boys have enjoyed their greatest success and have emerged as one of the very top acts in their field.[9]

Sydney Nathan, the head of King Records, was born on April 27, 1904, and founded the label in 1943 in Cincinnati, initially signing local country music talent such as Grandpa Jones, the Delmore Brothers, and Merle Travis. Country music continued to be an important part of the company's catalog, but early on rhythm and blues also proved to be a significant part of the mix. Eventually, R & B performer James Brown emerged as the label's biggest selling artist. Nathan grew King Records to become the largest independent label in the nation, and the sixth largest label overall. His operation was unique in that, unlike other companies at the time, he was able to do everything in-house under one roof. King Records had its own recording studio, art and printing departments, and pressing machines for manufacturing the records. Nathan also owned several publishing companies and was quick to make full use of the songs he controlled. Frequently, if a song was popular in country music, he would have one of his R & B artists cover it, thus selling the same song to a completely different audience. Syd was a very hands-on head of the company and frequently sat in on the recording sessions of various bands, much to the chagrin of those making the music. He is rumored to have joined the Stanleys in the studio for their King first recordings, but he appears to have left most, if not all, of the producing to Carter and Ralph.

King #1: September 30, 1958 (Session 580930)

The Stanley Brothers' first sessions for King, recorded in the label's Cincinnati studio, resulted in their legendary debut album for that label, King 615, which was called, simply enough, *The Stanley Brothers*. The twelve selections were recorded over a two-day period on September 30 and October 1, 1958. Bill Napier plays mandolin and Al "Towser Murphy" Elliott plays bass and sings baritone. Ralph Mayo makes a guest appearance on fiddle.

The very first number recorded at the September 30 session is "Love Me, Darling, Just Tonight," a duet by Carter and Ralph that they learned from their *Farm & Fun Time* friend Red Malone. On this song Carter shares the composer credits with Red, using the pen name Ruby Rakes (the name of his half sister on his mother's side of the family) to identify his contribution to the song. The name Ruby Rakes appears on nearly all of Carter and Ralph's compositions during their first few years at King. Ralph related that possible monetary damages from an auto accident threatened their income stream. "That was one of the reasons me and Carter copyrighted some of our songs in our half sister Ruby Rakes's name, to keep the royalties safe."[10]

Al Elliott wrote the next two selections. The first is "Heaven Seemed So Near." In an interview that was conducted by Stanley enthusiasts Doug Gordon and Roy Burke III,[11] Elliott related how the song came to be written:

> [It was] about two months before the session [and I was] sitting at a drive-in theater up in West Virginia. We were sitting there waiting for the show that night . . . well, I was just thinking about the girl back home, you know, and it just come to my mind. It all come together, the melody and the words, too. Carter liked it. That night after we did the show there, coming back in why I sang it [for him].[12]

The second Al Elliott composition, "Your Selfish Heart," was written "much earlier." In the same Gordon and Burke interview, he related,

> I wrote this song about my niece and her boyfriend . . . I mean, it's just a little story there that come in my mind and I just wrote it. Carter liked it and they recorded that. It gave me a real good feeling to know that they were gonna record two of my songs for a big recording company like that. In fact, the songs did real well, too.[13]

The melody is reminiscent of the Carter Family favorite "The Storms Are on the Ocean."

The final two tunes from the September 30 day of recording are songs that Carter Stanley wrote shortly before the session. He had introduced "How Mountain Girls Can Love" and "The Memory of Your Smile" as "new ones"[14] during their New River Ranch show three weeks earlier. In the same show, Carter included an extra verse in "The Memory of Your Smile" that was omitted at the recording session. It went as follows:

> Now there is a man over yonder
> With a far and distant look in his eye

> Maybe we have things in common
> But he too just then passed me by

King #2: October 1, 1958 (Session 581001)

On October 1, six more tunes were recorded to complete the King 615 album. The first four are instrumentals that feature Ralph. "Mastertone March" is a Ralph Stanley composition, while "Clinch Mountain Backstep" is Ralph's masterful interpretation of the breakdown tune "Lost John." Some have maintained that the tune is merely "Old Joe Clark" in a minor key.[15] Southwest Virginia multi-instrumentalist Scott Fore notes, "I can vaguely see a resemblance to the 'Old Joe Clark' chorus in the 'B' section of 'Backstep,' and a resemblance to 'Cluck Old Hen' in the 'A' section of the tune."[16] "Midnight Ramble" is Ralph's reworking of Bill Monroe's "Tennessee Blues," an instrumental he recorded for Bluebird Records in 1940 at his first session with the Blue Grass Boys. "Tennessee Blues" is also the very first mandolin instrumental that Monroe wrote and the first of his compositions that he recorded. His recording is a mandolin tour de force augmented by two brief bass solo passages. The Stanleys turned it into a banjo-driven bluegrass instrumental with full breaks by mandolin and fiddle as well.

The remaining instrumental is "Train 45"; Carter mentioned on personal appearances that he learned the tune from the old-time fiddler G. B. Grayson.[17] For the session, the Stanleys worked up a spoken exchange for "Train 45" that resembles the spoken exchange in Bill Monroe's Bluebird release of "Orange Blossom Special." Carter Stanley asks each of the band members where he is going and each replies by naming his hometown. The Stanley

Carter and Ralph had been at Starday barely long enough for one session when they hopped on board with Cincinnati's King Records. One side of their first single release for King was a smoking version of an old fiddle tune, "Train 45."

Besides "Train 45," two days of recording in Cincinnati netted twelve other songs that were released as the self-titled album *The Stanley Brothers and the Clinch Mountain Boys*. Often referred to by long-time fans simply as "King 615," the album rates as one of their best releases.

brothers are headed, of course, to Dickenson County, Virginia. Ralph Mayo, identified as Fiddlin' Mayo, is going to Kingsport, Tennessee. Al Elliott, pegged as "Towser Murphy," his stage name for his comedic alter ego, is bound for Big Stone Gap, Virginia. Bill Napier, using his old man Pap Napier voice, announces his destination as Grundy, Virginia. This bit of novelty banter gives the first hint on record of the comedy element that had long been a staple of Stanley Brothers live performances.

Two vocal selections, "Think of What You've Done" and "Keep a Memory," fall at the end of the session. Both were previewed at the New River Ranch show a few weeks earlier, and both are credited to Carter. The melody to "Think of What You've Done" is based on an older song, "Darling, Do You Know Who Loves You," that was written by West Virginian Billy Cox, the author of the World War II hit "Filipino Baby."

Suwannee River Jamboree: November (Session 581129)

Five weeks after recording for King, the Stanley Brothers left Bristol and their radio home, WCYB. They journeyed 550 miles to Live Oak, Florida, to be headliners on a weekly Saturday evening program called the *Suwannee River Jamboree*, which aired locally on radio station WNER. The show began airing in 1952 and, starting in 1955, sported as featured attractions another set of Virginians, Jim and Jesse McReynolds. The program folded in 1957, but local businessman Aubrey Fowler knew the potential for attracting tourists to the area with a country music program and worked to re-establish the show. Carter Stanley's working Florida vacation in September—evidently a meeting with Aubrey Fowler to discuss the band headlining a revitalized *Suwannee River Jamboree*—set the stage for the group's relocation. Bill Napier, Al Elliott, and fiddler Paul Mullins made the move south. Their debut on the *Jamboree* took place on November 8.

To promote the *Jamboree*, a half-hour segment of the program was syndicated to nearby radio stations. One of several tracks from a surviving circa 1958 transcription disc, "Gonna Paint the Town," was included in a 2005 CD designed to advance awareness of the diversity of items on deposit in the Florida state archives.

King #3 and #4: February 1959 (Sessions 590210 and 590211)

On February 10 and 11, 1959, the Stanleys returned to the King studios to record their first all-gospel album, *Hymns and Sacred Songs* (K-645). By the time of the sessions, Bill Napier had left the band to play with the Goins Brothers. Al Elliott switched from bass to take Napier's place on the mandolin. Paul Mullins's stay with the group was short-lived. When Carter Stanley returned to Bristol at Christmastime, he ran into Chubby Anthony and arranged for him to rejoin the band on fiddle. Playing bass for the session, although not a working band member at the time, was George Shuffler.

The music recorded for the gospel album is a mixture of original compositions by Carter and Ralph and some well-chosen standards. The first two selections, "Old Daniel Prayed" and "He Said If I Be Lifted Up," were "old standards," according to Ralph.[18] The first song dates from 1936, when G. T. Speer copyrighted it and published it in a James D. Vaughan

Carter and Ralph's next visit to the King studios took place in February of 1959. It produced their first all-gospel album, *Hymns and Sacred Songs*. The album's cover photo was taken in Cincinnati's Mount Storm Park, just down the hill from the Temple of Love monument.

publication called *Christian Choruses*. Speer was a fixture in the gospel music community, having taught at the Stamps-Baxter School of Music in Dallas and also at the Vaughan School of Music in Lawrenceburg, Tennessee. Raised near Fayetteville, Georgia, he formed the popular family gospel singing group The Speers in 1921. "He Said If I Be Lifted Up" dates to at least 1937. A 1937 Stamps-Baxter publication called *Virgil O. Stamps Favorite Radio Songs* credits the song to Charles H. Pace, with an arrangement by V. O. Stamps.

The next two songs were written and previously recorded by Bill Monroe. He recorded the first one, "This Wicked Path of Sin," for Columbia on September 17, 1946. Bill did the second one, "I'll Meet You in Church Sunday Morning," for Decca Records on April 8, 1950. The Stanleys' performances on both of these songs adhere to the structures of the original Monroe recordings, using quartet singing with mandolin accompaniment.

Ralph Stanley remembered "Are You Afraid to Die" as a Louvin Brothers song.[19] Carl Story and his Rambling Mountaineers Quartet were the first to record it, for Mercury on August 3, 1952. Carl related that Ira Louvin heard a Billy Graham broadcast from Charlotte, North Carolina, that dealt with the topic of death and being afraid to die. Soon after hearing the sermon, Ira wrote the song.[20] The Stanleys feature it as a trio with Chubby Anthony singing the high baritone part. "The White Dove," another song with a high baritone arrangement, is a re-recording of the Stanley classic that Carter and Ralph first recorded for Columbia, ten years earlier, on March 1, 1949.

A series of originals follows next. "How Can We Thank Him for What He Has Done" was written in Cincinnati the night before the recording session. Al Elliott related to Doug Gordon and Roy Burke III,

> [The] night we got into Cincinnati, Carter . . . well, he sat down and he said, "I want us to write this song. It's on my mind [and] me, you, and Ralph can sit here and write it." So, we got together and wrote that there that night and had it ready to record the next day. We switched instruments on that. Carter did the recitation and I played the guitar and then we got three-part harmony on it.[21]

Carter composed "Mother's Footsteps Guide Me On," "The Angel of Death," and "Wings of Angels," while Ralph wrote "That Home Far Away" and "My Lord's Gonna Set Me Free." The Stanleys waited some time after writing "The Angel of Death" to record it, as it was featured in a songbook that they issued in 1956,[22] almost three years prior to this session.

The final selection recorded at these sessions is a fiddle number, "Suwannee River Hoedown," that, for obvious reasons, was not included on the gospel album. Chubby Anthony related, "In 1958 I wrote or put together 'Suwannee River Hoedown' along with Carter. I was asked to cut it in Cinn[cinatti]. to see how it would sound. So it was released with Ruby Rakes's name on it."[23] Chubby was staying at the Suwannee Hotel in Live Oak when the tune was written, shortly after he joined the band.

Jim Walter Homes: March 1959

On March 7, 1959, the Stanley Brothers made their first appearance on television in Jacksonville, Florida. Their show, *The Suwannee River Jamboree*, was a program that ran for several years on WJXT-TV, Channel 4, and was sponsored by Jim Walter Homes, a shell home manufacturer located in Tampa. Aubrey Fowler, the same person who brought the Stanleys to Live Oak, aided in securing Jim Walter's sponsorship of the band. Eventually, the group was seen on television in other Florida towns such as Tallahassee, Ft. Myers, Orlando, and Tampa. A series of fifteen-minute radio shows were also created for syndication to stations near Jim Walter showrooms. In addition to appearing on the air, the Stanley Brothers performed at Sunday open houses for the company, attracting customers to view models of shell homes that Jim Walter offered for sale. The sponsorship package gave the band a level of financial stability that was perhaps the best of their career. Also, with all of their work taking place in north and central Florida, Carter and Ralph actually had time to devote to family life.

Starday #2: 1959 (Session 590300)

Not long after the sessions for *Hymns and Sacred Songs*, the Stanleys recorded several sessions to fulfill their obligation to Starday. They recorded eight songs in two different sessions, both of which were recorded at radio station WNER in Live Oak, the Stanley Brothers' then home base. Bill Savitz, who worked at the radio station, engineered the sessions. He recalled, "We'd meet Sunday night about six, cut a session and it'd take about four hours. It

As part of his agreement to release the Stanleys Brother from their Starday contract, which allowed them to move on to King Records, Don Pierce stipulated that they record twenty-four additional songs for him. The group worked at completing this task by making recordings for Starday at sessions in 1959 and 1960. One session was issued in its entirety on a four-song 45 rpm extended play (EP) disc, SEP-107. The disc was pressed on red wax. Shown here are two selections from the B side, "Carolina Mountain Home" and "Trust Each Other."

was laid back, relaxed. They knew what they were doing. It was simple, straight. There was no stereo or any mixing to do with it, it was straight two mikes right into the board and then into the recorder."[24] Bill Napier had returned to play mandolin on the sessions, and Al Elliott switched back to play bass. Chubby Anthony remained on fiddle.

The first tune recorded at the first session is "Choo Choo Comin'," which Carter learned from a musician by the name of Cuddles Newsome. Cuddles later related how he taught the song to Carter Stanley:

> I knew Carter from back in the '40s and he knew of me. I sang it one day up in Blue-field, West Virginia, on a television station there . . . it was downstairs and he said, "Hey! Wait little hoss, I want that song . . ." and I sung it to him right there at the bottom of the stairs. He told me, and Ralph has told me later, that it was one of their good ones. In 1953 I had a train wreck. I ran into a train, it beat me to the crossing. I told the other guy in the car, I said, "You drive son, I'm gonna ride a while." The choo choo beat me. That was one of those old coal dregs, you know, they put coal in the engines.[25]

The Wright Brothers, Len and Tommy, had released "Carolina Mountain Home" earlier on Starday. The song was cowritten by Estel Lee Scarborough and Len Wright. It's possible that Carter and Ralph learned the song through their association with Estel Scarborough, a music promoter who featured the Stanleys at a venue he was running in Felicity, Ohio, in 1954. "Trust Each Other" is a Stanley composition, while "Maple on the Hill" was the first of a number of songs composed by African American songwriter Gussie L. Davis. It was

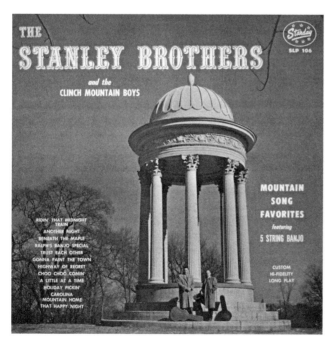

By the time the Stanley Brothers had completed three sessions for Starday, they had enough material for a twelve-song album, *Mountain Song Favorites*. The disc was pressed for Starday by King, which also provided the photo for the cover. The photo was taken on the same day that Carter and Ralph posed for the cover of their *Hymns and Sacred Songs* album. The duo is pictured here on the steps of the Temple of Love in Mount Storm Park in Cincinnati.

published in 1880 and was a successful recording for Wade Mainer in the 1930s; it's likely that Mainer's recording was the Stanleys' source for this selection. Bill Savitz had a hand in suggesting it for the session:

> I was the one that talked them into putting it on there. They were short one cut and they were arguing back and forth. It was one that Ralph did so well and I always loved to hear 'em do it. I asked them would they please do it. "No," they said, "that would never go anywhere." I said, "I think it will and since I'm doing this recording at no pay, I think you owe me that." So they said, "Ok, we will," and it became the hit song from the album.[26]

Starday #3: 1959 (Session 590700)

The songs from the second session include "Highway of Regret," a Chubby Anthony composition; "A Little at a Time," which Carter and Ralph learned in Bristol from local musician Red Malone; "Another Night," which was written by Hobo Jack Adkins; and "Riding That Midnight Train," a song that is now a Stanley classic. "Highway of Regret" has gained some notoriety in recent years, thanks to Bob Dylan. Several lines from the chorus ("Ain't talkin', just walkin' . . . heart burning, still yearning") show up in the choruses of a Dylan song—appropriately titled "Ain't Talkin'"—on his Grammy award–winning album *Modern Times*. The album debuted at number one on the *Billboard* 200 chart in August of 2006 and by the end of 2007 had sold in excess of six million copies.

Personnel for the session remained essentially the same, with the exception of Johnnie Bonds replacing Al Elliott on bass. After the previous session, about a week before the birth of their first child at the end of May, Elliott and his wife had left Florida and returned to Virginia.

Johnnie Bonds was a musician living in Live Oak, Florida, when the Stanley Brothers arrived there. He was born on March 17, 1915. He played bass off and on for several years with the Stanleys, appearing on at least one recording session with them as well as on their television and radio programs. In addition to his work with the Stanley Brothers, he also performed with a local group known as the Suwannee River Boys. Johnnie was the owner of the Amoco gas station in Live Oak. He died on July 9, 2003.

Blue Ridge: Summer 1959 (Session 590701)

Blue Ridge Records was a label started in North Carolina in the early 1950s by the father-daughter team of Noah and Drucilla Adams. Initial releases for the label included classic cuts by the Church Brothers, Jim Eanes, and Bill Clifton. In the late 1950s, the label was sold to Bill Clifton and Washington, DC, disc jockey Don Owens, who together continued to record and release material by Jim Eanes and others.

Exactly when the idea was conceived for the Stanley Brothers to record for Blue Ridge is not known. The first direct evidence comes from Walter V. Saunders, who is a contributor to *Bluegrass Unlimited*. On September 6, 1958, he attended a personal appearance of the

Although it was recorded in 1959, the Stanleys' lone single on the Blue Ridge label (#514) was not released until 1962.

Stanley Brothers at the Vienna, Virginia, Volunteer Fire Department Carnival. Years later, Walter remembered Don Owens announcing from the stage that the Stanley Brothers would be recording an album for Blue Ridge.

However, the album Don Owens referred to never materialized. In 1959, while working out of Live Oak, the Stanleys recorded two songs at radio station WNER. Featured on the session are Chubby Anthony on fiddle, Bill Napier on mandolin, and (most likely) Johnnie Bonds on bass. Before his death in 1980, Chubby Anthony recalled that four tunes were recorded for Blue Ridge.[27] However, the two additional masters have never surfaced, and the only ones known to exist are those that were used for a 45 rpm single.

Although the songs featured on the Blue Ridge single were recorded in 1959, they were not released until 1962 and remained in print for only a short time. They are among the scarcest recordings that the Stanley Brothers ever made. The two songs, "Meet Me Tonight" and "Nobody's Business," are older, traditional pieces that the band performed at personal appearances. Carter and Ralph were evidently saving their original material for their major label obligations. These songs were not, however, throw-away performances, but spirited renditions of two old-timers. "Meet Me Tonight" is most associated with the Carter Family, while "Nobody's Business" was popular in both white and black communities, starting in 1919 and continuing through the 1920s, when old-time artists such as Riley Puckett, Emry Arthur, and Earl Johnson's Dixie Entertainers were among those who recorded it.

Newport Folk Festival: July 1959 (Session 590712)

On July 12, 1959, the Stanley Brothers made one of their few out-of-state appearances that year when they performed at the first Newport Folk Festival. The event was the creation of Theodore Bikel; Oscar Brand; Pete Seeger; and George Wein, the organizer of the successful and influential Newport Jazz Festival, which got its start in 1954. The nationally publicized Folk Festival was held over a two-day period on July 11 and 12 and attended by 12,300 people, but it paled in comparison to the previous weekend's Jazz Festival turnout of 54,100. Appearing at the festival were headliners such as the Kingston Trio, Pete Seeger, Earl Scruggs with Hylo Brown and the Timberliners, Rev. Gary Davis, Jimmy Driftwood, Odetta, the New Lost City Ramblers, Sonny Terry and Brownie McGhee, and Oscar Brand. Making an unscheduled appearance was eighteen-year-old budding folk singer Joan Baez.

The Stanley Brothers were featured in the Sunday evening concert, the highlight of the two-day event. The group was introduced by folk icon Oscar Brand. Band members included Bill Napier, Chubby Anthony, and Lindy Clear. Vanguard Records recorded most, if not all, of the festival. Three albums were issued on the label shortly after the festival and featured a broad cross section of artists, though with a few glaring exceptions: the Kingston Trio, Jimmy Driftwood, and the Stanley Brothers. Presumably these omissions were due to the artists' contractual obligations with their parent recording companies. Portions of Carter and Ralph's performance eventually surfaced on a Vanguard CD in 1994. The disc contains only five songs and two comedy routines (by Lindy Clear); the remainder is fleshed out with tracks from the group's 1964 spot at Newport. The selections feature standard fare from the Stanley repertoire such as "Orange Blossom Special," "How Mountain Girls Can Love," "I'm a Man of Constant Sorrow," "Gathering Flowers for the Master's Bouquet," and the recently recorded "Choo Choo Comin'" (titled on the Vanguard CD as "Choo Choo Coming").

King #5: September 1959 (Session 590914)

The Stanleys recorded again for King in September of 1959, cutting two albums: *Everybody's Country Favorites* (K-690) and *For the Good People* (K-698). At these sessions, Syd Nathan encouraged the Stanleys to use the guitar as a lead instrument, something that until then had seldom been done in bluegrass. The Stanleys took a full band, including fiddle, with them to the sessions, but the only instruments heard on the recordings are banjo, guitar, and bass. Ralph acknowledged,

> Syd was most responsible for us starting to use lead guitar. He wanted something that the Delmore Brothers had. They'd been successful with the guitars. They thought we ought to get away from the mandolin because nearly all the bluegrass bands used a mandolin. And they wanted us to get the lead guitar in and get a different sound, which we did. Bill Napier was the first we played the guitar with. He was on the first session.[28]

Apparently Nathan also had a hand in selecting material for the sessions as most of the songs were remakes of titles that other artists had earlier made popular on King. If Carter or Ralph had any new original songs or tunes they wanted to showcase, these sessions weren't the place to do it.

To ensure that the Stanleys adhered to the new formula, Syd personally oversaw the recording of the first song, "Mountain Dew," on September 14, 1959. George Shuffler recalled, "Syd came in and engineered 'Mountain Dew.' That was the first number we did, and he said 'Just get that damn fiddle out of here, I don't want no fiddle on this,' . . . said, 'I want you to go.'"[29] Chubby Anthony, who went to the session to play fiddle, found himself beating out a rhythm on the fiddle. "Mountain Dew" was written by Bascomb Lamar Lunsford, a trial lawyer from Asheville, North Carolina, in the 1930s, who based the song on humorous incidents he witnessed in court. Lunsford was famous as a collector of old songs and for being a major force behind the folk festival that was held in Asheville for many years. "Mountain Dew" was a big song for Grandpa Jones, who recorded it for King in 1947.

"Sunny Side of the Mountain" dates back to 1944, when Harry C. McAuliff copyrighted it. Lester Flatt featured it as a solo when he worked as a Blue Grass Boy on the *Opry* in the mid-1940s. Many people remember it as Hawkshaw Hawkins's theme song in the late 1940s, and in 1947 he recorded it for King. It was later a popular song for bluegrass performer Jimmy Martin, who no doubt was inspired by it when he named his group the Sunny Mountain Boys.

King credited Grandpa Jones as the composer of "Tragic Romance," though there appears to be some controversy surrounding the true authorship of the song. It was most likely written by Wiley and Zeke Morris, the Morris Brothers, of North Carolina,[30] but Grandpa Jones did make a popular recording of it for King in 1947. Probably the most popular recording of this song is Cowboy Copas's, who made it at his very first session for King in July of 1945. He later recorded it again for King on February 28, 1955. "Tragic Romance" was, however, a number that the Stanley Brothers performed when they first organized their band in the late 1940s. After they began writing their own material, songs like "Tragic Romance" were discarded and replaced with their own songs. During an August 1962 appearance at the Ash Grove in Hollywood, California, Carter Stanley declined a request for "Tragic Romance," stating, "That's one we learned off a sheet of paper;"[31] apparently it was not retained in their list of stage songs.

Clyde Moody, the "hillbilly waltz king," and Chubby Wise wrote "Shenandoah Waltz." Recorded in 1947, this song was probably the biggest hit in Moody's career, selling over a million copies for King by the early 1950s. The Stanleys featured it often in their stage shows, introducing it as a song that was written about their home state of Virginia.

"Next Sunday, Darling, Is My Birthday" was a feature song in Carter and Ralph's 1947 Bristol radio shows. Mellow-voiced crooner Jim Eanes, from Martinsville, Virginia, wrote it, though his authorship has been overlooked because Knoxville songwriter Arthur Q. Smith pirated it. According to Eanes, he was working in Knoxville in the late 1940s with the Blue Mountain Boys when he made the acquaintance of Smith, who "borrowed" several of Jim's songs and took them to King Records. Consequently, Smith's name appeared on

Clyde Moody's late 1947 release of "Next Sunday, Darling, Is My Birthday" along with the maiden name of Syd Nathan's wife, Lois Mann. Syd frequently used his wife's name as a pseudonym for publishing purposes.

West Virginia songwriter Buddy Starcher, who wrote, among other songs, "I'll Still Write Your Name in the Sand," composed "Sweet Thing." Cowboy Copas had recorded the song for King in August of 1946. In October of 1993, Buddy Starcher recalled how "Sweet Thing" was popularized:

> The song "Sweet Thing" was originally called "Sweet Heart" when I first wrote it. The Franklin Brothers recorded it first, and while I was on radio in Fairmont, West Virginia, I got a call from a couple of boys who were on WWVA in Wheeling, West Virginia, wanting the words and music to "Sweet Heart." Well, to make a long story short, I took the song up to Wheeling and gave it to the boys, who said they wanted to record it and would be singing it over WWVA. I came back to Fairmont and started listening to the boys to see if they were actually going to use it. Here is what I heard them say: "We have just written a new song and want to see what you folks who are listening think of it. It's called 'Sweet Thing.'" Well, you can imagine what that done to me. So I called the manager of WWVA, whom I knew very well, and told him what had happened, that the Callahan Brothers had stolen my song and changed the title from "Sweet Heart" to "Sweet Thing" but had not changed the tune or the words, but claimed they had written the song. The manager of the station said very casually that he would look into it, not to worry. Well, to make a long story short the Callahans departed from Wheeling two weeks later and went to Nashville, where they recorded "Sweet Thing." The song was a hit and has been recorded by eight different groups that I know of on Columbia, Decca, and several other major labels.[32]

Esco Hankins recorded "Sweeter Than the Flowers" for King in 1949. His voice bore a strong resemblance to Roy Acuff's, and many of his recordings for King were covers of Acuff songs. Carter and Ralph crossed paths with him in the fall of 1950 when they worked on the *Kentucky Mountain Barn Dance* in Lexington. The song's inclusion on this session probably owes more to the urging of King Records than to any sentimental attachment the brothers might have had to it.

"It's Raining Here This Morning" is credited to Grandpa Jones, who recorded the song in 1944 at one of his first sessions for King. It was his second disc for the label and is reported to have sold in excess of 50,000 copies in the months after its release.[33]

King #6: September 1959 (Session 590915)

On September 15, the Stanleys completed the material for *Everybody's Country Favorites* and recorded the gospel album *For the Good People*. It was a marathon session. Carter Stanley remarked, "The most records I think we ever got done was seventeen sides in one day. That started probably about ten o'clock in the morning and lasted till about that time that night."[34] He partially explained their extraordinary output by saying, "We knew the material better." The first number to lead off this session is "Shackles and Chains," a song that belonged to Jimmie Davis, a former governor of Louisiana. Mac Wiseman had recorded an early bluegrass version for Dot in November of 1952.

"Weeping Willow" came from the Carter Family. Speaking to an urban New York audience on November 30, 1962, Carter Stanley made the following observations of the Carter Family and "Weeping Willow":

> Where folk music is played, I always like to mention the Carter Family. I've always had great admiration and respect for them people. While some of the original people are passed and gone, their songs will be with us, I think, as long as people like you and I get together and enjoy folk music. We did . . . tried to record one of their songs, well, we've recorded a number of 'em I guess. But here's one I have always enjoyed so much called "Bury Me Beneath the Willow."[35]

"Old Rattler" is a traditional number that was previously recorded in 1947 on King by Grandpa Jones. Carter makes an amusing reference to Grandpa in the Stanley Brothers' recording of the song. A line in the original version describes an "old yeller hen" that was "set on three buzzard eggs . . . [and] hatched out one old crow." Carter reconfigures the song to hatch out Grandpa Jones instead!

The last song recorded for the *Everybody's Country Favorites* album is a remake of the mountain ballad "I'm a Man of Constant Sorrow." The Stanleys had previously recorded it for Columbia Records on November 3, 1950, with Ralph singing the verses solo all the way through. Here, Ralph still sings the verses, but a vocal refrain by other members of the band is worked up and added. Ralph's voice, matured in the nine years since the song's first recording, makes for a more forceful rendition. Another contrast with the original is the substitution of Bill Napier's lead guitar work for the mandolin and fiddle. The changes make for a unique arrangement that would earn huge financial rewards for the Stanley families when the song, as sung by Dan Tyminski, was featured in the 2000 movie *O Brother, Where Art Thou?*

The format of the gospel material is the same as the secular album's in that the guitar is the dominant lead instrument. The first selection recorded for it was "My Main Trial Is Yet to Come," a song that was copyrighted in 1947 by promoter J. L. Frank and Pee Wee King. The Cope Brothers recorded it on King in late 1946 or early 1947. However, Jimmie Osborne, an entertainer best remembered for "The Death of Little Cathy Fiscus," recorded the most popular version of the song in 1953 for King. Recorded next was another song done previously by Esco Hankins, "Mother Left Me Her Bible."

Of the song "Jacob's Vision," Ralph Stanley stated, "We learned [that] from Enoch Rose, he was a Free Will Baptist preacher from Caney Ridge, Virginia."[36] "I'll Not Be a Stranger" was originally titled as "I Will Not Be a Stranger," and James B. Singleton copyrighted it in 1956. It first appeared in a Stamps Quartet Music Company songbook entitled *Christian Way* and was later reprinted in various songbooks.

Cowboy Copas had recordings on King of the next four songs: "From the Manger to the Cross," recorded on September 7, 1950; "Four Books in the Bible," recorded on February 18, 1951; "Purple Robe," recorded on September 25, 1952; and "When Jesus Beckons Me Home," recorded on February 4, 1954. "From the Manger to the Cross," "Four Books in the Bible," and "Purple Robe" were all written by Mac Odell in the early 1950s. Odell, who wrote a number of songs during the late 1940s and early 1950s, performed as a duet with his wife, and they recorded quite a few songs, most of them original, for King and Mercury in the early 1950s.

"Jordan" is thought by many to be an older traditional song, but Fred Rich, a gospel songwriter from northern Georgia, wrote it in 1954. He conceived the song's chorus at the co-op where he worked in Blairsville, Georgia. Carter Stanley said on a show once, "This is another song that we got from one of the revival meetings up in southwestern Virginia, up around Abingdon . . . Bristol and through that part of the country."[37]

"Pass Me Not" first appeared in 1912, when it was copyrighted by Fanny J. Crosby and W. H. Doane. Crosby was a prolific gospel songwriter during the late 1800s and early 1900s, and her name appears on hundreds of hymns. Perhaps her best known is "Blessed Assurance."

King listed "Lonely Tombs" as traditional. The song dates from the 1880s, when songwriter William M. Golden introduced it under the title "Oh Those Tombs"; he penned other favorites such as "Where the Soul Never Dies" and "A Beautiful Life." Old-time groups, such as the Blue Sky Boys, recorded the song in the 1930s, and country-oriented performers like Roy Hall and Roy Acuff recorded it in the early 1940s. J. E. Mainer recorded it for King in October of 1946. It was a featured part of the Stanley Brothers repertoire when they began doing radio work on WCYB in the mid-1940s.

The last gospel song recorded at the session was "Over in the Glory Land," which was copyrighted in 1915 by J. E. Reynolds and W. P. Snyder. Like "Lonely Tombs," this song also dates back to the early days of the Clinch Mountain Boys. Fiddler Les Woodie, who joined the band in 1949, recalled,

> The first show I did with 'em we played a ballpark and I came in that day and we went out and played the ballpark that night. I wasn't familiar with their songs and they did some quartets and I started singing bass with 'em. I remember the first song we tried to sing was "Over in the Glory Land," which was wide open, you know. I didn't know all the words and Carter said, "Well, just fake it." But, somehow or another we struggled through it.[38]

Following the completion of the two album projects, one additional song was recorded, one of the most popular and commercial pieces of the Stanleys' career: "How Far to Little Rock." Ralph Stanley noted that it was not their number one most popular song, but added that it had the most activity in the shortest amount of time. It debuted (and peaked) at number seventeen on the *Billboard* charts on March 21, 1960, and it remained on the charts for a total of twelve weeks. According to Carter,

Complete with a preprinted sleeve from King Records, "How Far to Little Rock" (#5306) was the Stanley Brothers' only release to appear on *Billboard*'s chart of top country singles. It debuted on the chart at number seventeen on March 21, 1960, and stayed on for a total of twelve weeks.

We hadn't planned to do it . . . we started doing "How Far to Little Rock" and somebody in the studio heard it and they said "Why not let's record that thing?" We didn't want to record it but they said, "Let's record it." No, we hadn't planned to ever record it. This fellow that taught us that tune was Fletcher Moss. He was a carpenter. He come to build one of our brothers a house and stayed with some family while he was doing that. He played the fiddle and he called it the "Arkansas Traveler." He'd play a verse of the "Arkansas Traveler" then he'd talk this "Hello stranger" deal and answer his own questions . . . ask the question and then answer it. So we learned it that way. [That was] before we ever played anywhere. That was one of the first that we ever learned.[39]

George Shuffler noted that "How Far to Little Rock" was "the last thing we cut and our fingers was so sore and so tired and they cut it. We cut it twice and took the first half of one and the last half of the other and patched it together, and if I can hear it, I can show you where the time varies. One cut was just a little bit faster than the other one."[40]

Starday #4: January 1960 (Session 600100)

In January of 1960, Carter and Ralph again recorded for Starday, doing a four-song session of gospel material. Prominent on this session is the lead guitar work of Bill Napier, a carryover from the King sessions of the previous September. Also appearing are Ralph Mayo on fiddle and Bill Slaughter, a local musician from Live Oak, Florida, on bass. Like the other recent Starday sessions, this one, too, was recorded at radio station WNER in Live Oak.

Featured are "A Few More Seasons," "Where We'll Never Die," "Mother No Longer Awaits Me at Home," and "In Heaven We'll Never Grow Old," which at the time was a rare vocal solo for Ralph. Although credited to William York, a pseudonym for Starday owner Don Pierce, "In Heaven We'll Never Grow Old" was written by N. D. Johnson and L. D. Huffstutler and first appeared under the title "We'll Never Grow Old in Heaven" in a 1941 songbook that was issued by Stamps-Baxter called *Pilgrim Songs*. By the time of the Stanleys' recording, the song had been in their repertoire for some time and had appeared in a songbook that the group issued in 1951.[41] The last song recorded at the session, "Mother No Longer Awaits Me At Home," is a remake of one side of the Stanley Brothers' first record, which was released in 1947.

William R. "Bill" Slaughter was a seventeen-year-old high school student when he recorded with the Stanley Brothers. A Live Oak resident, he had a disc jockey shift at WNER in the afternoon after school. His opportunity to record with the Stanley Brothers came when their regular bass player, Johnnie Bonds, took a brief leave of absence from the group. As a station employee, Bill also assisted with the recording of several other sessions by the Stanley Brothers at WNER. He later served three and a half years in the army, part of that time in Vietnam, and attained the rank of captain. Following his discharge, he worked toward receiving a law degree. He then spent the next five years working in partnership with his father, who was also a lawyer. In 1994 he was appointed a judge for Suwannee County, Florida. He later won election to the position and served for seventeen years, retiring in early 2011. Music has continued to be a part of his life, and as of 2011 he was playing bass in three different groups: Simple Gifts, the Twang Gang, and the Suwannee Trio.

Jim Walter Jamboree: March 1960 (Session 600300)

In addition to their considerable television exposure to Florida audiences, the Stanley Brothers also had coverage throughout the South from their affiliation with Jim Walter Homes, which sponsored their series of syndicated fifteen-minute radio programs. In all, eighteen of these programs are known to have been recorded, most (if not all) of them in Atlanta at a place called Samuel Candler Enterprises. Copies of the programs were mailed to radio stations on April 1, 1960, suggesting that they were recorded sometime in March. Carter, Ralph, and Bill Napier appear on all of the programs. Chubby Anthony is the fiddler on most, although Ralph Mayo is featured on several. Completing the personnel on most shows is George Shuffler on bass. Not a member of the band at the time, he took the bus from North Carolina to Atlanta to record the shows. The programs appeared on a number of stations, including:

WDKD in Kingstree, South Carolina
WGBA in Columbus, Georgia
WPAQ in Mount Airy, North Carolina
WHCC in Waynesville, North Carolina
WFVA in Fredericksburg, Virginia

WBSC in Bennettsville, South Carolina
WBCA in Bay Minette, Alabama
WLTC in Gastonia, North Carolina
WJDB in Thomasville, Alabama
WHAR in Baxley, Georgia.

Each of the programs starts with an opening Jim Walter jingle, followed by a friendly greeting from Carter Stanley. An up-tempo duet number usually follows, typically one of the band's recent record releases. Afterward, an advertisement for Jim Walter Homes is featured, with the pitch delivered by Carter. Another jingle, a sacred song, a quick fiddle or banjo number, and a closing theme make up the rest of each program.

The shows, for the most part, consist of versions of the Stanleys' popular recordings. However, a few performance tunes appear, such as "Uncle Pen," "Roll in My Sweet Baby's Arms," and "Heaven" (then a popular recording by Flatt & Scruggs), as well as fiddle tunes and instrumentals that the group had no intention of recording, including "Black Mountain Blues," "Mississippi Sawyer," and "Whoa Mule."

Antioch College: May 1960 (Session 600514)

On May 14, 1960, the Stanley Brothers ventured to Antioch College in Yellow Springs, Ohio, for their first college concert performance. They were the second bluegrass group to ever perform at a college, the first being the Osborne Brothers, who appeared two months earlier at the same venue. Mike Seeger and Jeremy Foster recorded the performance. Two sets were played, and a total of thirty-three songs, instrumentals, and comedy routines were taped, seventeen of which were issued on a ca. 1981 unauthorized album called *Live at Antioch College: 1960*. For the performance, the group featured Ralph Mayo on fiddle, Curley Lambert—who replaced the recently departed Bill Napier—on mandolin, and Lindy Clear on bass.

The unsigned notes on the album observe, "Realizing that bluegrass is now acceptable to an audience that doesn't necessarily like C & W, Carter and Ralph soft-pedal the honky-tonk aspect of their music, and dig back for a program of old time tunes and songs."[42] Some of the band's standard fare is offered, such as "How Mountain Girls Can Love," "Sunny Side of the Mountain," and "Orange Blossom Special," but traditional selections like "Cripple Creek," "Cumberland Gap," "John Henry," "Mountain Dew," "Bound to Ride," and "Little Birdie" make up a large percentage of the show. On the recording, the band seems to be in a good groove. Carter's emcee work is relaxed and engaging and the audience is very appreciative. Two songs from this show, "Bound to Ride" and "Shake My Mother's Hand for Me," later appeared on Rebel Records' *Legendary Stanley Brothers* series of albums.

New River Ranch: May 1960 (Session 600515)

Following the appearance at Antioch College, Carter and Ralph and their three sidemen drove nearly five hundred miles to appear at a Sunday afternoon show at New River

Ranch. It would have been a grueling all-night drive, even by today's standards. Making the trip today by interstate would take eight and a half hours; no telling how long it took the group to travel the same distance in 1960. Most likely, they arrived just in time for their first show of the afternoon.

In spite of the long car ride, Carter and Ralph and company sounded fresh and energetic as they sailed through three sets of material. Bill Offenbacher and Lamar Grier, a Maryland native living in the DC suburbs who landed a job playing banjo with Bill Monroe in 1966, recorded the shows. Material from the sets has been issued on releases from three separate labels. Rebel Records used four songs ("He'll Set Your Fields on Fire," "Mother's Not Dead," "Roll in My Sweet Baby's Arms" and "Knoxville Girl") on their *Legendary Stanley Brothers* albums. Copper Creek Records issued the entire first set as part of its *Stanley Series*. Lastly, Ralph Stanley issued on his StanleyTone label a CD combining material from the first two sets of the day that was available for sale only at his concert performances.

Not surprisingly, the Antioch and New River Ranch shows are fairly similar in terms of band sound and repertoire. Some interesting exceptions include Curley Lambert's performances of "Please Help Me, I'm Falling," which was then a popular song for country performer Hank Locklin, and "Baby Blue Eyes," a Jim Eanes song that was popularized by Flatt & Scruggs a decade earlier. The group had yet to record "Paul and Silas"; a studio version would appear on a 1962 album they recorded for King. At the time of the show, the group was in the planning stages of recording a session for Starday and they were perhaps audience testing songs such as "God Gave You to Me," "Don't Go Out Tonight," and "Let the Church Roll On."

Starday #5: June 1960 (Session 600600)

At the end of May or the very early part of June of 1960, the Stanley Brothers made their last formal recordings for Starday. The sessions, held at Magnum Studios in Jacksonville, Florida, resulted in twelve songs. Even with the absence of Bill Napier, who left to form a partnership with singer/guitarist Charlie Moore, the sound of the lead guitar continued to be featured in the Stanley band. On this session, Curley Lambert and Ralph Mayo shared the lead guitar chores.

Also on hand playing bass was Audie Webster, a member of the Webster Brothers duo from the Knoxville, Tennessee, area. The Webster Brothers had recently relocated to Alabama and were about to, or had already, recruited Ralph Mayo as part of their act. It is most likely that Audie's appearance as a guest on the session was due to his association with Mayo.

The owners of Magnum Studios were Tom Markham and Tom Rose. In 1981 Tom Rose offered vivid recollections of the recording sessions.

> We met the Stanley Brothers at a show in Live Oak, Florida, and talked to 'em and gave 'em our business card and told 'em we had a studio. It wasn't too long after that that they contacted us wanting to do some tapes for an album for Starday. We had just a small studio and I think our standard charge for recording was something like ten dollars an

hour and the union scale in those days for a recording studio was fifty dollars an hour. So, we were paid fifty dollars an hour by Starday! They came out to the studio three nights and they did probably fifteen or twenty songs. We listened to the tape with Carter and Ralph and picked the twelve cuts that they wanted to send to Starday. The rest of the cuts I had for three or four years but they got lost. My partner, Tom Markham, at that time was not really into bluegrass and he didn't know who the Stanley Brothers were. But they came in and set up and about half way through the first song he turned to me and he says, "My God, Tom, I've been in this recording business for six or eight years and for the first time I'm recording professionals." All the sessions were night sessions and they came over three nights in a row in the middle of the week. The studio was a twenty by twenty wooden garage with a concrete slab floor. The recordings were made on an Ampex 500 tape machine and three Electrovoice microphones. They had a mike on the bass and I guess a mike on Ralph and a mike on Carter. They just kind of worked the mikes the way they wanted the sound. They did more of engineering the session than my engineering partner did.[43]

The material recorded in Jacksonville is predominantly gospel, but the first four selections are secular. "If I Lose" was first recorded in the 1920s by Charlie Poole, and a 1930s version was waxed by Wade Mainer. "Little Maggie" is a re-recording of one of Ralph's first solo efforts of the late 1940s. Carter wrote "God Gave You to Me" not long before the session. On the recent show at Antioch College, Carter had introduced "Don't Go Out Tonight," saying,

One of the Stanley Brothers' most enduring songs was recorded for Starday in late May or early June of 1960. "Rank Stranger" was composed by famed gospel songwriter Albert E. Brumley, but came to the Stanleys' attention through the Willow Branch Quartet, a gospel group that appeared on the radio in the Bristol area in the 1950s. The Library of Congress added the Stanley Brothers' recording of this song to its National Recording Registry in 2009.

A number of songs from the May/June Starday session made their way to a 1962 album called *The Mountain Music Sound of the Stanley Brothers.* There weren't enough tracks to make a full album of Stanley Brothers material, however, and selections by Red Allen, Hylo Brown, Vern & Ray, and others rounded out the collection.

Here's an old folk song. I think this was one of the first songs ever recorded, and it was recorded by a blind fiddler from down in Shouns, Tennessee, and a fellow from Galax, Virginia . . . they went by the name of Shannon & Grayson[44] [actually Grayson & Whitter] back in those days and they recorded this tune about thirty-five years ago and it's called "Don't Go Out Tonight, Little Darling."[45]

The remaining eight songs from this session were recorded with the intention of combining them with the four gospel songs from the band's previous Starday session to produce an album called *Sacred Songs from the Hills* (SLP-122). Of the sacred songs, one of two that appear to have been written by the Stanleys is "The Darkest Hour Is Just Before Dawn." It was also featured in a songbook that the Stanleys issued shortly before the session, indicating that it was perhaps a new song.[46] "Rank Stranger," the Albert E. Brumley classic, was the Stanleys' biggest selling recording for Starday and has since become one of *the* songs most associated with them. In 2009 the Library of Congress added the Stanley Brothers' recording of "Rank Stranger" to its National Recording Registry, a list of culturally significant audio recordings. Carter and Ralph learned the song from the Willow Branch Quartet, a gospel group that appeared on radio in the Bristol area in the 1950s. The Carter Family recorded "Let the Church Roll On" in May of 1931, almost twenty-nine years before the Stanleys' recording was made. Among the more widely known hymns recorded at this session are "Rock of Ages," "I Saw the Light," which was written by Hank Williams, and "What a

Friend We Have in Jesus." An Irishman by the name of Joseph Scriven wrote this last hymn. Just before his wedding day, his bride-to-be accidentally drowned. Instead of giving up hope, he took refuge in his faith and spent the rest of his life at simple labor among poor people. The hymn expresses the comfort and consolation he received from his religion. "Gathering Flowers for the Master's Bouquet" is a re-recording of a song that the Stanleys had earlier recorded at their first Columbia session on March 1, 1949. The final selection recorded at the session is "I'm Ready to Go." George Shuffler recalled that he and Carter Stanley wrote this song while standing over a piano bench in the studio of King Records.

Starday #6: 1960 (Session 600601)

In October of 1960, Starday Records released a various artists album, *Y'All Come, Have a Country Christmas* (SLP-123). The Stanley Brothers song "Christmas Is Near" was included on the album among songs by Arlie Duff, Leon Payne, Jim Eanes, and several others. The Stanley track first appeared on a Starday single in the latter part of 1958. The original master apparently disappeared at some point, and when Starday started to assemble the *Country Christmas* album, a replacement master was needed. Exactly when it was recorded, or where, and who participated on the session to cut it are unknown. If Starday started to assemble the album in the summer of 1960, it would seem likely that the new master was recorded at this time, probably at radio station WNER in Live Oak. The fiddler sounds like Ralph Mayo, who recorded with the Stanleys in May or June of 1960. The mandolin could be by Curley Lambert.

King #7: July 1960 (Session 600711a)

The Stanleys were back in the studio for King Records again on July 11, 1960, in Cincinnati. Only eight titles were recorded that day, which produced the bulk of their fifth King album, *The Stanleys in Person* (K-719). To fill the album with twelve songs, four cuts from previous King sessions were used: "Suwannee River Hoedown," "It's Raining Here This Morning," "How Mountain Girls Can Love," and "Sweet Thing." Personnel for the session included George Shuffler and Curley Lambert. Making his first appearance on record with the Stanleys was fiddler Vernon Derrick.

Vernon Derrick was born on November 7, 1933, and grew up in Arab, Alabama. He began playing guitar at the age of five. His career in music got started soon after he graduated from high school in 1952 when he began playing in a local band, the Powell Brothers. The following year, he played briefly with Mac Wiseman, and another year later he performed with the Dixieland Drifters, a group headed up by Norman Blake. In the summer of 1960, while visiting with a cousin in Florida, he auditioned for a guest spot on a program at an Orlando television station. Waiting offstage, Bill Napier and Ralph Mayo overheard Vernon's performance of "Orange Blossom Special" and waved over nearby Ralph Stanley to listen. Vernon received a call shortly thereafter inviting him to join the Stanley Brothers. He worked with them off and on through the early part of 1963, helping record three

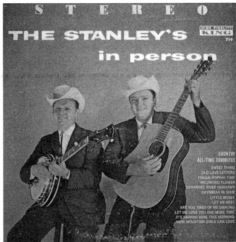

The Stanley's in Person was first issued as a monaural album, even though it was recorded in stereo. As stereo became more accepted in the marketplace, King decided to issue *In Person* in stereo. Initially, record jackets that were on hand in the warehouse received a "stereo" sticker (above left). When the jackets were depleted, the word *stereo* was incorporated into the actual artwork of the album jacket (above right).

albums for King. He then joined up with Jimmy Martin and recorded at least five albums with him. Vernon's most visible job was with Hank Williams Jr. in the 1980s. He later did a four-year stint with Hank Williams III. He died on January 4, 2008.[47]

The first track recorded, "Let Me Love You One More Time," bears Ralph Stanley's name as the composer. It was a popular song in the Stanley Brothers' personal appearances in the early 1960s. "Little Benny" is an older traditional song that Carter introduced several times on personal appearances as a "story song that I've always liked."[48]

King credited Ralph Stanley and Dean Bence with writing "Old Love Letters." Bence was a mandolin player, presumably from Georgia. In the late 1940s, he appeared on Atlanta's WSB as a part of "Cotton" Carrier and His Plantation Gang. Along with his guitar-playing wife, Marie, he was a member of a Georgia gospel quartet headed by Robert Hefner. By the 1960s, the pair was located in Jacksonville, Florida, where it is likely they encountered the Stanley Brothers when the band was in town for their Saturday evening program for Jim Walter Homes on WJXT-TV. Dean and Marie contributed a song, "Lord, I'm Ready to Go," to the repertoire of the gospel-singing Masters Family, then likewise located in Jacksonville. The duo also made appearances at the Jamboree Barn in Live Oak in 1963 and later recorded an album of gospel material for the Rem label.

Though the Stanleys and Bence frequently crossed paths, it appears that King's crediting of "Old Love Letters" to Ralph and Dean was an error. In actuality, popular country performer Johnny Bond wrote and, in 1955, copyrighted it. It was first an early recording for up-and-coming country music performer Jim Reeves, who made it the first recording of his first album for RCA, *Singing Down the Lane*, which was released in February of 1956.

King Records experimented with the format of the single with the release of two songs from the *In Person* album. Pictured here is "Little Benny" on a 33 1/3 rpm (as opposed to a 45 rpm) single with a small hole. Evidently, this didn't catch on with the buying public.

Reeves continued to feature the song throughout his career. Covering a song popularized by a crooning country star seems a bit out of character for such a tradition-oriented band as the Stanley Brothers. However, the group did occasionally make use of Reeves's material in radio and concert performances. One such example is the chart-topping "Four Walls," though the Stanleys adopted it only after it had been recorded by Bill Monroe.[49] Melodically, the Stanley rendering of "Old Love Letters" is very similar to the Reeves version. Lyrically, many of the same verses appear in both recordings, but in a few instances lines of verse are completely rewritten. The overall feeling is that the Stanleys recalled the song from memory, and where original lines couldn't be remembered, new ones were substituted. Or perhaps the Stanleys followed Bence's arrangement of the song. *Grand Ole Opry* personality Porter Wagoner released a popular version of "Your Old Love Letters" in January of 1961.

"Daybreak in Dixie" is an instrumental that was written in the late 1950s as a mandolin showpiece by Bill Napier. The Stanleys recorded it with Napier for Mercury in November of 1957. On the King recording, Ralph alters the tune by adding an extra chord and converting the piece to a banjo showcase. He apparently even thought of changing its name, as the original King ledgers list the title as "Daddy-O." George Shuffler related,

> We overdubbed guitar rhythm on "Daybreak in Dixie." Me and Curley [Lambert] both. He's a dragging time and I kicked knots on his shins. We set facing each other, we had earphones on, we was dubbing back, and he was wanting to drag a little bit and I kept bumping his shins with my foot.[50]

"Daybreak in Dixie" was issued in two different versions. The mono version of the *In Person* album contains the original, unaltered take. The later stereo version of the album makes use of the same track, but with an added guitar rhythm. George Shuffler noted that King studio musician Gene Redd "played drums on that 'Daybreak in Dixie.' I think the drums was a little obvious, a little dominant, and that might have been one of the reasons that we cut the choke- and slap-type guitars, you know, to kindly help cover up a little bit of the drums."[51]

"Wildwood Flower," which features George Shuffler on lead guitar, is, of course, the old Carter Family favorite. Often credited to A. P. Carter, the song actually dates to 1860 and was written by Maud Irving and J. D. Webster; the original title was "I'll Twine Mid the Ringlets."

"Let Me Rest" is an original that is credited to both Carter and Ralph. A line from a tribute that Ralph assembled for Carter after his passing notes of this tune, "This is your song, that was your request."[52]

"Are You Tired of Me, Darling" comes, again, from the Carter Family. Like "Wildwood Flower," it, too, has an earlier history that predates the Family's recording: G. P. Cook and Ralph Roland introduced the song in 1877.

The final selection is "Finger Poppin' Time," a tune that was written and recorded earlier by King rhythm and blues artist Hank Ballard. An item in *Billboard* magazine noted,

> The Stanley Brothers were at the King studios here Wednesday (13) to cut a session. One side was their own country version of "Finger Poppin' Time," which is slated for immediate release. "Finger Poppin' Time," as done by Hank Ballard and the Midnighters, is King's top seller at the moment and is moving up rapidly on the national charts.[53]

Syd Nathan of King requested that Carter and Ralph record the song, perhaps in an attempt to broaden their appeal, but definitely to add exposure to a song from his publishing catalog, Lois Music. To add to the R & B feel of the song, George Shuffler noted,

> We had every colored person in Cincinnati a-poppin' his fingers. They's about ten. [They had] little Gene Redd and they even called Roy, our good buddy [that was] a shipping clerk up there, he was colored. They's about eight or ten in there poppin' our fingers on that. We was a-pickin' and they was poppin' their fingers. We done it up right![54]

When asked if the Stanleys objected to the song, George replied, "Naw, they didn't care. Old man Syd thought it'd sell records and that's what we was up there for."[55] The inclusion of the finger pops, and drums, was made with overdubs after the session. After the song was released, the Stanley Brothers performed it in several of their shows. During an August 28 concert at Lake Whippoorwill near Warrenton, Virginia, Carter Stanley commented,

> We'd like to do a little tune for some of the folks that requested it, we need a few "poppers" on this tune here. So, if you all want to pop, just pop, it'll be all right. A little tune here that somebody talked us into recording one time called "Finger Poppin' Time."[56]

An outtake from the *In Person* photo shoot was later used as the cover of a live album that was initially issued by Ralph Stanley after Carter's passing. *Together for the Last Time* was later purchased by Rebel and has remained a part of that label's catalog ever since.

Starday #7: July 1960 (Session 600711b)

Following the completion of the session for the *In Person* project, the Stanleys visited with Wayne Raney, a popular evening disc jockey on WCKY in Cincinnati who gave the Stanley Brothers broad exposure on his show. His program was broadcast on a clear channel frequency, similar to WSM in Nashville, which gave the signal for his show wide coverage. While the group was busy recording the *In Person* project, Curley Lambert noted, "Wayne came out to the studio and insisted that we come out to his house that night after we got through recording. And we decided to cut a session. Why, I'll never know. But we did."[57] Two songs were recorded, most likely during the late evening of July 11 or the early morning hours of July 12, 1960. One was a remake of "Rank Stranger" that remained unissued until it appeared on a 1992 boxed-set compilation. The other was "Come All Ye Tenderhearted," a song that can be found in some older Southern hymnals.

Despite the age of the song, the Stanley Brothers appear to be the first group to have commercially recorded "Tenderhearted." The song relates the events of a house fire that took place in Carter County, Kentucky. Conflicting sources give the date of the fire as either 1867 or the early 1870s. The fire claimed the lives of two young children, Annie and Suvenia, belonging to Floyd Alson McCormack and Francis Jane Ratliff McCormack.[58] The song's words, and perhaps the melody as well, were reportedly written by M. J. Williams. The tune, which is somewhat akin to that used by the Stanley Brothers, is reported to have been added by Louise McGlone McMeans Rider. Kentucky fiddler and balladeer

James W. Day, aka Jilson Setters, used the song as part of his repertoire until his passing in 1942. The words to the song appeared in several hymnals, including 1936 and 1957 editions of *The New Baptist Song Book*. Exactly how the song made its jump to the Stanley Brothers is unknown, but it was a part of their early performance repertoire and made appearances in songbooks that the group issued in 1947 and 1949.[59]

The earliest known recorded version of this song by Carter and Ralph appeared on their *An Evening Long Ago* project that was recorded by Larry Ehrlich in March of 1956 (see session 560324). Carter Stanley was later reminded of the song when he saw it in a hymnbook that belonged to ballad singer Roscoe Holcomb when the Stanleys performed at the University of Chicago Folk Festival on February 4, 1961 (an event discussed in more detail later in this chapter).[60] After that, Carter began featuring a lovely version of the song as a solo on their personal appearances. On the session at Wayne Raney's house, Carter performs it as a recitation. Curley Lambert later described the recording of "Come All Ye Tenderhearted:"

> We took about two hours to cut that thing. We laughed ourselves to death, you see. Carter was trying to do the recitation on it. Me and Shuffler and Ralph and maybe Vernon Derrick or Chick or somebody, I forget who all was there. We got so tickled we couldn't do a thing for laughing. So finally we got it cut. Wayne, he was sitting back in the studio, you know, working the knobs, big tears running down his cheeks. I never thought it would be released. So some years later I was listening to the radio and heard it. I said, "Now this just can't be what we done in Cincinnati . . ." It was! They put it on one of those package deals, Starday. Oh lord, it was the worst thing I've ever seen in my life. Everybody was just dying laughing trying to get it cut. It was really a mess. That's the story on that now.[61]

King #8: January 1961 (Session 610115)

In January of 1961, Carter and Ralph returned to the King studios to record a two-day session that netted material for one and a half albums, all of *The Stanley Brothers Play and Sing the Songs They Like Best* (K-772) and part of *Folk Song Festival* (K-791). On hand for the session were Curley Lambert on mandolin, Art Stamper on fiddle, and George Shuffler on bass. Stamper was not working with the band at the time of the sessions, but appeared as a guest at Carter Stanley's request.

The first session occurred on January 15. Leading off is "The Window up Above," which was then a new release for George Jones. Jones's version appeared on the country charts in the early part of November of 1960 and stayed on the charts for a total of thirty-four weeks. It peaked at number two. Ralph recalled, "Carter and me played with George Jones and he had just written or wrote part of 'The Window up Above' one night in Orlando, Florida. I remember that he sung it backstage and I sung it with him. We told him we'd like to record it and he gave us the words that night."[62] At the time the Stanleys recorded it, Jones's recording was still on the country charts. Curley Lambert plays lead guitar on this one cut then reverts back to his more familiar mandolin for the balance of the session.

Two traditional selections are featured next. "Lover's Quarrel" is a duet by Carter and

In January of 1961, Carter and Ralph put in two long days in the studios at King. Helping out were Curley Lambert, bass player George Shuffler, and guest fiddler Art Stamper. Enough material was recorded for one and a half albums, and photos for two albums were taken at this time. *The Stanley Brothers Play and Sing the Songs They Like Best* (King-772) appeared first; *Folk Song Festival* (King-791) appeared later and was fleshed out with songs recorded later that summer.

Ralph that was popular in the 1930s. The Monroe Brothers had recorded a version of it called "Let Us Be Lovers Again," and the Carter Family had recorded it as well. The next song, "The Story of the Lawson Family," dates back to 1929. On the March 1956 recording by Larry Ehrlich, Carter Stanley observes,

> Friends, this is a true story that happened in the hills of western North Carolina in the year 1928 [actually 1929]. This tragedy occurred near the little town of Danbury in Stokes County in the state of North Carolina. It's absolutely true. This man murdered his family, his wife, and himself. His name was Charlie Lawson and this song is entitled "The Story of the Lawson Family."[63]

Walter "Kid" Smith wrote the song soon after the tragedy occurred; he recorded it with his old-time band the Carolina Buddies.

"Hey! Hey! Hey!" is a re-recording of a song that the Stanleys had recorded for Columbia in the early 1950s. "The Wild Side of Life" was a hit for country singer Hank Thompson in the early 1950s. Kitty Wells's answer to it, "It Wasn't God Who Made Honky Tonk Angels," catapulted her to national stardom.

Another bit of traditional material was "Jenny Lynn," a fast tune that featured Art Stamper on fiddle. The original King ledgers list the title as "Jenny Lind," but it was released as "Jenny Lynn." The tune was written in honor of a Swedish popular singer, Jenny Lind. Born in 1820, she was brought to the United States in 1850 for a tour that was sponsored by the famous circus promoter P. T. Barnum.

"What About You" was one of the first hits for the country duo of Johnnie & Jack. Carter Stanley used to sing it when he worked for Bill Monroe in the summer of 1951.

The last three songs in this session are devoted to Ralph. Two are vocal solos of old mountain ballads and one is an instrumental. The first ballad, "Little Willie," was collected, under various titles, by folklorists starting in the early 1900s. One of the earliest publications to feature it, as "Sweet Willie," was *Lover's Melodies*, which was published in 1910 or '11 by Balis Ritchie, the father of folk singer Jean Ritchie. It was collected as "Come All You Young and Handsome Girls" by Mrs. Olive Dame Campbell in Perry County, Kentucky, in 1908. It was subsequently included in folklorist Cecil Sharp's 1917 book *English Folk Songs from the Southern Appalachians*. A 1937 publication, *A Song Catcher in the Southern Mountains*, contained a version of the song that was collected from Ethel Owens of Dog Pen Branch, Council, Virginia, a locality situated thirty-five miles from the Stanley home place. Ms. Owens stated that the lyrics were "from a text in her mother's collection."[64] A more recent, and probable, source of the song for the Stanley Brothers is Bob Baker's recording of it on an album assembled in 1959 by Mike Seeger called *Mountain Music Bluegrass Style*. His recording is the first known published version of the song, in printed or recorded form, to be called "Little Willie." A native of Pike County, Kentucky, Baker, who migrated to Baltimore in 1955, learned "Little Willie" from his mother.[65] Musicologist Dick Spottswood explains,

> I don't know of any recorded versions before Bobby Baker's on *Mountain Music Bluegrass Style*. It created some excitement because it was clearly an ancient ballad that no one had heard before, and it worked as bluegrass. I don't know if Mike Seeger or Baker was the conveyor—maybe they both were—but Ralph began singing it soon afterwards—it was his kind of song and the folkies loved it.[66]

"Big Tilda" is an instrumental that Ralph wrote and the Stanley Brothers recorded for Mercury Records in December of 1955; they recorded it again at this session for King. Coincidentally, both Curley Lambert and Art Stamper appear on the original Mercury recording as well as the King version. The King recording remained unissued until the mid-1980s when Gusto Records prepared a special reissue for County Records that contained the unreleased version. The final tune recorded at the January 15 session is "Wild Bill Jones," a song of American origin that was first collected in 1916 by Cecil Sharp. It appeared in later collections, such as Alan Lomax's *Folk Songs of North America*[67] and Malcolm Laws's *Native American Balladry* (E10). The song was collected in Dickenson County as early as 1932.[68] There are old-time recordings of it from the 1920s and '30s by Wade Mainer as well as Virginians Dock Boggs, Kelly Harrell, and Ernest V. Stoneman.

King #9: January 1961 (Session 610116)

The next session to complete the *Sing the Songs They Like Best* project was held the following day, January 16. It has the distinction of being the only Stanley Brothers session to feature electric bass. According to George Shuffler,

This colored boy up at King was a staff musician and he was one of the finest old boys that you ever met. He recorded with Chubby Checker, Otis Redding, and all these guys. He bought him a new Fender bass, one of these big jazz masters, the first that they come out with. So we went in to record and he hooked it up and said "I want you to try this." And I hooked it up and it was easier to play. So, I just sort of made it easy on myself.[69]

The first three songs from the session are Carter Stanley originals. A trio called "You're Still to Blame" lay dormant until 1986 when it, too—like "Big Tilda"—was released on a custom reissue, this time for Old Homestead Records.[70] A note by Syd Nathan on a King Records' session report states that the tune and theme to "You're Still to Blame" had been "used a thousand times." This more than likely accounts for the song being held from release at the time. During an August 1960 concert, Carter introduced the song as "a brand new tune we just wrote, like to try it for you now, it's a trio number called 'I'll Take The Blame.'"[71] "I'll Just Go Away" was not issued until after Carter's passing; King released it as a 45 rpm single only.

Recorded next is a banjo instrumental that was never issued by King and was discovered when the author was working on assembling a four-CD boxed set of Stanley Brothers material for King Records in 1992.[72] "Steel Guitar Rag" was cut in three different takes, but apparently never gelled sufficiently to warrant release. As such, it was not even logged in at the time of the session, and all involved forgot its existence. "I'd Worship You" is a duet by Carter and Ralph that was written by Ralph.

The remaining four songs from this session appear on the *Folk Song Festival* album. "Just Dreamin'" is a Carter Stanley original that is featured as a trio with Curley Lambert. Especially noteworthy is Art Stamper's fiddle work on the tune. Art related, "That's what Carter referred to as the Georgia bull work and of course it's better referred to as, I guess, a Cajun bully."[73] Old-time fiddler James Leva noted, "Art's right on the money calling what he's doing here Cajun bully. There's a Georgia shuffle that is 4/4 but generally really only accents the first beat (ONE two three four, ONE two three four). As you can hear here, it's pretty much the same 4/4 shuffle that's so basic to Cajun fiddling, but it accents ONE and a TWO and a THREE and a FOUR . . . accenting every other beat . . . and you fit the notes into that structure."[74]

Of the remaining songs, "The Drunken Driver" dates back to the 1940s, when Molly O'Day recorded it for Columbia. "Little Joe" and "Handsome Molly" are both solos by Carter. The Monroe Brothers and the Carter Family, among others, recorded "Little Joe" in the 1930s, while G. B. Grayson and Henry Whitter introduced "Handsome Molly."

University of Chicago Folk Festival: February 1961

The first week of February was a busy one for the Stanley Brothers. On February 2, they stopped in Goodlettsville, Tennessee, to sign a booking agreement with Hal Smith of Curtis Artist Productions. It was one of the few times in their career that a professional booking agent represented Carter and Ralph. The next three days brought them to Chicago for the first University of Chicago Folk Festival.

As they edged farther into the 1960s, the Stanley Brothers were finding more and more of their work at college campuses and folk festivals. They were suggested for the Chicago event in part by Larry Ehrlich, the same person who recorded Carter and Ralph at an informal session at WCYB in March of 1956. Also appearing on the bill were the New Lost City Ramblers and Kentucky ballad singer Roscoe Holcomb. Mike Seeger recorded the events with an Ampex 600 reel-to-reel tape recorder.

Three selections ("Come All Ye Tender-Hearted," "Little Birdie," and "Rabbit in the Log") from Seeger's recordings were issued on a 1964 album on Folkways called *Friends of Old Time Music* (FOTM). The album features various artists who appeared in Friends of Old Time Music concerts in New York City in the early 1960s. The album's four-page booklet contains a reprint of a poster advertising a Stanley Brothers concert for the FOTM on June 9, 1961. Most of the tracks on the LP are concert recordings from actual FOTM events. With several songs on the album, including songs by the Stanley Brothers, recordings of FOTM concert material were not available and selections from other sources were presented as representative samplings of an artist's music. Consequently, selections from the Stanley Brothers' University of Chicago shows are featured. In 2001, all three days of Carter and Ralph's concerts in Chicago were issued on Ralph Stanley's StanleyTone label as a two-CD set called *Folk Festival*. Making up the Clinch Mountain Boys on these recordings are Curley Lambert on mandolin, Vernon Derrick on fiddle, and Chick Stripling on bass.

James Wilson "Chick" Stripling was born on March 4, 1916, in Tifton, Georgia. He spent his early youth in Tifton as well as at a family farm in nearby Lenox. He had a number of relatives who were musical, and by his early teens, Chick was playing the fiddle, competing in contests, and performing locally in bands with family members. Eventually, Chick incorporated three distinct elements into his entertainment package: dancing (often performing what he called a butter paddle buck and wing dance), comedy, and fiddling. He spent a good bit of the 1940s working at WSB in Atlanta. He also logged time on the road with Bill Monroe. By the mid-1950s, Chick had signed on to play with Jim & Jesse when they were headquartered out of Live Oak, Florida, and on the *Suwannee River Jamboree*. For a time, he served as the house comedian at country music parks such as New River Ranch and Sunset Park. In late 1960 or early 1961, Chick began an association with the Stanley Brothers that lasted, off and on, for the next five years. He recorded on numerous occasions with them for King Records, traveled on personal appearances, and accompanied the group on their 1966 tour of Europe. The last years of his life were spent in the northern Virginia area. He died in Alexandria, Virginia, on November 19, 1970.[75]

University of Chicago Folk Festival: February 1961 (Session 610203)

The Stanley Brothers performed one set per day over the three-day festival. Seeger's recording shows the first day, February 3, starting off with a fiddle tune by Vernon Derrick, "Old Joe Clark." The group quickly follows up with another fiddle tune, the popular "Orange

Blossom Special." Curley Lambert shines on his solo vocal number, "I Know What It Means to be Lonesome," a tune that originated with the Carter Family by way of their friend and fellow song collector Lesley Riddle. The song became associated with Clyde Moody in the 1940s and '50s. Ralph Stanley is featured on the banjo with a quick rendition of "Cripple Creek." A series of duets showcasing Carter and Ralph follow: "Gonna Paint the Town," "The Window up Above," and "Sunny Side of the Mountain." The Stanleys had recorded "The Window up Above" only three weeks earlier, but King Records had the song mastered and pressed on a 45 rpm single and available for sale by the time of the concert.

Chick Stripling devotes a fair amount of time to part of his comedy routine and performance of a butter paddle buck and wing dance to the tune of "The Chicken Reel." Mike Seeger notes that Chick was "a good fiddle player and a tolerable bass player and a great dancer. He was right on the money. He was an old-time vaudeville song and dance man really, but he was down to earth. He was a real asset when he was right."[76] Closing out the set are two of the Stanleys' popular songs at the time, "Rank Stranger" and "How Far to Little Rock." Vernon Derrick concludes things with a quick bit of "Old Joe Clark."

Larry Ehrlich recalled that the best music of the weekend occurred after the first night's show:

> Curley Lambert and Ralph and Carter and I sat in the basement of Mandel Hall and it must have been for a good hour. Carter would just strum a chord and the three of them would sing the most gorgeous harmonies you ever heard in your life. It was much, much, much better than the concerts. I'd give anything if there was a recording of that but there never was.[77]

University of Chicago Folk Festival: February 1961 (Session 610204)

Day two of the festival follows pretty much the same format as the first day. Vernon Derrick opens the show with a fiddle tune, "Turkey in the Straw," followed by a full-length version of "Black Mountain Blues." Curley Lambert solos with "The Wreck of the Old 97." The Stanley Brothers are featured on several instrumentals and duets, including "Jack and May," "Cumberland Gap," "Jenny Lynn," and "The Story of the Lawson Family." Chick Stripling fills a good segment of the program with comedy, his rendering of the old fiddle tune "Johnson Had an Old Gray Mule," and more dancing to the tune of "The Chicken Reel." Carter and Ralph close the show with "Nine Pound Hammer," the ever-popular "I'm a Man of Constant Sorrow," and a lovely solo rendition of "Come All You Tenderhearted."

A gathering at the home of Larry Ehrlich preceded the third day of the festival. Mike Seeger confirmed,

> Ralph and Carter were there and so was Chick and I don't remember who else was in the band . . . I don't remember for sure whether they were there but I know that Chick was there. There were some drinks being served and [in the process] Chick knew exactly what to say to Carter and Ralph to kinda just needle them against one another. I think we might have been listening to some Monroe Brothers or he kidded them

about the Monroe Brothers or something . . . but I don't remember the specifics. In any case, Chick got out of the way and they asked me to play bass with them [on the Sunday night performance].[78]

Seeger's recording captures Carter making light of Chick Stripling's absence, announcing, "Helping out tonight in Chick's Stripling's place, Chick's a little bit under the weather . . ."[79] The audience, who has obviously been in attendance throughout the weekend, erupts in laughter.

University of Chicago Folk Festival: February 1961 (Session 610205)

The third performance's recording shows it consisting of a short fiddle opening and then a full-length version of "Sally Goodin'" by Vernon Derrick. Carter and Ralph dominate much of the rest of the show. They do two duets, "Long Journey Home" and "East Virginia Blues." Ralph features one of his banjo instrumentals, "Big Tilda," while Carter performs a solo rendition of "Dream of a Miner's Child." Two sacred selections follow next: "Angel Band" and "This Wicked Path of Sin." Ralph sings "Little Birdie" and plays the banjo in the old-time clawhammer style. The group closes the show with "How Far to Little Rock" and "Rabbit in a Log," complete with a mandolin goof by Curley Lambert that Carter asks him to redo correctly. The audience roars with laughter.

King #10: February 1961 (Session 610207)

The Stanley Brothers' next trip to the King studios resulted in twelve songs being recorded for the gospel album *Old Time Camp Meeting* (K-750). The sessions were held over a two-day period on February 7 and 8 in 1961. Though King had tinkered with the Stanleys' sound earlier by dropping the mandolin and fiddle and adding a lead guitar, these sessions marked a return to the old style. On hand for the occasion were Curley Lambert on mandolin, Vernon Derrick on fiddle, and Chick Stripling on bass.

As the album's title suggests, the collection is a compilation of older songs, ones that the Stanley Brothers had been familiar with for many years. The first tune recorded is "Little Bessie," a song that laments the passing of a small child due to illness. Though the age of the song is uncertain, the lyrics are known to have appeared in songbooks dating from the late 1800s. Speaking of old songs like "Little Bessie," Carter Stanley recalled, "Dad knew some of 'em. He couldn't play a thing as far as an instrument but he, his voice was just the same as ours is. He sang 'Pretty Polly' and 'A Man of Constant Sorrow,' 'Little Bessie,' I believe. So, I guess that's where we got what little singing we know."[80] The song seems to have originated from around 1875, when R. S. Crandall and W. T. Porter published it. Among the first recorded versions is a 1928 waxing by Kentucky balladeer Buell Kazee.[81] The Blue Sky Boys recorded one of the most influential versions a decade later.[82]

"Mother's Only Sleeping" has an interesting history. Carter and Ralph associated it with both Charlie and Bill Monroe. According to Carter,

With a group that included mandolin player Curley Lambert,
fiddler Vernon Derrick, and bass
player Chick Stripling, the Stanley Brothers recorded one of their
best gospel albums for King, *Old
Time Camp Meeting* (King 750).

Charlie Monroe wrote a letter to the station where we was at and told 'em he didn't
want to hear the Stanleys doing any songs that he owned. And he wrote down a list there
about as long as your leg and included "Roll in My Sweet Baby's Arms." Of course, you
know that's older than several Charlie Monroes as far as I know, but I guess he owned
it. Well, anyhow, that was one of the numbers. "Mother's Not Dead" is another one that
he didn't want us to do and the station just said it's best that you don't . . . just don't do
'em. And we was gonna do 'em anyway. So, one day we was singing "Mother's Only
Sleeping" and they turned us off the air . . . said, "Don't do these songs." That was the
end of it. We didn't do them songs for a long time. It all kindly died away, you know.[83]

Both Bill and Charlie Monroe recorded "Mother's Only Sleeping" within a two-week
period in 1946. Charlie recorded it for Victor on September 30, 1946, and Bill recorded it
for Columbia on September 16, 1946. Bill related, "Lester Flatt brought this one to me. He
put it in both our names, but it was the first time I'd ever heard it. We used to share some
songs that way; when he first came to work with me he thought it was the most wonderful
thing in the world that I could get advance money for him from BMI."[84]

Although both Monroes claimed the song, Maynard and Lance Spencer, an old-time
duo from Dickenson County, Virginia, wrote it. Lance Spencer recalled,

The correct title of it is "Mother's Just Sleeping," that's the way it was originally written. The Monroes changed it to "Mother's Not Dead, She's Only Sleeping" when they

recorded it. We, Lance and Maynard Spencer, wrote the song in '41 [while we were working with Charlie Monroe]. We started with Charlie in about November 1940. We was with him a little over two years. We were two young guys out of the hills of Virginia, we trusted everybody, we didn't know about the tricks of the trade. We never thought about getting the song copyrighted. And when the war came along we both volunteered for the Marine Corps. It was a time when everything was in turmoil and we just didn't [copyright] it before we left and then after we left it sort of went wild. About the time my brother and I left [Charlie] the band sort of broke up. Some of the guys went in the service and then [Charlie] got ahold of Lester [Flatt], he was in Burlington, [North Carolina,] then. Lester played with Charlie for a while and then, of course, Bill [Monroe] got ahold of him and he went to Nashville. When Lester went with Bill, he took the song with him and I think that's how Bill got ahold of it. I believe that Bill's name is on the song. It was just a case where we didn't copyright it and the song went to whomever was latched onto it. The Stanley Brothers were raised at the same county we were, Dickenson County. In fact, we went to the same school together, we were just ahead of them. I like to go back and visit but our mother and father are dead. That's what brought the song on, "Mother's Just Sleeping," that's where we got the idea for that.[85]

The next several songs are ones that appeared in shape-note hymnals in the 1920s and '30s. "The Old Country Church" first appeared in 1933 when J. W. Vaughan copyrighted it. The Stanleys feature it as a quartet. Albert E. Brumley wrote "Campin' in Canaan Land" in 1937. Decades after the session, Ralph Stanley recalled hearing "Charlie Monroe do that on the radio years ago."[86] Charlie recorded it for Victor on November 7, 1947. "I Heard My Mother Call My Name in Prayer" was copyrighted in 1919 by E. M. Bartlett. It appeared in several songbooks during the 1920s and '30s. The original King ledgers listed the song as "P. D." (i.e., public domain or traditional), but when it appeared on the *Old Time Camp Meeting* album, it was mistakenly credited to country singer Webb Pierce. He had recorded a song with a similar title, "Mother Call My Name in Prayer," for Decca on May 7, 1953.

"Working on a Building" is a song that, according to Ralph, "we heard Bill [Monroe] do."[87] Monroe, who recorded the song for Decca on January 25, 1954, related, "I believe that I heard the Carter Family sing that song, and we got requests for it on our show dates and I thought that I should learn it. It's a holiness number, I would say. You know, there's holiness singing in my music . . ."[88] The Carter Family recorded the piece for Victor on May 8, 1934, and it was credited to A. P. Carter. The song's origins are unknown, but it did appear as early as 1927 in a songbook called *Plantation Melodies and Spiritual Songs*.[89] The Stanleys feature it as a quartet on the album, with Ralph handling the verses' lead vocals, his solo on the project.

"Somebody Touched Me" represents another case of King incorrectly crediting a song to someone else. The album lists its author as Ahmet Ertegun, a popular music composer of the 1950s and an executive for Atlantic Records; he worked with Ray Charles and, later, Crosby, Stills, Nash, and Young. Yet the song was actually written by eastern Kentucky musician John Reedy and was recorded by him and his Stone Mountain Hillbillys for Twin

City Records, allegedly on the same day that the Stanley Brothers recorded "The White Dove." Inspiration for the song came from an actual experience in church; Reedy related, "We was at church and you know how the preacher goes around and touches everybody."[90]

The last song recorded at the February 7 session is "Dying a Sinner's Death." Though the song is credited to Roy Acuff, it was Jim Anglin, a brother of Jack Anglin of the famous Johnnie and Jack duo, who composed it. The song first appeared in a 1941 songbook that was copyrighted by Johnnie Wright, Jack Anglin, and George Peek. In the early 1940s, it was sold in a batch of twenty-one Jim Anglin songs to Roy Acuff. Charlie Monroe featured it on the radio in 1944 on the *Noonday Jamboree—1944*.[91] Lester Flatt and his wife, Gladys, who was known as Bobby Jean on the program, performed it as a duet. Roy Acuff eventually recorded it for Columbia on November 19, 1947, as "A Sinner's Death." Lester Flatt continued to feature the song as part of the Flatt & Scruggs repertoire during the 1950s.

King #11: February 1961 (Session 610208)

On February 8, 1961, the Stanleys recorded the balance of the material for the *Old Time Camp Meeting* album. One of the most traditional pieces on the project is a duet by Carter and Ralph called "Village Church Yard." Ralph recalled, "We learned that at the McClure Church. Our dad and his brother, Jim Henry Stanley, used to lead that one. He worked for Dad; used to drive a team of horses for him in the woods, logging. And he would come home with Dad now and then and they would set up late at night and sing a lot of the old songs."[92] The Stanleys recorded the song in a quick, moderately up-tempo style that was closer to bluegrass than the style in which Carter and Ralph first heard the song. In March of 1966, while on a tour of Europe with eastern Kentucky ballad singer Roscoe Holcomb, the Stanleys and Roscoe performed a much slower, unaccompanied version that was more in-line with the way the song was sung at the McClure church.[93] Ralph Stanley recorded a similar a cappella version for Rebel in 1971.[94]

Carter had introduced "A Few More Years" on a July 4, 1961, personal appearance in Luray, Virginia, as "a brand new one,"[95] indicating that the band had written it only recently. Although the song is credited to Ralph, he felt that Carter was its actual composer.[96] In fact, the hymn was written by neither of the brothers: it dates back to 1842, when it was composed by Horatius Bonar (1808–89). At the time, Bonar was an ordained minister in the Church of Scotland. Although he authored several books on theology, he is widely known for his hymn writing. His "A Few More Years Shall Roll" was sung for the first time at St. James Church, Leith, in Edinburgh, Scotland, on New Years Day 1843.[97] It was later included in a number of hymnals in the United States, including the *Primitive Baptist Hymn Book*. Many of the Baptist hymnals of the time printed the texts only, leaving the congregations to supply their choice of traditional melodies. It is quite probable that Carter arranged one of these melodies to suit the band's rendition of the hymn.

Charles Ernest Moody, a member of the string band the Georgia Yellow Hammers, copyrighted "Kneel at the Cross" in 1924. He related,

I had been working all day in my brother's grocery store. As I was coming home, the Baptists were having a prayer meeting. I stopped for the last of it, and the preacher said, "Let us all kneel at the cross." My ears shot forward and I went home and wrote down the title. The next night I developed it into a song. The preacher's name was Sam Hare.[98]

It was recorded in the early part of 1930 by the Moody Quartet, and again by the Blue Sky Boys for Bluebird on October 7, 1940.

The final selection recorded for the album is a Carter Stanley original called "My Sinful Past." It first appeared in a songbook that the Stanley Brothers issued in the latter part of 1951.[99]

At the conclusion of the sessions for the *Old Time Camp Meeting* album, the band recorded a stereo version of "How Mountain Girls Can Love." The Stanley Brothers had recorded it previously for King—in mono—on September 30, 1958, and it appeared on their first King album, *The Stanley Brothers* (K-615). The song was later used on another Stanley Brothers' album, *The Stanleys in Person* (K-719), which was initially issued in mono with the 1958 mono take of the song. In 1961 the decision was made to issue the *In Person* album in stereo. With all of the other selections for the album having already been recorded in stereo, a new, stereo version of the song was recorded to make the entire album true stereo.

New River Ranch: May 1961 (Session 610521)

On May 21, 1961, the Stanley Brothers and George Shuffler appeared at New River Ranch. They traveled as a trio. Chick Stripling was apparently part of the band but unable to make the trip. Carter mentions on a recording of the show that Chick had been in Miami, Florida, recently (for a show at the Dinner Key Auditorium that was part of a country music spectacular held in conjunction with a Country Music Association board meeting) and that he "ate or drank something that didn't agree with him."[100] Taking Chick's place in the show was Jack Cooke. Having worked with the Stanleys several years earlier, he adapted easily. Carter and Ralph's second set of the day appeared on LP as the first issue in Copper Creek's *Stanley Series*. Lamar Grier recorded the day's proceedings.

Grier's recording shows the group sailing through eighteen songs and tunes, all of which are pretty standard fare. A few exceptions are Jack Cooke's performance of "Long Black Veil" and Carter and Ralph's rendering of "Little Bessie." A review in the May 15, 1961, issue of *Billboard* indicates that "Little Bessie" was the group's latest release ("Heartfelt chanting by team on tear-jerking weeper").[101] The brothers perform the song in answer to a request, but have to use a hymnbook to remember all the words.

Oak Leaf Park: May 1961 (Session 610528)

The Stanley Brothers evidently stayed in the Maryland–northern Virginia area for the week. On the evening of Saturday, May 27, they headlined the *New Dominion Barn Dance* in Richmond. The next day, they traveled northwest to appear near Luray, Virginia, at a venue called Oak Leaf Park. The facility was being leased for the summer by Bill Clifton for the purpose of promoting country music shows. The Stanleys were one of his first acts of the season. They performed two sets and were still without a regular bass player. An unidentified musician filled in for the first set, and Tom Gray, known today for his work with the Country Gentlemen and the Seldom Scene, filled in on the second set. The afternoon performance was issued on record as part of Copper Creek's *Stanley Series*. Like the Stanleys show of a week earlier, this one was also recorded by Lamar Grier.

With a few exceptions, the material performed is a sampling of songs recently released on record. Of interest is George Shuffler's version of "On Top of Old Smoky" and Ralph's rendering of "Steel Guitar Rag." Shuffler noted,

> I sung that everywhere we went for five years. The Weavers had the big hit on that, when Pete Seeger was with the Weavers. So, we kind of followed up on that. When we were going into a lot of northern country that we'd never been into before, we knew that was a song they could relate to because it had been so popular. That and "Old Mountain Dew," you could never stick them two wrong. We were thrown between bluegrass and the folk because we were authentic mountain and seemed like that old song, everybody could relate to it and sing it.[102]

Ralph had recorded "Steel Guitar Rag" for King, but it was not commercially released at the time of this performance.

Watermelon Park: June 1961 (Session 610618)

On June 18, 1961, Carter and Ralph appeared at Watermelon Park in Berryville, Virginia. Al Elliott was back in the band to play mandolin, and George Shuffler appeared on lead guitar. An unidentified bass player was also present. Of at least eighteen songs recorded that day, five were chosen for inclusion on the second volume of Rebel's *Legendary Stanley Brothers*. Many of the tracks appearing on these two *Legendary* albums are songs that the group didn't recorded commercially. To give Stanley fans something they might be familiar with, five fairly recognizable songs from this show are included: "If I Lose," "Rank Stranger," "A Few More Years," "Little Bennie," and "I'm a Man of Constant Sorrow."

Oak Leaf Park: July 1961 (Session 610704)

On July 4, 1961, Oak Leaf Park hosted one of the first all-day, multiartist bluegrass events. Promoted by Bill Clifton, the show featured Bill Monroe, Mac Wiseman, the Stanley Brothers, Bill Clifton, the Country Gentlemen, and Jim & Jesse. Although Don Owens had presented a similar event the year before, Clifton's was the first to acknowledge the central role of Bill Monroe in developing and defining bluegrass as a genre of music. In addition to individual performances by each of the bands, the day also included a segment that reunited Monroe with a number of his former sidemen, notably Mac Wiseman and Carter Stanley. Mike Seeger recorded much of the festivities, including a duet by Carter and Bill on a song they had recorded together for Decca in 1951, "Sugar Coated Love." The track appeared on the Stanley Brothers Time Life anthology *The Definitive Collection (1947–1966)*.

Tapes of the July 4 show, although never issued commercially, created quite a bit of controversy at the time. Several additional groups were invited to attend the event, most notably Reno & Smiley and Flatt & Scruggs. However, when Flatt & Scruggs learned that Bill Monroe and the Stanley Brothers were going to be on the same bill, they declined the offer to appear.[103] During the performance Carter Stanley initiated a series of remarks about Flatt & Scruggs's absence from the program. He was joined, without much prodding, by Bill Monroe. Both chided Flatt & Scruggs for deciding to boycott the event. The comments were caught on tape and eventually found their way to Earl Scruggs and his wife, Louise, who was the duo's business manager. As a number of people were taping that day, exactly who sent the tape to the couple has remained a mystery. In any event, the comments didn't do anything to quell the animosity between Monroe and Flatt & Scruggs, and it is rumored that Louise Scruggs threatened legal action over the comments. The incident created mistrust between a number of artists and the fans who wanted to tape record their performances.

King #12: July 1961 (Session 610720)

Three weeks later, on July 20, 1961, Carter and Ralph returned to King studios to record four songs, most of which would appear on their *Folk Song Festival* album (K-791). The band consisted of Al Elliott on mandolin, Chubby Anthony on fiddle, and George Shuffler on lead guitar and bass. Al Elliott and Chubby Anthony had returned earlier to play several months with the Stanley Brothers during the summer of 1961. These recordings are the last that Al Elliott made with the Stanley Brothers. Shuffler, a mainstay in the Stanley band, plays lead guitar on the original tracks and the overdubbed bass. These songs represent some of the first for King on which he plays lead guitar.

All four of the songs from the session are duets by Carter and Ralph. Curiously, no Stanley Brothers originals are featured; King supplied all of the songs. "There Is a Trap" was a fairly new song at the time. It was written by Bill J. Lindsey and copyrighted on April 16, 1962. Ralph Stanley believed that "we got that through Syd Nathan,"[104] the owner of King Records. "I See Through You" was held back from immediate release and made its first appearance on the 1964 album *The Remarkable Stanley Brothers Play and Sing Bluegrass Songs For You* (KLP-924). Because of its title, the song has the dubious distinction of being known as the Stanley Brothers' "x-ray song."[105] Pee Wee King copyrighted "Thy Burdens Are Greater Than Mine" on February 20, 1950. It was recorded by Roy Acuff for Columbia and was also featured by Hank Williams on his *Health and Happiness Show*. After Williams's death, MGM issued a Williams version of the song that was taken from transcriptions of the show. Carter once introduced "Fast Express" during a show as "one of the Delmore Brothers' numbers,"[106] and Ralph recalled, "We got that through King Records."[107] The Delmore Brothers had recorded the song for King in 1945, and it was one of their scarcer releases. The name "Jim Scott," which appears as the composer's credit on the Stanley recording, is a pseudonym for Alton Delmore.

On August 25, 1961, the Stanley Brothers completed several days of performing in the Baltimore area. At least three days were spent at the Hi-Fi Club, a venue located about five miles from downtown in nearby Rosedale. One of those days included a double bill with Reno & Smiley. Sadly, these were probably not the happiest of times for Carter and Ralph, as their father had passed away slightly less than a week earlier. They had cancelled a gig in Trenton, New Jersey, an American Folk Singing Festival, to attend the funeral. Following the stint at the Hi-Fi Club, the group made an hour-long trip up Route 1 to appear at New River Ranch. A recording of their performance by Baltimore-area audio enthusiast Leon Kagarise later appeared as a release on Ralph's StanleyTone label. The disc was called *Riding That New River Train*.

Roughly two dozen songs were recorded, most of which are fairly standard performance pieces for the group. A notable exception is "I'm on My Way Back to the Old Home," which features Ralph singing lead. Other deviations include George Shuffler's solos on "Willy Roy" and "On Top of Old Smoky" and guest musician Jack Cooke's versions of "Molly and Tenbrooks" and "Used to Be."

King #13: September 1961 (Session 610922)

The Stanley Brothers recorded a subsequent session for King on September 22, 1961, completing the *Folk Song Festival* material. As with the previous session, only four songs were recorded. With the exception of Al Elliot's departure, the personnel remained the same. George Shuffler confined his participation to lead guitar while Chubby Anthony doubled on fiddle and bass. Curiously, Chubby dubbed the bass on only two selections ("String, Eraser, and Blotter" and "Keep Them Cold Icy Fingers off of Me"), while the remaining two tracks ("I'm Only Human" and "Still Trying to Get to Little Rock") were featured without a bass. This session was the last that Chubby recorded with the Stanley Brothers.

"I'm Only Human" was a new song that was copyrighted by Jimmy Wells on September 15, 1961, only a few days before the session. "String, Eraser, and Blotter" was another new song that, according to Ralph Stanley, "Syd Nathan at King Records put us on to."[108] Three composers share credit for the song: Pop Eckler, Shorty Long, and Johnny Speca. Eckler had recorded it earlier for King, in the late 1940s. His lone session for the label produced a minor hit, "Money, Marbles and Chalk," that Reno & Smiley recorded for King in 1959. Shorty Long and Johnny Speca added another song to the Stanley repertoire in 1962, when Carter and Ralph recorded "My Deceitful Heart." John Lair, the genial master of ceremonies for the Renfro Valley Barn Dance, copyrighted "Keep Them Cold Icy Fingers off of Me" on October 3, 1946. It was recorded for King by Fairly Holden, also in 1946, and was later covered by Pee Wee King and Homer and Jethro. "Still Trying to Get to Little Rock," an attempt to duplicate the success of the Stanley Brothers' 1960 hit "How Far to Little Rock," unfortunately failed to attract as much attention.

Bill Clifton: March 1962 (Session 610304)

In early March of 1962, the Stanley Brothers, along with George Shuffler and Chick Stripling, spent several days in Charlottesville, Virginia, at the home of Bill Clifton. They used the location as a hub while they worked several dates in the area, including a Friday evening show in nearby Calverton, Virginia. On Sunday, March 4, Clifton hosted a party at his home to introduce some of the "movers and shakers" of the area to bluegrass music. Acting as master of ceremonies for the day was Eddie Matherly of WKCW radio from Warrenton, Virginia. Appearing on the showcase were the Stanley Brothers, the Country Gentlemen, and portions of the New Lost City Ramblers. Much of the event was recorded, and two tracks by the Stanley Brothers are included on the first volume of Rebel's *Legendary Stanley Brothers*: "Let Us Be Lovers Again" (as "Lover's Quarrel") and "Dream of a Miner's Child." The group had recorded "Let Us Be Lovers Again" a year or so earlier for King with lots of mandolin and fiddle. In contrast to the staccato chop of the mandolin and the lonesome wail of the fiddle, this live version with George Shuffler's lead guitar takes on a softer, gentler feel. "Dream of a Miner's Child" is performed in answer to a request from Eddie Matherly, and it is Matherly who is heard introducing the band at the beginning of the first volume of the *Legendary* album.

Oberlin College: March 1962 (620317)

Two weeks later, on March 17, 1962, the same foursome was in Oberlin, Ohio, to present an afternoon concert for the Oberlin College Folk Music Club. Three songs and one comedy routine from this show are used as part of Copper Creek's *Shadows of the Past* album. "John Henry" is a song the Stanley Brothers performed in a number of different ways over the years. Earlier performances have Ralph leading the song in a fast, up-tempo manner; on this recording, Carter offers a more relaxed version. Chick Stripling goes through several of his comedy routines on the show; he makes Carter the straight man in a bit that involves Chick's misuse of the word "propaganda." Other tunes include two songs associated with the Monroe Brothers, "Katy Cline" and "Long Journey Home." The Oberlin Folk Music Club pulled one track from the concert, "How Mountain Girls Can Love," for inclusion in a various artists album, *Oberlin College Folk Music Club: The Audience Pleased, Live Recordings 1959–1975*, which they assembled to highlight the diversity of talent that had appeared at the school over the years.[109]

King #14: May 1962 (Session 620502)

In May of 1962, the Stanley Brothers spent three days at King studios, producing a total of twenty-one masters. The bulk of the material, fourteen tunes, was for the gospel album *Good Old Camp Meeting Songs* (K-805). The remaining tracks were scattered over later King albums and singles. George Shuffler continued on lead guitar, veteran Clinch Mountain Boy Ralph Mayo appeared on fiddle, and Chick Stripling played bass. The material for the gospel album consists entirely of quartets and features Ralph Mayo singing baritone and George Shuffler singing bass. With a few exceptions, most of the material is gleaned from old songbooks the Stanleys were familiar with.

The first day of recording began on May 2 with "Where We'll Never Grow Old," a song that was written by James C. Moore on April 22, 1914. The Carter Family recorded it for Victor some years later, on February 24, 1932. Ralph Stanley, however, later cited Ralph

GOOD OLD CAMP MEETING SONGS

STEREO

STANLEY BROTHERS

The cover of this 1962 gospel album features Ralph and Carter Stanley in front of the Church of the Redeemer on Erie Avenue in Cincinnati. The photo was most likely taken on May 2, 3, or 4, 1962.

Mayo as their source for the hymn, saying, "I believe we learned that from Ralph Mayo, he's an old-time fiddle player."[110] "When the Savior Reached Down for Me" was written by G. E. Wright and was copyrighted in 1921. "Paul and Silas" evolved from African American traditions as a spiritual in the 1800s. In bluegrass circles, the first person to record it was Red Allen, who released a version on the Kentucky Records label in 1953. Carl Story released a recording of the song for Starday in 1959. The Stanley Brothers were performing the song on personal appearances in 1960. Flatt & Scruggs recorded the song in the spring of 1963 for their *Recorded Live at Vanderbilt University* album on Columbia.

"Who Will Sing for Me" is a song that found favor with several bluegrass bands in the 1950s and '60s, most notably Flatt & Scruggs and Carl Story. The song first appeared in 1922 when John Thomas Ely, a Texas farmer and singing school teacher, published it.[111] The Flatt & Scruggs and Carl Story versions make use of the first and fourth verses and the chorus of Ely's text. They both also feature a call-and-response technique that was popular in gospel music. Carl Story recorded the tune for Mercury in 1952, but this version lay dormant until 2011, when it appeared on a Bear Family reissue. He later recorded it again, in 1959, for Starday, who released it as a single. Flatt & Scruggs recorded it for Columbia in 1956, but their version also remained unissued for a time, finally appearing on a 1966 gospel album called *When the Saints Go Marching In*. The Stanley Brothers version differs somewhat from the Flatt & Scruggs and Story versions. Carter and Ralph don't use the call-and-response technique on the verses; Carter sings the verses straight through. The band keeps the lyrics of the chorus and, with some modifications, the first verse. However, the Stanley version contains a second verse ("When crowds shall gather around . . .") that does not appear in the printed or other recorded versions. It is, most likely, an example of Carter Stanley's adaptive process at work. Ralph Stanley associated the song with Charlie Monroe.[112]

One of the most popular songs in the collection is Albert E. Brumley's "I'll Fly Away." Albert related,

> I was picking cotton on my father's farm and was humming the old ballad that went like this: "If I had the wings of an angel, over these prison walls I would fly," and suddenly it dawned on me that I could use this plot for a gospel-type song. About three years later, I finally developed the plot, titled it "I'll Fly Away," and it was published in 1932. Those familiar with the song will note that I paraphrased one line of the old ballad to read, "Like a bird from prison bars have flown." When I wrote it, I had no idea that it would become so universally popular.[113]

Two older hymns completed the recording session for May 2. The hymn "Drinking from the Fountain," Ralph Stanley said, "is from an Old Regular Baptist songbook. Of course we heard that years ago, used to sing that in church."[114] This hymn is related to a spiritual called "I've Just Come from the Fountain," pieces of which date to 1872.[115] A more complete text can be found in an 1880 publication of songs by the Fisk Jubilee Singers. Another of the old songs on the album is "Leaning on the Everlasting Arms." Rev. E. A. Hoffman and A. J. Showalter copyrighted it in 1887. The Stanleys had performed this hymn earlier in their career, and a taped version exists from a July 1958 guest appearance on the WWVA *Jamboree* in Wheeling, West Virginia.

King #15: May 1962 (Session 620503)

The Stanley Brothers continued recording on May 3, leading off the session with a Carter Stanley original called "Memories of Mother." They had recorded it as a duet eight years earlier for Mercury Records. "Heaven's Light Is Shining on Me" is an old song of unknown origin. The Delmore Brothers had recorded the tune as "Heavenly Light Is Shining on Me" for Bluebird on August 3, 1937. They also included the words in a songbook they issued in 1937 and claimed an arrangement of the composition.[116] Wade Mainer recorded a variant called "Heaven Bells Are Ringing" in 1939.

"Let Me Walk, Lord, by Your Side" and "Harbor of Love" are both Carter Stanley songs that the band had recorded in the mid-1950s for Mercury Records. The original recordings were most likely out of print at the time of this session, and the Stanleys made these new versions to keep the songs available to their fans. "Hallelujah, We Shall Rise" was copyrighted in 1904 by J. E. Thomas; it appeared in many Winsett songbooks of the 1930s and '40s.

Following the recording of the twelve gospel selections, five secular songs were taped. The first, "Can You Forgive," was written by Roy Hall and recorded by him for Bluebird in 1941. Wilma Lee and Stoney Cooper cut it for Columbia a decade later. During the March 17, 1962, concert at Oberlin College, Carter Stanley introducing it, saying,

Here's a song, it's a trio number we'd like to try, it was recorded I expect about 1936, somewhere along there by a boy by the name of Roy Hall down at Roanoke, Virginia. He used to have a group there called the Blue Ridge Entertainers. It's an old song, it never did do very much at that time, but I always thought that it was well worth re-cording again, which we plan to do. It's called 'Can You Forgive'. . . . I guess everybody has their little pet songs, that's one of mine, I've always liked it.[117]

"If That's the Way You Feel" is yet another re-recording of a song that the Stanley Brothers had recorded previously for Mercury Records. At the time the Stanley Brothers made this re-recording, the original Mercury version had yet to be released. The King version contrasts quite a bit with the original Mercury recording, which was made on November 15, 1957. The original uses a trio and has the distinction of being the only Stanley Brothers song to feature a steel guitar. The King remake is featured as a quartet and the steel guitar is replaced by George Shuffler's acoustic lead guitar. Curiously, this version, too, remained unissued for years, first appearing in 1986 as a bonus cut on a limited pressing reissue of *Country Folk Music Spotlight* (K-864) that was prepared for County Records.

"Drunkard's Dream" is an old song and one Ralph Stanley thought "we heard our daddy do some of that."[118] The liner notes of the album on which it appears, *Country Folk Music Spotlight*, claim that it was a song "which was taught to Carter Stanley in his early boyhood by one of the neighbors down the road."[119] The song circulated in the mountains of Virginia and North Carolina in the early 1900s and is a variant of the British ballad "The Husband's Dream."[120] "I Just Came from Your Wedding" had been released earlier, in May of 1960, by the Wright Brothers, the same duo who supplied "Carolina Mountain Home" to the Stanleys.[121] Carter and Ralph were evidently unaware of the song's origin, as they copyrighted it in their names on August 26, 1962. The final tune recorded on May 3, the old song "Mama Don't Allow," highlights all of the instrumentalists present on the session; it also displays the dancing talents of bass player Chick Stripling, who often performed a dance routine on stage when he worked with the Stanley Brothers.

King #16: May 1962 (Session 620504)

The third day of recording, May 4, started with another song that showcases Chick Stripling, "Chickie's Old Gray Mule." Chick related, "I was born and raised on a farm and used to plow with a mule quite a bit, back before we had tractors, and I learned this old tune way back in them days."[122] The song was written by Thomas P. Westendorf, a composer who contributed other songs to old-time music, such as the 1884 song "Sweet Fern," which the Carter Family later adopted.[123] Originally titled "Thompson's Old Gray Mule," it was copyrighted by the Georgia Yellow Hammers as "Johnson's Mule" on April 25, 1927. It was recorded by them on February 18, 1927, and later recorded by another popular Georgia string band, the Skillet Lickers.

Two additional gospel songs were recorded for the *Good Old Camp Meeting Songs* project: "If We Never Meet Again," which was copyrighted by Albert E. Brumley in 1945, and

"Hand in Hand with Jesus," which was copyrighted by L. D. Huffstutler and Rev. Johnson Oatman, Jr. in 1923.

The final song recorded at the session was "My Deceitful Heart," a recent composition by Shorty Long and Johnny Speca that was copyrighted on August 8, 1962. It was initially issued as a single and later became part of a various artists album on King; it was not included on any Stanley Brothers albums while the duo was together.

After the release of *Good Old Camp Meeting Songs*, Baltimore disc jockey Ray Davis was instrumental in promoting the disc to his listeners. He would advertise recordings on his radio program, then ship them to his customers using the mail order service he had set up at Johnny's Used Cars, his sponsor. Whenever the Stanley Brothers had a new gospel album released on King, Davis arranged for the distributor to ship him two hundred copies as soon they were available. This allowed him to get a head start over other retailers in the area. The market for bluegrass was not especially big in Baltimore, but it was large enough for Davis to sell quite a bit of Stanley Brothers merchandise.[124]

Ash Grove: August 1962

From August 28 through September 16, 1962, the Stanley Brothers played at the trendy Hollywood, California, coffeehouse known as the Ash Grove. Club owner Ed Pearl had seen the Stanley Brothers in person when they performed at Bill Clifton's Blue Grass Day event on July 4, 1961, in Luray, Virginia. Appearing with Carter and Ralph at the Ash Grove were Curley Lambert and Vernon Derrick. Roger Bush of the Country Boys (soon to be renamed the Kentucky Colonels) filled in on bass. Vernon Derrick remembered the Ash Grove as, " . . . kind of a folk place. Of course, some of the movie stars would come in that liked that type music. I think the ones that used to play Hoss Cartwright and Little Joe, Dan Blocker and Michael Landon. We played . . . jammed a lot with Clarence White."[125] Between shows the group visited historic forts, an Appaloosa horse ranch, Knott's Berry Farm; saw a roundup; and helped produce an album by the Kentucky Colonels titled *The New Sound of Bluegrass America* (Briar 109). Old-time fiddler Leslie Keith visited with Carter and Ralph and sat in on one of their sets.

Following their engagement at the Ash Grove, the Stanleys ventured north for shows in Berkeley, San Jose, and Sacramento. It was while in Sacramento that Ralph acquired his Gibson Granada banjo. James Shelton, Ralph's lead guitarist from 1994 to 2014 and his road manager, had high praise for the instrument:

> I always thought it was one of the best banjos I've ever heard. It's like it had a bell in it or something. It really is a great banjo in the hands of Ralph . . . a lot of it was just the case of the right man being paired up with the right instrument, much like Bill and his mandolin, Earl and his Granada, or Tony Rice with the herringbone. It certainly was the perfect tool for Ralph and it served him well for a lot of years. That thing had a tone all its own.[126]

Ash Grove #1: August 1962 (Session 620829)

Several sets of music were recorded while the Stanley Brothers were at the Ash Grove. One set, from August 29, was released on Copper Creek's *Stanley Series* and features fourteen songs and tunes including "How Mountain Girls Can Love," "Clinch Mountain Backstep," "Let Me Love You One More Time," "The Flood," and others. One notable deviation on the set is Curley Lambert's rendition of a Bill Monroe recording from the early 1940s called "The Coupon Song."

Ash Grove #2: August 1962 (Session 620830)

Another recording, made on August 30 and later issued on the *Stanley Series*, starts off with a few songs from the Stanley repertoire but quickly morphs into a tribute to the Monroe sound. The last half of the set includes Monroe favorites such as "Uncle Pen," "Molly and Tenbrooks," "True Life Blues," "Sugar Coated Love," "The Little Girl and the Dreadful Snake," and "Drifting Too Far from the Shore."

Ash Grove #3: August 1962 (Session 620831)

Three songs from an August 31 show at the Ash Grove found their way on to other music releases. Time Life's *The Definitive Collection (1947–1966)* features a track that the duo never commercially recorded, "Tell Me Why My Daddy Don't Come Home." The song was cowritten by Bill Boyd, Hal Burns, and Earl Nunn, and was recorded by Boyd and his Cowboy Ramblers for Bluebird on October 12, 1941. The Stanley Brothers featured it early in their career while on the radio in Bristol. Two other songs from this set appear on Rebel's *Legendary Stanley Brothers* LPs. The first *Legendary* volume features Carter and Ralph on an old-time duet, "On the Banks of the Ohio." The second volume contains a solo by Carter on "Train 45," which he's heard performing in answer to a request. He uses the opportunity to tell a little of the background of the song's origin, and to express his admiration for the old-time duo of Grayson and Whitter. The tune also offers a nice showcase for Vernon Derrick's versatility on the fiddle.

New York University: November 1962 (Session 621130)

On November 30, 1962, the Stanley Brothers were in New York City to appear at a concert for the Friends of Old-Time Music. It was their second time performing for the organization, having appeared there previously on June 9, 1961. For this outing, the band included Curley Lambert on mandolin, Vernon Derrick on fiddle, and guest Carl Chatzky on bass. A veteran of the Baltimore bluegrass scene, Carl filled in with the Stanley Brothers on several occasions in the early 1960s. He adopted the stage name of Carl Hawkins for his guest spots with Carter and Ralph.

In 2006 Smithsonian Folkways issued a three-CD boxed set of material recorded at various Friends of Old-Time Music concerts. The boxed set was an expansion of a 1964 FOTM album issued on Folkways. While the original 1964 LP contained three selections by the Stanley Brothers that were recorded at the University of Chicago Folk Festival in February of 1961, the 2006 compilation deleted these tracks and replaced them with four selections from the November 30, 1962, NYU show. These new selections include "The Dream of the Miner's Child," "Have a Feast Here Tonight," "Mansions for Me," and "Hard Times."

In a lot of ways, the years from 1958 through 1962 were among the best for the Stanley Brothers. They hooked up with a label, King Records, that gave them plenty of exposure and opportunities to record. Their stylistic innovations, notably the inclusion of the lead guitar, gave them a unique sound that separated them from other bluegrass-styled bands of the time, and the group added one of the seminal songs of their career to their repertoire, "Rank Stranger." They also opened up a whole new market for their music, the Deep South, and became headliners of a well-promoted weekly jamboree program. Affiliation with a sponsor, Jim Walter Homes, gave them broad exposure on television and radio and provided a steady income. Numerous appearances at country music parks in the Northeast and Midwest kept them in touch with their many fans. Acceptance at major folk venues such as the Newport Folk Festival, the University of Chicago Folk Festival, and Hollywood's Ash Grove legitimized their music to yet another market. It was still a very demanding way to make a living, but the Stanley Brothers were staying ahead of the curve.

DISCOGRAPHY, 1958–1962

580800   Starday session; producer: Stanley Brothers
Radio station WCYB, Bristol, Virginia
ca. August 1958
Carter Stanley: g | Ralph Stanley: b | Bill Napier: m | Lowell Eugene "Gene" Meadows: lg
Joe Meadows: f | Albert H. "Al" Elliott: sb

2814	**Holiday Pickin'** (Ralph Stanley) Instrumental	413	NLP-2014, GD-5026, CCS-106/7, KBSCD-7000
2815	**Gonna Paint the Town** (Ralph Stanley) C. Stanley–L, R. Stanley–T, Elliott–B	406	SLP-106, NLP-2014, CCS-106/7, KBSCD-7000, B0007883-02
2816	**That Happy Night** (Ralph Stanley) C. Stanley–L, A. Elliott–T, R. Stanley–HB	406	SLP-106, NLP-2014, CCS-106/7, KBSCD-7000
2817	**Christmas Is Near** (Ralph Stanley) C. Stanley–L, R. Stanley–T, Elliott–B (last line only)	413	CCS-106/7, KBSCD-7000

580907   Copper Creek reissue of show, recorded by Pete Kuykendall and Bill Offenbacher
New River Ranch, Rising Sun, Maryland
September 7, 1958
Carter Stanley: g | Ralph Stanley: b | Bill Napier: m
Peter V. "Pete" Kuykendall: f | Al Elliott: sb

Dickenson County Breakdown Instrumental	CCCD-5512
Boil Them Cabbage Down C. Stanley–L, R. Stanley–T	SLP-1487, CCCD-5512
Nobody's Business C. Stanley–L, R. Stanley–T	CCCD-5512
If That's the Way You Feel C. Stanley–L, R. Stanley–T, Elliott–B	CCCD-5512
Big Tilda Instrumental	CCCD-5512
Gonna Paint the Town C. Stanley–L, R. Stanley–T, Elliott–B	CCCD-5512
How I Long to See the Old Folks C. Stanley–L, R. Stanley–T	CCCD-5512
Daybreak in Dixie Instrumental	CCCD-5512

The Memory of Your Smile
C. Stanley–L, R. Stanley–T, Elliott–B

CCCD-5512

How Mountain Girls Can Love
C. Stanley–L, R. Stanley–T, Elliott–B

CCCD-5512

Little Birdie
R. Stanley–L

CCCD-5512

The Fields Have Turned Brown
C. Stanley–L, Elliott–T, R. Stanley–HB

CCCD-5512

East Virginia Blues
C. Stanley–L, R. Stanley–T

SLP-1495, CCCD-5512

Old Salty Dog Blues
C. Stanley–L, R. Stanley–T, Napier (possibly)–B

CCCD-5512

Pretty Polly
R. Stanley–L

CCCD-5512

I'm a Man of Constant Sorrow
R. Stanley–L

CCCD-5512

Mother's Not Dead
C. Stanley–L, R. Stanley–T

CCCD-5512

Send Me the Pillow That You Dream On
Elliott–L

CCCD-5512

Baby Girl
C. Stanley–L, R. Stanley–T, Elliott–B

CCCD-5512

Dickson County Breakdown
Instrumental

CCCD-5512

John Henry
R. Stanley–L

CCCD-5512

Just a Little Walk with Jesus
C. Stanley–L, R. Stanley–T, Elliott–B, Napier–BS

CCCD-5512

That Happy Night
C. Stanley–L, Elliott–T, R. Stanley–HB

CCCD-5512

They're at Rest Together
C. Stanley–L, R. Stanley–T

CCLP-0101, CCCD-5512

Think of What You've Done
C. Stanley–L, R. Stanley–T, Elliott–B

SLP-1495, CCCD-5512

Uncle Pen
C. Stanley–L, R. Stanley–T, Elliott–B

CCCD-5512

White Dove
1st chorus: C. Stanley–L, R. Stanley–T, Napier (possibly)–B
Remainder of song: C. Stanley–L, Elliott–T, R. Stanley–HB

CCCD-5512

Handsome Molly C. Stanley–L		CCCD-5512	
Pike County Breakdown Instrumental		CCCD-5512	
If That's the Way You Feel C. Stanley–L, R. Stanley–T, Elliott–B		CCCD-5512	

580930	King session; producer: Bernard "Bernie" Pearlman King Studio, Cincinnati, Ohio September 30, 1958 Carter Stanley: g | Ralph Stanley: b | Bill Napier: m Ralph Mayo: f | Al Elliott: sb		
4192	**Love Me, Darling, Just Tonight** (Malone-Rakes) C. Stanley–L, R. Stanley–T	45-5165, EP-441	KLP-615, SD-3003, GD-5026, KBSCD-7000
4193	**She's More to Be Pitied** (Ruby Rakes) C. Stanley–L, R. Stanley–T	45-5155, EP-439	KLP-615, KBSCD-7000
4194	**Heaven Seemed So Near** (Rakes-Elliott) C. Stanley–L, R. Stanley–T, Elliott–B	45-5306, EP-439	KLP-615, KBSCD-7000
4195	**Your Selfish Heart** (Rakes-Elliott) C. Stanley–L, R. Stanley–T, Elliott–B	EP-440	KLP-615, KLP-924, OHCS-323, KBSCD-7000
4196	**How Mountain Girls Can Love** (Ruby Rakes) C. Stanley–L, R. Stanley–T, Elliott–B	45-5269, EP-439	KLP-615, KLP-1046, SD-3003, KBSCD-7000, B0007883-02, M-19493
4197	**The Memory of Your Smile** (Ruby Rakes) C. Stanley–L, R. Stanley–T, Elliott–B	45-5210, EP-441	KLP-615, KBSCD-7000

581001	King session; producer: Bernie Pearlman} King Studio, Cincinnati, Ohio October 1, 1958 Carter Stanley: g | Ralph Stanley: b | Bill Napier: m Ralph Mayo: f | Al Elliott: sb		
4198	**Mastertone March** (Ruby Rakes) Instrumental	45-5180, EP-439	KLP-615, KBSCD-7000
4199	**Clinch Mountain Backstep** (Ruby Rakes) Instrumental	EP-441	KLP-615, KBSCD-7000
4200	**Midnight Ramble** (Ruby Rakes) Instrumental	45-5165, 45-6236, EP-441	KLP-615, GD-5026, KBSCD-7000
4201	**Train 45** (Ruby Rakes) Instrumental with spoken exchange	45-5155, EP-440	KLP-615, SD-3003, KBSCD-7000, B0007883-02
4202	**Think of What You've Done** (Carter Stanley) C. Stanley–L, R. Stanley–T, Elliott–B	EP-440	KLP-615, KBSCD-7000, B0007883-02
4203	**Keep a Memory** (Carter Stanley) C. Stanley–L, R. Stanley–T, Elliott–B	45-5180, EP-440	KLP-615, KBSCD-7000

581129 *Suwannee River Jamboree*, recorded by unkown
Live Oak, Florida
ca. November, 1958
Carter Stanley: g | Ralph Stanley: b | Bill Napier: m
Paul "Moon" Mullins: f | Al Elliott: sb

       We Are Going to Paint the Town   No #
       C. Stanley–L, R. Stanley–T, Elliott–B

590210 King session; producer: Bernie Pearlman
King Studio, Cincinnati, Ohio
February 10, 1959
Carter Stanley: g | (except 4229) | Ralph Stanley: b | Al Elliott: m (g on 4229)
Chubby Anthony: f | George Shuffler: sb

4223	**Old Daniel Prayed** (G. T. Speer) C. Stanley–L, R. Stanley–T, Elliott–B, Shuffler–BS	EP-456	KLP-645, GT-0104, KBSCD-7000
4224	**He Said If I Be Lifted Up** (Charles H. Pace) C. Stanley–L, R. Stanley–T, Elliott–B, Shuffler–BS	EP-457	KLP-645, KBSCD-7000
4225	**This Wicked Path of Sin** (Bill Monroe) C. Stanley–L, R. Stanley–T, Elliott–B, Shuffler–BS	EP-457	KLP-645, KBSCD-7000
4226	**I'll Meet You in Church Sunday Morning** (Bill Monroe) C. Stanley–L, R. Stanley–T, Elliott–B, Shuffler–BS	EP-455	KLP-645, KBSCD-7000
4227	**Are You Afraid to Die** (Louvin–Louvin-Hill) C. Stanley–L, Anthony–T, R. Stanley–HB	EP-457	KLP-645, KBSCD-7000
4228	**White Dove** (Carter Stanley) C. Stanley–L, Elliott–T, R. Stanley–HB	45-5233, EP-456	KLP-645, GT-0016, KBSCD-7000
4229	**How Can We Thank Him** (Ruby Rakes) C. Stanley–L, R. Stanley–T, Elliott–B	45-5197, EP-455	KLP-645, SLP-384, KLP-1013, GT-0108, KBSCD-7000
4230	**Mother's Footsteps Guide Me On** (Ruby Rakes) C. Stanley–L, R. Stanley–T, Elliott–B	45-5233, EP-457	KLP-645, SLP-384, GT-0104, KBSCD-7000

590211 King session; producer: Bernie Pearlman
King Studio, Cincinnati, Ohio
February 11, 1959
Carter Stanley: g | Ralph Stanley: b | Al Elliott: m
Chubby Anthony: f | George Shuffler: sb

4231	**That Home Far Away** (Ruby Rakes) C. Stanley–L, R. Stanley–T, Elliott–B, Shuffler–BS	45-5197, EP-456	KLP-645, KLP-1013, GT-0062, KBSCD-7000
4232	**My Lord's Going to Set Me Free** (Ruby Rakes) C. Stanley–L, R. Stanley–T, Elliott–B, Shuffler–BS	EP-455	KLP-645, KLP-1013, GT-0062, KBSCD-7000
4233	**The Angel of Death** (Ruby Rakes) C. Stanley–L, R. Stanley–T, Elliott–B, Shuffler–BS	45-5441, EP-456	KLP-645, NLP-2112, KBSCD-7000

| 4234 | **Wings of Angels** (Ruby Rakes)
C. Stanley–L, R. Stanley–T, Elliott–B | EP-455 | KLP-645, SLP-384, GT-0108, KBSCD-7000 |
| 4235 | **Suwanee River Hoedown** (Ruby Rakes)
Instrumental | 45-5210, EP-467 | KLP-719, KBSCD-7000 |

590300 Starday session; producer: Stanley Brothers
Radio station WNER, Live Oak, Florida
ca. March 1959
Carter Stanley: g | Ralph Stanley: b | Bill Napier: m
Chubby Anthony: f | Al Elliott: sb

2918	**Choo Choo Comin'** (Newsome) C. Stanley–L, R. Stanley–T	587, SEP-107	SLP-106, NLP-2014, GT-0106, CCS-106/7, KBSCD-7000
2919	**Carolina Mountain Home** (Wright-Scarborough) C. Stanley–L, R. Stanley–T	565, SEP-107	SLP-106, NLP-2014, GT-0106, CCS-106/7, KBSCD-7000
2920	**Trust Each Other** (Ralph Stanley) C. Stanley–L, R. Stanley–T	438, SEP-107	SLP-106, NLP-2014, GT-0104, CCS-106/7, KBSCD-7000
2921	**Beneath the Maple** (Ralph Stanley–York) C. Stanley–L, R. Stanley–T	438, SEP-107	SLP-106, NLP-2014, GT-0108, CCS-106/7, KBSCD-7000, MERC-B0000534-02

590700 Starday session; producer: Stanley Brothers
Radio station WNER, Live Oak, Florida
ca. July 16, 1959
Carter Stanley: g | Ralph Stanley: b | Bill Napier: m
Chubby Anthony: f | Johnnie Z. Bonds: sb

2997	**Highway of Regret** (R. Stanley–Anthony) C. Stanley–L, R. Stanley–T, Elliott–B	466	SLP-106, NLP-2014, GT-0106, CCS-106/7, KBSCD-7000
2998	**A Little at a Time** (R. Stanley–Malone) C. Stanley–L, R. Stanley–T	494	SLP-106, NLP-2014, GT-0106, CCS-106/7, KBSCD-7000
2999	**Another Night** (Adkins) C. Stanley–L, R. Stanley–T	466	SLP-106, NLP-2014, GT-0106, CCS-106/7, KBSCD-7000
3000	**Ridin' That Midnight Train** (R Stanley) C. Stanley–L, R. Stanley–T	494, SEP-184	SLP-106, NLP-2014, GT-0106, CCS-106/7, KBSCD-7000, B0007883-02

590701 Blue Ridge session; producer: Stanley Brothers
Radio station WNER, Live Oak, Florida
ca. Summer 1959
Carter Stanley: g | Ralph Stanley: b | Bill Napier: m
Chubby Anthony: f | Johnnie Bonds (probably): sb

| 6215 | **Meet Me Tonight** (Stanley Brothers)
C. Stanley–L, R. Stanley–T | 514 | BCD-15681, B0007883-02 |
| 6216 | **Nobody's Business** (Stanley Brothers)
C. Stanley–L, R. Stanley–T | 514 | BCD-15681, B0007883-02 |

590712   Vanguard reissue of show, recorded by unknown
Newport Folk Festival, Newport, Rhode Island
July 12, 1959
Carter Stanley: g | Ralph Stanley: b | Bill Napier: m
Chubby Anthony: f | Lindy Clear: sb

    Introduction (by Oscar Brand)   VSD-77018

    Orange Blossom Special (Carter & Ralph Stanley)   VSD-77018
    C. Stanley–L, R. Stanley–T

    How Mountain Girls Can Love (Ruby Rakes)   VSD-77018
    C. Stanley–L, R. Stanley–T, Napier–B

    Model T [comedy routine]   VSD-77018
    Clear–L

    I'm a Man of Constant Sorrow (Carter Stanley)   VSD-77018
    R. Stanley–LV, C. Stanley–LC, Anthony–T, Napier–B

    Gathering Flowers for the Master's Bouquet (Marvin E. Baumgardner) VSD-77018
    C. Stanley–L, R. Stanley–T

    Choo Choo Coming (Newsome-York)   VSD-77018
    C. Stanley–L, R. Stanley–T

    All Aboard for Baltimore [comedy routine]   VSD-77018
    Clear–L

590914   King session; producer: SydNathan (4339 only) and Bernie Pearlman
King Studio, Cincinnati, Ohio
September 14, 1959
Carter Stanley: g | Ralph Stanley: b | Bill Napier: lg
George Shuffler: sb

4339	**Mountain Dew** (Scott Wiseman) C. Stanley–L, R. Stanley–T, Napier–B, Shuffler–BS	45-5347	KLP-690, SD-3003, KBSCD-7000
4340	**Sunny Side of the Mountain** (McAuliff-Gregory) C. Stanley–L, R. Stanley–T	45-5291	KLP-690, KLP-953, SD-3003, GD-5026, KBSCD-7000
4341	**Tragic Romance** (Grandpa Jones) C. Stanley–L, R. Stanley–T		KLP-690, GD-5026, KBSCD-7000
4342	**Shenandoah Waltz** (Moody-Wise) C. Stanley–L, R. Stanley–T	45-5291	KLP-690, KBSCD-7000
4343	**Next Sunday Darling Is My Birthday** (Mann-Smith) C. Stanley–L, R. Stanley–T	45-5355	KLP-690, KLP-1046, NLP-2078, SD-3003, KBSCD-7000
4344	**Sweet Thing** (Buddy Starcher) C. Stanley–L, R. Stanley–T	EP-467	KLP-690, KBSCD-7000

4345	**Sweeter Than the Flowers** (Rouse-Burns-Mann) C. Stanley–L, R. Stanley–T, Napier–B, Shuffler–BS	45-5355	KLP-690, KLP-953, KLP-1046, NLP-2078, GD-5026, KBSCD-7000
4346	**It's Raining Here This Morning** (Grandpa Jones) C. Stanley–L, R. Stanley–T, Shuffler–BS	EP-469	KLP-690, KLP-953, GD-5026, KBSCD-7000

590915	King session; producer: Bernie Pearlman King Studio, Cincinnati, Ohio September 15, 1959 Carter Stanley: g | Ralph Stanley: b | Bill Napier: lg George Shuffler: sb		
4347	**Shackles and Chains** (Jimmy Davis) C. Stanley–L, R. Stanley–T, Napier–B, Shuffler–BS		KLP-690, KLP-953, KBSCD-7000
4348	**Weeping Willow** (Traditional–P.D.) C. Stanley–L, R. Stanley–T, Napier–B, Shuffler–BS		KLP-690, GT-0105, KBSCD-7000
4349	**Old Rattler** (Traditional–P.D.) C. Stanley–L, R. Stanley–T, Napier–B, Shuffler–BS	45-5347	KLP-690, NLP-2078, GT-0105, KBSCD-7000
4350	**I'm a Man of Constant Sorrow** (Carter Stanley) R. Stanley–LV/TC, C. Stanley–LC, Napier–B, Shuffler–BS	45-5269, EP-468	KLP-690, SD-3003, GD-5026, KBSCD-7000, B0007883-02
4351	**My Main Trial Is Yet to Come** (Frank-King) C. Stanley–L, R. Stanley–T, Napier–B, Shuffler–BS	EP-462	KLP-698, KBSCD-7000
4352	**Mother Left Me Her Bible** (Esco Hankins) C. Stanley–L, R. Stanley–T, Napier–B, Shuffler–BS	45-5367, EP-462	KLP-698, GT-0016, KBSCD-7000
4353	**Jacob's Vision** (Ruby Rakes) C. Stanley–L, R. Stanley–T, Napier–B, Shuffler–BS	45-5582 EP-463	KLP-698, SLP-384, KLP-1013, GT-0016, KBSCD-7000, B0007883-02
4354	**I'll Not Be a Stranger** (Traditional–P.D.) C. Stanley–L, R. Stanley–T, Napier–B, Shuffler–BS	EP-461	KLP-698, KBSCD-7000
4355	**From the Manger to the Cross** (Odell McLeod) C. Stanley–L, R. Stanley–T, Napier–B, Shuffler–BS	EP-462	KLP-698, KBSCD-7000
4356	**Four Books in the Bible** (Odell McLeod) C. Stanley–L, R. Stanley–T, Napier–B, Shuffler–BS	EP-463	KLP-698, KBSCD-7000
4357	**Purple Robe** (Odell McLeod) R. Stanley–LV/TC, C. Stanley–LC, Napier–B, Shuffler–BS	EP-461	KLP-698, KBSCD-7000
4358	**When Jesus Beckons Me Home** (Gene Arnold) R. Stanley–LV/TC, C. Stanley–LC, Napier–B, Shuffler–BS	45-5313, EP-461	KLP-698, KBSCD-7000
4359	**Jordan** (Traditional–P.D.) C. Stanley–L, R. Stanley–T, Napier–B, Shuffler–BS	45-5441, EP-463	KLP-698, NLP-2112, GT-0016, KBSCD-7000
4360	**Pass Me Not** (Crosby-Doane) C. Stanley–L, R. Stanley–T, Napier–B, Shuffler–BS	45-5313, EP-461	KLP-698, NLP-2112, KBSCD-7000
4361	**Lonely Tombs** (Traditional–P.D.) C. Stanley–L, R. Stanley–T, Napier–B, Shuffler–BS	EP-463	KLP-698, KBSCD-7000

4362	**Over in the Glory Land** (Traditional–P.D.) C. Stanley–L, R. Stanley–T, Napier–B, Shuffler–BS	45-5367, EP-462	KLP-698, KLP-1013, NLP-2112, GT-0016, GT-0062, KBSCD-7000
4363	**How Far to Little Rock** (Ruby Rakes) Spoken exchanges by Carter and Ralph Stanley	45-5306	KLP-698, KLP-953, KLP-1046, SD-3003, KBSCD-7000, B0007883-02

600100	Starday session; producer: Stanley Brothers Radio station WNER, Live Oak, Florida ca. January 1960 Carter Stanley: g | Ralph Stanley: b | Bill Napier: lg Ralph Mayo: f | William "Bill" Randall Slaughter: sb		
3139	**A Few More Seasons** (Ralph Stanley) C. Stanley–L, R. Stanley–T, Napier–B, Mayo–BS	565, SEP-123	SLP-122, KLP-953, NLP-2037, CCS-106/7, KBSCD-7000
3140	**Where We'll Never Die** (Ralph & Peggy Stanley) C. Stanley–L, R. Stanley–T, Mayo–B	SEP-123	SLP-122, GT-0108, CCS-106/7, KBSCD-7000
3141	**In Heaven We'll Never Grow Old** (York) R. Stanley–LV/TC, C. Stanley–LC, Napier–B, Mayo–BS	SEP-123	SLP-122, GT-0062, CCS-106/7, KBSCD-7000
3142	**Mother No Longer Awaits Me** (Ralph Stanley) C. Stanley–L, R. Stanley–T	SEP-123	SLP-122, NLP-2037, GT-0107, CCS-106/7, KBSCD-7000

600300	County Records *Jim Walter Jamboree* programs, recorded by Samuel Candler Enterprises Atlanta, Georgia ca. March 1960 Carter Stanley: g | Ralph Stanley: b | Bill Napier: lg Chubby Anthony: f | Ralph Mayo: * f | George Shuffler: sb |	
	Theme C. Stanley–L, R. Stanley–T, Anthony (probably)–B	CO-780, REB-1115
	Roll in My Sweet Baby's Arms (P.D.) C. Stanley–L, R. Stanley–T, Anthony–B	CO-780, REB-1115
	A Few More Seasons (Stanley) C. Stanley–L, R. Stanley–T, Anthony–B, Napier–BS	CO-780, REB-1115
	Love Me Darling Just Tonight (Malone-Rakes) C. Stanley–L, R. Stanley–T	CO-780, REB-1115
	Black Mountain Blues (Keith) Instrumental	CO-780, REB-1115
	My Lord's Gonna Set Me Free (Rakes) C. Stanley–L, R. Stanley–T, Shuffler–BC/BSC, Napier–BS	CO-780, REB-1115
	How Mountain Girls Can Love (Rakes) C. Stanley–L, R. Stanley–T, Napier (probably)–B	CO-780, REB-1115
	Mississippi Sawyer (P.D.) Instrumental	CO-780, REB-1115

Orange Blossom Special (Rouse) C. Stanley—L, R. Stanley—T	CO-780, REB-1115
Daniel Prayed (Speer) C. Stanley—L, R. Stanley—T, Anthony—B, Napier—BS	CO-780, REB-1115
Shenandoah Waltz (Moody-Wise) C. Stanley—L, R. Stanley—T	CO-780, REB-1115
How Far to Little Rock (P.D.) Spoken exchange between Carter and Ralph Stanley	CO-780, REB-1115
Mother's Footsteps Guide Me On (Rakes) C. Stanley—L, R. Stanley—T, Anthony—B	CO-780, REB-1115
Pig in a Pen (Smith) C. Stanley—L, R. Stanley—T, Napier (probably)—B	CO-780, REB-1115
Cripple Creek (P.D.) Instrumental	CO-780, REB-1115
Theme C. Stanley—L, R. Stanley—T, Anthony—B	CO-780, REB-1115
Theme C. Stanley—L, R. Stanley—T, Anthony—B	CO-781, REB-1115
Uncle Pen (Monroe) C. Stanley—L, R. Stanley—T, Napier (probably)—B	CO-781, REB-1115
Little Glass of Wine (Stanley) C. Stanley—L, R. Stanley—T	CO-781, REB-1115
Midnight Ramble (Rakes) Instrumental	CO-781, REB-1115
Heaven (McSpadden) C. Stanley—L, R. Stanley—T, Shuffler—B, Napier—BS	CO-781, REB-1115
Don't Go Out Tonight (P.D.) C. Stanley—L, R. Stanley—T	CO-781, REB-1115
Fire on the Mountain (P.D.) Instrumental	CO-781, REB-1115
Carolina Mountain Home* (Wright-Scarborough) C. Stanley—L, R. Stanley—T	CO-781, REB-1115
Mother No Longer Awaits Me at Home* (Stanley) C. Stanley—L, R. Stanley—T	CO-781, REB-1115
He Will Set Your Fields on Fire* (P.D) C. Stanley—L, R. Stanley—T, Mayo—B, Napier—BS	CO-781, REB-1115
Big Tilda* (Stanley) Instrumental	CO-781, REB-1115

If We Never Meet Again* (Brumley)		CO-781, REB-1115
C. Stanley—L, R. Stanley—T, Mayo—B, Napier—BS		
Whoa Mule* (P.D.)		CO-781, REB-1115
Napier—L, R. Stanley—T, Mayo—B		
Theme		CO-781, REB-1115
C. Stanley—L, R. Stanley—T, Mayo—B		

600514 Vintage Collectors Club reissue of show, recorded by Mike Seeger and Jeremy Foster
Antioch College, Yellow Springs, Ohio
May 14, 1960
Carter Stanley: g | Ralph Stanley: b | Curley Lambert: m
Ralph Mayo: f | Lindy Clear: sb

How Mountain Girls Can Love		ZK-002
C. Stanley—L, R. Stanley—T, Lambert—B		
Sunny Side of the Mountain		ZK-002
C. Stanley—L, R. Stanley—T		
Cripple Creek / Cumberland Gap		ZK-002
Instrumental		
I Hear a Voice Callin'		ZK-002
R. Stanley—high lead, Lambert—low tenor, C. Stanley—B		
White Dove		ZK-002
C. Stanley—L, Lambert—T, R. Stanley—HB		
Uncle Pen		ZK-002
C. Stanley—L, R. Stanley—T, Lambert—B		
Cluck Ol' Hen		ZK-002
Instrumental		
John Henry		ZK-002
R. Stanley—LV/TC, C. Stanley—LC, Lambert—B		
Mountain Dew		ZK-002
C. Stanley—L, R. Stanley—T, Lambert—B		
Bound to Ride		SLP-1495, ZK-002
C. Stanley—L		
Little Birdie		ZK-002
R. Stanley—L		
Shake My Mother's Hand for Me		SLP-1487, ZK-002
C. Stanley—L, R. Stanley—T, Lambert—B		
Are You Afraid to Die		ZK-002
C. Stanley—L, R. Stanley—T, Lambert—B		
Pig in a Pen		ZK-002
C. Stanley—L, R. Stanley—T		

Home Sweet Home Instrumental		ZK-002
Don't Go Out Tonight C. Stanley–L, R. Stanley–T		ZK-002
Orange Blossom Special C. Stanley–L, R. Stanley–T		ZK-002

600515 Copper Creek reissue of show, recorded by Lamar Grier
New River Ranch, Rising Sun, Maryland
May 15, 1960
Carter Stanley: g | Ralph Stanley: b | Curley Lambert: m
Ralph Mayo: f | Lindy Clear: sb

Watermelon on the Vine (Traditional) Instrumental	CCSS-V1N2
Cacklin' Hen (Traditional) Instrumental	CCSS-V1N2
Please Help Me, I'm Falling (Hal Blair–Donald Robertson) Lambert–L	CCSS-V1N2
Turkey in the Straw / Mule Imitation (Traditional) Clear–L	CCSS-V1N2
Gonna Paint the Town (Ralph Stanley) C. Stanley–L, R. Stanley–T	CCSS-V1N2
Sunny Side of the Mountain (McAuliff-Gregory) C. Stanley–L, R. Stanley–T	CCSS-V1N2
Cripple Creek (Traditional) Instrumental	CCSS-V1N2
Mountain Dew (Scott Wiseman) C. Stanley–L, R. Stanley–T	CCSS-V1N2
How Far to Little Rock (Ruby Rakes) Spoken exchange between Carter and Ralph Stanley	CCSS-V1N2
I'm a Man of Constant Sorrow (Carter Stanley) R. Stanley–LV/TC, C. Stanley–LC, Lambert–B	CCSS-V1N2, ST-no #
Climate routine (Traditional) Spoken exchange between Carter and Ralph Stanley	CCSS-V1N2, ST-no #
Are You Afraid to Die? (Louvin–Louvin-Hill) C. Stanley–L, R. Stanley–T, Lambert–B	CCSS-V1N2, ST-no #
Black Mountain Blues (Leslie Keith) Instrumental	CCSS-V1N2, ST-no #
In Heaven We'll Never Grow Old (Traditional) R. Stanley–LV/TC, C. Stanley–LC, Lambert–B	CCSS-V1N2, ST-no #

Cumberland Gap (Traditional)   CCSS-V1N2, ST-no #
Instrumental

God Gave You to Me (Ralph Stanley)   CCSS-V1N2, ST-no #
C. Stanley—L, R. Stanley—T, Lambert—B

Songbook sales pitch   CCSS-V1N2
Spoken dialogue by C. Stanley

Don't Go Out Tonight   ST-no #
C. Stanley—L, R. Stanley—T

Little Glass of Wine   ST-no #
C. Stanley—L, R. Stanley—T

So Blue   ST-no #
C. Stanley—L, R. Stanley—T, Lambert—B

Uncle Pen   ST-no #
C. Stanley—L, R. Stanley—T, Lambert—B

Come All You Tenderhearted   ST-no #
C. Stanley—L

Mountain Dew   ST-no #
C. Stanley—L, R. Stanley—T

Baby Blue Eyes   ST-no #
Lambert—L

How Far to Little Rock   ST-no #
Spoken exchanges by Carter and Ralph Stanley

Let the Church Roll On   ST-no #
C. Stanley—L, R. Stanley—T, Lambert—B, Mayo—BS

He'll Set Your Fields on Fire   SLP1487, ST-no #
C. Stanley—L, R. Stanley—T, Lambert—B, Mayo—BS

Paul and Silas   ST-no #
C. Stanley—L, R. Stanley—T, Lambert—B, Mayo—BS

The Cry from the Cross   ST-no #
C. Stanley—L, R. Stanley—T, Lambert—B

John Henry   ST-no #
R. Stanley—LV/TC, C Stanley—LC, Lambert—B

No School Bus in Heaven}   ST-no #
C. Stanley—L, Lambert—T, R Stanley—high baritone

Mother's Not Dead   SLP-1495
C. Stanley—L, R. Stanley—T

Roll in My Sweet Baby's Arms
C. Stanley–L, R. Stanley–T, Lambert–B   SLP-1487

Knoxville Girl
C. Stanley–L, R. Stanley–T   SLP-1487

600600 Starday session; producer: Stanley Brothers
Magnum Studio, 5610 Lovegrove Road, Jacksonville, Florida
ca. June 1960
Carter Stanley: g | Ralph Stanley: b | Curley Lambert: lg (* m)
Ralph Mayo: f († lg) | James Austin "Audie" Webster: sb

3333 **If I Lose** (Ralph Stanley)   546, SEP-184   SLP-201, NLP-2037, GT-0106, CCS-106/7, KBSCD-7000
C. Stanley–L, R. Stanley–T, Lambert–B

3334 **Little Maggie** (Stanley-York)   522, SEP-184   SLP-201, MGW-12327, KLP-953,NLP-2037, SD-3003,
R. Stanley–L   GD-5026, CCS-106/7, KBSCD-7000, MERC-B0000534-02,
B0007883-02

3335 **God Gave You to Me** (Ralph Stanley)   522   SLP-201, GT-0107, CCS-106/7, KBSCD-7000, B0007883-02
C. Stanley–L, R. Stanley–T, Lambert–B

3336 **Don't Go Out Tonight** (York)   546   SLP-201, NLP-2037, GD-5026, CCS-106/7, KBSCD-7000
C. Stanley–L, R. Stanley–T

3337 **The Darkest Hour Is Just Before Dawn** (Ralph Stanley)   SLP-122, NLP-2037, GT-0107, CCS-106/7,
C. Stanley–L, R. Stanley–T, Lambert–B   KBSCD-7000

3338 **Rank Stranger***† (York)   506, SEP-184   SLP-122, KLP-953, NLP-2037, NLP-2112, GT-0016,
C. Stanley–L, R. Stanley–T, Lambert–B   CCS-106/7, KBSCD-7000, B0007883-02, M-19493

3339 **Let the Church Roll On***† (York)   SLP-122, CCS-106/7, KBSCD-7000
C. Stanley–L, R. Stanley–T, Lambert–B, Mayo–BS

3340 **Rock of Ages** (York)   SLP-122, GT-0104, CCS-106/7, KBSCD-7000
C. Stanley–L, R. Stanley–T, Lambert–B, Mayo–BS

3341 **I Saw the Light** (York)   SLP-122, CCS-106/7, GT-0062, KBSCD-7000
C. Stanley–L, R. Stanley–T, Lambert–B, Mayo–BS

3342 **What a Friend** (York)   SLP-122, CCS-106/7, GT-0062, KBSCD-7000
C. Stanley–L, R. Stanley–T, Lambert–B

3343 **Gathering Flowers for the Master's Bouquet** (York)   506   SLP-122, KLP-953, GT-0016, CCS-106/7, KBSCD-7000
C. Stanley–L, R. Stanley–T

3344 **I'm Ready to Go*** (York)   SLP-122, GT-0104, CCS-106/7, KBSCD-7000
C. Stanley–L, R. Stanley–T, Lambert–B

600601   Starday session; producer: unknown
Possibly WNER, Live Oak, Florida
ca. June 1960
Carter Stanley: g | Ralph Stanley: b | Curley Lambert (possibly): m
Ralph Mayo (possibly): f | unknown: sb

2817   **Christmas Is Near** (Ralph Stanley)   SLP-123, KLP-811, K4CD-0950
C. Stanley–L, R. Stanley–T, Mayo (possibly)–B

600711a   King session; engineer: Charles L. "Chuck" Seitz Jr.
King Studio, Cincinnati, Ohio
July 11, 1960
Carter Stanley: g | Ralph Stanley: b | Vernon Derrick: f
Curley Lambert: lg (sb on 4741 and 4744) | George Shuffler: sb (lg on 4741 and 4744) | Gene Redd: drums

4737   **Let Me Love You One More Time** (Ralph Stanley)   EP-468   KLP-719, KLP-1046, GD-5026, KBSCD-7000
C. Stanley–L, R. Stanley–T, Lambert–B

4738   **Little Benny** (Traditional–P.D.)   45-5415, EP-468   KLP-719, KLP-1046, GD-5026, KBSCD-7000
C. Stanley–L, Lambert–T, R. Stanley–HB, Shuffler–BS

4739   **Old Love Letters** (Stanley–Bence)   45-5415, EP-469   KLP-719, KLP-1046, SD-3003, GD-5026, KBSCD-7000
C. Stanley–L, R. Stanley–T

4740   **Daybreak in Dixie** (Ralph Stanley)   45-5384, EP-467   KLP-719, GD-5026, KBSCD-7000
Instrumental

4741   **Wildwood Flower** (Arr. Carter Family)   EP-469   KLP-719, KLP-953, KBSCD-7000
Instrumental

4742   **Let Me Rest** (Ralph & Carter Stanley)   EP-467   KLP-719, KBSCD-7000, B0007883-02
C. Stanley–L, R. Stanley–T, Lambert–B

4743   **Are You Tired of Me, Darling** (Traditional– P.D.)   EP-468   KLP-719, KBSCD-7000
C. Stanley–L, R. Stanley–T, Lambert–B, Shuffler–BS

4744   **Finger Poppin' Time** (Hank Ballard)   45-5384, EP-469   KLP-719, KBSCD-7000
C. Stanley–L, R. Stanley–T

600711b   Starday session; producer: Wayne Rainey
Home of Wayne Rainey, Cincinnati, Ohio
July 11, 1960
Carter Stanley: g | Curley Lambert: lg |
George Shuffler: sb

Rank Stranger   KBSCD-7000
C. Stanley–L, R. Stanley–T, Lambert–B, Shuffler–BS

3389   **Come All Ye Tenderhearted** (York)   587   SLP-201, NLP-2037, GT-0107, CCS-106/7, KBSCD-7000
C. Stanley–L, R. Stanley–T, Lambert–B, Shuffler–BS

610115   King session; engineer: Chuck Seitz
King Studio, Cincinnati, Ohio
January 15, 1961
Carter Stanley: g | Ralph Stanley: b | Curley Lambert: m (lg on 10587)
Art Stamper: f | George Shuffler: sb

10587	**The Window up Above** (George Jones)	45-5460	KLP-772, KBSCD-7000
	C. Stanley–L, R. Stanley–T		
10588	**Lover's Quarrel** (Ralph & Carter Stanley)		KLP-772, KBSCD-7000
	C. Stanley–L, R. Stanley–T		
10589	**The Story of the Lawson Family** (Ralph & Carter Stanley)		KLP-772, KBSCD-7000
	C. Stanley–L, R. Stanley–T		
10590	**Hey! Hey! Hey!** (Ralph & Carter Stanley)		KLP-772, KBSCD-7000
	C. Stanley–L, R. Stanley–T		
10591	**The Wild Side of Life** (W. Warren–A. Carter)	45-5460	KLP-772, KLP-1046, GD-5026, KBSCD-7000
	C. Stanley–L, R. Stanley–T, Lambert–B		
10592	**Jenny Lynn** (R.alph & Carte.r Stanley)		KLP-772, KBSCD-7000
	Instrumental		
10593	**What About You** (Wright-Anglin)		KLP-924, OHCS-323, KBSCD-7000
	C. Stanley–L, Lambert–T, R. Stanley–HB		
10594	**Little Willie** (Arr. Ralph & Carter Stanley)		KLP-772, KBSCD-7000
	R. Stanley–L		
10595	Big Tilda (Ralph Stanley)		KBSCD-7000
	Instrumental		
10596	**Wild Bill Jones** (P.D.)		KLP-772, KBSCD-7000
	R. Stanley–L		

610116   King session; engineer: E. Smith
King Studio, Cincinnati, Ohio
January 16, 1961
Carter Stanley: g | Ralph Stanley: b | Curley Lambert: m
Art Stamper: f | George Shuffler: electric bass

10597	**You're Still to Blame** (Carter Stanley)		OHCS-323, KBSCD-7000
	C. Stanley–L, R. Stanley–T, Lambert–B		
10598	**I'll Take the Blame** (Carter Stanley)	45-5518	KLP-772, KBSCD-7000
	C. Stanley–L, R. Stanley–T, Lambert–B		
10599	**I'll Just Go Away** (Carter Stanley)	45-6236	OHCS-323, KBSCD-7000
	C. Stanley–L, R. Stanley–T, Lambert–B		
	Steel Guitar Rag		KBSCD-7000
	Instrumental		

10600	**I'd Worship You** (Ralph Stanley) C. Stanley–L, R. Stanley–T	45-5518	KLP-772, KBSCD-7000
10601	**Just Dreamin'** (Carter Stanley) C. Stanley–L, Lambert–T, R. Stanley–HB		KLP-791, KBSCD-7000
10602	**The Drunken Driver** (Paul Westmoreland) R. Stanley–L		KLP-791, KLP-1046, KBSCD-7000
10603	**Little Joe** (Traditional–P.D.) C. Stanley–L		KLP-791, KBSCD-7000
10604	**Handsome Molly** (Traditional–P.D.) C. Stanley–L		KLP-791, KBSCD-7000

610203	StanleyTone reissue of show, recorded by Mike Seeger University of Chicago Folk Festival, Chicago, Illinois February 3, 1961 Carter Stanley: g | Ralph Stanley: b | Curley Lambert: m Vernon Derrick: f | James Wilson "Chick" Stripling: sb	
	Old Joe Clark Instrumental	ST-5003
	Orange Blossom Special C. Stanley–L, R. Stanley–T	ST-5003
	I Know What It Means to Be Lonesome Lambert–L	ST-5003
	Cripple Creek Instrumental	ST-5003
	Gonna Paint the Town C. Stanley–L, R. Stanley–T	ST-5003
	The Window up Above C. Stanley–L, R. Stanley–T	ST-5003
	Sunny Side of the Mountain C. Stanley–L, R. Stanley–T	ST-5003
	Comedy with Chick Stripling Spoken dialogue by Chick Stripling	ST-5003
	Chicken Reel Spoken dialogue by Chick Stripling	ST-5003
	Rank Strangers C. Stanley–L, R. Stanley–T, Lambert–B	ST-5003
	How Far to Little Rock Spoken exchanges by Carter and Ralph Stanley	ST-5003
	Old Joe Clark Instrumental	ST-5003

610204   StanleyTone reissue of show, recorded by Mike Seeger
University of Chicago Folk Festival, Chicago, Illinois
February 4, 1961
Carter Stanley: g | Ralph Stanley: b | Curley Lambert: m
Vernon Derrick: f | Chick Stripling: sb

Turkey in the Straw Instrumental	ST-5003
Black Mountain Blues Instrumental	ST-5003
Wreck of the Old 97 Lambert—L	ST-5003
Jack and May C. Stanley—L, R. Stanley—T	ST-5003
Cumberland Gap Instrumental	ST-5003
Jenny Lynn Instrumental	ST-5003
The Story of the Lawson Family C. Stanley—L, R. Stanley—T	ST-5003
Comedy with Chick Stripling Spoken dialogue by Chick Stripling	ST-5003
Johnson Had an Old Gray Mule Stripling—L	ST-5003
Chicken Reel Instrumental	ST-5003
Nine Pound Hammer C. Stanley—L, R. Stanley—T	ST-5003
I'm a Man of Constant Sorrow R. Stanley—LV/HBC, C. Stanley—LC, Lambert—T	ST-5003
Come All You Tenderhearted C. Stanley—L	FA-2390, ST-5003

610205   StanleyTone reissue of show, recorded by Mike Seeger
University of Chicago Folk Festival, Chicago, Illinois
February 5, 1961
Carter Stanley: g | Ralph Stanley: b (* m) | Curley Lambert: m
Vernon Derrick: f | Michael "Mike" Seeger: b

Sally Goodin' Instrumental	ST-5003
Long Journey Home C. Stanley—L, R. Stanley—T	ST-5003

East Virginia Blues* C. Stanley–L, R. Stanley–T		ST-5003	
Big Tilda Instrumental		ST-5003	
Dream of a Miner's Child C. Stanley–L	.	ST-5003	
Angel Band C. Stanley–L, R. Stanley–T, Lambert–B		ST-5003	
Wicked Path of Sin C. Stanley–L, R. Stanley–T, Lambert–B, Derrick–BS		ST-5003	
Little Birdie R. Stanley–L		FA-2390, ST-5003	
How Far to Little Rock Spoken exchanges by Carter and Ralph Stanley		ST-5003	
Rabbit in a Log C. Stanley–L, R. Stanley–T		FA-2390, ST-5003	

610207 King session; producer/engineer: Ed Smith
King Studio, Cincinnati, Ohio
February 7, 1961
Carter Stanley: g | Ralph Stanley: b | Curley Lambert: m
Vernon Derrick: f | Chick Stripling: sb

10613	**Little Bessie** (Traditional) C. Stanley–L, R. Stanley–T	45-5494, EP-479	KLP-750, GT-0084, K4CD-0950
10614	**Mother's Only Sleeping** (Bill Monroe) C. Stanley–L, R. Stanley–T		KLP-750, GT-0062, GT-0084, K4CD-0950
10615	**Old Country Church** (Traditional) C. Stanley–L, R. Stanley–T, Lambert–B, Derrick–BS		KLP-750, GT-0084, K4CD-0950,
10616	**Campin' in Canaan Land** (Traditional) C. Stanley–L, R. Stanley–T, Lambert–B, Derrick–BS	EP-479	KLP-750, KLP-1013, GT-0084, K4CD-0950
10617	**Mother Call My Name in Prayer** (Davis-Pierce) C. Stanley–L, R. Stanley–T, Lambert–B, Derrick–BS	EP-479	KLP-750, GT-0084, K4CD-0950
10618	**Working on a Building** (Bowles-Noyes) R. Stanley–LV/TC, C. Stanley–LC, Lambert–B, Derrick–BS	EP-479	KLP-750, GT-0084, K4CD-0950
10619	**Somebody Touched Me** (Ahmet Ertegun) C. Stanley–L, R. Stanley–T, Lambert–B, Derrick–BS		KLP-750, K4CD-0950
10620	**Dying a Sinner's Death** (Roy Acuff) C. Stanley–L, R. Stanley–T, Lambert–B	EP-480	KLP-750, K4CD-0950

610208   King session; producer/engineer: Ed Smith
King Studio, Cincinnati, Ohio
February 8, 1961
Carter Stanley: g | Ralph Stanley: b | Curley Lambert: m
Vernon Derrick: f | Chick Stripling: sb

10621	**Village Church Yard** (Ralph Stanley) C. Stanley—L, R. Stanley—T	45-5494	KLP-750, GT-0016, GT-0084, K4CD-0950
10622	**A Few More Years** (Ralph Stanley) C. Stanley—L, R. Stanley—T, Lambert—B	EP-480	KLP-750, GT-0084, K4CD-0950
10623	**Kneel at the Cross** (Charles Moody) C. Stanley—L, R. Stanley—T, Lambert—B, Derrick—BS	EP-480	KLP-750, GT-0084, K4CD-0950
10624	**My Sinful Past** (Carter Stanley) C. Stanley—L, R. Stanley—T, Lambert—B, Derrick—BS	EP-480	KLP-750, KLP-1013, GT-0084, K4CD-0950
	How Mountain Girls Can Love (R. Rakes) C. Stanley—L, R. Stanley—T		KLP-719 **, K4CD-0950 **this master released on the stereo version of the album

610521   Copper Creek reissue of show, recorded by Lamar Grier
New River Ranch, Rising Sun, Maryland
May 21, 1961
Carter Stanley: g | Ralph Stanley: b | George Shuffler: lg (* sb)
Jack Cooke: sb († g)

	Wild Side of Life (Wm. Warren—Arlie Carter) C. Stanley—L, R. Stanley—T	CCSS-V1N1
	Long Black Veil*† (Marijohn Wilkins—Danny Dill) Cooke—L	CCSS-V1N1
	Intro Spoken introduction by George Shuffler	CCSS-V1N1
	Little Benny (Traditional) C. Stanley—L, R. Stanley—T	CCSS-V1N1
	How Mountain Girls Can Love (Ruby Rakes) C. Stanley—L, R. Stanley—T	CCSS-V1N1
	I'm a Man of Constant Sorrow (Carter Stanley) R. Stanley—LV/TC, C. Stanley—LC, Shuffler—B	CCSS-V1N1
	Little Joe (Traditional) C. Stanley—L	CCSS-V1N1
	Knoxville Girl (Traditional) C. Stanley—L, R. Stanley—T	CCSS-V1N1
	Little Maggie (Traditional) R. Stanley—L	CCSS-V1N1

Home Sweet Home (Traditional) Instrumental	CCSS-V1N1
Don't Go Out Tonight (Traditional) C. Stanley–L, R. Stanley–T	CCSS-V1N1
Sunny Side of the Mountain (McAuliff-Gregory) C. Stanley–L, R. Stanley–T	CCSS-V1N1
Keep a Memory (Carter Stanley) C. Stanley–L, R. Stanley–T	CCSS-V1N1
Little Bessie (Traditional) C. Stanley–L, R. Stanley–T	CCSS-V1N1
Clinch Mountain Backstep (Ruby Rakes) Instrumental	CCSS-V1N1
Long Journey Home (Traditional) C. Stanley–L, R. Stanley–T	CCSS-V1N1
In Heaven We'll Never Grow Old (Traditional) R. Stanley–LV/TC, C. Stanley–LC, Shuffler–B	CCSS-V1N1
Rank Strangers (Traditional) C. Stanley–L, R. Stanley–T, Shuffler–B	CCSS-V1N1
If I Lose (Traditional) C. Stanley–L, R. Stanley–T, Shuffler–B	CCSS-V1N1

610528 Copper Creek reissue of show, recorded by Lamar Grier
Oak Leaf Park, Luray, Virginia
May 28, 1961
Carter Stanley: g | Ralph Stanley: b | George Shuffler: lg
unknown: sb

Riding That Midnight Train (R. Stanley) C. Stanley–L, R. Stanley–T	CCSS-V2N2
On Top of Old Smokey (Traditional) Shuffler–L	CCSS-V2N2
Steel Guitar Rag (L. McAuliffe) Instrumental	CCSS-V2N2
Old Love Letters (Stanley–Bence) C. Stanley–L, R. Stanley–T	CCSS-V2N2
If I Lose (R. Stanley) C. Stanley–L, R. Stanley–T, Shuffler–B	CCSS-V2N2
Big Tilda (R. Stanley) Instrumental	CCSS-V2N2
Shenandoah Waltz (Moody-Wise) C. Stanley–L, R. Stanley–T	CCSS-V2N2

Propaganda routine (Traditional)	CCSS-V2N2
Spoken exchanges by Carter and Ralph Stanley	
I Saw the Light (H. Williams)	CCSS-V2N2
C. Stanley–L, R. Stanley–T, Shuffler–B	
Jordan (Traditional)	CCSS-V2N2
C. Stanley–L, R. Stanley–T, Shuffler–BS	
A Few More Years (R. Stanley)	CCSS-V2N2
C. Stanley–L, R. Stanley–T, Shuffler–B	
Mountain Dew (S. Wiseman)	CCSS-V2N2
C. Stanley–L, R. Stanley–T	
Sunny Side of the Mountain (McAuliff-Gregory)	CCSS-V2N2
C. Stanley–L, R. Stanley–T	
Clinch Mountain Backstep (R. Rakes)	CCSS-V2N2
Instrumental	

610618   Rebel Records reissue of show, recorded by unknown
Watermelon Park, Berryville, Virginia
June 18, 1961
Carter Stanley: g | Ralph Stanley: b | Al Elliott: m | George Shuffler: lg
unknown: sb

If I Lose	SLP-1495
C. Stanley–L, R. Stanley–T, Elliott–B	
Rank Stranger	SLP-1495
C. Stanley–L, R. Stanley–T, Elliott–B, Shuffler–BS	
A Few More Years	SLP-1495
C. Stanley–L, Elliott–T, R. Stanley–HB, Shuffler–BS	
Little Benny	SLP-1495
C. Stanley–L, Elliott–T, R. Stanley–HB	
I'm a Man of Constant Sorrow	SLP-1495
R. Stanley–LV/TC, C. Stanley–LC, Shuffler–B	

610704   Time Life reissue of show, recorded by Mike Seeger
Oak Leaf Park, Luray, Virginia
July 4, 1961
Carter Stanley: g | Bobby Smith: g | Anthony Paul "Tony" Ellis: b | William Smith "Bill" Monroe: m
Billy Baker: f | : Bessie Lee Mauldin: sb

Sugar Coated Love (A. Butler)	B0007883-02
Stanley–L, Monroe–T	

610720 King session; engineer: Chuck Seitz Jr.
King Studio, Cincinnati, Ohio
July 20, 1961
Carter Stanley: g | Ralph Stanley: b | Al Elliott: m
Chubby Anthony: f | George Shuffler: lg and sb (dubbed)

10912	**There Is a Trap** (Bill J. Lindsey) C. Stanley–L, R. Stanley–T	45-5557	KLP-791, SD-3003, K4CD-0950
10913	**I See Through You** (F. Lidell–B. Ledley) C. Stanley–L, R. Stanley–T	45-5869	KLP-924, OHCS-323, K4CD-0950
10914	**Thy Burdens Are Greater Than Mine** (Pee Wee King) C. Stanley–L, R. Stanley–T	45-5582	KLP-791, NLP-2112, GT-0016, K4CD-0950
10915	**Fast Express** (Jim Scott) C. Stanley–L, R. Stanley–T	45-5557	KLP-791, K4CD-0950

610826 StanleyTone reissue of show, recorded by Leon Kagarise
New River Ranch, Rising Sun, Maryland
August 26, 1961
Carter Stanley: g | Ralph Stanley: b | Carl Chatzky (aka Carl Hawkins): m | George Shuffler: lg
Jack Cooke: sb

Steel Guitar Rag Instrumental	ST-5002
Old Love Letters C. Stanley–L, R. Stanley–T	ST-5002
Riding That Midnight Train C. Stanley–L, R. Stanley–T	ST-5002
Molly and Tenbrooks Cooke–L	ST-5002
If I Lose C. Stanley–L, R. Stanley–T, Shuffler–B	ST-5002
Jordan C. Stanley–L, R. Stanley–T, Shuffler–BS	ST-5002
I'm on My Way Back to the Old Home R. Stanley–L, Cooke–T	ST-5002
Clinch Mountain Backstep Instrumental	ST-5002
God Gave You to Me C. Stanley–L, R. Stanley–T, Shuffler–B	ST-5002
Willy Roy Shuffler–L	ST-5002

How Mountain Girls Can Love C. Stanley–L, R. Stanley–T, Shuffler–B	ST-5002	
Next Sunday Darling Is My Birthday C. Stanley–L, R. Stanley–T	ST-5002	
Happy Birthday Shuffler–L, and others	ST-5002	
The Window up Above C. Stanley–L, R. Stanley–T	ST-5002	
The White Dove C. Stanley–L, Shuffler–T, R. Stanley–HB	ST-5002	
Used to Be Cooke–L	ST-5002	
I'm a Man of Constant Sorrow R. Stanley–LV/TC, C. Stanley–LC, Shuffler–B	ST-5002	
Rank Strangers C. Stanley–L, R. Stanley–T, Shuffler–B	ST-5002	
On Top of Old Smoky Shuffler–L	ST-5002	
A Few More Years C. Stanley–L, Shuffler–T, R. Stanley–HB	ST-5002	
Pretty Polly R. Stanley–L	ST-5002	
Daybreak in Dixie Instrumental	ST-5002	
How Far to Little Rock Spoken exchanges by Carter and Ralph Stanley	ST-5002	
Cumberland Gap Instrumental	ST-5002	

610922 King session; engineer: Chuck Seitz
King Studio, Cincinnati, Ohio
September 22, 1961
Carter Stanley: g | Ralph Stanley: b | George Shuffler: lg
Chubby Anthony: f (sb overdubbed on 10972 and 10973)

10971	**I'm Only Human** (Jimmy Wells) C. Stanley–L, R. Stanley–T	45-5637	KLP-791, K4CD-0950
10972	**String, Eraser, and Blotter** (Long-Speca-Eckler) C. Stanley–L, R. Stanley–T, Anthony–B	45-5629	KLP-791, K4CD-0950

| 10973 | **Keep Them Cold Icy Fingers off Me** (John Lair) | 45-5637 | KLP-791, K4CD-0950 |
| | C. Stanley–L, R. Stanley–T, Shuffler–B | | |

| 10974 | **Still Trying to Get to Little Rock** (Ralph Stanley) | 45-5629 | KLP-791, NLP-2078, GD-5026, K4CD-0950 |
| | Spoken exchange between Carter and Ralph Stanley | | |

620304 Rebel Records reissue of show, recorded by Pete Kuykendall
Glen Echo (home of Bill Clifton), Charlottesville, Virginia
March 4, 1962
Carter Stanley: g | Ralph Stanley: b | George Shuffler: lg
Chick Stripling: sb

| | **Let Us Be Lovers Again** | SLP-1487 |
| | C. Stanley–L, R. Stanley–T | |

| | **Dream of a Miner's Child** | SLP-1487 |
| | C. Stanley–L | |

620317 Copper Creek reissue of show, recorded by Nancy Decker for the Oberlin College Folksong Club
Wilder Lounge, Oberlin College, Oberlin, Ohio
March 17, 1962
Carter Stanley: g | Ralph Stanley: b | George Shuffler: lg
Chick Stripling: sb

| | **John Henry** (Traditional) | CCLP-0101 |
| | C. Stanley–L, R. Stanley–T, Shuffler–B | |

| | **Propaganda routine** (Traditional) | CCLP-0101 |
| | Spoken exchanges by Carter Stanley and Chick Stripling | |

| | **Katy Cline** (Traditional) | CCLP-0101 |
| | C. Stanley–L, R. Stanley–T | |

| | **How Mountain Girls Can Love** | OCF-42-756 |
| | C. Stanley–L, R. Stanley–T | |

| | **Long Journey Home** (Traditional) | CCLP-0101 |
| | Instrumental | |

620502 King session; producer: Harold "Hal" G. Neely; engineer: Chuck Seitz
King Studio, Cincinnati, Ohio
May 2, 1962
Carter Stanley: g | Ralph Stanley: b | George Shuffler: lg
Ralph Mayo: f | Chick Stripling: sb

| 11175 | **Where We'll Never Grow Old** (Jab. C. Moore) | | KLP-805, KLP-1013, K4CD-0950 |
| | C. Stanley–L, R. Stanley–T, Mayo–B, Shuffler–BS | | |

| 11176 | **When He Reached Down His Hand for Me** (A. E. Brumley–G. E. Wright) | | KLP-805, K4CD-0950 |
| | C. Stanley–L, R. Stanley–T, Mayo–B, Shuffler–BS | | |

| 11177 | **Paul and Silas** (Ralph Stanley) | 45-5754 | KLP-805, GT-0016, K4CD-0950 |
| | C. Stanley–L, R. Stanley–T, Mayo–B, Shuffler–BS | | |

| 11178 | **Who Will Sing for Me** (Carter Stanley) | 45-5708 | KLP-805, KLP-1013, GT-0016, K4CD-0950, B0007883-02 |
| | C. Stanley–L, R. Stanley–T, Mayo–B, Shuffler–BS | | |

| 11179 | **I'll Fly Away** (Albert E. Brumley) | | KLP-805, GT-0016, K4CD-0950 |
| | C. Stanley–L, R. Stanley–T, Mayo–B, Shuffler–BS | | |

| 11180 | **Drinking from the Fountain** (Ralph Stanley) | 45-5708 | KLP-805, GT-0016, K4CD-0950 |
| | R. Stanley–LV/TC, C. Stanley–LC, Mayo–B, Shuffler–BS | | |

| 11181 | **Leaning on the Everlasting Arms** (Arr. E. A. Hoffman–A. J. Showalter) | | KLP-805, K4CD-0950 |
| | C. Stanley–L, R. Stanley–T, Mayo–B, Shuffler–BS | | |

620503 King session; producer: Hal Neely; engineer: Chuck Seitz
King Studio, Cincinnati, Ohio
May 3, 1962
Carter Stanley: g | Ralph Stanley: b | George Shuffler: lg
Ralph Mayo: f | Chick Stripling: sb

| 11182 | **Memories of Mother** (Ralph and Carter Stanley) | 45-5754 | KLP-805, K4CD-0950 |
| | C. Stanley–L, R. Stanley–T, Mayo–B, Shuffler–BS | | |

| 11183 | **Heaven's Light Is Shining on Me** | | KLP-805, K4CD-0950 |
| | C. Stanley–L, R. Stanley–T, Mayo–B, Shuffler–BS | | |

| 11184 | **Let Me Walk, Lord, by Your Side** (Ralph and Carter Stanley) | | KLP-805, K4CD-0950 |
| | C. Stanley–L, R. Stanley–T, Mayo–B, Shuffler–BS | | |

| 11185 | **Harbor of Love** (Carter Stanley) | | KLP-805, K4CD-0950 |
| | C. Stanley–L, R. Stanley–T, Mayo–B, Shuffler–BS | | |

| 11186 | **We Shall Rise** (J. E. Thomas) | | KLP-805, K4CD-0950 |
| | C. Stanley–L, R. Stanley–T, Mayo–B, Shuffler–BS | | |

| 11187 | **(Dear Girl) Can You Forgive** (Carter Stanley) | | KLP-864, GT-0103, K4CD-0950 |
| | C. Stanley–L, R. Stanley–T, Shuffler–BS | | |

| 11188 | **It's Alright If That's the Way You Feel** (Ralph Stanley) | | K4CD-0950 |
| | C. Stanley–L, R. Stanley–T, Shuffler–B | | |

| 11193 | **Drunkard's Dream** (Carter Stanley) | 45-5674 | KLP-864, GT-0103, K4CD-0950 |
| | C. Stanley–L, R. Stanley–T, Shuffler–BS | | |

| 11194 | **I Just Came from Your Wedding** (Ralph and Carter Stanley) | 45-5688 | KLP-864, GT-0103, K4CD-0950 |
| | C. Stanley–L, Shuffler–T, R. Stanley–HB | | |

| 11195 | **Mama Don't Allow** (Traditional) | 45-5688 | GT-0105, K4CD-0950 |
| | C. Stanley–L | | |

620504	King session; producer: Hall Neely; engineer: Chuck Seitz		
	King Studio, Cincinnati, Ohio		
	May 4, 1962		
	Carter Stanley: g | Ralph Stanley: b | George Shuffler: lg		
	Ralph Mayo: f | Chick Stripling: sb		
11196	**Chickie's Old Gray Mule** (Traditional)		KLP-924, GT-0105, K4CD-0950
	Stripling—L		
11197	**If We Never Meet Again** (Albert E. Brumley)		KLP-805, K4CD-0950
	C. Stanley—L, R. Stanley—T, Mayo—B, Shuffler—BS		
11198	**Hand in Hand with Jesus** (Oatman-Huffstutler)		KLP-805, K4CD-0950
	C. Stanley—L, R. Stanley—T, Mayo—B, Shuffler—BS		
11199	**My Deceitful Heart** (Shorty Long—Johnny Specca)	45-5674	GT-0106, K4CD-0950
	C. Stanley—L, R. Stanley—T		

620829	Copper Creek reissue of show, recorded by Eric Thompson	
	Ash Grove, Hollywood, California	
	August 29, 1962	
	Carter Stanley: g | Ralph Stanley: b | Curley Lambert: m	
	Vernon Derrick: f | Roger Bush: sb	
	How Mountain Girls Can Love (Ruby Rakes)	CCSS-V3N2
	C. Stanley—L, R. Stanley—T	
	The Coupon Song (Traditional—P.D.)	CCSS-V3N2
	Lambert—L	
	Clinch Mountain Backstep (Ruby Rakes)	CCSS-V3N2
	Instrumental	
	Let Me Love You One More Time (R. Stanley)	CCSS-V3N2
	C. Stanley—L, R. Stanley—T, Lambert—B	
	The Flood (Carter & Ralph Stanley)	CCSS-V3N2
	C. Stanley—L, R. Stanley—T	
	Turkey in the Straw (Traditional—P.D.)	CCSS-V3N2
	Instrumental	
	The Lonesome River (Carter Stanley)	CCSS-V3N2
	C. Stanley—L, Lambert—T, R. Stanley—HB	
	John Henry (Traditional—P.D.)	CCSS-V3N2
	C. Stanley—L, R. Stanley—T, Lambert—B	
	The Wild Side of Life (W. Warren—A. Carter)	CCSS-V3N2
	C. Stanley—L, R. Stanley—T, Lambert—B	
	The White Dove (Carter Stanley)	CCSS-V3N2
	C. Stanley—L, Lambert—T, R. Stanley—HB	

Hard Times (Ralph Stanley) Instrumental	CCSS-V3N2
Don't Go Out Tonight (Traditional–P.D.) C. Stanley–L, R. Stanley–T	CCSS-V3N2
How Far to Little Rock (Ruby Rakes) Spoken exchanges by Carter and Ralph Stanley	CCSS-V3N2
Cripple Creek (Traditional–P.D.) Instrumental	CCSS-V3N2

620830   Copper Creek reissue of show, recorded by Eric Thompson
Ash Grove, Hollywood, California
August 30, 1962
Carter Stanley: g | Ralph Stanley: b | Curley Lambert: m
Vernon Derrick: f | Roger Bush: sb

Cluck Old Hen Instrumental	SLP-1487
Working on a Building R. Stanley–LV/TC, C. Stanley–LC, Lambert–B	SLP-1487
Late Last Night (Traditional) C. Stanley–L, R. Stanley–T, Lambert–B	CCSS-V2N4
Little Benny (Traditional) C. Stanley–L, Lambert–T, R. Stanley–HB	CCSS-V2N4
Banks of the Ohio (Traditional) C. Stanley–L, R. Stanley–T	CCSS-V2N4
The Memory of Your Smile (Ruby Rakes) C. Stanley–L, R. Stanley–T, Lambert–B	CCSS-V2N4
Salty Dog Blues (Wiley and Zeke Morris) C. Stanley–L, R. Stanley–T, Lambert–B	CCSS-V2N4
Uncle Pen (Bill Monroe) C. Stanley–L, R. Stanley–T, Lambert–B	CCSS-V2N4
Molly and Tenbrooks (Traditional) C. Stanley–L	CCSS-V2N4
True Life Blues (Bill Monroe) C. Stanley–L, R. Stanley–T	CCSS-V2N4
Sugar Coated Love (Audrey Butler) C. Stanley–L, R. Stanley–T	CCSS-V2N4
The Little Girl and the Dreadful Snake (Albert Price) C. Stanley–L, R. Stanley–T	CCSS-V2N4

Drifting Too Far from the Shore (Charles E. Moody)   CCSS-V2N4
C. Stanley–L, R. Stanley–T

Cripple Creek (Traditional)   CCSS-V2N4
Instrumental

620831   Time Life / Rebel Records reissue of show, recorded by Eric Thompson
Ash Grove, Hollywood, California
August 31, 1962
Carter Stanley: g | Ralph Stanley: b | Curley Lambert: m
Vernon Derrick: f | Roger Bush: sb

Tell Me Why My Daddy Don't Come Home (B. Boyd–H. Burns–E. Nunn)   B0007883-02
C. Stanley–L, R. Stanley–T, Lambert–B

Banks of the Ohio   SLP-1487
C. Stanley–L, R. Stanley–T

Train 45   SLP-1495
C. Stanley–L

621130   Smithsonian Folkways reissue of show, recorded by Peter K. Siegel
New York University, New York, New York
November 30, 1962
Carter Stanley: g | Ralph Stanley: b | Curley Lambert: m
Vernon Derrick: f | Carl Chatzky (aka Carl Hawkins): sb

The Dream of a Miner's Child (Robert Donnelly–Will Geddes)   SFW CD 40160
C. Stanley–L, R. Stanley–T

Have a Feast Here Tonight (Charlie Monroe)   SFW CD 40160
C. Stanley–L, R. Stanley–T

Mansions for Me (Bill Monroe)   SFW CD 40160
C. Stanley–L, R. Stanley–T

Hard Times (Ralph Stanley)   SFW CD 40160
Instrumental

5

"STONE WALLS AND STEEL BARS"

The Later King Years, 1963–1966

As the Stanley brothers entered 1963, their career, which had been on an upward trajectory, seemed to be leveling off. Losing the support of their sponsor, Jim Walter Homes, put them back on the road, chasing an endless succession of gigs to earn an income. The folk music boom that had embraced their authentic brand of old-time music, while not dead, was waning and becoming less of a haven for the duo. More often than not, Carter and Ralph carried only one or two full-time musicians with them on the road and hoped they could flesh out the group with a few local musicians once they arrived at a venue for a show. Regardless of what conditions were like on the road, King Records remained intent on recording and promoting the duo, and Carter and Ralph settled in for another year of recording.

King #17: January 1963 (Session 630128)

In January of 1963, the Stanley Brothers spent several days at the King studios recording an album that was decidedly aimed at the folk market. The album, appropriately titled *Folk Concert*, was a studio production that included fake applause to give the impression of a live concert. The recording's concept most likely lay with the session's producer, Ray Pennington.

Ramon Daniel "Ray" Pennington was born on January 1, 1933, in Clay County, Kentucky. He received a guitar at age fifteen, and by nineteen he had a twelve-piece band called the Western Rhythm Boys. The band toured a number of cities in southern Ohio and made their way to Detroit and Canada. Pennington started recording for King in 1958 and was hired by the label a year later. Eventually, he became a producer there and recorded country acts such as Hawkshaw Hawkins, the Stanley Brothers, and Reno & Smiley. He also produced a number of rhythm and blues acts at King. He maintained an interest in performing throughout the early 1960s and fronted two different bands: Ray Pennington and the Western Rhythm Boys, which he played country with, and the Starliners, which he played R & B with under the pseudonym Ray Starr. In 1964 he moved to Nashville to work for Pamper Music as a songwriter. He then returned to producing, first for Pamper and later for Capitol, Monument, RCA, and several smaller labels. In 1984 he headed up the newly formed Step One label and produced a series of freshly recorded albums by

Recorded over a two-day period at the end of January 1963 in the studios of King Records in Cincinnati, the *Folk Concert* album contained phony applause and Carter Stanley's spoken introductions to the songs. It was an attempt to cash in on the success of other recent live albums in the country and bluegrass markets.

Nashville stars of years gone by. Several releases featured him paired with steel guitar legend Buddy Emmons.[1]

Although the liner notes to the *Folk Concert* album claim that it is a collection of authentic folk songs, the first track recorded was a recent composition put together by several King staffers. According to recording engineer Chuck Seitz,

> "I Don't Want Your Rambling Letters" and "He Went to Sleep and the Hogs Ate Him," those song titles were Syd's idea. How he came up with them, I don't know, but he used to do it all the time. He gave those titles to his two A & R men, Gene Redd and Ray Pennington, to write, and then Syd would claim half writer on the thing just because he came up with the title. And [in] this particular case he gave his one third to Nat Nathan, which was his son. Syd's pen name was Lois Mann, and going through a lot of the old Lois publication things you'll find Lois Mann named through a whole lot, although he never wrote a word of music and he still claimed half. Also, that's the place where Lois Publishing came from. Lois Mann was the maiden name of his first wife as I recall."[2]

"I Don't Want Your Rambling Letters" features Ralph Mayo playing the guitar on what he called "that old Delmore Brothers note in there," on which he achieved the feel of one of that duo's most popular recordings, "Blues Stay Away from Me."[3] Recorded next is a solo by Carter, "Just Because," a tune that was written and recorded by the old-time duo the Shelton Brothers. Bob and Joe Shelton recorded it on February 23, 1935, at their second session for Decca Records. The song is probably the most popular one that the Sheltons recorded, and it has been covered by numerous artists including Elvis Presley.

King credited Frankie Brown, a pseudonym for Ted Daffan, with writing "No Letter Today." His song was copyrighted in 1943, but the version the Stanleys recorded is based on an older piece. Bill Monroe recorded "No Letter Today" for Bluebird on October 7, 1940, and his version is credited to Bill Carlisle, who recorded it with his Kentucky Home Boys for Decca on June 11, 1938. In August of 1962, Carter and Ralph performed the song at the Ash Grove. In speaking of the song, Carter noted, "It's always been one of my favorites . . . I don't remember all the words to that, I've always thought it was a good song and our good friend Bill Monroe now has it out in a new album."[4]

"He Went to Sleep and the Hogs Ate Him" is one of the few novelty songs that the Stanleys ever recorded. Hal Neely's liner notes to the album state that it is "an adaptation of a song which Ray Starr, King country A & R director, says was taught to him by his great grandfather in the hills of Kentucky."[5] Neely's notes also state that "My Brother's Bride" was "taken from an old folklore tale and adapted and put to music by a songwriter in Florida by the name of Elsa [sic] Straley and is a story which has been handed down from father to son for several generations."[6] Ralph Stanley stated, "That's another song that sounds like it could have happened, you know. This fellow went into the army and the news got out that he got killed but he didn't, and when he went back, his brother had married his bride."[7] A 1964 newspaper article reported, "It is built around a story about a young man who returns from war to find his sweetheart has married his brother. Mrs. Straley said she tried to imagine how her husband would have felt in the same situation and then wrote the words and music."[8] This selection features the guitar work of Vernon Derrick.

One of the oldest songs from the session is "Six Months Ain't Long." It had previously been recorded by several old-time groups, including the Monroe Brothers (June 21, 1936), Emry Arthur (January 17, 1935), and John Foster (November 14, 1930). At a concert in New York in November of 1962, Carter had announced that he and Bill Monroe would be recording the song in the near future:

> I'd like to mention to you that very soon now, during the Christmas holidays, I'm going to Nashville to record twelve sides of the old original Monroe/Carter songs with Bill Monroe. It'll be Bill Monroe on the mandolin, me on the guitar, singing lead, and a bass fiddle, and that'll be all there'll be to it. We're gonna do "Six Months Ain't Long," "Rabbit in a Log," oh, that "Moonshine Still" deal, and twelve in all. So, that'll be something coming out for you on the Decca label by Bill Monroe and Carter Stanley real soon, and I'd appreciate it if you'd watch for it. It'll come out sometime after the first of the year.[9]

The recording project described by Carter never materialized, most likely because the Stanley Brothers and Bill Monroe were under exclusive recording contracts to different companies. Obviously not wishing to let go of a good song, Carter and Ralph elected to record "Six Months Ain't Long" for their *Folk Concert* album.

Hal Neely's liner notes describe "Old and in the Way" as a "narration which comes from a song that Carter learned back in his early days in Virginia."[10] Composer credits show it as a joint composition between Carter and Ralph Mayo. Mayo recalled, "They sung the words and chorus for six weeks and then I wrote 'em a recitation and they never would do nothing else and I got tired of hearing it."[11]

King #18: January 1963 (Session 630129)

Another of the old songs the Stanleys recorded was "The Hills of Roan County." Carter related,

> In the old days they recorded three minutes, three and a half was okay. Now they want 'em down to anywhere from a minute forty to two ten. Of course that's the jukebox deal that brought that around. The nickels are not flying, or the dimes, fast enough if the record's still on. That was one of the reasons we put off recording "The Hills of Roane County" so long, and Syd Nathan heard us do it and he realized, I think, that without telling the story it was a waste of time and he says, "I don't give a damn if it takes five minutes." So, it took about four something to do it.[12]

Ralph Stanley recalled that this was one of the songs the brothers did when they were first learning music and performing. He went on to say, "I hear that's a true song that was written about Roane County, Tennessee. I heard that that actually happened."[13] Ralph related additional commentary to *Muleskinner News* editor Fred Bartenstein: "I believe, Fred, the first I remember hearing the 'Hills of Roane County' was by Molly O'Day. She was known at the time we heard it . . . she went by the name of Dixie Lee Williamson out of Bluefield, West Virginia. I believe now, the best I can remember that's the first time we ever heard 'The Hills of Roane County.'"[14] The song is in fact based on a true event: in September of 1884, Willis Maberry shot and killed his brother-in-law Tom Galbreath in Roane County, Tennessee. He eluded justice for twenty-five years until, upon his return to Roane County, he was apprehended, tried, and convicted for the murder. Maberry wrote the song while in prison.[15] In addition to Molly O'Day, other country music notables such as Roy Acuff and Bill Monroe made use of the song over the years.

Ralph's solo portion of the program features him on one of his showpieces, "Little Birdie." The Stanley Brothers had previously recorded this piece in 1952 for Rich-R-Tone Records. Ralph recreates the mood of the first recording with his unmistakable solo vocals and clawhammer banjo playing. "Pig in the Pen," though listed by King as traditional, is associated with Fiddlin' Arthur Smith. Country music historian Charles Wolfe notes that it is "another modern composition which Arthur composed around an older set of banjo tune verses."[16] Smith had recorded the tune with the Delmore Brothers for Bluebird on February 17, 1937. Carter and Ralph themselves would record the song a second time, in 1964, for Ray Davis on his Wango label. "Whiskey" features Carter on another recitation. To enable Carter to do the recitation, Curley Lambert plays rhythm guitar. Ralph later recalled, "We got that from the old man Syd Nathan, King Records."[17] King supplied "Lips That Lie," a then recent composition by Fred Stryker, who later in the year would contribute two additional songs for Stanley recordings, "Don't Step over an Old Love" and "I Just Stood There." "Lips That Lie" is the first of only a few songs by the Stanley Brothers to feature a harmonica. The instrument, played by Billy Lee Holmes, son of legendary country music harmonica player Floyd Lee "Salty" Holmes, was overdubbed on the master.[18]

The final two selections are traditional pieces. "Little Darlin', Pal of Mine" was recorded by the Carter Family for Victor on May 9, 1928. "Darling Nellie Gray," featured as a banjo and guitar instrumental with Ralph Mayo handling the lead guitar chores, is the album's closing track. During the song, Carter makes a humorous reference to Mayo's guitar work. Ralph Mayo recalled,

> They had an old wore out guitar there and my finger got to bleeding and that's when I told 'em, I said, "Now listen, I'm telling you right now, this is the end of my guitar picking. I didn't come up here to play the guitar. My finger's so sore it feels like it's ready to break out and bleed." I said, "Either get somebody else or bring me some gloves in here." Carter said, "Would you like to hear him [Mayo] pick it once with his gloves off now?" And then he said, "He took 'em off." I played the guitar on it and capoed up in G chord way up on the neck and played the Mother Maybelle style and Ralph played the banjo on it.[19]

The song, written by Benny Hanby, had made its debut in the 1800s when it was featured in the hit play *Dred, or the Dismal Swamp* that appeared at P.T. Barnum's American Museum in New York.

Reno & Smiley: Summer 1963 (Session 630700)

In the summer of 1963, Carter and Ralph were in Roanoke, Virginia, to appear as guest artists on a television pilot that Don Reno & Red Smiley were preparing for a new program. The audio was later issued on a CD by Rural Rhythm and the program itself was issued on DVD by Ronnie Reno's Man-do-lin Productions. The Stanleys are shown without the backing of the Clinch Mountain Boys and are presumably assisted by members of the Reno & Smiley band on their solo number, "In the Pines." Ralph Stanley and Don Reno feature a twin banjo number, "Home Sweet Home." The foursome of Carter, Ralph, Don, and Red sing a religious selection, "Just Over in the Glory Land." Closing out the show are two selections that feature Reno & Smiley with the Tennessee Cut-Ups along with the Stanley Brothers. Everyone takes turns playing and singing on "Nine Pound Hammer," while "John Henry" is featured instrumentally.

King #19: August 1963 (Session 630813)

In August and September of 1963, Carter and Ralph recorded sessions that resulted in two album releases on King, *Country Folk Music Spotlight* (K-864) and *America's Finest 5-String Banjo Hootenanny* (K-872).

On August 13, 1963, five instrumentals were recorded as part of the *Hootenanny* project. In the mid-1970s Jeth Mill, host of a series on bluegrass music for National Public Radio

(NPR), would note on an episode about the Stanley Brothers that *America's Finest 5-String Banjo Hootenanny* is a "good example of Ralph's banjo work. While on a recording trip to Cincinnati during the folk revival of the early sixties, Ralph was asked to put together a banjo album for King Records. According to the story, Ralph took his banjo to a hotel room and returned in three hours with twelve songs ready to record."[20]

This set of recordings marks Henry Dockery's recording debut with the Clinch Mountain Boys. He was born on May 18, 1938, in South Carolina. Unfortunately, little is known of Henry's early musical training. He was twenty-five when he joined the Stanley Brothers in the summer of 1963, playing bass. He stayed with the group for six months or so and appeared on several recording sessions. He spent a number of years in the 1970s working with Charlie Moore. He died in December of 1990 in South Carolina.

The session features the work of Ralph Stanley on banjo, George Shuffler on guitar, and Ralph Mayo on fiddle. It proves to be an excellent instrumental workout. The first selection is a remake of a tune the Stanley Brothers recorded for their first album release on King in 1958, "Train 45." In fact, the vocal introduction from the original 1958 version is spliced onto the 1963 recording. Ralph Mayo is the fiddle player on both versions.

Of the proceedings, Ralph Stanley noted that "we just put some old tunes together and named 'em . . . there's a lot of good tunes on there."[21] One song that was put together for the session, "Lonesome Traveler," bears Ralph's name as its composer. Another selection, "Shout Little Lulie," features Ralph playing clawhammer banjo. In the spoken introduction to a re-recording of this tune for Rebel Records in 1973, Ralph notes, "This is the first tune I ever learned to play from my mother many years ago. I'm gonna try to play it just as close as I can to the way she did."[22] "Shamrock" is another original that Ralph put together for the project.

"Stoney Creek" is Ralph's adaptation of "Salt Creek," a tune that Bill Monroe had recently recorded with banjo player Bill Keith. At the time Keith had just introduced the chromatic style of banjo playing on Monroe's 1963 recordings for Decca Records. The tune "Salt Creek," more commonly known in old-time music as "Salt River," is derived from an Irish fiddle selection called "Red Haired Boy."

On August 14, 1963, the Stanleys recorded five songs for their *Country Folk Music Spotlight* album. Ralph Mayo's fiddle takes a very subdued role on these songs, taking only one break and providing minimal backup on the rest. Ralph Stanley noted,

> Syd [Nathan] didn't like a fiddle and he didn't want us to use a fiddle, he didn't like a banjo either. I think the sound he was looking for is the guitars like the Delmore Brothers. They were past and gone, I guess. He didn't like a fiddle or a banjo, either one . . . that's the reason we started using the lead guitar instead of the mandolin. I guess it's alright in a way but me, I prefer a mandolin. So, that's why we done that. Syd set in a little bit on one or two sessions and I remember one day he said, "Hell, you know more about it than I do, I ain't got no business here," and he just walked out.[23]

This was the last session that Mayo recorded with the Stanley Brothers for King.

The waning days of the folk boom found the Stanley Brothers being marketed to this segment of the music-buying public with albums such as *Country Folk Music Spotlight*. The disc contained one of the duo's most popular songs of the mid-1960s, "Stone Walls and Steel Bars."

King #20: August 1963 (Session 630814)

Session producer Ray Pennington contributed the next session's first two songs, "Stone Walls and Steel Bars" and "Standing Room Only (Outside Your Heart)." Ralph noted of Ray Pennington,

> [He was] sort of a writer for Syd, I think. We always saw him right there in the studio, we'd get 'em [the songs] right there and work 'em up and do 'em. We went into King Studios a many of a time and not knowing a thing we was gonna do . . . learn 'em and cut 'em right there. But everybody knew exactly what the other one could do . . . that means a lot.[24]

"Stone Walls and Steel Bars" proved to be one of the Stanley Brothers' most popular songs of the mid-1960s.

Carter and Ralph originally recorded "Lonesome Night" for Mercury in 1956, though at the time of the 1963 King session, the Mercury version remained unissued. Carter wrote the song, and the words to it appeared in a songbook that the Stanleys issued in the 1950s.[25] The songbook version, and the Mercury version as well, contain a third verse that is omitted from the King version.

The last two songs recorded are traditional selections. The Stanleys learned "Pretty Little Miss in the Garden" from the New Lost City Ramblers. Tracy Schwarz, a member of the Ramblers, recalled,

The basic tune came from Roscoe Holcomb from Daisy, Kentucky. However, we used Cousin Emmy's words. We liked her words a little bit better, so we pretty much adapted her words to Roscoe's melody. One day at John Cohen's apartment in New York City, the Stanleys had met us there 'cause they were gonna do a program that night, I think for the Friends of Old Time Music in New York City. [That was] an organization that John was a member of . . . Ralph Rinzler was in that organization. A bunch of people would bring artists up . . . Clarence Tom Ashley and people like that, and have them up to New York City in the early sixties. So the Stanleys came up and rested for an hour or so at John's apartment and we were there and Carter told us that they were recording an album and they needed a folk song and would we know anything. So, we said, "I'll bet you 'Pretty Little Miss Out in the Garden' would really be a good Stanley Brothers number," and we played it for them. They all ran to their instruments and backed us up and got right in with it. So, that's how they did it. I guess they did an arrangement on it, they dropped out some notes. The Stanleys didn't have any recorded version of it to go on or anything, and I guess they did it from memory and they left out some of the melody. They simplified it down. The Stanleys kept it just within about three notes of the lead, it was kind of relaxed the way they did it.[26]

Mike Seeger added that when the Ramblers were "singing it for them, Carter cracked a joke. 'Pretty fair miss out in the garden, strange young man comes riding by,' and Carter says 'strange young man named Phyllis.' What he meant was some gay man, I suppose."[27]

"Late Last Night" is a song the Stanley Brothers used frequently to open their shows in the early 1960s. Their source for the song is not known, though Uncle Dave Macon had recorded an old-time version of it in the 1930s.

King #21: September 1963 (Session 630916)

In September, eleven more songs were recorded to complete the projects started in August. Surprisingly, the entire band for this first September session consisted of Carter and Ralph Stanley and George Shuffler; Shuffler played lead guitar and dubbed the bass. The session's first seven tunes are instrumentals. As in the other session, they are a mixture of traditional pieces and Ralph Stanley originals. "When You and I Were Young, Maggie" / "Red Wing" is a medley of two traditional pieces. "Rang Tang" and "Five String Drag" are selections that George Shuffler and Ralph wrote together.

King #22: September 1963 (Session 630917)

The last four songs from the September sessions are all duets by Carter and Ralph. "Never Again" was written by fiddle player Benny Williams. Williams had an interesting career in the 1950s that included stints with Mac Wiseman, Reno & Smiley, Flatt & Scruggs, the Stanley Brothers, and Bill Monroe. He related,

I'd had the song a long time . . . when I was working in Indiana, before I went to work with Mac, working clubs up there, and wrote it at that time. I thought it was just a file thirteen song.[28] I worked with the [Stanley Brothers] a while in, I guess it was '58, I worked with Carter and Ralph in Bristol and they was just working personal appearances at that time and had a daily radio program. One day I was just kind of going over it and singing it in the car and Carter said, "Where'd you get that song?" "I wrote it." And he liked it and I guess they remembered it . . . just put it down when they went to record.[29]

Benny later recorded the song with Bill Monroe, cutting it for Decca on April 9, 1964.

"Don't Cheat in Our Home Town" is another song that was written by producer Ray Pennington. Like "Stone Walls and Steel Bars," it proved to be one of the Stanley Brothers' more popular releases of the early 1960s. "Don't Step over an Old Love" and "I Just Stood There," both Fred Stryker compositions, were supplied by King. Of "Don't Step over an Old Love," Ralph recalled, "One of the governors of Ohio wrote that. He was still governor or had been governor and was running again and he wrote 'Don't Step over an Old Friend,' . . . he used that in his campaign. Syd said 'That "friend" ain't no good, put "love" there,' so we put 'don't step over an old love.'"[30] It has yet to be determined which governor, if any, used "Don't step over an old friend" as a campaign slogan or song, but copyright records do indicate it is an alternate title to the song.

Ray Davis and Wango Records #1: December 1963 (Session 631209)

By the time the Stanley Brothers made their first recordings with Ray Davis, he was a fifteen-year veteran disc jockey and concert promoter. A native of the Eastern Shore of Maryland, Davis did some of his first professional work at WDOV in Dover, Delaware, at the age of fifteen. In 1950, he moved to Havre de Grace, Maryland, where he met Alex Campbell, the disc jockey and promoter who did much to shape Ray's tastes in traditional country music. By the end of the year, Ray was in Baltimore, doing radio work under the auspices of Tim Bright, a local car dealer. Davis's on-air persona attracted the attention of Bright's competitor, John Wilbanks of Johnny's Auto Sales. Thus began a more than thirty-year relationship in which Davis served as the on-air spokesman for Johnny's. In addition to spinning bluegrass and gospel recordings to promote the dealership, Ray developed a good sideline as a master of ceremonies at local country music parks, most notably New River Ranch and Sunset Park. His proximity to the artists allowed him to form a number of friendships that turned into booking opportunities; Ray frequently hired bands for weeks at a time, placing them in various venues in Baltimore and surrounding environs. The Stanley Brothers were one of the bands that Ray hired for such occasions. Yet another of Ray's endeavors was the creation of a recording label, Wango Records, named after his hometown. The recordings were rarely, if ever, distributed in stores. They were most often used by Davis as on-air sales pitches and sold directly by mail to people who responded to his advertisements.

In December of 1963, the Stanley Brothers were in Baltimore and hired for a week by Ray Davis to record a series of twenty-six fifteen-minute radio shows. The programs were designed so that the sponsor's ad could be inserted after the Stanleys left the studio. Most of the shows aired on WBMD for Johnny's Used Cars.

Ray made use of some of the radio performances almost immediately, inserting some of the instrumental selections, such as "Wildwood Flower" and "Mountain Pickin'," on albums that he produced with the Stanley Brothers the following year. A few tracks were issued on various 45s and extended-play discs (EPs). In 1976 Ray issued *On the Air*, a full album of material that was drawn from the various radio programs.

In 1985 Ray left the world of commercial (i.e., AM) radio to become an on-air personality at WAMU-FM, a public radio station in Washington, DC. To assist with fundraising for the station, Ray released a series of CDs made up of songs he had recorded over the years, including tracks from the Stanley Brothers radio shows. He released seven *Radio Series* discs, making much of this radio material available for the first time.

The programs feature the band as it existed in the winter of 1963: Carter and Ralph Stanley, George Shuffler on lead guitar, and Henry Dockery on bass and performing comedy. Carter Stanley, with a case of laryngitis, confines his participation to playing rhythm guitar and performing some of the MC duties. Ralph Stanley and George Shuffler, with Henry Dockery chiming in occasionally, share the bulk of the vocal chores. Most of the songs are covers of their record numbers, but George Shuffler adds some diversity, both instrumentally and vocally, with selections such as "Gathering Flowers from the Hillside," "Don't Let Your Sweet Love Die," and "Long Black Veil."

Ray Davis and Wango Records #2: December 1963 (Session 631214a)

At the end of the week of recording, Ray Davis employed the Stanley Brothers to perform live music for a Christmas party that took place in the lobby of Johnny's Used Cars. The program was broadcast live as part of Davis's daily radio show on WBMD; Ray worked the controls for the show from his second-story studio at Johnny's while the Stanleys played in the lobby below. He also tape recorded the event and offered selections as part of the *Radio Series* discs. On the recording, Carter Stanley is heard dedicating one of the songs to the Kentucky Colonels, a group the Stanleys had met a year or so earlier when playing at the Ash Grove in California. Coincidentally, the Colonels, who were then on their way from New England to perform a Saturday evening show in Washington, DC, heard the Stanley Brothers on the air and made their way to Johnny's for a visit.[31]

Ray Davis and Wango Records #3: December 1963 (Session 631214b)

It was after this party that Carter and Ralph made their next set of recordings, the first of several quickie albums they would become known for later in their career. The project was released on Ray's Wango label under the pseudonym "John's Country Quartet." In addition to honoring Ray's sponsor, John Wilbanks, the name also served as a cover for the Stanleys, who were taking liberties with their contract with their parent label by recording for another label.

Carter Stanley, still ill with a case of laryngitis, limits his participation on these recordings, with one exception, to providing guitar rhythm. He does sing lead on the choruses of one track, "Will You Miss Me," that was released on a later Wango project. Ralph Stanley, George

Shuffler, Henry Dockery, and Jack Cooke make up the quartet that appears on several of the selections. Jack, not a member of the band at the time but living in the Baltimore area, appears as a guest on the session.

Leading off the album is the Bill Monroe favorite "The Old Cross Road," a song he recorded for Columbia in October of 1947 with Lester Flatt and Earl Scruggs. Monroe recalled, "I wrote that song coming back from Texas when we were working the tent show. I wrote it in the car while everyone was asleep. When we got back to Nashville, we got to working on it."[32] Ray Davis was especially fond of the Stanley Brothers' recording of the song, and decades later he characterized it as one of his favorites from the sessions he did with the group. He noted that Ralph Stanley and George Shuffler were the singers on this track and cited Carter's guitar work on it as an example of what a gifted rhythm guitarist he was. Both the Stanleys and Ray knew of "The Old Cross Road" before the session. Carter and Ralph, of course, were aware of the song from Monroe's performances of it.

Another selection from the Monroe catalog is "Drifting Too Far from the Shore," which is featured as a duet between Ralph Stanley and George Shuffler. The Stanley Brothers performed this song for years on their live concerts. At the Ash Grove on August 30, 1962, Carter commented while introducing the song, "If you want to call this a copy, I hope it is a copy. I hope we can do it as well as they did back then."[33] The Monroe Brothers recorded it for Bluebird on February 17, 1936, at their very first recording session. The song can be found in many of the old shape-note hymnals throughout the South. It was composed by Charles E. Moody and copyrighted by him in 1923. Moody was also the source of another popular Stanley Brothers song, "Kneel at the Cross."

"Just a Little Talk with Jesus" is a re-recording of the Cleavant Derricks hymn that the Stanley Brothers had cut for Mercury in 1955. "Precious Memories" is another standard from the shape-note tradition. It was written by J. B. F. Wright and was published in a number of the Stamps-Baxter books. It had been recorded earlier, in March of 1958, as part of Bill Monroe's first gospel album, *I Saw the Light*. Ralph Stanley leads the vocals on the Stanley Brothers' rendition. The instrumental medley of "I'll Fly Away" / "In the Sweet By and By" is the final track recorded at the session, and completing side one of the album is "The Unclouded Day," a song that was written by Josiah K. Alwood in the 1880s.

Leading off side two are "Over in the Glory Land" and "Lonely Tombs," both of which the Stanleys had previously recorded for King, in September of 1959. The immensely popular hymn "Amazing Grace" remains a favorite among Ralph Stanley's fans to this day. Ralph would record the song again in 1977 in a lined-out a cappella style popular in Primitive Baptist traditions. "I Am a Pilgrim," a solo by Ralph, was one of guitar legend Merle Travis's signature songs. Merle recalled in later years, "[I] first heard a version of this song from Lyman Rager, who had learned it while he was in the Elkton, Kentucky, jail. I rewrote it, rearranged it, and added to it."[34] "A Beautiful Life" was written by William M. Golden and copyrighted by him in 1918. It was recorded in the 1930s by the Monroe Brothers and re-recorded by Bill Monroe in March of 1958 as part of his *I Saw the Light* album. Completing the Stanleys' first Wango release is a duet by Ralph Stanley and George

Shuffler on a familiar hymn, "Someone's Last Day." The song was copyrighted in 1924 by M. H. McKee and first appeared in a songbook entitled *Song Praise*.

Also recorded at this session, but not released until later, is a Carter Family favorite, "Will You Miss Me When I'm Gone?" It features Ralph handling the lead vocal chores and shows George Shuffler displaying his exquisite lead guitar work. Ray Davis noted that the song was recorded at the end of a Saturday night session in his studio at Johnny's Used Cars in Baltimore. The Stanleys were preparing to leave when Carter suggested one additional tune that he wanted do. Although Carter quoted a price to record the song, Davis recalled that in all likelihood it was thrown in as part of the session. After hearing Carter and Ralph audition the tune, Ray readily agreed to it and in retrospect judged the performance to be worth tenfold the agreed upon price. A case of laryngitis had limited Carter's work on the recording session to providing rhythm guitar accompaniment, but he was determined to contribute his vocals to "Will You Miss Me." Ralph admonished Carter to conserve his voice for a good-paying engagement the following day. Perhaps it was a compromise that the finished song features Ralph singing lead on the verses and Carter doing so on the choruses.[35]

King #23: April 1964 (Session 640401)

On April 1 and 2, 1964, Carter and Ralph recorded an album of gospel material for King that resulted in the release of *Hymns of the Cross* (K-918). Although George Shuffler had been an integral part of the Stanley Brothers sound for many years, this album was the first Stanley release to give him prominent billing. In addition to receiving a subtitle credit of "with George Shuffler," he also appeared with Carter and Ralph in the photograph on the front of the album. Shuffler's presence is definitely in evidence on the album, both vocally and instrumentally. All twelve songs are trios with George, and they all feature his distinctive cross-picked guitar.

Also performing on the album are Earl Taylor and Chick Stripling. Taylor was never an official Clinch Mountain Boy, but he appears on the album as a guest. A fixture of the bluegrass scene in Cincinnati in the early 1960s, he appeared at the Ken-Mill Club, a venue frequented many times by the Stanley Brothers. Earl was born on June 17, 1929, in Rose Hill, Virginia. He took up the mandolin early and was playing professionally by age seventeen. The next several years found him playing in Detroit, Washington, DC, and Baltimore. In the mid-1950s, he took time out for a stint with Jimmy Martin, helping him record some classic sides for Decca. After leaving Martin, Earl reactivated his Stoney Mountain Boys, and in 1959 they became the first bluegrass band to perform at Carnegie Hall. He recorded several fine albums for United Artists and Capitol. In 1961 the band relocated to Cincinnati, and it was during this period that he recorded with the Stanleys. His later work included a stint with Flatt & Scruggs. Earl also helped Ralph Stanley record his first solo album, for King Records, in 1967. He died on January 28, 1984, after suffering a heart attack, at the age of fifty-four.[36]

After having spent a number of years as an integral part of the Stanley Brothers' sound, guitarist George Shuffler was given prominent billing on the cover of the 1964 gospel album *Hymns of the Cross*.

Of the gospel album, Ralph Stanley recalled,

> We got all of these out of a book. I think this right here is one of our best, the one with George Shuffler's picture with Carter and me. We'd go along a lot of times riding in the car of a night, late at night, sometimes we'd drive all night and sing, seemed like we just happened to get on hymns, sing that more than anything else, so I guess that led us to record a lot of gospel songs.[37]

The first song recorded, "Will the Circle Be Unbroken," was popularized by the Carter Family, who first recorded it for Victor on June 17, 1933. That version, however, remained unissued, and the Carters recorded it again two years later, on May 6, 1935, for ARC as "Can the Circle Be Unbroken Bye & Bye." King credited an arrangement of the song to the Browns Ferry Four, who recorded it for King in 1945 as "Will the Circle Be Unbroken." "Jesus Savior Pilot Me" was first published as a poem in an 1871 edition of *The Sailor's Magazine*. The text was written by Edward Hopper, an American Presbyterian minister who was the pastor of the Church of the Land and Sea, located on what is currently the corner of Market and Henry Streets in lower Manhattan. It was his involvement in ministering to the needs of the many sailors in the area that inspired him to write the poem. The music to the hymn was composed later that same year by a music store owner named John E. Gould. It was also in 1871 that "Jesus Savior Pilot Me" made its first appearance in a hymnal, *The Baptist Praise Book*. Since that time it has become a church standard.

King credited the next two songs, "I Just Dropped By" and "Oh Death," to Kentucky songwriter John Reedy, who also composed a previous Stanley Brothers recording, "Somebody Touched Me." Both of the songs were featured on a 1961 Starday EP by Reedy. "I Just Dropped By" was copyrighted by him on November 9, 1960, but "Oh Death" is incorrectly attributed to him, though his recording of it is the model for the Stanley Brothers' rendition.

The song "Oh Death" has an interesting history. In 1978, the Blue Ridge Institute of Ferrum, Virginia, issued an album called *Virginia Traditions: Ballads from British Tradition.* The collection contains a version of the song as sung by noted southwest Virginia musician Moran Lee "Dock" Boggs. In the notes that accompany the album, Blanton Owen writes,

> The song "Oh Death," sometimes called "Conversations wth Death," has appeared in a number of southern song and hymn books. In oral tradition, "Oh Death" is most often found in far southwestern Virginia and western North Carolina. Polly Johnson recorded ten verses of the song in 1939 for Emory Hamilton and it has been recorded by John Cohen from a number of western North Carolina singers. For a full tracing of the song back to its British antecedents, see "Death and a Lady: Echoes of a Mortal Conversation in English and American Folksong Tradition," an unpublished M.A. thesis done at the University of North Carolina in 1966 by Katherine Susan Barks. Dock learned his version of "Oh Death" from his friend Lee Hunsucker in the 1930s.[38]

Charlie Monroe had recorded the song, as Charlie Monroe's Boys, for Bluebird on February 5, 1939. In addition to recording the song, Charlie also claimed a copyright on it on February 15, 1940. Ralph Stanley recorded a spirited remake of the song for Rebel in 1977 with Keith Whitley singing lead; it appeared as part of his *Clinch Mountain Gospel* album. The song went on to reap huge benefits for Ralph when he recorded it again, this time as a solo a cappella selection for the soundtrack to the movie *O Brother, Where Art Thou?* His rendition won a Grammy in 2002 for Best Male Country Vocal Performance. A CD of music from the movie sold in excess of 7 million copies and was the genesis of a successful star-studded tour called Down from the Mountain, of which Stanley was a headliner.

Two more traditional songs rounded out the first day's recording. "Shoutin' on the Hills of Glory" was originally listed in the King ledgers as public domain; Carter subsequently claimed it. An earlier variant of the song had appeared in the 1936 hymnal *Heartfelt Songs* as "There'll Be Shouting," an E. M. Bartlett composition.[39]

One of the most successful songs from the session is "Beautiful Star of Bethlehem." Since its release by the Stanley Brothers, it has become a Christmas standard in bluegrass music and been recorded by a number of artists, including Emmylou Harris and the Judds. Widely regarded as a traditional mountain hymn, it was copyrighted in 1940 and made its first appearance in the songbook *Beautiful Praise.* It was subsequently featured in four different songbooks during the 1940s and was reprinted in other books in the 1950s and '60s. It was written by a Murfreesboro, Tennessee, dairy farmer named Robert F. Boyce. According to Boyce's son Franklin,

Father initially tried to write his song in our farmhouse when we were little children, but the noise of the household filled with little children was distracting. That's when he took his pencil and paper, walked across the road to the barn and sat down on his milking stool. There, on the milking stool, was where the words began to flow for him.[40]

King #24: April 1964 (Session 640402)

On April 2, the Stanleys finished the recording for the *Hymns of the Cross* project. The Harlan County Four, a group that included Alton and Rabon Delmore and was similar to the Browns Ferry Four, was Carter and Ralph's source for "John Three-Sixteen." The quartet had recorded it for King in October of 1951. The song was credited to group members Alton Delmore and Ulysses "Red" Turner. Mac Odell, the composer of three other songs the Stanleys had featured in 1959 on their *For the Good People* album, wrote "A Crown He Wore" and had recorded it for King on February 15, 1954. In an attempt to recreate the sound of the original recording, Earl Taylor plays harmonica on the Stanleys' version. Mac stated that he didn't have a specific recollection concerning how the song was written but felt certain that his upbringing contributed greatly to many of the songs he wrote. He recalled growing up in the "Bible Belt" in Alabama and had fond memories from his childhood of being in the front row of church each Sunday morning.[41] "How Beautiful Heaven Must Be" dates back to 1933. A. S. Bridgewater and A. P. Bland wrote the song. The Monroe Brothers featured it on one of their early recording sessions for Bluebird, recording it on October 12, 1936, as "We Read of a Place That's Called Heaven." Its lyrics were also featured in an Uncle Dave Macon songbook of the 1930s. Although King credited "He's Passing This Way" to Wade Mainer, who recorded it for King on March 17, 1951, Harkins Frye had earlier copyrighted it under the title "He's Passing Along This Way."[42]

Fiddle player Paul Mullins was the source for "No Burdens Pass Through." Paul worked with the Stanley Brothers on three different occasions in 1959 and 1960, when they were headquartered in Florida. It was while working as a disc jockey in the early 1960s that he came in contact with the song. Paul related,

> I was working at WTCR [Huntington, West Virginia]. I had to work Sunday afternoons and there was some live ministers on the air and one of these guys, his name was Green Kitchen, was an Apostolic Gospel Church minister there at the tri-state, I think it was Huntington. He'd come to do the radio program once a month and I had to put him on the air live. He knew I was a fiddle player and a musician, that's when I had the Bluegrass Playboys, and he brought me the words to that song. I don't know where he got the words and it didn't have music to it, I set the music to it. I put together a PI,[43] me and some guys from some of the different bands around . . . Sid Campbell and the Log Cabin Boys helped me. I had twenty-four gospel recordings for $2.98, I think it was. That song was one of 'em. I'd pitch it on the air and people got to inquiring about it. I went and rerecorded it on REM Records in Lexington, Kentucky, me and Benny Birchfield, and it had pretty good success right here in this area. Carter and Ralph come

to see me one time, I guess that was right before they went to record that album, and Carter stayed with me that night and I played him that record. I said, "You can have half of this song if you'll record it." So, they did.[44]

"Building on That Rock" was credited by King to Julia Mainer, the wife of Wade Mainer, who had recorded the song with Wade for King on April 7, 1961. However, the Mainer and the Stanley Brothers selections are two different songs, and King's credit is obviously a mistake. The version recorded by the Stanley Brothers was written by Barney Warren and was copyrighted in 1903. The original title was "On the Rock." Warren is responsible for at least one other hymn popular in old-time music circles, "Beautiful," which was performed by the Blue Sky Boys.

Ray Davis and Wango Records #4: 1964 (Session 640518)

The Stanley Brothers returned to Baltimore to work for Ray Davis several times during 1964. On one of their outings, they took advantage of the occasion to record an album of secular material for Wango (104). The project portrays the group as they frequently appeared at the time, a trio composed of Carter, Ralph, and George Shuffler. In terms of material and performance, Wango 104 stands as one of the Stanleys' better-recorded triumphs of the mid-1960s. It contains a rich cross section of old ballads and tunes that they had been familiar with for years. Ray Davis asked Carter, who was in considerably better voice than he had been at the previous Wango session, for "just the old, authentic, original sound," to which Carter replied, "I'll be proud to give it to you."[45] Indeed, Ray remarked that Carter and Ralph's mother especially enjoyed the album because of its selection of old-time songs and the manner in which it was recorded, just two guitars and a banjo. The group was billed on the album as John's Country Quartet, a reference to Ray's sponsor, Johnny's Used Cars. The album has been unofficially dubbed "the green album" because of the color of the label that appeared on the disc.[46]

"Long Journey Home," which kicks off the album, comes from the Monroe Brothers catalog. Like "Drifting Too Far from the Shore," of the earlier Wango session, the Stanley Brothers often included it in their live performances in remembrance of the Monroes. "Will You Miss Me" appears next, although it was recorded at the previous session in December of 1963. "I'll Be True to the One That I Love" is a song popularized by country music performer Jimmie Davis in the 1930s and one that the Stanleys sang even before they became professional musicians. Ray Davis later remarked that Carter had trouble remembering where he learned the song. Sometime after the session, Ray conversed with Jimmie, who told him that the song was, in fact, his.[47] It appeared in his 1942 songbook, titled simply *Jimmie Davis Song Folio*, with words and music listed as being composed by Ike Cargill and E. Settlemyer. Carter and Ralph had recorded "No Letter in the Mail Today" for King barely a year earlier, on their *Folk Concert* album (K-834). "Pretty Polly," one of Ralph's signature songs and one he had routinely performed since the late 1940s, is an old ballad he learned from his father. The Stanley Brothers had recorded the tune earlier, for Columbia Records in 1950. "Wildwood Flower" is an instrumental highlighting the lead guitar work of George Shuffler. The tune was not recorded at the session but drawn from radio shows the group had recorded earlier for Ray Davis.[48] "Two More Years and I'll Be Free" is yet another Jimmie Davis tune, dating from 1939. Floyd Tillman was a co-contributor to the song. Ray Davis recalled that Carter and Ralph were reluctant to do the song because they were unfamiliar with it. Davis had a fondness for the song, having heard Mac Wiseman perform it a decade or so earlier on an early morning radio program that aired on the same station where Ray worked. Davis prevailed upon Carter and Ralph to do the song and noted later that the lyrics of the Wiseman and Stanley versions are slightly different. Ray cited Carter's ability to improvise on the spot as an example of his deft songwriting talents.[49] The Carter Family had recorded "Two More Years" on their *Last Sessions* album for the Acme label in 1956. Closing out side one of the Stanley Brothers' album is "Ramshackle Shack on the Hill," an old-time tune that was featured by Mainer's Mountaineers in the 1930s.

Leading off side two is "East Virginia Blues," another Carter Family favorite. The Stanleys occasionally featured the song on live performances, with Carter handling the lead guitar chores. Here, George Shuffler tackles the guitar leads. Though Ralph had played mandolin on this song in years past, he sticks to his more familiar banjo on this recording. Like "No Letter Today," "Pig in a Pen" is song Carter and Ralph had recently recorded for their *Folk Concert* album on King in January of 1963. Ray Davis first heard the album's third track, "Your Saddle Is Empty Ol' Pal," when Carter and Ralph performed it at the recording session. The Stanleys offered up the song when another selection was needed for the album. They noted that they had learned it years ago by hearing it on border radio stations and had performed it as youngsters before they embarked on a professional musical career.[50] Merle Travis popularized "Nine Pound Hammer." George Shuffler plays the guitar leads in the Travis-style of picking, taking a break from his more familiar cross-picking techniques. "Cluck Old Hen" is another old-time tune that Ralph features as a solo on the banjo. Ray Davis noted that Ralph suggested it because Davis and the group wanted to include an instrumental on the album. After Ralph played a snippet of it for George Shuffler, who was unfamiliar with the tune, the trio proceeded to lay down a recording of the tune in one take. Ralph would later record the tune for Rebel in the early 1970s.[51] "Wild and Reckless Hobo"[52] is another tune that Carter and Ralph performed in their younger, preprofessional days, while "Rabbit in a Log" is yet another Monroe Brothers favorite. Closing out the album is an instrumental titled "Mountain Pickin'." It was drawn from radio shows that were recorded the previous December; Carter Stanley handles the lead guitar chores.

In addition to the Stanley Brothers LPs that Ray Davis produced on Wango, he also released several extended-play 45 rpm singles and at least one conventional single. The six hymns that formed most of this material were recorded at the same time as the album of nongospel songs. It's likely that Davis suggested most of them, all or in part from Stamps-Baxter/Albert E. Brumley songbooks that he sold on the radio.

Though found in a number of Southern hymnals, "Hold Fast to the Right" can also be classified as a subset of gospel that was popular with first-generation bluegrass performers and fans: mother songs. Ray Davis delighted in having the groups that recorded for him make use of such selections; his mother was still living at the time, and he would often dedicate "mother songs" to her on his radio program.[53] The song dates to 1878, when it was written by prolific gospel composer Fanny Crosby; the melody was supplied by William Howard Doane. The song's initial title was "The Mother's Goodbye." A quarter of a century later, it had taken on a life of its own and its origins were clouded. Gospel publisher James D. Vaughan issued the song as "Hold Fast to the Right" in a 1906 publication. He listed the words as anonymous but took credit for adding the music. Throughout the twentieth century, other composers and publishers, such as Albert E. Brumley and R. E. Winsett, likewise claimed arrangements of the song. It appeared in a number of shape-note hymnals in the 1930s through the '50s.

"If I Could Hear My Mother Pray Again" was another "mother song" that Ray prevailed upon the Stanleys to record, in part for his mother.[54] Like "Hold Fast to the Right," it, too, is an old hymn from gospel traditions. It was written in 1922 by James Rowe, an English immigrant who came to the United States in 1889, and an Alabama native by the name of John Whitfield Vaughan. It appeared in numerous shape-note hymnals and was popular with many old-time groups, including Wade Mainer, who recorded it for Bluebird in 1936.

"Standing in the Need of Prayer" is a selection the Stanley Brothers performed in the formative days of their career, when Carter introduced it as "an old-time spiritual."[55] When the group was searching for additional material to record at this session, Carter suggested it. Davis later remembered being initially skeptical until Carter previewed it for him, getting really into the performance and dancing in the studio while the tape was running. His enthusiasm was contagious, and Ray found himself bouncing along at the controls of the recording equipment.[56]

The Stanley Brothers apparently brought "Sunny Side of Life" to the session as well. Davis recalled the song, also released as "Happy, Sunny Side of Life," as one Carter and Ralph used to sing in their younger days.[57] It was written in 1918 by Tillit S. Teddlie, a Texas-born gospel composer with some 130 songs to his credit. Old-time and bluegrass aficionados often cite a 1936 recording of the song by the Blue Sky Boys as the model for later versions. Tracy Schwarz, one of the members of the New Lost City Ramblers, recalled an incident from a 1966 tour of Europe that included the Ramblers, the Stanley Brothers, and several others:

> . . . [Carter] walked over to me and Mike [Seeger] and remarked how much he liked the Blue Sky Boys' song *The Sunny Side of Life*. His enthusiasm sparked him to sing it right there, and I noticed him nodding to me—could he mean for me to tenor him, the great Carter Stanley, sing with him? I threw caution to the winds and joined him with my best tenor harmony and even got a compliment from him ("good note").[58]

"What Would You Give in Exchange for Your Soul" was known to the Stanley Brothers as an early hit for the Monroe Brothers, supposedly outselling "any song put on record by an 'oldtime' group."[59] Their 1936 recording for Bluebird has been characterized as one of the biggest hillbilly hits of the 1930s. The song was written in 1911 by the duo of F. J. Berry and James J. Carr, the latter an Arkansas native who traveled as a singing schoolteacher for the Texas-based Trio Publishing Company. Aside from the fact that the Stanley Brothers' rendition replaces Bill Monroe's mandolin with George Shuffler's lead guitar, both recordings are quite similar. Clearly, the Stanleys were paying homage to the Monroes with this performance.

King #25: July 1964 (Session 640716)

The Stanley Brothers made their last secular bluegrass recordings for King on July 16 and 17, 1964. Only eight songs were done at the session. Earlier sessions were culled for the remaining four tracks: "Your Selfish Heart" (September 30, 1958), "What About You" (January 15, 1961), "I See Through You" (July 20, 1961), and "Chickie's Old Gray Mule" (May 4, 1962). The album was called *The Remarkable Stanley Brothers Play and Sing Bluegrass Songs for You*. In contrast to their other King album covers, this one featured Carter and Ralph in an informal outdoor setting. Ralph observed, "We look relaxed there, didn't we? I believe it was a hot day and we got out and made these pictures. Seemed like just outside of the studio there. We usually wore a suit and tie and maybe a hat and we said we're just gonna look relaxed on this one."[60]

In addition to regular Clinch Mountain Boy George Shuffler on lead guitar, also appearing on the album are Art Stamper on fiddle, Earl Taylor on mandolin and harmonica, and Vernon McIntyre Jr. on bass. Starting the session are "Bully of the Town," "Back Up

George Shuffler was supposed to receive billing on the Stanleys' next release, *The Remarkable Stanley Brothers Play and Sing Bluegrass Songs For You*, as he had on the *Hymns of the Cross* album. However, when the album went into production, he was cropped out of the cover photo. In the original session photography, he was standing off to the left, beside Ralph.

and Push," and "Careless Love," three instrumentals that highlight the instrumental work of Shuffler, Stamper, Taylor, and Ralph Stanley.

"How Bad I Do Feel" is an old song related to several other tunes, including "Jack of Diamonds," "Rye Whiskey," "The Rabble Soldier," and "Frosty Mornin'." In fact, the original ledgers for the session initially listed the song's title as "Frosty Morn." Not one of the Stanley Brothers' better efforts, it required twenty-one takes to obtain an acceptable version. Session engineer Ron Lenhoff recalled, "We spent eight hours one time at a session because they wouldn't give it up. It was just a bad tune right from the very start. They just wouldn't let go of it. That was one of the first things that they did [at the session] . . . they just put everybody in a bad mood."[61] It is one of two tunes from the session that feature Earl Taylor on harmonica.

"Rollin' on Rubber Wheels," a Carter Stanley original, represents the Stanley Brothers' first entry into the truck driver craze of country music in the mid-1960s. Other King artists, Moore & Napier and Reno & Smiley, had recently completed entire albums of truck driver material.

"Our Darlin's Gone" is a re-recording of a song the Stanley Brothers had cut at their second session, for Rich-R-Tone Records, in the early part of 1948. This track also contains the harmonica work of Earl Taylor.

King #26: July 1964 (Session 640717)

"How You've Tortured My Mind" is an original composition by Carter Stanley and Peggy Stanley, Ralph's first wife. It is featured as a trio with George Shuffler. The final selection, "I'm Bound to Ride," was popularized by the old-time duo of Sam and Kirk McGee. The Stanleys had been performing this tune for years, with Carter singing the lead vocals and Ralph playing clawhammer banjo. In an obvious tip of the hat to the song's first performers, Carter would sometimes call out the names of Sam and Kirk McGee during Ralph's banjo breaks. The Stanleys had changed the arrangement of the song by the time of the session, putting Ralph Stanley front and center, playing three-finger banjo and singing the song as a solo.

Newport Folk Festival: July 1964 (Sessions 640723–640726)

Barely a week after their recording session in Cincinnati for King, the Stanleys were in Rhode Island for the 1964 Newport Folk Festival. The proceedings were recorded by Vanguard Records, which had taped previous Newport festivals and issued albums of the various concerts. The core trio of Carter and Ralph Stanley and George Shuffler was augmented by the talents of a new Clinch Mountain Boy, Harold "Red" Stanley. He evidently joined the group after the recording session for King, and his appearance with the Stanleys at Newport was one of his first show dates—if not *the* first—with them.

Fiddle player Harold "Red" Stanley was born on May 4, 1922, and grew up in the Jamestown, Tennessee, area. His father, Elmer, was an old-time fiddler. Red was a veteran of World War II. Some of his early work included a stint with the Rhythm Serenaders, a group that appeared on the WLBC *Hoosierland Jamboree* out of Muncie, Indiana, in 1952. He later worked with Bill Monroe, helping him record several sessions for Decca in 1962. One of his career highlights was a performance at Carnegie Hall with Mac Wiseman and Benny Williams. He worked with the Stanley Brothers for about a year, starting in July of 1964 and ending in the late spring of 1965. He died on February 8, 1987.[62]

The Stanley Brothers' appearance at Newport was in all likelihood before the largest audience that they ever played for. The event spanned four days, from July 23 to July 26, and was estimated to have had seventy thousand people in attendance. The festival was a mixture of evening concerts on the main stage in Freebody Park (a sports arena) and morning and afternoon workshops at nearby St. Michaels School. An afternoon blues workshop was touted to have three thousand in attendance, up drastically from the previous year's workshop high of six hundred.

The opening Thursday night concert was hosted by Alan Lomax and consisted entirely of traditional performers, with thirty separate acts. With such a massive array of talent, each group was allotted two songs. As such, the Stanley Brothers' contribution to the evening consisted of "The White Dove" and "Hard Times." The recording shows Carter Stanley, suffering from laryngitis again, limiting his involvement to making song introductions and singing on the choruses to "The White Dove"; George Shuffler sings lead. Ralph's banjo work on "Hard Times" is one of the highlights of the evening.

Workshops on Friday included several banjo sessions, with one devoted to bluegrass stylings and another to old-time. Ralph plays two songs in the clawhammer manner on the old-time segment: "Little Birdie" and "Shout Little Luly." The bluegrass set includes "Clinch Mountain Backstep," "Hard Times," and "Little Maggie." George Shuffler backs up Ralph by playing bass, and Carter presumably plays guitar.

Saturday morning's workshop, hosted by Ralph Rinzler and Mike Seeger, was devoted to string bands and included such notables as Clayton McMichen, the Osborne Brothers, Hobart Smith, and the Watson Family. Up-and-coming or lesser-known groups included the Greenbriar Boys and the Phipps Family. The Stanley Brothers and the Osborne Brothers evidently traded musicians during the workshop, as the recordings shows George Shuffler playing bass with Bob and Sonny, thus allowing Benny Birchfield to play guitar and sing in the trios. Birchfield in turn fills in with the Stanleys, playing bass so that Shuffler can play lead guitar and sing. Photos from this set show an interesting collection of performers seated around the stage, including cohost Ralph Rinzler and Doc and Merle Watson. Carter is heard on the recording acknowledging a request from Doc for the "Orange Blossom Special." Other songs include "How Mountain Girls Can Love," "Man of Constant Sorrow," "Little Glass of Wine," and "Big Tilda." Carter is still straining with his voice and as such minimizes the amount of singing he does on the show. Consequently, show pieces by Ralph and instrumentals make up the bulk of the set.

The Sunday morning Concert of Religious Music features two songs by the Stanley Brothers, "Jordan" and "Rank Stranger." Both are trios consisting of Carter and Ralph Stanley and George Shuffler. The music from all four days of Stanley Brothers appearances at Newport was issued on two Vanguard CDs in the 1990s called *Clinch Mountain Bluegrass* and *Bluegrass Breakdown*.

Ray Davis and Wango Records #5: November 1964 (Session 641122)

On November 21, 1964, the Stanley Brothers were in Baltimore, Maryland, to perform at the Lyric Theater with Flatt & Scruggs and the Stoneman Family. Appearing with the Stanleys on the show that night was Red Stanley and bass player Barry Glickman. The latter related, "I grew up in Baltimore . . . played with Jack Cooke for a couple of years. [The Stanley Brothers] just came into town and called me at six o'clock, the night of the concert. I mean, I had tickets to the concert. I was kind of nervous; I don't know how well I did."[63]

Ray Davis had a hand in producing the event at the Lyric, though he noted that the venue probably wasn't the most appropriate one for bluegrass. Built in 1894 and originally called The Music Hall (it was renamed The Lyric in 1909), the auditorium was usually home to more sophisticated social events. Still, a big crowd with a lot of appreciative bluegrass fans attended the event. It was one of the few occasions when the Stanley Brothers and Flatt & Scruggs appeared on the same bill. Even though Ray had booked the show, he didn't attend it. The manager of the station where Ray's programs were broadcast, WBMD, oversaw the show and paid the bands. The manager was somewhat peeved with the Stanley Brothers because legendary fiddle player Chubby Wise, who apparently had worked recently with Carter and Ralph, wasn't on the program; he even wanted a rebate because of Wise's absence.[64]

The following day, Carter and Ralph ventured into the tiny second-story studio of Johnny's Used Cars for more recording sessions with Ray Davis. These produced the final two Stanley albums (Wango 105 and 106) released on Ray's label. Both projects were gospel, and most of the selections were drawn from a hymnbook Ray Davis had at the sessions.

Baltimore native Barry Glickman also lent a hand on these sessions. He was a fan of bluegrass and had made numerous trips to country music parks in the area, such as New River Ranch and Sunset Park, to see the Stanley Brothers, Jim & Jesse, Reno & Smiley, and others. For several years in the early 1960s, he played bass in Jack Cooke's band. One memorable event during this time period was a show when Cooke's band backed up Mac Wiseman. It was Barry's association with Jack that led to his recording with the Stanley Brothers. He currently lives in California, where he is an in-demand graphic artist.

Jack Cooke was present at the sessions, too, playing rhythm guitar and singing an occasional harmony part. Also on hand was Red Stanley. The recordings he made for these two Wango albums represent his only studio work with the Stanley Brothers.

The first selection on Wango 105 is "Hold to God's Unchanging Hand," a song from Ray's gospel songbook that was written by Jenny Wilson and F. L. Eiland in 1905. "When I Lay My Burdens Down" has been classified over the years as a "negro spiritual."[65] Alternately known as "Happy in Prison," it was recorded by old-time groups such as the Carter Family and Ernest Phipps & His Holiness Quartet in the 1920s and '30s. However, a 1940 recording by Roy Acuff, released as "When I Lay My Burden Down," appears to be the likely model for the Stanley Brothers' version. The song dates back to the very early days of the Stanleys' career. Ralph recalled in 1966,

> The very first song we ever sang on a radio [May of 1941] was in Elizabethton, Tennessee. It was a Saturday morning show that they had there called the *Barrel of Fun*, and I believe the first song we sang was "When I Lay My Burden Down." And way back then, Carter always liked to cut up a little bit and holler maybe during a song. The first time we played on the radio, why he tried to holler and it wouldn't come out, he was scared so bad it wouldn't come out.[66]

The Stanley Brothers had recorded "In Heaven We'll Never Grow Old" for Starday in the very early part of 1960. The Starday version features Ralph singing the lead vocals; on this version, Carter handles the lead vocal chores. Ray Davis recalled that when he recorded the song, he didn't have any speakers in the studio—just a single headphone—and it was difficult to gauge exactly what he was getting, performance-wise. Upon listening to the song in 2009, Ray Davis felt that Carter offered up a very heartfelt and meaningful rendition.[67]

Three songs included on the Wango 105 album were not recorded at the sessions that produced the bulk of the material for the disc: duets by George Shuffler and Ralph Stanley, all presumably drawn from the radio shows that Ray recorded in December of 1963. The first is a tune the Stanleys had recorded earlier for King, called "Somebody Touched Me." The other two songs are also remakes of earlier recordings; "Paul and Silas" previously appeared on King, and "I Saw the Light" was earlier issued by Starday.

"Lord, I'm Coming Home" was written in the late 1800s by prolific gospel songwriter William J. Fitzpatrick. Ray Davis commented that this tune happens to be the very last song the Stanleys recorded for Wango—it was Ray's idea for Carter and Ralph to trade lead vocals on the verses. James Rowe and R. H. Cornelius copyrighted "Give Me the Roses While I Live" in the early 1920s. Like Fitzpatrick, Rowe was very active in composing gospel songs in the early part of the 1900s. Ralph Stanley would record the song again in 1971 for Rebel Records.[68]

Side two of the Wango 105 release starts off with the "negro spiritual" "Swing Low, Sweet Chariot," a tune that for many years was a favorite of Bill Monroe's. Two years later, Monroe sang the song at Carter Stanley's funeral. "Paul and Silas" had been previously recorded by the Stanley Brothers, in 1962, for their King album *Good Old Camp Meeting Songs*. "Gathering Flowers for the Master's Bouquet" had been recorded twice before by the Stanley Brothers, once for Columbia in 1949 and again for Starday in 1960. The Stanley Brothers had recorded "The Old Country Church" previously as well, as a quartet in 1961. It appears as an instrumental on the Wango recording. Making its third appearance on Wango is the December 1963 recording of "Will You Miss Me When I'm Gone?" Hank Williams is represented with his "I Saw the Light," a song that the Stanley Brothers had recorded for Starday in May of 1960. Closing out the album is the J. B. Coats standard "Where Could I Go?"

Wango 106 opens up with "Little Country Church House," a song the Masters Family recorded for Mercury in the early 1950s. They also provided "The Cry from the Cross" for the Stanley Brothers. For some time, the original release of "Little Old Country Church House" was surrounded by confusion. One side of a Flatt & Scruggs' Mercury 78 rpm single from New Year's Day in 1951, "Cora Is Gone," was backed, not with another Flatt & Scruggs title, but with the Masters Family version of the song. Because of the odd coupling of the two titles, Flatt & Scruggs began receiving requests for the song and consequently added it to their repertoire for a period of time.[69] Mercury compounded the mistake nearly a decade later by including the track in an album of Flatt & Scruggs material.

The Stanley Brothers' recording of "Little Country Church House" features Jack Cooke prominently, starting with the opening guitar notes. Ray Davis recalled that Carter read the song's lyrics from an Albert E. Brumley hymnbook that Ray had at the session, the source of many of the session's songs. As Carter was reading the words, Jack Cooke provided the guitar rhythm.[70] Years later, Ray compiled a gospel CD called *Little Old Country Church House* that was used as a fundraising premium on radio station WAMU in Washington, DC. The cover of the CD featured a picture of the church that he attended as a youth.[71]

"Little Country Church House" had a special meaning for Ray at the time. The church that his mother attended, the one that was featured on the cover of the fundraiser CD, had recently closed. His mother had loved to keep the church decorated with fresh flowers and enjoyed playing the piano there. It was a time of sadness for her when the church closed, and it was these circumstances that prompted Ray to ask Carter and Ralph to record the song. Happily, the church reopened not long after the session, and Ray felt that possibly the song was a good omen. There was some discussion about how to end the song, and this is probably the only Stanley song on Wango that is gradually faded out as the Stanleys repeat the last line of the chorus.[72]

Appearing next is "Nobody Answered Me," which was copyrighted in 1937 by Albert E. Brumley. The song was popularized by Roy Acuff on one of his Columbia recordings from that era. It was Ray Davis who suggested the song to the Stanleys, and again it was Ray's book of hymns compiled by Albert E. Brumley that provided the lyrics.[73] "Shake My Mother's Hand for Me" appeared in several shape-note hymnals of the 1930s and '40s and is credited to a 1937 arrangement by Eugene Wright. Bill Monroe recorded the song as a quartet at his second session for Bluebird on October 2, 1941. Preparing to record it at the Wango session, Carter warned Ray that his performance would be over the top. Davis had an old tube-type recorder with a built in compressor that supposedly compensated for loud spikes of volume in the recording process. Despite this technology, Carter managed to peak the meters that measured the input levels into the red danger zone. Ray feared that the equipment would overload and breakdown, but such was not the case, and the Stanleys managed to turn in an energetic performance.[74]

"I Heard My Mother Call My Name in Prayer" and "Mother's Only Sleeping" had both been recorded earlier by the Stanley Brothers, in February 1961 at sessions for their *Old Time Camp Meeting* album on King. Completing the trio of mother songs is "Shake Hands with Mother Again," a song composed by a W. A. Berry that appeared in a number of shape-note hymnals in the 1930s, '40s and '50s. As he had with one of the other Wango tracks, Carter read its words from a Brumley hymnbook. Consequently, Jack Cooke, whom Carter referred to as "Cookie Bird," fills in on rhythm guitar; he also contributes harmony vocals.[75]

Side two of Wango 106 leads off with the up-tempo "Hide Ye in the Blood," a song that dates at least to the early 1900s, when it appeared, uncredited, in a shape-note hymnal. "Give Me Your Hand" was copyrighted 1923 by Rev. Johnson Oatman Jr. and gospel music publishing giant James D. Vaughan. Ralph Stanley sings this as a solo. "Where We'll Never Grow Old" and "Leaning on the Everlasting Arms" had both been recorded by the Stanley Brothers in May of 1962 as part of their *Good Old Camp Meeting Songs* album for King. "Angel Band" was likewise recorded earlier, in 1955 for Mercury. Rev. Elisha A. Hoffman, a composer who wrote several songs that have become standards in the field of gospel music, copyrighted "Are You Washed in the Blood?" in 1879. Closing out Wango 106 is "Farther Along." Ray Davis later noted that Jack Cooke was playing the guitar because Carter was reading the words from the Brumley hymn book."[76] Most shape-note hymnals of the 1930s, '40s, and '50s use an arrangement of the song that was copyrighted in 1937, crediting the composition to Rev. W. B. Stevens and the arrangement to J. R. Baxter Jr.

University of Chicago Folk Festival: January 1965 (Session 650129)

In January of 1965, the Stanley Brothers appeared once again at the University of Chicago Folk Festival. The event took place over a three-day period, and Carter and Ralph appeared twice, once on January 29 and again on the 31st. The band included Red Stanley on fiddle, Larry Sparks on lead guitar, and Ray Tate on bass. With the exception of one new song, Carter's recently composed "Sharecropper's Son," the material presented was fairly typical Stanley fare. The shows were presented in the school's Mandel Hall. Other performers throughout the weekend included Mississippi John Hurt, the Beers Family, Glenn Ohrlin, Stringbean, Sarah Gunning, and the Phipps Family.

Larry Sparks was born on September 15, 1947, in Lebanon, Ohio. With the help of his older sister, Bernice, he started learning to play guitar at age five. Among his influences were radio stations in Nashville (WSM) and Cincinnati (WCKY) as well as performers such as the Stanley Brothers, Wayne Raney, and Paul "Moon" Mullins. It was Mullins who arranged an audition for Larry with the Stanley Brothers, sometime in the middle or latter part of 1964. Larry played with the Stanleys off and on until October of 1966, when he left to pursue other performance opportunities. Following the death of Carter Stanley in December of 1966, Larry became Ralph Stanley's first new lead singer, a spot he held for three years. He recorded five albums with Ralph, leaving him in 1969 to organize his own band, the Lonesome Ramblers, a group he has headed for more than forty years. A two-time winner of the International Bluegrass Music Association's award for Male Vocalist of the Year, he remains a vibrant and in-demand performer on the bluegrass concert and festival circuit.

A native of Illinois, Ray Tate was by the early 1960s a fixture of the Chicago traditional music scene and an instructor at the Old Town School of Music. His appearance with the Stanley Brothers at the University of Chicago Folk Festival happened by chance; the group needed a bass player, and he just happened to be there. In the 1970s and early '80s, he served as the director of the Old Town School of Music. Later music opportunities took him to Texas and then to Europe for an extended stay. He currently resides near Akron, Ohio.

Oscar Brand—World of Folk Music: Spring 1965 (650500)

In the late spring of 1965, the Stanley Brothers appeared as guests of Oscar Brand on his *World of Folk Music* program, which was sponsored by the Social Security Administration. Appearing with Carter and Ralph were Curley Lambert and Red Stanley. Brand was a well-known figure in folk music circles, having started in radio in 1945. He had introduced the Stanley Brothers for their appearances at the Newport Folk Festival in 1959. His *World of Folk Music* episodes were assembled at a radio studio in New York City then pressed on albums and distributed to about 1,800 radio stations nationwide. The shows were fifteen minutes long and included selections by Brand, narrative pieces about the Social Security Administration, and songs by guest artists. The Stanley Brothers performed two of their more popular selections for their appearance, "How Mountain Girls Can Love" and "Stone Walls and Steel Bars."

Cabin Creek: June 1965 (650605)

Yet another of Carter and Ralph's quickie albums was recorded in June of 1965, this time for Alex Campbell's Cabin Creek label. Campbell, along with his sister, Ola Belle Reed is best remembered as New River Ranch's house band in the 1950s. Alex's Cabin Creek label had relatively few releases, most of them by Campbell and Reed and their New River Boys. However, there were two fine collections by the Stanley Brothers and the duo of Don Reno and Benny Martin.

The Stanley and Reno-Martin releases were both originally titled *Bluegrass Gospel Favorites* and produced specifically to be sold on Alex's radio show that was heard on Saturday nights after the *Jamboree* on WWVA in Wheeling, West Virginia. With a keen eye towards marketing, Alex produced these albums in a manner that let him advertise them as containing an incredible twenty-two songs. This was accomplished by making most of the songs relatively short, only about a minute each. Nearly all contained only a verse and a chorus. The original issues of these albums did not stay on the market very long. When Alex's radio offer expired, they were allowed to go out of print. Rebel Records reissued them as cassette-only releases in the 1980s.

The band that recorded the Stanley LP was composed of Carter and Ralph, Jack Cooke on guitar, Sonny Miller on fiddle, and Curley Lambert on mandolin. Curiously, Ralph Stanley sings lead on only one track, "An Empty Mansion," and harmony on only one other, "Dust on the Bible." The majority of the remaining tunes are trios with Carter Stanley singing lead, Jack Cooke singing tenor, and Curley Lambert singing baritone. Virtually all of the selections appear to have been drawn from shape-note hymnals and would have resonated well with traditional country audiences of the day.

Arthur K. "Sonny" Miller was born on May 2, 1932. In his late teens, he got his start

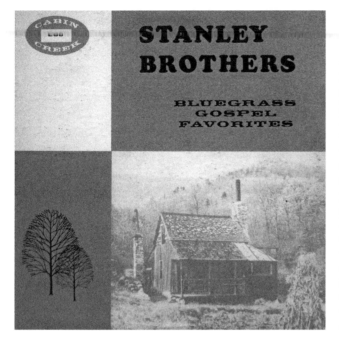

In June of 1965, the Stanley Brothers moonlighted to record an album of gospel songs for their longtime friend Alex Campbell. In addition to being part of the house band at Sunset Park, Campbell hosted a number of radio shows over the years. He was able to promote this album on his program on the powerful WWVA station in Wheeling, West Virginia. Part of his sales pitch was calling attention to the fact that there were an amazing "twenty-two songs on one LP." He achieved this by having the group record abbreviated versions of the songs, with usually just a verse and a chorus on each.

playing fiddle with Alex Campbell and Ola Belle Reed and the New River Boys and Girls, performing with them for most of the next thirty years. He took time out for a stint in the Air Force that was followed by a brief stay with Charlie Monroe and the Kentucky Pardners. He then returned to Alex and Ola Belle, who were then the house band at Sunset Park. He recorded several albums with the group, as well as the album with the Stanley Brothers and a few sides with Ted Lundy. Towards the end of his career, he appeared on recordings by Herschel Sizemore, Joe Val, and Del McCoury. In November of 1978, he joined up with McCoury's Dixie Pals. He stayed with them until his untimely passing on November 24, 1981, when his car slid off an icy bridge in northeastern Maryland and he drowned.[77] He was forty-nine.

King #27: September 1965 (Session 650908)

In September of 1965, the Stanleys and George Shuffler returned to King Studios in Cincinnati to record what would be their final album for the label. The project was recorded at two different sessions: the first on September 8 and the second two weeks later, on September 20. On this final set of recordings for King, the entire band consisted of Carter, Ralph, and George Shuffler. Shuffler was used to the maximum, playing lead guitar, dubbing in the bass, and singing baritone on all the selections.

In April of 1966, shortly before the release of the album, Carter said of the session, "I felt like the last time we was there we got the best [sound] we've ever got at King. I haven't heard any of it yet, but it was a sacred album and I believe it's supposed to be released

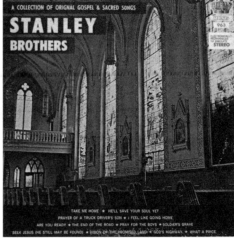

The Stanley Brothers recorded their last album for King Records in September of 1965. A collection of gospel songs, it was released the following year. Unfortunately, the art department was not clued in to the gospel nature of the material and created a somewhat gaudy album cover and title, *The Greatest Country & Western Show on Earth*. At Ralph Stanley's insistence, the album was quickly changed to the more appropriate *A Collection of Orignal* [*sic*] *Gospel & Sacred Songs*.

most any time. But I know I was well pleased with the sound."[78] The album was originally released with a gaudy jacket that was totally inappropriate for the material and billed the Stanley Brothers as the *Greatest Country and Western Show on Earth*. Ralph Stanley related, "I got Syd Nathan to see into this . . . a gospel album and he calls us the *Greatest Country and Western Show on Earth* and I told him that would never do and he changed the cover and it's a big brown church or something. He agreed real quick with me on that. He probably wasn't paying any attention to the songs."[79] A later, and more appropriate, jacket was made correctly describing the material as *A Collection of Orignal* [*sic*] *Gospel and Sacred Songs*.

Reviews of the album were generally favorable. A review by Dick Spottswood in the August 1966 issue of *Bluegrass Unlimited* read,

> This is probably the most unusual title ever given to an album of hymns, but we'll be charitable and assume it was a mistake. In any case, don't let it interfere with your enjoyment of this first-class album, the best from the Stanleys in years. No small part of the credit goes to George Shuffler whose style meshes perfectly with the Stanleys. These are beautiful hymns performed by one of the very best bluegrass bands around, and no one will want to be without it.[80]

Most of the songs from the September 8 session are indeed recent original compositions. These include "God's Highway," "The End of the Road," "Seek Jesus (He Still May Be Found)," "He'll Save Your Soul Yet," and "I Feel Like Going Home." Carter and Ralph

This single contained one of the last songs that the Stanley Brothers recorded for King, "God's Highway." The preprinted sleeve calls attention to the variety of sublabels owned by King Records.

wrote all but one of the songs, "Take Me Home." In a Stanley Brothers personal appearance at Bean Blossom, Indiana, on October 16, 1966, Carter related,

> To be honest with you, we learned it in a Baptist meeting down home a long time ago, when they used to have the old-timers outside and the dinner on the ground . . . all day preaching and dinner on the ground or all day dinner and preaching on the ground usually the way it turned out to be. We learned this number there. It's in our new album, too, it's called "Take Me Home, Savior, Take Me Home."[81]

The song is known to have circulated in the mountains of western North Carolina in the 1880s, and a printed version appeared in an 1868 book titled *Slave Songs of the United States*.[82]

King #28: September 1965 (Session 650920)

On September 20, the Stanleys recorded the final six songs to finish the album. Recorded first, "Are You Ready" was written by the Stanleys' friend Gene Duty. Ralph recalled,

> He worked as a mechanic up in the state of Michigan. He was originally from Dickenson County, down in Council and Haysi. We met him after he went to Michigan. He got some fingers cut off, he worked for Cadillac up there, and of course he got disability and he was just about free to do . . . he could work when he wanted to and he traveled with us a lot and him and Carter were great friends. He took Carter under his wing and waited on him like a mother would a child. He just sort of . . . he worked when

he wanted to and then when he didn't he traveled with us and wrote songs, wrote a lot of songs. He wrote that . . . one I sung solo, "Beautiful Woman." He wrote several.[83]

"Prayer of a Truck Driver's Son" is one of the few recitations that the Stanleys ever recorded, Ralph related. "I was living in Florida and I got up about three o'clock one morning and I got three songs on my mind and, afraid I'd forget it, I got up and wrote three songs. 'Prayer of a Truck Driver's Son' was one of 'em. 'I Feel Like Going Home,' I wrote that. And 'Vision of the Promised Land,' I wrote that."[84] "What a Price" is another song written by Gene Duty.

The last two songs of the session are patriotic war songs that were recorded in response to the growing conflict in Vietnam. Flatt & Scruggs had recorded "Pray for the Boys" in the early 1950s, during the Korean War; it was featured in several shape-note hymnals at that time. The last song recorded is "Soldier's Grave." During the Stanley's 1966 Bean Blossom show, Carter introduced it, saying,

> [This is] a song that I guess was popular during World War II, some of you folks might remember it, some of you men folks that is, of course none of the women are that old but some of you men might remember this number. Johnnie and Walter, the Bailes Brothers from Charleston, West Virginia, recorded this song during World War II. I thought it was a good song then, I always have liked it. We recorded it and it's out now on King Record and it's called "A Soldier's Grave." We used that song on all of our shows in Europe this past spring, in about six different countries, and I believe it went over better, the folks seemed to like it better than any song that we did. I might mention this, too, while we're speaking of the war songs and the like, I know most of you have some connections, either friends or relatives, that are stationed in or near Vietnam. I'd consider it a real favor if you'd write to 'em and tell 'em that the Stanley Brothers are coming to South Vietnam in January, the latter part of January.[85] We'll be in that country, in and around there for six weeks. So if you do have friends or relatives that you think would enjoy our down-home playing and singing, drop 'em a note and tell 'em we're coming, and I'd like to see 'em all while we're there.[86]

Though credited to Roy Acuff, "Searching for a Soldier's Grave" was written by Jim and Jack Anglin and Johnnie Wright during the early 1940s. Like "Dying a Sinner's Death," which the Stanleys recorded in February of 1961, the song was sold to Roy Acuff as part of a package of twenty-one songs that the trio had written. Johnnie Wright recalled, "We used to sing it ['Searching For A Soldier's Grave'] . . . when we were up in Knoxville at WNOX, during the war. Eddie [Hill] did a real high part then and did a recitation on it." Their inspiration for the song came from "all the people over there who got killed and buried, a lot of them didn't have tombstones."[87]

Rimrock: December 1965 (Session 651208)

Shortly after completing the album for King, the Stanleys traveled to Arkansas to visit and work with their old friend Wayne Raney, who owned Rimrock Records. Fan club president

Fay McGinnis noted with an item in the November 1965 issue of the *Stanleys Brothers Fan Club Newsletter* [*sic*], "I believe the second week of Dec. will be spent around Concord, Ark. playing shows with Wayne Rainy [*sic*], there will also be some radio shows."[88] The group recorded twenty-five songs while moonlighting with Raney.

Appearing on the Rimrock sessions are George Shuffler on lead guitar and Ralph Mayo on fiddle, the same combination that had recorded the *Good Old Camp Meeting Songs* project for King in May of 1962. Ralph Mayo later recalled that the Rimrock projects were "recorded at Concord, Arkansas. Wayne had a pretty nice studio set up in his . . . he had a big fine brick mansion way out there in the middle of nowhere. [He] had four or five chicken houses outside."[89] George Shuffler remembered that Wayne had a "big old ranch down there [with] about fifty thousand chickens and a thousand head of steers, and boy, he had it alright. That was when these mail orders was still so heavy and he had his own little old pressing place and shipping."[90]

Much of the material that appears on the Rimrock sessions is the same as what the Stanley Brothers had just recorded for Wango. Ray Davis, despite his friendship and admiration for Wayne Raney, seemed a little perturbed in later years that Carter and Ralph re-recorded so many of the same songs that they had cut for him.[91] Unfortunately, the Rimrock recordings are probably the most lackluster of the Stanley Brothers' career. Wayne's wife, Loys Raney, later noted, "At that time Carter was very sick. I cooked all of their meals while they were there."[92] One bright spot in the proceedings occurs when Wayne Raney teams up on harmonica with the Stanleys to produce a lively rendition of "Where the Soul Never Dies."

Thomas Wayne Raney was born on August 17, 1921, in Wolf Bayou, Arkansas. He learned to play harmonica at an early age and by age thirteen was working on radio station XEPN in Piedras Negras, Mexico. In 1936 he met his long-time partner, Lonnie Glosson. They moved to Little Rock, Arkansas, in 1938 and later wound up at WCKY in Cincinnati. Raney and Glosson formed a harmonica mail-order business and are reported to have sold millions of instruments. Raney teamed up with the Delmore Brothers to make a series of recordings for King Records in the late 1940s. During this same time, he also recorded as a solo artist for King, introducing popular selections such as "Lost John Boogie" and "Jack and Jill Boogie." His biggest hit was "Why Don't You Haul Off and Love Me." In the 1950s, he worked at WSM, on the KOVR-TV *California Hayride* and the WWVA *Jamboree*, and at Cincinnati's WCKY. Of Raney's time in Cincinnati, Ralph Stanley noted,

> We had heard and admired him since we were all very young, but when he started spinning the country records on WCKY in Cincinnati, Ohio, we had the privilege of meeting him. We began to visit him at his home when we were in that part of the country . . . Wayne Raney did more for the Stanley Brothers by playing our records and promoting us than anyone else living today.[93]

WCKY was a clear-channel station, with a signal that blanketed the South during the evening and nighttime hours. Raney's show was listened to by a large number of people throughout the region. While in Cincinnati, Raney was also connected with Jimmie Skinner

Music Center, one of the leading mail-order outlets for country and bluegrass recordings. It was during this time that he made another influential recording, "We Need a Lot More Jesus (And a Lot Less Rock and Roll)." After returning to Arkansas in the early 1960s, he formed Rimrock Records. Like King Records, Raney did everything in-house. He had his own recording studio and pressed his own records. It was in Raney's studio in December of 1965 that the Stanley Brothers made their last commercial recordings. Raney published his autobiography, *Life Has Not Been a Bed of Roses*, in 1990. He died of cancer on January 23, 1993.[94]

Pete Seeger's *Rainbow Quest*: February 1966 (Session 660224)

On February 24, 1966, the Stanley Brothers were in Newark, New Jersey, ten miles from New York City's center, preparing for their first and only overseas tour. A number of bands made the trip, including the New Lost City Ramblers, Roscoe Holcomb, Cousin Emmy, and Cyp Landreneau's Cajun Band. While in Newark, the Stanley Brothers and Cousin Emmy appeared on Pete Seeger's *Rainbow Quest* television program, which aired over public television stations. The band was made up of George Shuffler on lead guitar, Don Miller on fiddle, and Chick Stripling on bass.

Fiddle player Don Miller was introduced by Carter on the Seeger program as being from Point Pleasant, West Virginia. Unfortunately, little of substance is known about his life or career. At some point, Don made his way to the Northern Virginia area where he worked in a group called Ed Cassady and the Hidden Valley Ramblers. Also in the band were noted DC-based musicians Bill and Wayne Yates. Don appeared on one album with the Ramblers, *From the Heart of Bluegrass Country*. As preparations were being made for the Stanley Brothers' upcoming tour of Europe, fiddle player Biller Baker was sought for the trip. But with him unable to make the tour, Don Miller was a last-minute replacement. Various newspaper articles in support of the tour listed his name as James Miller. When the group returned to the States, Don parted ways with the Stanleys and drifted into obscurity. He is reported to have died in the Northern Virginia area some time in the 1990s.

Although the Stanley Brothers appeared on television quite often throughout their career, very few of their performances were saved on film or videotape. For a number of years, the *Rainbow Quest* appearance was thought to be the only surviving footage of the band. While other footage has come to light over the years, it is nevertheless probably the best of what is available. The recording quality is good, and the band is in a good groove. Carter Stanley is in good voice and displays his amicable emcee work. A nice cross section of material is presented, including a duet by Carter and Ralph on a song they never commercially recorded, "It Takes a Worried Man"; an instrumental by Ralph, "Clinch Mountain Backstep"; a bit of comedy with Chick Stripling, as well as a sample of his "butter paddle buck and wing dance"; a sacred song, "Jacob's Vision"; and a solo by Carter on another song that the duo never recorded, "Single Girl."

American Folk and Country Music Festival, Germany: March 1966 (Session 660301)

A week later, the band was in West Germany preparing a television documentary on country music for broadcast to European audiences. Narrated, in German, by one of the New Lost City Ramblers, Tracy Schwarz, the documentary has various members of the Clinch Mountain Boys appearing throughout it to back up other performers. The Stanley Brothers perform on their own twice, showcasing "How Mountain Girls Can Love" and "Rank Stranger."

American Folk and Country Music Festival, Germany: March 1966 (Session 660317)

On March 17, as the European tour was nearing its completion, the ensemble performed in the town of Bremen in West Germany. The show was recorded and later issued by Bear Family in a deluxe two-CD set that contained an exquisite hardcover book with a huge selection of photos. On the recording, the Stanley Brothers are introduced on stage by John Cohen of the New Lost City Ramblers. Carter and Ralph perform one of their standards, "How Mountain Girls Can Love," and then offer up a duet with "Nobody's Business." Roscoe Holcomb is introduced next, and he is joined by Carter and Ralph on an a cappella version of "Village Church Yard," probably one of the first examples of a bluegrass band performing songs in an unaccompanied manner. Another set features the Clinch Mountain Boys soloing on a few instrumentals such as the fiddle tune "Leather Britches" and a guitar rendering of "Cannonball Blues." Closing out the set is a medley the Stanley Brothers featured on a number of their shows that year. The trio of songs consists of "Roll in My Sweet Baby's Arms," "Long Journey Home," and "Katie Cline."

Last Performance: Brown County Jamboree, October 1966 (Session 661016a)

On October 16, 1966, the Stanley Brothers—along with George Shuffler on guitar and Melvin Goins on bass—played their last full program together. They appeared at Bill Monroe's Brown County Jamboree in Bean Blossom, Indiana. The person running the sound equipment, Marvin Hedrick, recorded the show that day. He also made patches into the soundboard available to other tapers, including Bill Ivey, later the director of the Country Music Foundation and the chairman of the National Endowment for the Arts. The Stanley Brothers performed three sets of music that day: an afternoon show, an evening show, and a short closing set.

Last Performance: Brown County Jamboree, October 1966 (Session 661016b)

A number of selections from the first set of the day were used for the Joy/Rebel release *Together for the Last Time*. Ralph Stanley later issued the entire set on his StanleyTone label. In his book *Bluegrass*, Bob Artis observes, "Carter's voice was little more than a shadow of what it had been only a few years before, but he sang with the strength and conviction and depth of feeling that characterized everything he had ever done."[95]

In contrast to a number of other recordings of live concerts, this set seems to offer a lot more variety and less rehashing of recent record selections. Leading off is a duet by Carter and Ralph on "Nobody's Business." George Shuffler solos on "Another Day, Another Dollar," written by West Coast country star Wynn Stewart, whose single release of the song on the Challenge label had charted in November of 1962, eventually peaking at number twenty-seven. Porter Wagoner then covered the song, and it appeared as the opening track of his 1965 album on RCA, *The Thin Man from West Plains*. "Somebody Loves You, Darling," not previously recorded by the Stanley Brothers, was written by the Morris Brothers, a duo noted for writing "Salty Dog Blues." George Shuffler offers an instrumental version of "Little Rosewood Casket," and the group performs several sacred selections, including a quartet arrangement of a Bill Monroe song, "Boat of Love," that featured Bill's brother, Birch, singing bass. Other songs not commercially recorded are "Single Girl" and "Worried Man Blues." Several songs from the Stanleys' recent gospel album are highlighted, including "Searching for a Soldier's Grave," "Are You Ready," and "Take Me Home."

The Stanley Brothers came back for an evening performance at Bean Blossom, a set that appeared in its entirety as an issue in Copper Creek's *Stanley Series*. While not as lengthy as the first program of the day, it does contain more fresh material, including a take on Monroe's "My Dixie Home" and a repeat of "Somebody Loves You, Darling." George Shuffler offers up "I Know What It Means to Be Lonesome" and another instrumental version of "Little Rosewood Casket." Melvin Goins is highlighted with some comedy routines with George Shuffler and Carter Stanley and sings a solo on "Charming Betsy." The last part of the set is spent with Birch Monroe on stage. He does two fiddle tunes, "Down Yonder" and "Lost Train Blues," then sings the bass part in two sacred selections, "Canaan's Land" and "A Beautiful Life." Carter acknowledges on the program that this is the first time they ever tried to perform "Canaan's Land."

Melvin Goins has had a long and distinguished career in bluegrass. He was born on December 30, 1933, in Bramwell, West Virginia. His first professional work came in 1951 when he and his brother Ray had a radio show on WKOY in Bluefield. Two years later, the boys were asked to join the Lonesome Pine Fiddlers, an association that lasted for most of the next decade. The group worked out of WLSI in Pikeville, Kentucky, and made some memorable recordings for RCA and Starday. In January of 1966, Melvin went to work with the Stanley Brothers, playing bass and doing comedy. He also assisted with bookings. After Carter Stanley's passing, Melvin stayed on with Ralph for another three years. Then Melvin and Ray reunited as the Goins Brothers, a partnership that lasted for twenty-five years. Ray was forced to retire from traveling in 1997 for health reasons, but Melvin has fronted his group, Windy Mountain, as a solo bandleader since the mid-1990s. In 2009 he was inducted into the International Bluegrass Music Association's Hall of Fame.[96]

Birch Monroe was born on May 16, 1901, in Rosine, Kentucky. A brother of Bill and Charlie Monroe, he performed music in the Chicago area with them in the 1930s, but

In 1970 Rebel Records released
a two-volume live album called
The Legendary Stanley Brothers. At
the time, many of the duo's recordings were out of print, and
the release helped fill a void that
had existed for several years. The
cover photo by Walt Saunders was
taken at American Legion Park
in Culpeper, Virginia, on June 26,
1966. Shot barely six months before Carter Stanley's passing, it is
perhaps the most iconic photo of
the Stanleys' career.

declined to go professional when the duo began broadening their horizons. After the split
of the Monroe Brothers, Birch worked with Charlie's group, the Kentucky Pardners. In
the mid-1940s, he worked with Bill's Blue Grass Boys and helped record one session for
Columbia Records. In the 1950s, he began managing Bill Monroe's music park, the Brown
County Jamboree. He occasionally played a tune or two on stage with some of the more
traditionally oriented groups, such as Bill Monroe or the Stanley Brothers. Such was the
case when he appeared on stage with Carter and Ralph at the Brown County Jamboree on
October 16, 1966. Birch continued to manage the park for a number of years afterwards.
He died on May 15, 1982.[97]

The Stanley Brothers' appearance at the Brown County Jamboree represented the last
full concert that they would ever perform. From there, they journeyed to Nashville, where
they were honored by their fan club for their twenty years in the music business. While
there, they visited in the Nugget recording studio with Roy McGinnis, the husband of
Carter and Ralph's fan club president, Fay McGinnis, who was there recording a 45 rpm
single with his partner Sonny Nelson. Carter is reported to have played a few selections
on stage with Bill Monroe during Monroe's appearance at a club called the Black Poodle
in Nashville. The Stanleys' next engagement was at the Red River School in Hazel Green,
Kentucky. The foursome took to the stage, but after a few songs, Carter developed a nose-
bleed and excused himself. Ralph, George, and Melvin completed the show. It was the last
time Carter ever appeared in public. Six weeks later, he was dead at the age of forty-one,
the result of an addiction to alcohol that plagued him during much of his adult life.

The bluegrass world was shocked and saddened by Carter Stanley's passing. The death of his brother left Ralph Stanley uncertain about his future as well. The encouragement and support he received from family, friends, and fans no doubt played a large part in his decision to continue his career in music. At the age of forty, he was not trained to do much else. As time bore out, he launched a successful solo career, one that would have earned him a highly respected spot in the annals of country music history even without his twenty-year tenure with the Stanley Brothers.

As for the Stanley Brothers themselves, the music speaks for itself. They were there at the start of it all. The recordings show how the group morphed from old-time string to bluegrass, how their songwriting efforts added to the core repertoire of the genre, and how they became the genre's most recorded group. Ample evidence of Carter and Ralph's staying power can be found in the demand for their recordings that continues to warrant reissues of their music and in the fact that today's bluegrass and country artists persist in mining the Stanley catalog for material. In the nearly fifty years since the demise of the Stanley Brothers, an aura has arisen around them. To their fans, they are larger than life. Along with the legend has come a fair amount of misinformation, or, in a lot of cases, lack of information, about the duo and their recordings. It is hoped that *The Music of the Stanley Brothers* will set and keep the record straight, for today and for generations to come.

DISCOGRAPHY, 1963–1966

630128   King session; producer: Ray Pennington
King Studio, Cincinnati, Ohio
January 28, 1963
Carter Stanley: g (except 11413) | Ralph Stanley: b | Ralph Mayo: lg (f 11407) | Curley Lambert: m (lg 11413)
| Vernon Derrick: sb

11407	**I Don't Want Your Rambling Letters** (N. Nath–R. Starr–G. C. Redd)	45-6089	KLP-834, KLP-1046, NLP-2078, SD-3003, K4CD-0950
	C. Stanley–L, R. Stanley–T		
11408	**Just Because** (Shelton-Shelton-Robin)		KLP-834, GD-5026, K4CD-0950
	C. Stanley–L		
11409	**No Letter Today** (F. Brown)		KLP-834, K4CD-0950
	C. Stanley–L, R. Stanley–T		
11410	**He Went to Sleep and the Hogs Ate Him** (N. Nath–R. Starr–G. C. Redd)	45-5763	KLP-834, K4CD-0950
	C. Stanley–L, R. Stanley–T		
11411	**My Brother's Bride** (Elesa Straley)		KLP-834, K4CD-0950
	C. Stanley–L, R. Stanley–T		
11412	**Six Months Ain't Long** (Traditional)	45-5732	KLP-834, K4CD-0950
	C. Stanley–L, R. Stanley–T		
11413	**Old and in the Way** (Carter Stanley–Ralph Mayo)	45-5732	KLP-834, NLP-2078, K4CD-0950
	C. Stanley–L, R. Stanley–T, Lambert–B		

630129   King session; producer: Ray Pennington
King Studio, Cincinnati, Ohio
January 29, 1963
Carter Stanley: g (except 11417) | Ralph Stanley: b | Curley Lambert: m (lg 11417)
Ralph Mayo: f (lg 11418) | Vernon Derrick: sb (lg 11418) | Billy Lee Holmes: harmonica (11418)

11414	**Hills of Roan County** (Traditional)	45-6089	KLP-834, SD-3003, K4CD-0950
	C. Stanley–L, R. Stanley–T		
11415	**Little Birdie** (Wade Mainer)	45-6079	KLP-834, SD-3003, K4CD-0950, B0007883-02
	R. Stanley–L		
11416	**Pig in a Pen** (Traditional)		KLP-834, K4CD-0950
	C. Stanley–L, R. Stanley–T		
11417	**Whiskey** (Kit Carson)	45-6079	KLP-834, K4CD-0950
	C. Stanley–L, R. Stanley–T		
11418	**Lips That Lie** (F. Stryker–D. Byrd–M. Byrd)	45-5763	KLP-834, K4CD-0950
	C. Stanley–L, R. Stanley–T		

| 11419 | **Little Darlin', Pal of Mine** (A. P. Carter) | | KLP-834, K4CD-0950 |
| | C. Stanley—L, R. Stanley—T | | |

| 11420 | **Darling Nellie Gray** (Traditional) | | KLP-834, K4CD-0950 |
| | Instrumental | | |

630700 Reissue of video; producer: WDBJ—TV
Roanoke, Virginia
ca. July 1963
Carter Stanley: g | Ralph Stanley: b | Arthur Lee "Red" Smiley: g
Donald Wesley "Don" Reno: b | Ronald Wesley "Ronnie" Reno: m | Mack Magaha: f
Steven R. "Steve" Chapman: g | John D. Palmer: sb

| | **In the Pines** | | MP-0108, MP-0108 (DVD) |
| | C. Stanley—L, R. Stanley—T | | |

| | **Home Sweet Home** | | MP-0108, MP-0108 (DVD) |
| | Instrumental | | |

| | **Over in the Gloryland** | | MP-0108, MP-0108 (DVD) |
| | C. Stanley—L, R. Stanley—T, D. Reno—B, Smiley—BS | | |

	Nine Pound Hammer		MP-0108, MP-0108 (DVD)
	Ronnie Reno—LV; 1st chorus: C. Stanley—L, R. Stanley—T;		
	2nd chorus: Smiley—L, Don Reno—T; 3rd chorus: C. Stanley—L; Group sing-along by others		

| | **John Henry** | | MP-0108, MP-0108 (DVD) |
| | Instrumental | | |

630813 King session; producer: Ray Pennington
King Studio, Cincinnati, Ohio
August 13, 1963
Carter Stanley: g | Ralph Stanley: b | George Shuffler: lg
Ralph Mayo: f | Henry Dockery: sb

| 11675 | **Train 45** (Ruby Rakes) | 45-5916 | KLP-872 K4CD-0950 |
| | Instrumental | | |

| 11676 | **Lonesome Traveler** (Ralph Stanley) | | KLP-872 K4CD-0950 |
| | Instrumental | | |

| 11677 | **Shout Little Lulie** (Ralph Stanley) | 45-5934 | KLP-872 SD-3003 K4CD-0950 |
| | Instrumental | | |

| 11678 | **Shamrock** (Ralph Stanley) | | KLP-872 K4CD-0950 |
| | Instrumental | | |

| 11679 | **Stoney Creek** (Ralph Stanley) | | KLP-872 K4CD-0950 |
| | Instrumental | | |

630814 King session; producer: Ray Pennington
King Studio, Cincinnati, Ohio
August 14, 1963
Carter Stanley: g | Ralph Stanley: b | George Shuffler: lg
Ralph Mayo: f | Henry Dockery: sb

11680	**Stone Walls and Steel Bars** (R. Pennington–R. Marcum) C. Stanley–L, R. Stanley–T, Mayo–B, Shuffler–BS	45-5809	KLP-864, KLP-1046, NLP-2078, SD-3003, GD-5026, K4CD-0950, B0007883-02
11681	**Standing Room Only (Outside Your Heart)** (Ray Pennington) C. Stanley–L, R. Stanley–T		KLP-864, NLP-2078, GT-0103, K4CD-0950
11682	**Lonesome Night** (Carter Stanley) C. Stanley–L, Shuffler–T, R. Stanley–HB	45-5809	KLP-864, K4CD-0950, B0007883-02
11683	**Pretty Little Miss in the Garden** (Carter Stanley) C. Stanley–L, R. Stanley–T		KLP-864, GT-0103, K4CD-0950
11684	**Late Last Night** (Carter Stanley) C. Stanley–L, R. Stanley–T, Mayo–B, Shuffler–BS		KLP-864, GT-0103, K4CD-0950

630916 King session; producer: Ray Pennington
King Studio, Cincinnati, Ohio
September 16, 1963
Carter Stanley: g | Ralph Stanley: b | George Shuffler: lg and sb (dubbed)

11701	**When You and I Were Young, Maggie / Red Wing** (Traditional) Instrumental		KLP-872, K4CD-0950
11702	**Big Booger** (Ralph Stanley) Instrumental		KLP-872, K4CD-0950
11703	**Sourwood Mountain** (Traditional) Instrumental		KLP-872, K4CD-0950
11704	**Ground Hog / Red River Valley** (Traditional) Instrumental		KLP-872, K4CD-0950
11705	**Rang Tang** (R. Stanley–G. Shuffler) Instrumental		KLP-872, K4CD-0950

630917 King session; producer: Ray Pennington
King Studio, Cincinnati, Ohio
September 17, 1963
Carter Stanley: g | Ralph Stanley: b | George Shuffler: lg and sb(dubbed)

11706	**Snow Deer** (Traditional) Instrumental		KLP-872, K4CD-0950
11707	**Five String Drag** (R. Stanley–G. Shuffler) Instrumental	45-5934	KLP-872, GD-5026, K4CD-0950
11708	**Never Again** (Benny Williams) C. Stanley–L, R. Stanley–T	45-6046	GT-0103, K4CD-0950

11709	**Don't Cheat in Our Home Town** (R. Pennington–R. Marcum) C. Stanley–L, R. Stanley–T	45-5869	KLP-864, GT-0103, K4CD-0950, B0007883-02
11710	**Don't Step over an Old Love** (Fred Stryker) C. Stanley–L, R. Stanley–T	45-5933	KLP-864, GD-5026, K4CD-0950
11711	**I Just Stood There** (D. Byrd–M. Byrd–F. Stryker) C. Stanley–L, R. Stanley–T	45-5916	KLP-864, GT-0103, K4CD-0950

631209 Wango reissue of radio shows; producer: Ray Davis
Johnny's Used Cars, 4801 Harford Rd., Baltimore, Maryland
ca. week of December 9, 1963
Carter Stanley: g | Ralph Stanley: b | George Shuffler: lg
Henry Dockery: sb

Somebody Touched Me Shuffler–L, R. Stanley–T		Wango LP-105
Paul and Silas Shuffler–L, R. Stanley–T		Wango LP-105
I Saw the Light Shuffler–L, R. Stanley–T		Wango LP-105
Cripple Creek Instrumental		Wango LP-115
God Gave You to Me Shuffler–L, R. Stanley–T		Wango LP-115
Little Birdie R. Stanley–L		Wango LP-115
Gathering Flowers from the Hillside Instrumental		Wango LP-115
In the Pines Shuffler–L, R. Stanley–T	EP-110	Wango LP-115, Wango CD-117
Banjo Boogie Instrumental		Wango LP-115
Comedy routine Spoken exchange between Carter Stanley and Henry Dockery		Wango LP-115
Man of Constant Sorrow R. Stanley–L, Dockery–T, Shuffler–B		Wango LP-115
Wildwood Flower Instrumental		Wango LP-115
Six Months Ain't Long Shuffler–L, R. Stanley–T		Wango LP-115
Sunny Side of the Mountain Instrumental		Wango LP-115

Jordan Dockery–L, R. Stanley–T, Shuffler–BS		Wango LP-115
Shout Little Luly Instrumental		Wango LP-115
Comedy routine Spoken exchange between Carter and Ralph Stanley and Henry Dockery		Wango LP-115
Cripple Creek Instrumental		Wango LP-115
Stanley's Theme—Cripple Creek Instrumental		Wango CD-109
Sunny Side of the Mountain Shuffler–L, R. Stanley–T		Wango CD-109
Don't Let Your Sweet Love Die Instrumental	EP-110	Wango CD-109
Little Maggie R. Stanley–L	EP-110	Wango CD-109
Mountain Pickin' Instrumental		Wango CD-109
Comedy—Uncle Henry Spoken exchange between Henry Dockery and Ralph Stanley		Wango CD-109
Good Ole Mountain Dew Dockery–L		Wango CD-109
Clinch Mountain Backstep Instrumental		Wango CD-109
Whoa Mule Whoa Instrumental		Wango CD-09
Weeping Willow Instrumental		Wango CD-109
Rank Stranger R. Stanley–LV/TC, Dockery–LC, Shuffler–B		Wango CD-109
Cripple Creek Instrumental		Wango CD-109
Stanley's Theme Instrumental		Wango CD-110
He Went to Sleep and the Hogs Ate Him Dockery–L, R. Stanley–T		Wango CD-110
Weeping Willow Instrumental		Wango CD-110

The Long Black Veil Shuffler—L	Wango CD-110
Wildwood Flower Instrumental	Wango CD-110
Late Last Night Shuffler—L, R. Stanley—T	Wango CD-110
Red River Valley Instrumental	Wango CD-110
Drinking from the Fountain R. Stanley—LV/TC, Shuffler—LC	Wango CD-110
Banjo Picking Instrumental	Wango CD-110
Stone Walls and Steel Bars Shuffler—L, R. Stanley—T	Wango CD-110
Comedy & Theme Spoken exchange between Henry Dockery and Ralph Stanley / Instrumental	Wango CD-110
Theme——Cripple Creek Instrumental	Wango CD-113
Little Birdie R. Stanley—L	Wango CD-113
Gathering Flowers from the Hillside Instrumental	Wango CD-113
Comedy Spoken exchange between Henry Dockery and Carter Stanley	Wango CD-113
How Far to Little Rock Spoken exchange between Henry Dockery and Ralph Stanley	Wango CD-113
Sunny Side of the Mountain Instrumental	Wango CD-113
I Know What It Means to Be Lonesome Shuffler—L	Wango CD-113
Cumberland Gap Instrumental	Wango CD-113
Someone's Last Day Shuffler—L, R. Stanley—T	Wango CD-113
Carter's Boogie [listed as "Mountain Pickin'" on Wango 104] Instrumental	Wango CD-113
Theme——Cripple Creek Instrumental	Wango CD-113

Theme—Cripple Creek Instrumental	Wango CD-114
Going to Georgia R. Stanley–LV/TC, Shuffler–LC	Wango CD-114
Big Tilda Instrumental	Wango CD-114
Pretty Polly R. Stanley–L	Wango CD-114
In the Mood Instrumental	Wango CD-114
Comedy Spoken exchange between Henry Dockery and Carter Stanley	Wango CD-114
Old Love Letters Shuffler–L, R. Stanley–T	Wango CD-114
Cotton Eyed Joe [actually Cumberland Gap] Instrumental	Wango CD-114
Old Crossroads Shuffler–L, R. Stanley–T	Wango CD-114
Pike County Breakdown Instrumental	Wango CD-114
God Gave You to Me Shuffler–L, R. Stanley–T	Wango CD-114
Comedy Spoken exchange between Henry Dockery and Ralph Stanley	Wango CD-114
I Cried Again Shuffler–L	Wango CD-114
Theme—Cripple Creek Instrumental	Wango CD-114
Pretty Polly R. Stanley–L	Wango CD-115
Little Willie R. Stanley–L	Wango CD-116
Mother's Not Dead (She's Only Sleeping) Shuffler–L, R. Stanley–T	Wango CD-116
Man of Constant Sorrow R. Stanley–L, Dockery–T, Shuffler–B	Wango CD-116
Train 45 Instrumental	Wango CD-118

Ridin That Midnight Train R. Stanley—LV/TC, Shuffler—LC	Wango CD-118
Late Last Night Shuffler—L, R. Stanley—T	Wango CD-125
Long Black Veil Shuffler—L	Wango CD-125
Pike County Breakdown Instrumental	Wango CD-125
Rank Stranger R. Stanley—LV/TC, Dockery—LC, Shuffler—B	Wango CD-125
Little Birdie R. Stanley—L	Wango CD-125
Comedy Spoken exchange between Henry Dockery and Ralph Stanley	Wango CD-125
I'm a Man of Constant Sorrow R. Stanley—L, Dockery—T, Shuffler—B	Wango CD-125
Comedy Spoken exchange between Henry Dockery and Ralph Stanley	Wango CD-125
Drinking from the Fountain R. Stanley—LV/TC, Shuffler—LC	Wango CD-125
Boogie Woogie Instrumental	Wango CD-125
Theme Instrumental	Wango CD-127
Pig in a Pen Shuffler—L, R. Stanley—T	Wango CD-127
Cotton Eyed Joe [actually "Cumberland Gap"] Instrumental	Wango CD-127
Mother's Only Sleepin' Ralph Stanley—LV/TC, Shuffler—LC	Wango CD-127
Arkansas Traveler Instrumental	Wango CD-127
Comedy Spoken exchange between Henry Dockery and Ralph Stanley	Wango CD-127
Mountain Dew Dockery—L	Wango CD-127
Are You Tired of Me My Darlin' Instrumental	Wango CD-127

My Main Trial Is Yet to Come Shuffler–L, R. Stanley–T		Wango CD-127
Comedy Spoken exchange between Henry Dockery and Ralph Stanley		Wango CD-127
Daybreak in Dixie Instrumental		Wango CD-127
Cripple Creek Instrumental		Wango CD-127
In the Pines Shuffler–L, R. Stanley–T	EP-110	Wango CD-0117
Little Maggie R. Stanley–L	EP-110	
Don't Let Your Sweet Love Die Instrumental	EP-110	

631214a Wango reissue of Christmas party; producer: Ray Davis
Johnny's Used Cars, 4801 Harford Rd., Baltimore, Maryland
December 14, 1963
Carter Stanley: g | Ralph Stanley: b | George Shuffler: lg
Henry Dockery: sb

How Mountain Girls Can Love Shuffler–L, R. Stanley–T	Wango CD-126
Comedy Spoken exchange between Henry Dockery and Ralph Stanley	Wango CD-126
Mountain Dew Dockery–L	Wango CD-126
On Top of Old Smokey Shuffler–L	Wango CD-126
Comedy Spoken dialog by Henry Dockery	Wango CD-126
Little Birdie R. Stanley–L	Wango CD-126
Jordan Dockery–L, R. Stanley–T, Shuffler–BS	Wango CD-126
Heavenly Light Is Shining on Me Shuffler–L, Stanley–T, Dockery–BS	Wango CD-126
Someone's Last Day Shuffler–L, R. Stanley–T	Wango CD-126
Rank Stranger R. Stanley–LV/TC, Dockery–LC, Shuffler–BT	Wango CD-126

631214b   Wango session; producer: Ray Davis
Johnny's Used Cars, 4801 Harford Rd., Baltimore, Maryland
December 14, 1963
Carter Stanley: g | Ralph Stanley: b | George Shuffler: lg
Jack Cooke: g | Henry Dockery: sb

The Old Cross Roads   Wango LP-103, CO-753, Wango CD-108
Shuffler—L, R. Stanley—T, Dockery—B

Drifting Too Far from the Shore   Wango LP-103, CO-753, Wango CD-120
Shuffler—L, R. Stanley—T

Just a Little Talk with Jesus   Wango LP-103, CO-753
R. Stanley—L, Cooke—T, Dockery—B, Shuffler—BS

Precious Memories   Wango LP-103, CO-753, Wango CD-108
R. Stanley—L, Cooke—T, Dockery—B, Shuffler—BS

I'll Fly Away / In the Sweet Bye and Bye   EP-109   Wango LP-103, CO-753, Wango CD-108
Instrumental

Uncloudy Day   Wango LP-103, CO-753, Wango CD-108
Shuffler—L, R. Stanley—T

Over in the Gloryland   Wango LP-103, CO-753
Cooke—L, R. Stanley—T, Dockery—B, Shuffler—BS

Lonely Tombs   Wango LP-103, CO-753
Shuffler—L, R. Stanley—T

Amazing Grace   Wango LP-103, CO-753, Wango CD-120
Cooke—L, R. Stanley—T, Dockery—B, Shuffler—BS

I Am a Pilgrim   Wango LP-103, CO-753, Wango CD-108
R. Stanley—L

A Beautiful Life   Wango LP-103, CO-753
Cooke—L, R. Stanley—T, Dockery—B, Shuffler—BS

Someone's Last Day   EP-108   Wango LP-103 CO-753
Shuffler—L, R. Stanley—T

Will You Miss Me When I'm Gone?   Wango-104, Wango-105, CO-739, CO-754,
R. Stanley—LV/TC, C. Stanley—LC, Dockery—B, Shuffler—BS   REB-1110, B0007883-02

640401   King session; producer: Don Cahall
King Studio, Cincinnati, Ohio
April 1, 1964
Carter Stanley: g | Ralph Stanley: b | Earl Taylor: m and harmonica
George Shuffler: lg | Chick Stripling: sb

11850   **Will the Circle Be Unbroken** (Arr. Browns Ferry Four)   KLP-918, K4CD-0950
C. Stanley—L, R. Stanley—T, Shuffler—B

11851	**Jesus Savior Pilot Me** (Traditional)		KLP-918, KLP-1013, NLP-2112, K4CD-0950
	C. Stanley–L, R. Stanley–T, Shuffler–B		
11852	**I Just Dropped By** (John Reedy)		KLP-918, K4CD-0950
	C. Stanley–L, R. Stanley–T, Shuffler–B		
11853	**Oh, Death** (John Reedy)		KLP-918, NLP-2112, K4CD-0950, B0007883-02
	C. Stanley–L, R. Stanley––L/T, Shuffler–B		
11854	**Shoutin' on the Hills of Glory** (Carter Stanley)	45-5932	KLP-918, KLP-1013, GT-0016, K4CD-0950
	C. Stanley–L, R. Stanley–T, Shuffler–B		
11855	**Beautiful Star of Bethlehem** (Traditional)		KLP-918, K4CD-0950, B0007883-02
	C. Stanley–L, R. Stanley–T, Shuffler–B		

640402   King session; producer: Don Cahall
King Studio, Cincinnati, Ohio
April 2, 1964
Carter Stanley: g | Ralph Stanley: b | Earl Taylor: m and harmonica
George Shuffler: lg | Chick Stripling: sb

11856	**John Three-Sixteen** (A. Delmore–V. Turner)	45-5902	KLP-918, GT-0016, K4CD-0950
	C. Stanley–L, R. Stanley–T, Shuffler–B		
11857	**A Crown He Wore** (Mac Odell–Lois Mann)	45-5902	KLP-918, K4CD-0950
	C. Stanley–L, R. Stanley–T, Shuffler–B		
11858	**How Beautiful Heaven Must Be** (Traditional)		KLP-918, NLP-2112, K4CD-0950
	C. Stanley–L, R. Stanley–T, Shuffler–B		
11859	**He's Passing This Way** (Wade Mainer)	45-5932	KLP-918, K4CD-0950
	C. Stanley–L, R. Stanley–T, Shuffler–B		
11860	**No Burdens Pass Through** (Carter Stanley–Paul Mullins)		KLP-918, K4CD-0950
	C. Stanley–L, R. Stanley–T, Shuffler–B		
11861	**Building on That Rock** (J. Mainer)		KLP-918, K4CD-0950
	C. Stanley–L, R. Stanley–T, Shuffler–B		

640518   Wango session; producer: Ray Davis
Johnny's Used Cars, 4801 Harford Rd., Baltimore, Maryland
ca. May 1964
Carter Stanley: g | Ralph Stanley: b | George Shuffler: sb

	Long Journey Home	Wango LP-104, CO-739, REB-1110
	C. Stanley–L, R. Stanley–T	
	I'll Be True to the One That I Love	Wango LP-104, CO-739, REB-1110
	C. Stanley–L	
	No Letter in the Mail Today	Wango LP-104, CO-739, REB-1110
	C. Stanley–L, R. Stanley–T	
	Pretty Polly	Wango LP-104, CO-739, REB-1110, B0007883-02
	R. Stanley–L	

Two More Years and I'll Be Free C. Stanley–L, R. Stanley–T		Wango LP-104, CO-739, REB-1110
Ramshackle Shack on the Hill C. Stanley–L, R. Stanley–T		Wango LP-104, CO-739, REB-1110
East Virginia Blues C. Stanley–L, R. Stanley–T		Wango LP-104, CO-739, REB-1110, B0007883-02
Pig in a Pen C. Stanley–L, R. Stanley–T, Shuffler–B		Wango LP-104, CO-739, REB-1110, B0007883-02
Your Saddle Is Empty Ol' Pal C. Stanley–L, R. Stanley–T		Wango LP-104, CO-739, REB-1110
Nine Pound Hammer C. Stanley–L, R. Stanley–T		Wango LP-104, CO-739, WANGOCD117, REB-1110
Cluck Ol' Hen Instrumental		Wango LP-104, CO-739, Reb-1110
Wild and Reckless Hobo C. Stanley–L, R. Stanley–T		Wango LP-104, CO-739, REB-1110, WANGO118
Rabbit in a Log C. Stanley–L, R. Stanley–T		Wango LP-104, CO-739, REB-1110
Hold Fast to the Right C. Stanley–L, R. Stanley–T	EP-108 EP-1784	Wango CD-107, WANGOCD0119
If I Could Hear My Mother Pray Again C. Stanley–L, R. Stanley–T	EP-1784	Wango CD-107
Life's Railway to Heaven C. Stanley–L, R. Stanley–T, Shuffler–B	EP-1784	Wango CD-118
Standing in the Need of Prayer C. Stanley–L, R. Stanley–T, Shuffler–BS	45-1783	Wango CD-108
Sunny Side of Life C. Stanley–L, R. Stanley–T	45-1783	Wango LP 115, Wango CD-0119
What Would You Give in Exchange for Your Soul C. Stanley–L, R. Stanley–T	EP-1784	Wango CD-0119
Will You Miss Me When I'm Gone C. Stanley–L, R. Stanley–T, Shuffler–B/BS		Wango CD-116

640716	King session; producer: Don Cahall		
	King Studio, Cincinnati, Ohio		
	July 16, 1964		
	Carter Stanley: g | Ralph Stanley: b | Earl Taylor: m and harmonica		
	Art Stamper: f | George Shuffler: lg | Vernon McIntyre, Jr.: sb		
11949	**Bully of the Town** (Traditional) Instrumental	45-5920	KLP-924, OCHS-323, GT-0105, K4CD-0950
11950	**Back Up and Push** (Traditional) Instrumental		KLP-924, OCHS-323, GT-0105, K4CD-0950
11951	**Careless Love** (Traditional) Instrumental		KLP-924, OCHS-323, GT-0105, K4CD-0950
11952	**How Bad I Do Feel** (Carter Stanley) C. Stanley–L, R. Stanley–T, Shuffler–B	45-5920	KLP-924, OCHS-323, GT-0105, K4CD-0950
11953	**Rollin' on Rubber Wheels** (Carter Stanley) C. Stanley–L, R. Stanley–T	45-6005	KLP-924, OCHS-323, NLP-2078, K4CD-0950
11954	**Our Darlin's Gone**(Carter Stanley) C. Stanley–L, R. Stanley–T		KLP-924, OCHS-323, K4CD-0950

640717	King session; producer: Don Cahall		
	King Studio, Cincinnati, Ohio		
	July 17, 1964		
	Carter Stanley: g | Ralph Stanley: b | Earl Taylor: m and harmonica		
	Art Stamper: f | George Shuffler: lg | Vernon McIntyre, Jr.: sb		
11955	**How You've Tortured My Mind** (Carter Stanley–Peggy Stanley) C. Stanley–L, R. Stanley–T, Shuffler–B	45-6005	KLP-924, OCHS-323, GT-0105, K4CD-0950
11956	**I'm Bound to Ride** (Traditional) R. Stanley––L	45-5933	KLP-924, OCHS-323, GT-0105, K4CD-0950

640723	Vanguard reissue of opening night concert		
	Newport Folk Festival, Newport, Rhode Island		
	July 23, 1964		
	Carter Stanley: g | Ralph Stanley: b | George Shuffler: lg		
	Red Stanley: f | unknown: sb		
	The White Dove (Carter Stanley) Shuffler–L, C. Stanley–T, R. Stanley–HB		VSD-77018
	Hard Times (Ralph Stanley) Instrumental		VSD-77018

640724 Vanguard reissue of banjo workshop
Newport Folk Festival, Newport, Rhode Island
July 24, 1964
Carter Stanley: g | Ralph Stanley: b | George Shuffler: sb

Little Birdie (Traditional; Arr. and adpt. Ralph Stanley) R. Stanley—L	77018
Shout Little Luly (Traditional; Arr. and adpt. Ralph Stanley) Instrumental	77018
Clinch Mountain Backstep (Ruby Rakes) Instrumental	77018
Hard Times (Ralph Stanley) Instrumental	77018
Little Maggie (Stanley-York)} R. Stanley—L	77018

640725 Vanguard reissue of string bands workshop
Newport Folk Festival, Newport, Rhode Island
July 25, 1964
Carter Stanley: g | Ralph Stanley: b | George Shuffler: lg
Red Stanley: f | Benny Howard Birchfield: sb

How Mountain Girls Can Love (Ruby Rakes) Shuffler—LV/BC, C. Stanley—LC, R. Stanley—T	VCD-77006, VSD-77018
Man of Constant Sorrow (Carter Stanley) R. Stanley—L	VCD-77006, VSD-77018
Little Glass of Wine (Carter & Ralph Stanley) C. Stanley—L, R. Stanley—T	77018
Big TildY (Ralph Stanley) Instrumental	VCD-77006, VSD-77018
Orange Blossom Special (Carter & Ralph Stanley) Instrumental	VCD-77006, VSD-77018

640726 Vanguard reissue of Sunday morning concert of religious music
Newport Folk Festival, Newport, Rhode Island
July 26, 1964
Carter Stanley: g | Ralph Stanley: b | George Shuffler: lg
Red Stanley: f | unknown: sb

Jordan (Traditional; Arr. and adpt. by Carter & Ralph Stanley C. Stanley—L, R. Stanley—T, Shuffler—B	77018
Rank Stranger (Albert E. Brumley) R. Stanley—LV/TC, C. Stanley—LC, Shuffler—B	77018

641122   Wango session; producer: Ray Davis
Johnny's Used Cars, 4801 Harford Rd., Baltimore, Maryland
November 22, 23, and 24, 1964
Carter Stanley: g | Ralph Stanley: b |
Jack Cooke: g | Harold "Red" Stanley: f | Barry Glickman: sb

Hold to God's Unchanging Hand   Wango LP-105, CO-754
R. Stanley—LV/TC, C. Stanley—LC

When I Lay My Burden Down   Wango LP-105, CO-754, REB-8002
C. Stanley—L, R. Stanley—T

In Heaven We'll Never Grow Old   Wango LP-105, CO-754
C. Stanley—L, Cooke—T, R. Stanley—B

Lord, I'm Coming Home   Wango LP-105, CO-754, Wango CD-120
R. Stanley—L (1st half of verse)/TC , C. Stanley—L (2nd half of verse)

Give Me the Roses While I Live   Wango LP-105, CO-754
C. Stanley—L, R. Stanley—T, Cooke—B

Swing Low, Sweet Chariot   Wango LP-105, CO-754
R. Stanley—LV/TC, C. Stanley—LC

Gathering Flowers for the Master's Bouquet   Wango LP-105, CO-754
C. Stanley—L, R. Stanley—T

The Old Country Church   Wango LP-105, CO-754
Instrumental

Where Could I Go?   Wango LP-105, CO-754
C. Stanley—L, R. Stanley—T, Cooke—B

Little Old Country Church House   Wango LP-106, CO-738, Wango CD-108
C. Stanley—L, Cooke—T, R. Stanley—B

Nobody Answered Me   Wango LP-106, CO-738
C. Stanley—L, R. Stanley—T

Shake My Mother's Hand for Me   Wango LP-106, CO-738
R. Stanley—LV/BC, C. Stanley—LC, Cooke—T

I Heard My Mother Call My Name in Prayer   Wango LP-106, CO-738
C. Stanley—L, Cooke—T, R. Stanley—B

Mother's Only Sleeping   Wango LP-106, CO-738
C. Stanley—L, R. Stanley—T

Shake Hands with Mother Again   Wango LP-106, CO-738, Wango CD-107
C. Stanley—L, R. Stanley—T, Cooke—B

Hide Ye in the Blood   Wango LP-106, CO-738, B0007883-02
C. Stanley—L, R. Stanley—T

Give Me Your Hand   Wango LP-106, CO-738
R. Stanley—L

Where We'll Never Grow Old C. Stanley–L, Cooke–T, R. Stanley–B	Wango LP-106, CO-738
Leaning on the Everlasting Arms C. Stanley–L, R. Stanley–T	Wango LP-106, CO-738
Angel Band R. Stanley—LV/TC, C. Stanley–LC, Cooke–B	Wango LP-106, CO-738
Are You Washed in the Blood? C. Stanley–L, R. Stanley–T	Wango LP-106, CO-738
Farther Along C. Stanley–L, Cooke–T, R. Stanley–B	Wango LP-106, CO-738

650129 StanleyTone reissue of show, recorded by unknown
University of Chicago Folk Festival, Chicago, Illinois
January 29, 1965
Carter Stanley: g | Ralph Stanley: b | Larry Sparks: lg
Red Stanley: f | Ray Tate: sb

How Mountain Girls Can Love C. Stanley–L, R. Stanley–T	ST-5003
Cacklin' Hen Instrumental	ST-5003
When You and I Were Young, Maggie Instrumental	ST-5003
Don't Go Out Tonight C. Stanley–L, R. Stanley–T	ST-5003
Sharecropper's Son C. Stanley–L, R. Stanley–T	ST-5003
I'm a Man of Constant Sorrow R. Stanley–LV/TC, C. Stanley–LC, Red Stanley–B	ST-5003
Single Girl, Married Girl C. Stanley–L	ST-5003
Shouting on the Hills of Glory C. Stanley–L, R. Stanley–T	ST-5003
Cumberland Gap Instrumental	ST-5003

650500 Transcription session; producer: Fred Hertz
Social Security Administration, radio, New York City
ca. June 1965
Carter Stanley: g | Ralph Stanley: b | Curley Lambert: m
Red Stanley: f

How Mountain Girls Can Love C. Stanley–L, R. Stanley–T	GXTV 103000 (show #209)
Stone Walls and Steel Bars C. Stanley–L, R. Stanley–T	GXTV 103000 (show #209)

650605 Cabin Creek session; producer Alex Campbell
Ken-Del Productions, Wilmington, Delaware
June 5, 1965
Carter Stanley: g | Ralph Stanley: b | Curley Lambert: m
Sonny Miller: f | Jack Cooke: g

Where Could I Go C. Stanley–L, Cooke–T, Lambert–B	CC-203
An Empty Mansion R. Stanley–L, Cooke–T, Lambert–B	CC-203
Where the Soul Never Dies C. Stanley–L, Lambert–T	CC-203
Dust on the Bible C. Stanley–L, R. Stanley–T	CC-203, B0007883-02
Farther Along J. Cooke–LV/TC, C. Stanley–LC, Lambert–B	CC-203
I Feel Like Traveling On C. Stanley–L, Cooke–T, Lambert–B	CC-203
I Need the Prayers Lambert–LV/BC, C. Stanley–LC, Cooke–T	CC-203
Softly and Tenderly C. Stanley–L, Cooke–T, Lambert–B	CC-203
When the Saints Go Marching In C. Stanley–L, Lambert–T	CC-203
The Sweet Bye and Bye C. Stanley–L, Cooke–T, Lambert–B	CC-203
Take My Hand Precious Lord C. Stanley–L, Cooke–T, Lambert–B	CC-203
When I Reach That City C. Stanley–L, Cooke–T, Lambert–B	CC-203

Won't It Be Wonderful There C. Stanley–L, Cooke–T, Lambert–B		CC-203
Hold Fast to the Right C. Stanley–L, Cooke–T, Lambert–B		CC-203
Matthew Twenty-Four C. Stanley–L, Cooke–T		CC-203
Lonesome Valley C. Stanley–L, Cooke–T, Lambert–B		CC-203
Keep on the Sunny Side of Life C. Stanley–L, Cooke–T, Lambert–B		CC-203
How About You C. Stanley–L, Cooke–T, Lambert–B		CC-203
The Glory Land Way C. Stanley–L, Cooke–T, Lambert–B		CC-203
Precious Memories C. Stanley–L, Cooke–T, Lambert–B		CC-203
Heaven's Light Is Shining on Me C. Stanley–L, Cooke–T, Lambert–B		CC-203
Lord I'm Coming Home C. Stanley–L, Cooke–T, Lambert–B		CC-203

650908 King session; producer:
King Studio, Cincinnati, Ohio
September 8, 1965
Carter Stanley: g | Ralph Stanley: b | George Shuffler: lg and sb(dubbed)

12053	**God's Highway** (C. Stanley–R. Stanley) C. Stanley–L, R. Stanley–T, Shuffler–B	45-6059	KLP-963, GT-0062, K4CD-0950
12054	**The End of the Road** (C. Stanley–R. Stanley) C. Stanley–L, R. Stanley–T, Shuffler–B	45-6023	KLP-963, KLP-1013, GT-0108, K4CD-0950
12055	**Seek Jesus (He Still May Be Found)** (C. Stanley–R. Stanley) C. Stanley–L, R. Stanley–T, Shuffler–B		KLP-963, GT-0108, K4CD-0950
12056	**He'll Save Your Soul Yet** (C. Stanley–R. Stanley) C. Stanley–L, R. Stanley–T, Shuffler–B		KLP-963, K4CD-0950
12057	**I Feel Like Going Home** (C. Stanley–R. Stanley) C. Stanley–L, R. Stanley–T, Shuffler–B	45-6059	KLP-963, K4CD-0950
12058	**Take Me Home** (C. Stanley–R. Stanley) R. Stanley–LV/TC, C. Stanley–LC, Shuffler–B	45-6053	KLP-963, GT-0108, K4CD-0950

650920   King session; producer:
King Studio, Cincinnati, Ohio
September 20, 1965
Carter Stanley: g | Ralph Stanley: b | George Shuffler: lg and sb (dubbed)

12067   **Are You Ready** (R. Stanley–G. Duty)   KLP-963, GT-0107, K4CD-0950
C. Stanley–L, R. Stanley–T, Shuffler–B

12068   **Prayer of a Truck Driver's Son** (C. Stanley–R. Stanley)   45-6046   KLP-963, KLP-1046, NLP-2078, GT-0108,
C. Stanley–L, R. Stanley–T, Shuffler–B   K4CD-0950

12069   **What a Price** (R. Stanley–G. Duty)   KLP-963, GT-0103, K4CD-0950
C. Stanley–L, R. Stanley–T, Shuffler–B

12070   **Vision of the Promised Land** (C. Stanley–R. Stanley)   KLP-963, NLP-2112, GT-0062, K4CD-0950
C. Stanley–L, R. Stanley–T, Shuffler–B

12071   **Pray for the Boys** (C. Stanley–R. Stanley)   45-6023   KLP-963, K4CD-0950
C. Stanley–L, R. Stanley–T, Shuffler–B

12072   **Soldier's Grave** (Bailes Brothers)   45-6053   KLP-963, GT-0107, K4CD-0950, B0007883-02
C. Stanley–L, R. Stanley–T, Shuffler–B

651208   Rimrock Records session; producer: Wayne Raney
Concord, Arkansas
ca. December 8, 1965
Carter Stanley: g | Ralph Stanley: b | George Shuffler: lg and sb
Ralph Mayo: f | Thomas Wayne Raney: * harmonica

If I Could Hear My Mother Pray Again   RLP-200, GT-0104
C. Stanley–L, R. Stanley–T, Shuffler–B

Jesus Savior Pilot Me   RLP-200
C. Stanley–L, R. Stanley–T, Shuffler–B

Over in the Glory Land   RLP-200
C. Stanley–L, R. Stanley–T, Mayo–B, Shuffler–BS

A Beautiful Life   RLP-200, SLP-384, GT-0107
C. Stanley–L, R. Stanley–T, Mayo–B, Shuffler–BS

Nobody Answered Me   RLP-200
C. Stanley–L, R. Stanley–T

Precious Memories   RLP-200, SLP-384, GT-0104
C. Stanley–L, R. Stanley–T, Mayo–B, Shuffler–BS

We Shall Meet Someday   RLP-200, GT-0104
C. Stanley–L, R. Stanley–T, Shuffler–B

Amazing Grace   RLP-200, SLP-384, GT-0108
C. Stanley–L, R. Stanley–T, Mayo–B, Shuffler–BS

How Beautiful Heaven Must Be   RLP-200
C. Stanley–L, R. Stanley–T, Mayo–B, Shuffler–BS

Farther Along	RLP-200, GT-0107
C. Stanley–L, R. Stanley–T, Mayo–B, Shuffler–BS	
Just a Little Talk with Jesus	RLP-200
C. Stanley–L, R. Stanley–T, Mayo–B, Shuffler–BS	
An Empty Mansion (Baxter)	RLP-153
C. Stanley–L, R. Stanley–T, Mayo–B, Shuffler–BS	
This World Is Not My Home	RLP-153, GT-0104
C. Stanley–L, R. Stanley–T	
I'll Meet You in the Morning	RLP-153
C. Stanley–L, R. Stanley–T, Mayo–B, Shuffler–BS	
Hand in Hand with Jesus	RLP-153
C. Stanley–L, R. Stanley–T, Shuffler–B	
Lord, I'm Coming Home	RLP-153, GT-0104
C. Stanley–L, R. Stanley–T, Mayo–B, Shuffler–BS	
Softly and Tenderly	RLP-153
C. Stanley–L, R. Stanley–T, Mayo–B, Shuffler–BS	
Hold to God's Unchanging Hand	RLP-153 SLP-384 GT-0108
C. Stanley–L, R. Stanley–T, Mayo–B, Shuffler–BS	
The Blood That Stained the Old Rugged Cross (Baxter)	RLP-153
C. Stanley–L, R. Stanley–T, Mayo–B, Shuffler–BS	
Where Could I Go (Baxter)	RLP-153
C. Stanley–L, R. Stanley–T, Mayo–B, Shuffler–BS	
Leaning on the Everlasting Arms	RLP-153
C. Stanley–L, R. Stanley–T, Mayo–B, Shuffler–BS	
Are You Washed in the Blood	RLP-153, SLP-384, GT-0107
C. Stanley–L, R. Stanley–T	
What Would You Give in Exchange (Baxter)	RLP-153
C. Stanley–L, R. Stanley–T	
Where the Soul Never Dies*	RLP-153, GT-0107, B0007883-02
C. Stanley–L, R. Stanley–T	
I'll Meet You in Church Sunday Morning	RLP-153
C. Stanley–L, R. Stanley–T, Mayo–B, Shuffler–BS	

660224 Central Sun Video Company reissue of *Rainbow Quest* television program; producer: Sholon Rubinstein
WNJU–TV, Newark, New Jersey
February 24, 1966
Carter Stanley: g | Ralph Stanley: b | George Shuffler: lg (* sb)
Don Miller: f | Chick Stripling: sb (†f)

It Takes a Worried Man	A-108, Shanachie 605
C. Stanley–L, R. Stanley–T, Shuffler–BS	

Clinch Mountain Backstep Instrumental	A-108, Shanachie 605
Chicken Reel*† Instrumental	A-108, Shanachie 605
Jacob's Vision C. Stanley—L, R. Stanley—T, Shuffler—BS	A-108, Shanachie 605
I'm Thinking Tonight of My Blue Eyes Cousin Emmy—L; Group sing-along by others	A-108, Shanachie 605
I Never Will Marry Pete Seeger—L; Group sing-along by others	A-108, Shanachie 605
Single Girl C. Stanley—L	A-108, Shanachie 605
Knick Knack Song Cousin Emmy—L	A-108, Shanachie 605
Down in the Valley Pete Seeger—L; Group sing-along by others	A-108, Shanachie 605

660301 Bear Family reissue of a television program; producer: Horst Lippmann
SWF-Fernsehproduktion, Baden—Baden, West Germany
March 1–3, 1966
Carter Stanley: g | Ralph Stanley: b | George Shuffler: lg
Don Miller: f | Chick Stripling: sb

How Mountain Girls Can Love C. Stanley—L, R. Stanley—T, Shuffler—B	BVD-20101 AT
Rank Stranger C. Stanley—L, R. Stanley—T, Shuffler—B	BVD-20101 AT

660317 Bear Family reissue of a live show; producers: John Cohen and Chris Strachwitz
Bremen, West Germany
March 17, 1966
Carter Stanley: g | Ralph Stanley: b | George Shuffler: lg
Don Miller: f | Tracy Schwarz: sb

Introduction by John Cohen	BCD-16849 BK
How Mountain Girls Can Love C. Stanley—L, R. Stanley—T, Shuffler—B	BCD-16849 BK
Nobody's Business C. Stanley—L, R. Stanley—T, Shuffler—B	BCD-16849 BK
Village Church Yard Holcomb—L; Congregational/unison singing by Carter and Ralph Stanley and others	BCD-16849 BK
Introduction of New Lost City Ramblers by Carter Stanley	BCD-16849 BK

Introduction of Stanley Brothers by Carter Stanley and Mike Seeger	BCD-16849 BK
Riding on the Midnight Train C. Stanley–L, R. Stanley–T, Shuffler–B	BCD-16849 BK
Leather Britches Instrumental	BCD-16849 BK
Cannonball Blues Instrumental	BCD-16849 BK
Stone Walls and Steel Bars C. Stanley–L, R. Stanley–T, Shuffler–B	BCD-16849 BK
Little Birdie R. Stanley–L	BCD-16849 BK
Rank Stranger C. Stanley–L, R. Stanley–T, Shuffler–B	BCD-16849 BK
Jordan C. Stanley–L, R. Stanley–T, Shuffler–BS	BCD-16849 BK
Medley: Roll in My Sweet Baby's Arms / Long Journey Home / Katie Cline C. Stanley–L, R. Stanley–T, Shuffler–B	BCD-16849 BK
Chicken Reel [all bands on stage] Instrumental	BCD-16849 BK

661016a Joy Records, reissue of show, recorded by unknown
Rebel Records, reissue of show, recorded by unknown
StanleyTone reissue of show, recorded by unknown
Brown County Jamboree, Bean Blossom, Indiana
October 16, 1966, afternoon performance
Carter Stanley: g | Ralph Stanley: b | George Shuffler: lg
Melvin Goins: sb | Birch Monroe: * bass vocals

Nobody's Business C. Stanley–L, R. Stanley–T	Joy-10329, SLP-1512, NO RLS #
Another Day Another Dollar Shuffler–L	NO RLS #
I See Through You C. Stanley–L, R. Stanley–T	NO RLS #
Somebody Loves You Darling C. Stanley–L, R. Stanley–T	Joy-10329, SLP-1512, NO RLS #
Comedy routine Spoken exchange by Carter Stanley and Melvin Goins	NO RLS #
Clinch Mountain Backstep Instrumental	NO RLS #

Searching for a Soldier's Grave
C. Stanley–L, R. Stanley–T, Shuffler–B

NO RLS #

Little Rosewood Casket
Instrumental

NO RLS #

Never Again
C. Stanley–L, R. Stanley–T

NO RLS #

Boat of Love*
C. Stanley–L, R. Stanley–T, Shuffler–B, Monroe–BS

Joy-10329, SLP-1512

Let Me Walk Lord, by Your Side
C. Stanley–L, R. Stanley–T, Shuffler–B, Monroe–BS

NO RLS #

Comments by Birch Monroe

NO RLS #

Little Birdie
R. Stanley–L

Joy-10329, SLP-1512, NO RLS #

Single Girl
C. Stanley–L

Joy-10329, SLP-1512, NO RLS #

Takes a Worried Man / Worried Man Blues
C. Stanley–L, R. Stanley–T, Shuffler–B

Joy-10329, SLP-1512, NO RLS #

How Far to Little Rock
Spoken exchanges by Carter and Ralph Stanley

NO RLS #

Are You Ready
C. Stanley–L, R. Stanley–T, Shuffler–B

NO RLS #

Rank Stranger
C. Stanley–L, R. Stanley–T, Shuffler–B

NO RLS #

Jordan
C. Stanley–L, R. Stanley–T, Shuffler–BS

NO RLS #

Take Me Home Savior
R. Stanley–LV/TC, C. Stanley–LC, Shuffler–B

Joy-10329, SLP-1512, NO RLS #

Comments by Birch Monroe

NO RLS #

Stone Walls and Steel Bars
C. Stanley–L, R. Stanley–T, Shuffler–B

Joy-10329, SLP-1512, NO RLS #

She'll Be Coming Around the Mountain
Goins–L

NO RLS #

661016b   Copper Creek reissue of show, recorded by Bill Ivey
Brown County Jamboree, Bean Blossom, Indiana
October 16, 1966, evening performance
Carter Stanley: g | Ralph Stanley: b | George Shuffler: lg
Melvin Goins: sb | Birch Monroe: * f / † bass vocals

My Dixie Home (Traditional)   CCSS-V1N4
C. Stanley–L, R. Stanley–T

I Know What It Means to Be Lonesome (A. P. Carter)   CCSS-V1N4
Shuffler–L

I See Through You (F. Liddell–B. Ledley)   CCSS-V1N4
C. Stanley–L, R. Stanley–T

Somebody Loves You, Darling (Traditional)   CCSS-V1N4
C. Stanley–L, R. Stanley–T

Comedy   CCSS-V1N4
Spoken exchange by Carter Stanley and Melvin Goins

Wildwood Flower (A. P. Carter)   CCSS-V1N4
Instrumental

Searching for a Soldier's Grave (Bailes Bros.)   CCSS-V1N4
C. Stanley–L, R. Stanley–T, Shuffler–B

Little Rosewood Casket (A. P. Carter)   CCSS-V1N4
Instrumental

If I Lose (R. Stanley)   CCSS-V1N4
C. Stanley–L, R. Stanley–T, Shuffler–B

Comedy   CCSS-V1N4
Spoken exchange by George Shuffler and Melvin Goins

Charming Betsy (Traditional)   CCSS-V1N4
Goins–L

Down Yonder* (Traditional)   CCSS-V1N4
Instrumental

Lost Train Blues* (Arthur Smith)   CCSS-V1N4
Instrumental

Canaan's Land† (A. P. Carter)   CCSS-V1N4
C. Stanley–L, R. Stanley–T, Shuffler–B, Monroe–BS

Beautiful Life† (Wm. Golden)   CCSS-V1N4
C. Stanley–L, R. Stanley–T, Shuffler–B, Monroe–BS

NUMERICAL LISTING OF RELEASES

In the previous chapters of discographical information, song titles were followed by listings of release numbers for 78 rpm singles, 45 rpm singles, extended play singles, albums, compact discs, video cassettes, and DVDs. This section arranges those release numbers in groups according to what recording labels they were originally issued on. Within these groups, which are arranged alphabetically by label name, the releases are presented in numerical order by release number. The release numbers are followed by, in the case of singles, individual song titles or, in the case of albums, album titles. To the right of the titles appear the release dates for each selection.

Bear Family:

BCD-15423	*Bill Monroe: Bluegrass 1950–1958*	1989
BCD-15564	*The Stanley Brothers & the Clinch Mountain Boys, 1949–52*	1991
BCD-15681	*The Stanley Brothers & the Clinch Mountain Boys, 1953–1958 & 1959*	1993
BCD-16425 HK	*Bill Clifton, Around the World to Poor Valley*	2001
BCD-16849 BK	*American Folk & Country Music Festival*	2007
BVD-20101 AT	*American Folk & Country Music* (DVD)	2003

Bluegrass Special:

BS-1	*Bluegrass Special*	ca. 1975

Blue Ridge:

514	Meet Me Tonight	ca. April 1962
	Nobody's Business	ca. April 1962

Blue Ridge Institute:

BRI-002	*Virginia Traditions: Ballads from British Tradition*	1978

Cabin Creek:

CC-203	*Bluegrass Gospel Favorites*	1967

Central Sun Video Co.:

A-108	*Rainbow Quest with Pete Seeger, the Stanley Brothers, Clinch Mountain Boys, Cousin Emmy*	1985

CMH:

CMH-CD-8412	*High Lonesome: The Story of Bluegrass Music*	2003

Columbia singles (78/45):

20577	The White Dove	April 4, 1949
	Gathering Flowers for the Master's Bouquet	
20590	Little Glass of Wine	June 20, 1949
	Let Me Be Your Friend	
20617	The Angels Are Singing (in Heaven Tonight)	Sept. 26, 1949
	It's Never Too Late	
20647	A Vision of Mother	Dec. 5, 1949
	Have You Someone (in Heaven Awaiting)	
20667	The Old Home	Feb. 13, 1950
	The Fields Have Turned Brown	
20697	I Love No One but You	May 15, 1950
	Too Late to Cry	
20735	We'll Be Sweethearts in Heaven	Aug. 21, 1950
	The Drunkard's Hell	
20770	Hey! Hey! Hey!	Dec. 18, 1950
	Pretty Polly	
20816	The Lonesome River	May 7, 1951
	I'm a Man of Constant Sorrow	
20953	Sweetest Love	June 7, 1952
	The Wandering Boy	
54008	The White Dove	Oct. 9, 1954
	Gathering Flowers for the Master's Bouquet	

Columbia EP:

2833	The White Dove	ca. 1958
	Gathering Flowers For the Master's Bouquet	
	The Old Home	
	The Fields Have Turned Brown	

Columbia/SONY/CBS/Harmony albums in chronological order with dates of release where known.

Columbia (SONY/CBS) and Harmony (HL) albums and CDs:

HL-7291	*The Stanley Brothers*	April 1961
HL-7377	*Angels Are Singing*	June 11, 1966
HS-11177	*Angels Are Singing*	June 11, 1966
CK-53798	*The Complete Columbia Stanley Brothers*	March 1, 1996
CK-86747	*An Evening Long Ago*	March 23, 2004

Copper Creek:

CCLP-0101	*Shadows of the Past*	1981
CCSS-V1N1	*Stanley Series*, Vol. 1, No. 1.	1982
CCSS-V1N2	*Stanley Series*, Vol. 1, No. 2	1982
CCSS-V1N3	*Stanley Series*, Vol. 1, No. 3	1982
CCSS-V1N4	*Stanley Series*, Vol. 1, No. 4	1984
CCSS-V2N1	*Stanley Series*, Vol. 2, No. 1	1984

CCSS-V2N2	*Stanley Series*, Vol. 2, No. 2	1984
CCSS-V2N3	*Stanley Series*, Vol. 2, No. 3	1986
CCSS-V2N4	*Stanley Series*, Vol. 2, No. 4	1987
CCSS-V3N1	*Stanley Series*, Vol. 3, No. 1	1987
CCSS-V3N2	*Stanley Series*, Vol. 3, No. 2	1989
CCCD-5511	*Stanley Series*, Vol. 3, No. 3	1990
CCCD-5512	*Stanley Series*, Vol. 3, No. 4	1992
CCCD-5513	*Stanley Series*, Vol. 4, No. 1	1996

County:

CO-738	*Stanley Brothers of Virginia*, Vol. 1: *That Little Old Country Church House*	Aug. 1973
CO-739	*Stanley Brothers of Virginia*, Vol. 2: *Long Journey Home*	Aug. 1973
CO-753	*Stanley Brothers of Virginia*, Vol. 3: *Uncloudy Day*	1977
CO-754	*Stanley Brothers of Virginia*, Vol. 4	1976
CO-780	*On Radio*, Vol. 1	1984
CO-781	*On Radio*, Vol. 2	1984
CCS-106/7	*Starday Sessions*	1984
CCS-114	*In the Pines*	1993

The Department of Health, Education, and Welfare—Social Security Administration:

Show #209	*The World of Folk Music Starring Oscar Brand*	1965

Decca singles (78/45):

28608	**You're Drifting Away**	March 23, 1953
28749	**Cabin of Love**	July 13, 1953
46344	**Rotation Blues**	July 23, 1951
	Lonesome Truck Driver Blues	
46351	**Get Down on Your Knees And Pray**	Sept. 4, 1951
46369	**Sugar Coated Love**	Oct. 15, 1951

Decca EP:

ED 2354	**Get Down on Your Knees and Pray**	April 30, 1956

Decca (DL) and MCA albums and CDs:

DL-4780	*The High Lonesome Sound*	June 13, 1966
DL 7-5066	*Bill Monroe and Charlie Monroe*	Feb. 24, 1969
DL 7-5135	*A Voice from On High*	June 30, 1969
MCAD 4-11048	*The Music of Bill Monroe from 1936 to 1994*	1994
MCA 088 113 207-2	*Bill Monroe Anthology*	2003
MCA B0002907-2	*The Gospel Spirit*	2004

Florida Folklife Digitization and Education Project

	More Music from the Florida Folklife Collection	2005

Folkways:

FA-2390	*Friends of Old Time Music*	1964

Joy:

Joy-10329	*Together for the Last Time*	1971

King singles:

5155	She's More to Be Pitied	Nov. 3, 1958
	Train 45	
5165	Love Me Darlin' Just Tonight	Dec. 22, 1958
	Midnight Ramble	
5180	Keep a Memory	Feb. 16, 1959
	Mastertone March	
5197	How Can We Thank Him for What He Has Done	April 13, 1959
	That Home Far Away	
5210	Memory of Your Smile	ca. June 1959
	Suwanee River Hoedown	
5233	Mother's Footsteps Guide Me On	Aug. 10, 1959
	White Dove	
5269	How Mountain Girls Can Love	ca. Oct. 5, 1959
	I'm a Man of Constant Sorrow	
5291	Shenandoah Waltz	Dec. 14, 1959
	Sunny Side of the Mountain	
5306	Heaven Seemed So Near	Jan. 4, 1960
	How Far to Little Rock?	
5313	Pass Me Not	Feb. 22, 1960
	When Jesus Beckons Me	
5347	Mountain Dew	ca. May 1960
	Old Rattler	
5355	Next Sunday, Darling, Is My Birthday	May 30, 1960
	Sweeter Than the Flowers	
5367	Mother Left Me Her Bible	June 27, 1960
	Over in the Glory Land	
5384	Daybreak in Dixie	July 25, 1960
	Finger Poppin' Time	
5415	Little Benny	Oct. 31, 1960
	Old Love Letters	
5441	Angel of Death	Jan. 30, 1961
	Jordan	
5460	Wild Side of Life	Jan. 30, 1961
	Window up Above	
5494	Little Bessie	May 15, 1961
	Village Church Yard	
5518	I'd Worship You	June 12, 1961
	I'll Take the Blame	
5557	Fast Express	Sept. 14, 1961
	There Is a Trap	
5582	Jacob's Vision	Nov. 14, 1961
	Thy Burdens Are Greater Than Mine	
5629	Still Trying to Get to Little Rock	March 19, 1962
	String, Eraser, and Blotter	
5637	I'm Only Human	April 10, 1962
	Keep Them Cold Icy Fingers off Me	
5674	Drunkard's Dream	July 18, 1962
	My Deceitful Heart	
5688	I Just Came from Your Wedding	ca. Aug. 7, 1962
	Mama Don't Allow	
5708	Drinking from the Fountain	Nov. 20, 1962
	Who Will Sing for Me	
5732	Old and in the Way	March 11, 1963
	Six Months Ain't Long	

5754	Memories of Mother	April 24, 1963
	Paul and Silas	
5763	He Went to Sleep and the Hogs Ate Him	June 5, 1963
	Lips That Lie	
5809	Lonesome Night	Sept. 17, 1963
	Stone Walls and Steel Bars	
5869	Don't Cheat in Our Home Town	March 31, 1964
	I See Through You	
5902	A Crown He Wore	May 26, 1964
	John Three-Sixteen	
5916	I Just Stood There	July 13, 1964
	Train 45	
5920	Bully of the Town	Sept. 5, 1964
	How Bad I Do Feel	
5932	He's Passing This Way	ca. Sept. 1964
	Shoutin' on the Hills of Glory	
5933	Don't Step over an Old Love	ca. Sept. 1964
	I'm Bound to Ride	
5934	Five String Drag	ca. Sept. 1964
	Shout Little Lulie	
6005	How You've Tortured My Mind	ca. Sept. 1965
	Rollin' on Rubber Wheels	
6023	End of the Road	ca. Feb. 1966
	Pray for the Boys	
6046	Never Again	ca. May 1966
	Prayer of a Truck Driver's Son	
6053	Soldier's Grave	ca. Aug. 1966
	Take Me Home	
6059	God's Highway	ca. Oct. 1966
	I Feel Like Going Home	
6079	Little Birdie	ca. Feb. 1967
	Whiskey	
6089	Hills of Roan County	ca. April 1967
	I Don't Want Your Rambling Letters	
6236	I'll Just Go Away	ca. 1968
	Highway Ambush (actually "Midnight Ramble")	

King EPs:

EP-439	How Mountain Girls Can Love	ca. 1959
	Heaven Seemed So Near	
	Mastertone March	
	She's More to Be Pitied	
EP-440	Keep a Memory	ca. 1959
	Train 45	
	Think of What You've Done	
	Your Selfish Heart	
EP-441	Clinch Mountain Backstep	ca. 1959
	The Memory of Your Smile	
	Love Me Darling Just Tonight	
	Midnight Ramble	
EP-455	How Can We Thank Him for What He Has Done	ca. 1959
	My Lord's Going to Set Me Free	
	I'll Meet You in Church Sunday Morning	
	Wings of Angels	

EP-456	White Dove	ca. 1959
	That Home Far Away	
	The Angel of Death	
	Daniel Prayed	
EP-457	He Said If I Be Lifted Up	
	Are You Afraid to Die	
	Mother's Footsteps Guide Me On	
	The Wicked Path of Sin	
EP-461	I'll Not Be a Stranger	ca. 1960
	Purple Robe	
	When Jesus Beckons Me Home	
	Pass Me Not	
EP-462	Mother Left Me Her Bible	ca. 1960
	From the Manger to the Cross	
	Over in the Glory Land	
	My Main Trial Is Yet to Come	
EP-463	Jordan	ca. 1960
	Lonely Tombs	
	Four Books in the Bible	
	Jacob's Vision	
EP-467	Suwanee River Hoedown	ca. 1961
	Sweet Thing	
	Daybreak in Dixie	
	Let Me Rest	
EP-468	Little Benny	ca. 1961
	Are You Tired of Me Darling	
	I'm a Man of Constant Sorrow	
	Let Me Love You One More Time	
EP-469	Old Love Letters	ca. 1961
	It's Raining Here This Morning	
	Finger Poppin' Time	
	Wildwood Flower	
EP-479	Working on a Building	ca. 1961
	Campin' in Canaan Land	
	Little Bessie	
	Mother Call My Name in Prayer	
EP-480	Dying a Sinner's Death	ca. 1961
	A Few More Years	
	My Sinful Past	
	Kneel at the Cross	

King albums and CDs:

KLP-615	*The Stanley Brothers & the Clinch Mountain Boys*	March 1959
KLP-645	*Hymns and Sacred Songs*	Nov. 1959
KLP-690	*Sing Everybody's Country Favorites*	June 1960
KLP-698	*For the Good People*	Aug. 1960
KLP-719	*In Person*	Nov. 21, 1960
KLP-750	*Old Time Camp Meeting*	ca. April 1961
KLP-772	*Sing the Songs They Like Best*	ca. Nov. 1961
KLP-791	*Award Winners at the Folk Song Festival*	ca. March 1962
KLP-805	*Good Old Camp Meeting Songs*	ca. May 1962
KLP-811	*Christmas Songs*	Nov. 24, 1962
KLP-834	*Folk Concert*	ca. March 1963
KLP-864	*Country Folk Music Spotlight*	Dec. 1963
KLP-872	*America's Finest Five-String Banjo Hootenanny*	Jan. 1964

KLP-918	*Hymns of the Cross with George Shuffler*	July 1964
KLP-924	*The Remarkable Stanley Brothers Play and Sing Bluegrass Songs for You*	Nov. 1964
KLP-953	*Best of the Stanley Brothers*	1966
KLP-963	*A Collection of Original Gospel and Sacred Songs*	1966
KLP-1013	*Sing the Best-Loved Sacred Songs of Carter Stanley*	1967
KLP-1046	*How Far to Little Rock*	May 1969
KBSCD-7000	*The Early Starday/King Years, 1958–1961*	1993
K4CD-0950	*The King Years, 1961–1965*	2003

Man-do-lin:

MO-0108 (DVD)	*Bluegrass 1963*	2008

Melodeon:

MLP-7322	*Their Original Recordings*	Feb. 1966

Mercury singles (78/45):

70217	This Weary Heart You Stole Away	Aug. 20, 1953
	I'm Lonesome Without You	
70270	(Say) Won't You Be Mine	Nov. 3, 1953
	Our Last Goodbye	
70340	I Long to See the Old Folks	March 1, 1954
	A Voice from On High	
70400	Memories of Mother	June 2, 1954
	Could You Love Me One More Time	
70437	Poison Lies	Aug. 4, 1954
	Dickson County Breakdown	
70453	I Just Got Wise	Sept. 2, 1954
	Blue Moon of Kentucky	
70483	Calling from Heaven	Oct. 22, 1954
	Harbor of Love	
70546	Hard Times	Jan. 26, 1955
	I Worship You	
70718	I Hear My Savior Calling	Sept. 27, 1955
	Just a Little Talk with Jesus	
70612	So Blue	April 11, 1955
	You'd Better Get Right	
70663	Lonesome and Blue	July 11, 1955
	Orange Blossom Special	
70789	Nobody's Love Is Like Mine	Jan. 3, 1956
	Big Tilda	
70886	Baby Girl	May 24, 1956
	Say You'll Take Me Back	
71064	I'm Lost, I'll Never Find the Way	Feb. 14, 1957
	The Flood	
71135	The Cry from the Cross	June 4, 1957
	Let Me Walk, Lord, by Your Side	
71207	Fling Ding	Oct. 2, 1957
	Loving You Too Well	
71258	Life of Sorrow	Jan. 15, 1958
	I'd Rather Be Forgotten	
71292	Are You Alone	Feb. 25, 1958
71302	I'll Never Grow Tired of You	March 31, 1958
	No School Bus in Heaven	

Mercury albums and CDs:

MG-20349	*Country Pickin' & Singin'*	Sept. 1958
MG-20857	*Hootenanny Bluegrass Style*	Nov. 1, 1963
MG-20884	*Hard Times*	Nov. 1963
MGW-12262/SRW-16262	*Great Country Gospel Songs*	March 1964
MGW-12327/SRW-16327	*Hard Times*	July 20, 1966
MERC-314-528-191-2	*Angel Band: The Classic Mercury Recordings*	1995
MERC-088-170-222-2	*The Best of the Stanley Brothers: The Millennium Collection*	Oct. 11, 2002
MERC-B0000534-02	*The Complete Mercury Recordings*	2003
Old Homestead: OHCS-323	*The Remarkable Stanley Brothers Play and Sing Bluegrass Songs for You*	1986

Oberlin Folk Music Club:

OCF-42-756	*The Audience Pleased: Live Recordings 1959–1975*	1975

Rebel:

REB-854	*Live Again! WCYB Bristol Farm & Fun Time*	1988
REB-855	*The Stanley Brothers on WCYB Bristol*	1988
SLP-1487	*The Legendary Stanley Brothers Recorded Live*, Vol. 1	1970
SLP-1495	*The Legendary Stanley Brothers Recorded Live*, Vol. 2	1970
SLP-1512	*Together for the Last Time*	1972
REB-1110	*Long Journey Home*	1992
REB-1115	*On Radio*	1991
REB-2003	*Live Again! WCYB Bristol Farm & Fun Time*	1997
REB-4303	*Gospel Songs from Cabin Creek*	1990
REB-8002	*True Bluegrass Gospel*	May 22, 2007

Revenant:

REV-203	*Earliest Recordings*	1997

Rich-R-Tone:

RRT-418	**The Rambler's Blues**	Sept. 10, 1948
	Molly and Tenbrook	
RRT-420	**Mother No Longer Awaits Me at Home**	Dec. 29, 1947
	The Girl Behind the Bar	
RRTI-423	**Little Maggie**	April 17, 1948
	The Little Glass of Wine	
RRT-435	**The Jealous Lover**	March 20, 1949
	Our Darling's Gone	
RRT-466	**Death Is Only a Dream**	Feb. 28, 1950
	I Can Tell You the Time	
RRT-1055	**The Little Girl and the Dreadful Snake**	
	Are You Waiting Just for Me	
RRT-1056	**Little Glass of Wine**	
	Little Birdie	

Rimrock:

RLP-153	*In Memory of Carter Stanley: "An Empty Mansion"*	1967
RLP-200	*Stanley Brothers Goes to Europe* [Also two other titles]	1966

Rounder:

ROU-1110	*Earliest Recordings: The Complete Rich-R-Tone 78s (1947–1952)*	2005

| ROU-SS-09 | Columbia Sessions: 1949–'50, Vol. 1 | 1980 |
| ROU-SS-10 | Columbia Sessions, Vol. 2 | 1982 |

Rural Rhythm:

| MP-0108 | Bluegrass 1963 | 2010 |

Shanachie:

| Shanachie 605 | High Lonesome: The Story of Bluegrass Music | 1999 |

Smithsonian Folkways:

| SFW CD 40160 | Friends of Old-Time Music: The Folk Arrival, 1961—1965 | 2006 |

StanleyTone:

ST-5001	Old-Time Songs	2001
ST-5002	Ridin' That New River Train	2001
ST-5003	Folk Festival	2001
ST-no #	Brown County Jamboree	2004

Starday singles:

290	Gathering Flowers from the Hillside	April 1957
	Take Back the Heart	
406	Gonna Paint the Town	ca. Sept 7, 1959
	That Happy Night	
413	Holiday Pickin'	Dec. 1, 1958
	Christmas Is Near	
431	Corey	April 20, 1959
438	Trust Each Other	June 15, 1959
	Beneath the Maple	
444	You Go to Your Church	July 13, 1959
	When You Kneel at Mother's Grave	
466	Highway of Regret	Nov. 16, 1959
	Another Night	
494	A Little at a Time	May 9, 1960
	Ridin' That Midnight Train	
506	Rank Stranger	Aug. 8, 1960
	Gathering Flowers for the Master's Bouquet	
522	Little Maggie	Oct. 31, 1960
	God Gave You to Me	
546	If I Lose	April 24, 1961
	Don't Go Out Tonight	
565	Carolina Mountain Home	Dec. 4, 1961
	A Few More Seasons	
587	Choo Choo Comin'	April 1962
	Come All Ye Tenderhearted	

Starday EPs:

SEP-107	Beneath the Maple	June 1959
	Choo Choo Comin'	
	Carolina Mountain Home	
	Trust Each Other	

SEP-123	A Few More Seasons	March 1960
	Where We'll Never Die	
	In Heaven We'll Never Grow Old	
	Mother No Longer Awaits Me at Home	
SEP-184	Ridin' That Midnight Train	1962
	If I Lose	
	Little Maggie	
	Rank Stranger	

Starday (SLP, SD), Nashville (NLP), and Gusto (GD, GT) albums and CDs:

SLP-104	*Banjo in the Hills*	Aug. 3, 1959
SLP-106	*Mountain Songs Favorites Featuring Five-String Banjo*	Nov. 9, 1959
SLP-111	*Mountain Folk Songs*	March 28, 1960
SLP-116	*Old Time Religion, Country Style*	May 16, 1960
SLP-122	*Sacred Songs from the Hills*	Oct. 24, 1960
SLP-159	*Bluegrass Sound*	March 1962
SLP-201	*Mountain Music Sound of the Stanley Brothers*	Dec. 1, 1962
SLP-384	*Jacob's Vision*	Oct. 29, 1966
NLP-2014	*Mountain Song Favorites*	Aug. 1964
NLP-2037	*The Famous Song Hits of the Stanley Brothers*	Aug. 1967
NLP-2078	*Sweeter Than the Flowers*	April 1970
NLP-2112	*Rank Strangers*	1973
GD-5026	*20 Bluegrass Originals*	1978
GT-0016	*16 Greatest Gospel Hits*	1978
GT-0062	*I Saw the Light*	1980
GT-0084	*Old Country Church*	1981
GT-0103	*1983 Collector's Edition*, Vol. 1	1983
GT-0104	*1983 Collector's Edition*, Vol. 2	1983
GT-0105	*1983 Collector's Edition*, Vol. 3	1983
GT-0106	*1983 Collector's Edition*, Vol. 4	1983
GT-0107	*1983 Collector's Edition*, Vol. 5	1983
GT-0108	*1983 Collector's Edition*, Vol. 6	1983
SD-3003	*16 Greatest Hits*	1977

State Library and Archives of Florida:

| No # | *More Music from the Florida Folklife Collection* | 2005 |

Time Life:

| B0007883-02 | *The Definitive Collection (1947–1966)* | 2007 |
| M-19493 | *Classic Bluegrass Collection* | 2007 |

Vanguard:

| VCD-77006 | *Bluegrass Breakdown* | 1992 |
| 77018 | *Clinch Mountain Bluegrass* | 1994 |

Vintage Collector's Club:

| ZK-002 | *Live at Antioch College, 1960* | |

Wango:

1783	**Sunny Side of Live**	ca. 1965
	Standin' in the Need of Prayer	
1784	**Life's Railway to Heaven**	ca. 1965
	If I Could Hear My Mother Pray Again	
	What Would You Give in Exchange for Your Soul	
	Hold Fast to the Right	
EP-108	**Someone's Last Day**	ca. 1967
	Hold Fast to the Right	
EP-109	**I'll Fly Away**	ca. 1967
	In the Sweet Bye and Bye	
EP-110	**In the Pines**	ca. 1967
	Don't Let Your Sweet Love Die	
	Little Maggie	
Wango CD-102	*Freight Train Special*, Vol. 2	1996
Wango LP-103	*John's Gospel Quartet*	
Wango LP-104	*John's Country Quartet*	
Wango LP-105	*Joans's Gospel Quartet*	
Wango LP-106	*Songs of Mother and Home*	
Wango CD-107	*Memories of Mother*	1997
Wango LP-115	*On the Air*	1976
Wango CD-108	*Little Old Country Church House*	1997
Wango CD-109	*Radio Series*, Vol. 1	1998
Wango CD-110	*Radio Series*, Vol. 2	1998
Wango CD-113	*Radio Series*, Vol. 3	2000
Wango CD-114	*Radio Series*, Vol. 4	2000
Wango CD-115	*Plum Pitiful*, Vol. 1	2000
Wango CD-116	*Plum Pitiful*, Vol. 2	2000
Wango CD-117	*Freight Trains Ride Again*, Vol. 1	2000
Wango CD-118	*Freight Trains Ride Again*, Vol. 2	2000
Wango CD-119	*It's Hymn Time*, Vol. 1	2002
Wango CD-120	*It's Hymn Time*, Vol. 2	2002
Wango CD-125	*Radio Series*, Vol. 5	2005
Wango CD-126	*Radio Series*, Vol. 6	2005
Wango CD-127	*Radio Series*, Vol. 7	2005

NOTES

1. Death Is Only a Dream: 1947–1948

1. Ralph Rinzler, "Ralph Stanley: The Tradition from the Mountains," *Bluegrass Unlimited* 8 (March 1974): 8.

2. Ralph Stanley, interview with Mike Seeger, Stockholm, Sweden, March 1966.

3. Hal Neeley, liner notes to *Folk Concert*, King KLP-834, 1963.

4. Dr. Ralph Stanley, *Man of Constant Sorrow: My Life and Times*, with Eddie Dean (New York: Gotham Books, 2009), 46–47.

5. *The Stanley Brothers: Your Favorite Songs*, Folio No. 1 (ca. 1947), 8.

6. Larry Mitchell, "Dr. Ralph Stanley!" *Pickin'* 4 (August 1977): 6.

7. Army enlistment record for Carter G. Stanley, World War II Army Enlistment Records Data File, ca. 1938–1946 [Electronic Record], Record Group 64 (College Park, Md.: National Archives and Records Administration), accessed December 13, 2011, www.aad.archives.gov.

8. Fran Russell, *Stanley Brothers . . . and the Clinch Mountain Boys* (ca. 1955), 2.

9. Rinzler, "Ralph Stanley: The Tradition from the Mountains," 9.

10. Ralph Stanley, interview with Mike Seeger, Stockholm, Sweden, March 1966.

11. Carter Stanley, interview with Mike Seeger, West Germany, March 1966.

12. Robert Barton Puryear III, *Border Forays and Adventures: From the Manuscripts of Lyman Copeland Draper and the Wisconsin Historical Society* (Westminster, Md.: Heritage Books, 2007), 21.

13. "New Radio Station on Air Here Today," *Bristol Herald Courier*, December 13, 1946, 6.

14. Ibid.

15. Ibid.

16. Roy Webb, interview with the author, Bristol, Tenn., January 6, 2008.

17. Rinzler, "Ralph Stanley: The Tradition from the Mountains," 9.

18. "American Folk Tunes: Cowboy and Hillbilly Tunes and Tunesters," *Billboard*, October 4, 1947, 124.

19. Ralph Stanley, interview with Mike Seeger, Stockholm, Sweden, March 1966.

20. Quote of Mac Wiseman in Jack Tottle, liner notes to *Live Again! WCYB Bristol Farm and Fun Time*, Rebel REB-854, 1988.

21. Quote of Ralph Stanley in Jack Tottle, liner notes to *Live Again! WCYB Bristol Farm and Fun Time*, Rebel REB-854, 1988.

22. The history of the Rich-R-Tone label is discussed in detail in a booklet accompanying a

reissue of Rich-R-Tone 78 rpm records. Unsigned liner notes to *The Rich-R-Tone Story—The Early Days of Bluegrass*, vol. 5, Rounder ROU-1017, 1974, back cover and pp. 2–5.

23. Jim Stanton, telephone interview with the author, ca. September 1978.

24. Rinzler, "Ralph Stanley: The Tradition from the Mountains," 10.

25. Carter Stanley, interview with Pete Wernick, Fincastle, Va., September 1965.

26. Jim Stanton, telephone interview with the author, ca. September 1978.

27. Bill Malone, *Country Music U. S. A.: A Fifty-Year History* (Austin: University of Texas Press, 1968), 219.

28. Rinzler, "Ralph Stanley: The Tradition from the Mountains," 10.

29. Carter Stanley, interview with Pete Wernick, Fincastle, Va., September 1965.

30. *Greetings From . . . The Lambert Boys* (ca. 1947), 2.

31. Unsigned liner notes to Leslie Keith, *Black Mountain Blues*, Briar BF-4201, 1974.

32. Ibid.

33. Ralph Stanley, interview with Charlie Sizemore, March 1981.

34. *The Stanley Brothers on WCYB Bristol*, Rebel REB-855, 1988.

35. Neil V. Rosenberg, *Bluegrass: A History* (Urbana: University of Illinois Press, 1985), 85.

36. Mac Wiseman quoted in Charles Wolfe, "Bill Monroe," *Journal of the American Academy for the Preservation of Old-Time Country Music* 16 (August 1993): 8

37. Ralph Stanley, interview with the author, Glasgow, Del., Sept. 6, 1981.

38. Ibid.

39. Ibid.

40. Neil V. Rosenberg, "From Sound to Style: The Emergence of Bluegrass," *Journal of American Folklore* 80 (April–June 1967): 146.

41. Ralph Stanley, interview with Charlie Sizemore, March 1981.

42. Bob Sayers, "Leslie Keith: Black Mountain Odyssey," *Bluegrass Unlimited* (11 December 1976): 16.

43. Rosenberg, "From Sound to Style: The Emergence of Bluegrass," 146.

44. Dick Spottswood, "Carl Sauceman: The Odyssey of a Bluegrass Pioneer," *Bluegrass Unlimited* 11 (August 1976): 15.

2. To Us, That Would Have Been the Impossible: Columbia Records, 1949–1952

1. *News and Observer*, radio listing, July 5, 1948, 3.

2. Dr. Ralph Stanley, *Man of Constant Sorrow My Life and Times*, with Eddie Dean (New York: Gotham Books, 2009), 146.

3. Ralph Stanley, interview with Mike Seeger, Stockholm, Sweden, March 1966.

4. Ibid.

5. "James C. Petrillo," *WTTW.com*, accessed July 4, 2014, http://www.wttw.com/main.taf?p=1,7,1,1,38.

6. Carter Stanley, interview with Mike Seeger, West Germany, March 1966.

7. *The Stanley Brothers and the Clinch Mountain Boys: Picture and Song Favorites*, Folio No. 2 (ca. 1949), 4.

8. Ibid.

9. Jay Hughes, telephone interview with the author, September 8, 1978.

10. Carter Stanley, interview with Mike Seeger, West Germany, March 1966.

11. Ralph Stanley, interview with Mike Seeger, Stockholm, Sweden, March 1966.

12. Carter Stanley, interview with Mike Seeger, West Germany, March 1966.

13. Carter Stanley, interview with Mike Seeger, West Germany, March 1966.

14. Bob Cantwell, "The Lonesome Sound of Carter Stanley," *Bluegrass Unlimited* 10 (June 1976): 13.

15. Ibid.

16. Ralph Stanley, interview with the author, May 31, 1981.

17. Jack Tottle, liner notes to *Live Again! WCYB Bristol Farm & Fun Time*, Rebel REB-854, 1988.

18. Wayne Erbsen, "Lester Woodie: Coming Up the Hard Road," *Bluegrass Unlimited* 14 (March 1980): 44.

19. Ibid., 45–46.

20. Basic biographical information for Ernie Newton can be found in Walt Trott, "Ernie Newton," in *Encyclopedia of Country Music*, edited by Paul Kingsbury (New York: Oxford University Press, 1998), 360.

21. Ralph Stanley, interview with the author, May 31, 1981.

22. Guthrie T. Meade Jr., Dick Spottswood, and Douglas S. Meade, *Country Music Sources: A Biblio-Discography of Commercially Recorded Traditional Music* (Chapel Hill, N.C: University of North Carolina Press, 2002), 387.

23. Kyle Davis Jr., *Folk-Songs of Virginia: A Descriptive Index and Classification* (Durham, N.C.: Duke University Press, 1949), 309.

24. Lester Woodie, telephone interview with the author, March 26, 1981.

25. Ibid.

26. George Shuffler, interview with the author, Valdese, N.C., October 13, 1977.

27. Lester Woodie, telephone interview with the author, March 26, 1981.

28. *Huntington Herald-Dispatch*, radio listing, July 3, 1950, 16.

29. *Shreveport Times*, radio listing, October 9, 1950, 9.

30. *Shreveport Times*, radio listing, October 25, 1950, 8.

31. Ralph Stanley, interview with Mike Seeger, Stockholm, Sweden, March 1966.

32. Johnny Sippel, "Folk Talent and Tunes," *Billboard*, November 25, 1950, 29.

33. *Lexington Herald*, advertisement for the Kentucky Mountain Barn Dance, October 28, 1950, 9.

34. Lester Woodie, telephone interview with the author, March 26, 1981.

35. Carter Stanley, interview with Mike Seeger, West Germany, March 1966.

36. Neil V. Rosenberg and Charles K. Wolfe, *The Music of Bill Monroe* (Urbana and Chicago: University of Illinois Press, 2007), 105.

37. The Tennessee driver's license issued to Carter Stanley, with its July 2, 1951, date of issue, is on display at the Ralph Stanley Museum and Traditional Mountain Music Center in Clintwood, Virginia.

38. "At the 71 Drive-In Theatre," *Northwest Arkansas Times*, July 5, 1951, 11.

39. *Nashville Tennessean*, radio listing, July 7, 1951, 10.

40. *Cecil Democrat*, advertisement for concert at New River Ranch, July 5, 1951, 6.

41. Ray Davis, *The Ray Davis Show*, WAMU-FM's BluegrassCountry.org, December 2, 2007.

42. Rosenberg and Wolfe, *The Music of Bill Monroe*, 105.

43. Ray Davis, *The Ray Davis Show*, WAMU-FM's BluegrassCountry.org, December 2, 2007.

44. Rosenberg and Wolfe, *The Music of Bill Monroe*, 106.

45. Ibid.

46. Stanley, *Man of Constant Sorrow*, 153.

47. Johnny Sippel, "Folk Talent and Tunes," *Billboard*, September 1, 1951, 30.

48. *Favorite Songs and Picture Album,* "As featured by the Stanley Brothers, your Radio Friends" (ca. 1951), 17.

49. Bobby Osborne, telephone interview with the author, August 26, 1993.

50. Penny Parsons, "Curly Seckler, Bluegrass Pioneer," *Bluegrass Unlimited* 38 (June 2004): 41.

51. *Lexington Herald*, radio listing, April 5, 1952, 8.

52. Ralph Rinzler, "Ralph Stanley: The Tradition from the Mountains," *Bluegrass Unlimited* 8 (March 1974): 10.

53. Bill Monroe, "Out in the Cold World" [partial home recording], 1944, accessed July 4, 2014, http://www.youtube.com/watch?v=Qg62FL2i0Fk.

54. *The Stanley Brothers and the Clinch Mountain Boys*, vol. 2., CBS Sony 20AP 13, 1976.

55. *Pikeville Daily News*, radio listing, April 15, 1952, 7; *Pikeville Daily News*, radio listing, April 30, 1952, 7.

56. *Charleston Daily Mail*, radio listing, May 23, 1952, 8.

57. Jim Williams quoted in Ivan M. Tribe, "Sing Your Song Jimmy: The Jim Williams Story," *Bluegrass Unlimited* 11 (June 1977): 29.

58. Basic biographical information for Jimmy Williams can be found in Ivan Tribe, "Sing Your Song: The Jimmy Williams Story."

59. Jim Stanton, telephone interview with the author, ca. September 1978.

60. On August 30, 1962, in a show at the Ash Grove in Hollywood, California, Carter Stanley spoke of learning to sing this song with Bill Monroe when he first went to work with him, in 1951.

61. Ralph Stanley, interview with the author, Glasgow, Del, September 6, 1981.

62. Ibid.

3. Some of Our Best Recordings Were the Mercurys: 1953–1958

1. Ralph Stanley, interview with Mike Seeger, Stockholm, Sweden, March 1966.

2. Ralph Stanley, quoted in Barry Brower, "Ralph Stanley: Keeping It Right Down and Simple," *Bluegrass Unlimited* 21 (February 1987): 13.

3. Carter Stanley, interview with Mike Seeger, West Germany, March 1966.

4. General information on Kilpatrick's career can be found in Bernie Asbell, "'D' Kilpatrick as C&W 'Man of Year,'" *Billboard*, November 17, 1958, 18 and 22.

5. Bob Artis, *Bluegrass* (New York: Hawthorn Books, Inc.), 34.

6. Carter Stanley, interview with Mike Seeger, West Germany, March 1966.

7. George Shuffler, interview with the author, Valdese, N.C., October 13, 1977.

8. Basic biographical information for John Shuffler was obtained in a telephone interview with the author on July 23, 2009.

9. Basic biographical information for Ralph Mayo was taken from an unpublished article by Gary Reid, "Mayo's the Name, Fiddlin's My Game: The Life and Times of Ralph Mayo," last modified July 17, 2013, Microsoft Word file.

10. Carter Stanley, interview with Mike Seeger, West Germany, March 1966.

11. Basic biographical information for Joe Meadows can be found in Ivan Tribe, "Joe Meadows: Mountain State Fiddler," *Bluegrass Unlimited* 13 (October 1978): 30–35.

12. Walt Trott, "Lightnin' Chance," in *Encyclopedia of Country Music*, edited by Paul Kingsbury (New York: Oxford University Press, 1998), 90.

13. Bill Lowe, interview with the author, Sykesville, Md., January 7, 1978.

14. Basic biographical information for Charlie Cline can be found in Russ Cheatham, "Charlie & Lee Cline and the Lonesome Pine Fiddlers," *Bluegrass Unlimited* 14 (February 1980): 18–22.

15. Carter Stanley, interview with Mike Seeger, West Germany, March 1966.

16. Neil V. Rosenberg and Charles K. Wolfe, *The Music of Bill Monroe* (Urbana: University of Illinois Press, 2007), 96.

17. Neil V. Rosenberg, e-mail to the author, November 11, 2009.

18. David W. Johnson, *Lonesome Melodies: The Lives and Music of the Stanley Brothers* (Jackson, Miss.: University Press of Mississippi), 122.

19. Review of "Hard Times," *Billboard*, March 5, 1955, 34.

20. Review of "Hard Times," *Country & Western Jamboree* 1 (April 1955): 25.

21. "Reviews of New C & W Records," *Billboard*, February 11, 1956, 43.

22. "Reviews of New Pop Records," *Billboard*, June 24, 1957, 56.

23. "Reviews of New C & W Records," *Billboard*, March 9, 1957, 59.

24. "Reviews of New C & W Records," *Billboard*, June 16, 1956, 45.

25. Review of Mercury 71064, *Country & Western Jamboree* 3 (June 1957).

26. *Richmond Times-Dispatch*, advertisement, March 9, 1955, 15.

27. *Richmond Times-Dispatch,* advertisement, April 9, 1955, 9.

28. *Danville Bee* (Va.), advertisement, August 13, 1955, 10.

29. *Danville Bee* (Va.), advertisement, November 12, 1955, 13.

30. "RCA Victor—1525 McGavock St," Scotty Moore: The Official Website, accessed May 29, 2014, http://www.scottymoore.net/studio_mcgavock.html.

31. Carter Stanley, interview with Mike Seeger, West Germany, March 1966.

32. Ralph Stanley, interview with the author, Glasgow, Del., September 6, 1981.

33. Ibid.

34. Johnson, *Lonesome Melodies*, 179.

35. G. Malcolm Laws Jr., *Native American Balladry: A Descriptive Study and a Bibliographical Syllabus* (Philadelphia: The American Folklore Society, 1950), 217.

36. Kyle Davis Jr., *Folk-Songs of Virginia: A Descriptive Index and Classification* (Durham, N. C.: Duke University Press, 1949), 58.

37. *Favorite Songs and Picture Album,* "As featured by The Stanley Brothers, your Radio Friends" (ca. 1951), 5.

38. Leo Zabelin, "Upsets Mark First Readers' Poll," *Country & Western Jamboree* 10 (December 1955): 9.

39. Ray Davis, *The Ray Davis Show*, WAMU-FM's BluegrassCountry.org, December 2, 2007; *Cecil Democrat*, advertisement for concert at New River Ranch, July 5, 1951, 6.

40. *Cecil Democrat*, advertisement for concert at New River Ranch, June 30, 1955, 7.

41. Mike Seeger, as quoted in liner notes to Stanley Brothers, Stanley Series, vol. 1, no. 3. Copper Creek CCSS-V1N3, 1982, 4–5.

42. Basic biographical information for Doug Morris was obtained in a telephone interview with the author on July 22, 2009.

43. Dave Samuelson, liner notes to, Stanley Brothers, Stanley Series, vol. 4, no. 1. Copper Creek CCSS-5513, 1996, 5–6.

44. Harold Bradley, quoted in Michael Kosser, *How Nashville Became Music City, U.S.A.: 50 Years of Music Row* (Milwaukee: Hal Leonard Corporation, 2006), 14.

45. Basic biographical information for Curley Lambert can be found in: Ivan M. Tribe, "Curley Lambert: Bluegrass Evergreen," *Bluegrass Unlimited* 10 (February 1976): 12–15.

46. *The Stanley Brothers and the Clinch Mountain Boys*, vol. 1, Mercury FDX-9063–4, 1974.

47. Unsigned liner notes to Leslie Keith, *Black Mountain Blues*, Briar BF-4201, 1974.

48. Gary Reid, liner notes to Stanley Brothers, *Old-Time Songs*, Stanley Tone ST-5001, 1996, 3.

49. Ralph Mayo, interview with Frankie Moore, March 4, 1981.

50. Benny Cain, interview with Walt Saunders, Stanley Brothers, *Stanley Series*, vol. 2, no. 1, Copper Creek CCSS-V2N1, 1984.

51. Basic biographical information for Chubby Anthony can be found in Don Rhodes, "Make

That Fiddle Sing! Chubby Anthony," *Bluegrass Unlimited* 13 (February 1979): 30–33; and "Donald 'Chubby' Anthony," *Bluegrass Unlimited* 14 (March 1980): 7.

52. Barry Brower, "Keeping It Right Down and Simple," 14.

53. Ralph Stanley, interview with the author, Glasgow, Del., September 6, 1981.

54. Ibid.; George Shuffler, interview with the author, October 13, 1977

55. Ralph Stanley, interview with the author, Troutville, Va., ca. 2007.

56. *Songs for Home Folks*, "By the Stanley Brothers" (ca. 1957), 8.

57. Bill Clifton, interview with the author, December 2, 2006.

58. Carter Stanley, interview with Mike Seeger, West Germany, March 1966.

59. Red Malone, interview with the author, April 21, 1979.

60. Don Pierce, "A Biography on the Stanley Brothers," *The Stanley Brothers Clinch Mountain Song Review* (ca. 1957), 2.

61. Basic biographical information for Jack Cooke can be found in: Barry Brower, "Making the Blend: The Jack Cooke Story," *Bluegrass Unlimited* 21 (January 1987): 55–57.

62. Bill Napier, interview with the author, Detroit, Mich., May 15, 1977.

63. Gary Reid, "2005 Inductee—Benjamin Edward 'Benny' Martin," International Bluegrass Music Museum, accessed June 11, 2014, http://bluegrassmuseum.org./hall-of-fame/2005-inductee-benjamin-edward-benny-martin.

64. "Howdy Forrester: Artist Biography," AllMusic.com, accessed June 11, 2014, www.allmusic.com/artist/howdy-forrester-mn0000230143.

65. "'Little' Roy Wiggins," Brad's Page of Steel, accessed June 8, 2014, http://www.well.com/~wellvis/wiggins.html.

66. Bill Clifton, letter to the author, postmarked December 21, 2009.

67. Ibid.

68. "Nation's Worst School Bus Tragedy Kills 23 Children," *Lima News* (Lima, Ohio), March 1, 1958, 1.

69. Adkins was a prolific songwriter who contributed a number of songs to bluegrass, including "Another Night" for the Stanley Brothers and "Windy Mountain" for the Lonesome Pine Fiddlers. An overview of his life can be found in Walter V. Saunders, "Notes & Queries," *Bluegrass Unlimited* 43 (September 2008): 21–26.

4. "How Mountain Girls Can Love": The Early King/Starday Years, 1958–1962

1. John Broven, *Record Makers and Breakers: Voices of the Independent Rock 'n' Roll Pioneers* (Urbana: University of Illinois Press, 2009), 288.

2. Quote of Bill Clifton in Rienk Janssen, liner notes to Bill Clifton, *Around the World to Poor Valley*, Bear Family BCD-16425 HK, 2001, 30.

3. "Don Pierce Named C&W Man of Year," *Billboard*, November 9, 1959, 22.

4. Gene Meadows, telephone interview with the author, September 16, 1978.

5. Ibid.

6. Ibid.

7. Joe Meadows, telephone interview with the author, ca. 1982.

8. Carter Stanley, comments on live show, as heard on Stanley Brothers, *Stanley Series*, vol. 3, no. 4. Copper Creek Records CCSS-V3N4, 1992.

9. Hal Neely, liner notes to Stanley Brothers, *Folk Concert*, King 834, 1963.

10. Ralph Stanley, *Man of Constant Sorrow: My Life and Times*, with Eddie Dean (New York, Gotham Books, 2009), 155.

11. Gordon and Burke were active in the mid- and late 1970s researching the careers of the Stanley Brothers and Ralph Stanley. Gordon hosted a series of teach-ins featuring Ralph Stanley at Lincoln Memorial University and was responsible for Ralph's honorary doctorate of arts award.

12. Al Elliott, interview with Douglas Gordon and Roy Burke III, Coeburn, Va., May 28, 1977.

13. Ibid.

14. Carter Stanley, comments on live show, as heard on Stanley Brothers, Stanley Series, vol. 3, no. 4. Copper Creek Records CCSS-V3N4, 1992.

15. D. K. Wilgus, "Record Reviews," *Journal of American Folklore* 72 (July–September 1959): 290; on-air commentary by Dick Spottswood on the *Dick Spottswood Show*, October 14, 2007.

16. Scott Fore, e-mail to the author, March 20, 2013.

17. Carter Stanley, comments on live show, Ash Grove, Hollywood, California, August 30, 1962, *The Legendary Stanley Brothers*, vol. 2, Rebel SLP-1495, 1970.

18. Ralph Stanley, interview with the author, ca. 1982.

19. Ibid.

20. Carl Story, radio interview with Gary Henderson, July 1, 1976.

21. Al Elliott, interview with Douglas Gordon and Roy Burke III, Coeburn, Va., May 28, 1977.

22. *Songs for Home Folks*, "By the Stanley Brothers" (ca. 1957), 9.

23. Chubby Anthony, undated letter to the author, postmarked October 25, 1977.

24. Bill Savitz, telephone interview with the author, January 22, 1985.

25. Cuddles Newsome, telephone interview with the author, ca. January 1983.

26. Bill Savitz, telephone interview with the author, January 22, 1985.

27. Chubby Anthony, undated letter to the author, postmarked October 25, 1977.

28. Ralph Stanley, quoted in Fred Bartenstein, "The Ralph Stanley Story: An Interview with Fred Bartenstein," *Muleskinner News* 2 (March 1972): 16.

29. George Shuffler, interview with the author, Valdese, N.C., October 13, 1977.

30. Wayne Erbsen, "Wiley & Zeke: The Morris Brothers," *Bluegrass Unlimited* 15 (August 1980): 48–49.

31. Carter Stanley, comments on unpublished recording of live show, Ash Grove, Hollywood, California, August 29, 1962.

32. Buddy Starcher, interview with the author, Harrisonburg, Va., October 17, 1993.

33. Jack Palmer, "'Grandpa' Jones," *In the Groove* (June 2000): 15.

34. Carter Stanley, interview with Mike Seeger, West Germany, March 1966.

35. Carter Stanley, comments on unpublished live show, New York University, New York, Nov. 30, 1962.

36. Ralph Rinzler, "Ralph Stanley: The Tradition from the Mountains," *Bluegrass Unlimited* 8 (March 1974): 11.

37. Carter Stanley, comments on unpublished live show, New York University, New York, November 30, 1962.

38. Quote of Lester Woodie in Wayne Erbsen, "Lester Woodie: Coming Up the Hard Road," *Bluegrass Unlimited* 14 (March 1980): 45.

39. Carter Stanley, interview with Mike Seeger, West Germany, March 1966.

40. George Shuffler, interview with the author, Valdese, N.C., October 13, 1977.

41. *Favorite Songs and Picture Album*, "As featured by the Stanley Brothers, your Radio Friends" (ca. 1951), 14.

42. Unsigned liner notes to Stanley Brothers, *Live at Antioch College*, Vintage Collectors Club ZK-002, ca. 1981.

43. Tom Rose, telephone interview with the author, October 10, 1981.

44. Carter inadvertently substituted "Shannon & Grayson" for "Grayson & Whitter." Shannon Grayson, a North Carolina banjo player, led a group known as the Golden Valley Boys and made recordings for RCA and King in the late 1940s and early 1950s.

45. Carter Stanley, comments on unpublished live show, Antioch College, Yellow Springs, Ohio, May 14, 1960.

46. *The Stanley Brothers Clinch Mountain Song Review* (ca. 1957), 5.

47. Norman Carlson, "Vernon Derrick," *Bluegrass Unlimited* 4 (December 1969): 10; and David Moore, "Vernon Derrick: Master Musician and Great Friend," *Arab Tribune*, January 9, 2008, 1.

48. Carter Stanley, as heard on Stanley Brothers, Stanley Series, vol. 2, no. 4, Copper Creek CCSS-V2N4, 1987.

49. Two unpublished live recordings of the Stanley Brothers performing this song are known to exist: one from *Jim Walter Jamboree*, program no. 24, ca. March 1960, and the other from an appearance at the Famous Restaurant in Washington, DC, on October 16, 1961.

50. George Shuffler, interview with the author, Valdese, N.C., October 13, 1977.

51. Ibid.

52. Ralph Stanley, "Hills of Home (A Tribute to Carter Stanley)," *Hills of Home*, King KSD-1069, 1969.

53. "King A. & R. Men, Branch Mgrs. Confab," *Billboard*, July 18, 1960, 4.

54. George Shuffler, interview with the author, Valdese, N.C., October 13, 1977.

55. Ibid.

56. Carter Stanley, comments on unpublished live show, Lake Whippoorwill, Warrenton, Va., August 28, 1960.

57. Curley Lambert, interview with the author, Douglas Gordon, and Roy Burke III, Coeburn, Va., May 28, 1977.

58. Teresa Martin Klaiber, "Come All You Tender Hearted," Eastern Kentucky Genealogy, accessed July 10, 2014, http://easternkentuckygenealogy.blogspot.com/2010/12/come-all-you-tender -hearted.html; Robert E. McCormack, "The Fire Tragedy," Cherry Tree, WV, accessed July 10, 2014, http://wp.cherrytreewv.com/2012/04/2891/?doing_wp_cron=1405010212.8246290683746 337890625.

59. Walt Saunders, "Notes & Queries," *Bluegrass Unlimited* 43 (November 2008): 14–16; Jean Thomas, *Ballad Makin' in the Mountains of Kentucky* (New York: Henry Holt and Company, 1939), 108–9.

60. Peter Siegel, liner notes to *FOTM Friends of Old Time Music*, Folkways FA-2390, 1964, 2.

61. Curley Lambert, interview with the author, Douglas Gordon, and Roy Burke III, Coeburn, Va., May 28. 1977.

62. Ralph Stanley, quoted in Chris Skinker, liner notes to Ralph Stanley and Friends, *Clinch Mountain Country*, Rebel Records 5001, 1998, 16.

63. Comments by Carter Stanley, preceding the Stanley Brothers' performance of "The Story of the Lawson Family" on *The Stanley Brothers: An Evening Long Ago*, Columbia/DMZ/Legacy CK-86747, 2004.

64. Dorothy Scarborough, *A Song Catcher in the Southern Mountains: American Folk Songs of British Ancestry* (New York: Columbia University Press, 1937), 322.

65. Mike Seeger, liner notes to *Mountain Music, Bluegrass Style*, Folkways FA-2318, 1959.

66. Dick Spottswood, e-mail to the author, April 22, 2013.

67. Alan Lomax, *The Folk Songs of North America in the English Language* (Garden City, N.J.: Doubleday & Company, Inc., 1960), 270.

68. Kyle Davis, Jr., *Folk-Songs of Virginia: A Descriptive Index and Classification* (Durham, N.C.: Duke University Press), 277.

69. George Shuffler, interview with the author, Valdese, N.C., October 13, 1977.

70. Stanley Brothers, *The Remarkable Stanley Brothers Play and Sing Bluegrass Songs for You,* Old Homestead-323, 1986.

71. Carter Stanley, comments on unpublished live show, Lake Whippoorwill, Warrenton, Virginia, August 28, 1960.

72. Stanley Brothers, *The Early Starday King Years 1958–1961*, Highland Music-7000, 2003.

73. Art Stamper, telephone interview with the author, February 4, 1982.

74. James Leva, e-mail to the author, April 3, 2013.

75. Basic biographical information for Chick Stripling can be found in Wayne W. Daniel, "Chick Stripling: Dancer, Comedian, and Old-Time Fiddler," *Bluegrass Unlimited* 28 (November 1993): 36–39.

76. Quote of Mike Seeger in Gary Reid, liner notes to Stanley Brothers, *Folk Festival*, Stanley-Tone ST-5003, 2001, 4.

77. Ibid.

78. Quote of Mike Seeger in ibid, 6.

79. Quote of Carter Stanley in ibid, 7.

80. Carter Stanley, interview with Mike Seeger, West Germany, March 1966.

81. Buell Kazee, "Little Bessie" and "My Mother," Brunswick BR-215, 1928).

82. Wayne Erbsen, *Rural Roots of Bluegrass* (Asheville, N.C.: Native Ground Music, 2003), 111; and Blue Sky Boys, "Little Bessie," Bluebird B-8017, 1938.

83. Carter Stanley, interview with Mike Seeger, West Germany, March 1966.

84. Quote by Bill Monroe in Douglas B. Green, liner notes to Bill Monroe and His Blue Grass Boys, *The Classic Bluegrass Recordings*, vol. 1, County CCS-104, 1980.

85. Lance Spencer, telephone interview with the author, December 28, 1993.

86. Ralph Stanley, interview with the author, December 18, 1993.

87. Ibid.

88. Quote of Bill Monroe in Alice Foster and Ralph Rinzler, liner notes to Bill Monroe & His Blue Grass Boys, *A Voice from On High*, Decca 5135, 1969.

89. John Nelson Clark Coggin, *Plantation Melodies and Spiritual Songs*, 3rd ed. (Philadelphia: Hall Mack Co., 1927), 88.

90. Quote of John Reedy in unsigned liner notes to *The Early Days of Bluegrass*, vol. 1, Rounder-1013, 1974, 6.

91. Charlie Monroe, *On the Noon-day Jamboree*, County ROU-538, 1974.

92. Rinzler, "Ralph Stanley: The Tradition from the Mountains," 11.

93. *American Folk & Country Music Festival*, Bear Family BCD-16849 BK, 2007.

94. Ralph Stanley, *Cry from the Cross*, Rebel SLP-1499, 1971.

95. Carter Stanley, comments on unpublished live show, Oak Leak Park, Luray, Virginia, July 4, 1961.

96. Ralph Stanley, interview with the author, December 18, 1993.

97. Norman Mable, *Popular Hymns and Their Writers*, rev. ed. (London: Independent Press, 1951), 43–45.

98. Quote of Ernest Moody in Gene Wiggins and Tony Russell, "Hell Broke Loose in Gordon County, Georgia," *Old Time Music* (Summer 1977): 11.

99. *Favorite Songs and Picture Album*, "As featured by the Stanley Brothers, your Radio Friends" (ca. 1951), 18.

100. Carter Stanley, comments on unpublished live show , New River Ranch, Rising Sun, Md., May 21, 1961.

101. Review of "Little Bessie," *Billboard*, May 15, 1961, 48.

102. George Shuffler, telephone interview with the author, January 16, 1985.

103. Monroe had harbored resentment against the group for their success with the style of music that he developed. For many years, Monroe led the only bluegrass-styled band on the *Grand Ole Opry*; he was livid when Flatt & Scruggs obtained membership on the program.

104. Ralph Stanley, interview with the author, December 18, 1993.

105. On-stage comment by Melvin Goins, as heard on Stanley Brothers, Stanley Series, vol. 1, no. 4, Copper Creek Records CCSSV1N4, 1984.

106. Carter Stanley, comments on unpublished live show, Famous Restaurant, Washington, DC, October 17, 1961.

107. Ralph Stanley, interview with the author, December 18, 1993.

108. Ibid.

109. *The Audience Pleased*, Oberlin Folk Music Club OCF-42-756, 1975.

110. Ralph Stanley, interview with the author, December 18, 1993.

111. James D. Vaughan, et al., *Hallelujahs—For Sunday-Schools, Singing-Schools, Revivals, Conventions and General Use in Christian Work and Worship* (Lawrenceburg, Tenn.: James D. Vaughan, 1922), 73.

112. Ralph Stanley, interview with the author, December 18, 1993.

113. Quote of Albert E. Brumley in Dorothy Horstman, *Sing Your Heart Out, Country Boy* (Nashville: Country Music Foundation Press, 1975), 49–50.

114. Ralph Stanley, interview with the author, December 18, 1993.

115. George Pullen Jackson, *White and Negro Spirituals: Their Life Span and Kinship, Tracing 200 Years of Untrammeled Song Making and Singing Among Our Country Folk, with 116 Songs as Sung by Both Races* (New York: J. J. Augustin, 1944), 221.

116. Delmore Brothers, *Songs We Sing*, 1937, 19.

117. Carter Stanley, comments on unpublished live show, Oberlin College, Oberlin, Ohio, March 17, 1962.

118. Ralph Stanley, interview with the author, December 18, 1993.

119. Hal Neely, liner notes to Stanley Brothers, *Folk Concert*, King KLP-834, 1963.

120. Dorothy Scarborough, *A Song Catcher in the Southern Mountains: American Folk Songs of British Ancestry* (New York: Columbia University Press, 1937), 366–72.

121. Wright Brothers "I Just Came from Your Wedding," Gold Leaf 45–106, released May 1960.

122. Chick Stripling, as heard on Stanley Brothers, *Folk Festival*, StanleyTone ST-5003, 2001.

123. Guthrie T. Meade Jr., Dick Spottswood, and Douglas S. Meade, *Country Music Sources: A Biblio-Discography of Commercially Recorded Traditional Music* (Chapel Hill: University of North Carolina Press, 2002), 443.

124. Ray Davis, *The Ray Davis Show*, WAMU-FM's BluegrassCountry.org, December 2, 2007.

125. Vernon Derrick, quoted in unsigned liner notes to Stanley Series, vol. 2, no. 4, Copper Creek CCSS-V2N4, 1987.

126. James Alan Shelton, e-mail to the author, May 9, 2010.

5. "Stone Walls and Steel Bars": The Later King Years, 1963–1966

1. Basic biographical information for Ray Pennington can be found in: Colin Larkin, *The Encyclopedia of Popular Music*, 3rd ed. (London: MUZE UK Ltd, 1998), 4187–88.

2. Chuck Seitz, telephone interview with the author, December 3, 1979.

3. Ralph Mayo, interview with Frankie Moore, March 4, 1981.

4. Carter Stanley, comments on unpublished live show, Ash Grove, Hollywood, California, August 29, 1962.

5. Hal Neely, liner notes to Stanley Brothers, *Folk Concert*, King KLP-834. 1963.

6. Ibid.

7. Ralph Stanley, interview with the author, December 18, 1993.

8. "Songwriters to Appear at the Music Center," *Winter Haven Daily News-Chief*, October 21, 1964, 2.

9. Carter Stanley, comments on unpublished live show, New York University, New York, November 30, 1962.

10. Neely, liner notes to *Folk Concert*.

11. Ralph Mayo, interview with Frankie Moore, March 4, 1981.

12. Carter Stanley, interview with Mike Seeger, West Germany, March 1966.

13. Ralph Stanley, interview with the author, December 18, 1993.

14. Ralph Stanley, interview with Fred Bartenstein on "Ralph Stanley Day," Camp Springs, North Carolina, Labor Day weekend, 1969.

15. Jere Hall and Robert L. Bailey, "The Killer Poet," Roane County Heritage Commission, accessed December 31, 2011, http://www.roanetnheritage.com/research/m&m/05.htm.

16. Charles Wolfe, "The Odyssey of Arthur Smith," *Bluegrass Unlimited* 13 (August 1978): 53.

17. Ralph Stanley, interview with the author, December 18, 1993.

18. Correspondence from Norm Carlson to Fay McGinnis, Walter Saunders, R. J. Ronald, and Nick Barr, October 26, 1969.

19. Ralph Mayo, interview with Frankie Moore, March 4, 1981.

20. "The Stanley Brothers," *Bluegrass Hornbook*, National Public Radio, WAMU-FM, July 1976.

21. Ralph Stanley, interview with the author, December 18, 1993.

22. Ralph Stanley, spoken intro to "Shout Little Lulie," *Ralph Stanley: A Man and His Music*, Rebel SLP-1530, 1974.

23. Ralph Stanley, interview with the author, December 18, 1993.

24. Ibid.

25. *Songs for Home Folks*, "By the Stanley Brothers" (ca. 1956), 7.

26. Tracy Schwarz, telephone interview with the author, ca. 2002.

27. Mike Seeger, telephone interview with the author, January 26, 1994.

28. Williams meant he thought the song was not worth keeping.

29. Benny Williams, telephone interview with the author, February 26, 1992.

30. Ralph Stanley, interview with the author, December 18, 1993.

31. Roland White, interview with the author, Owensboro, Ky., June 26, 2009.

32. Douglas B. Green, liner notes to Bill Monroe and His Blue Grass Boys, *The Classic Bluegrass Recordings*, vol. 1, County CCS-104, 1980.

33. Carter Stanley, comments on live show, Ash Grove, Hollywood, California, August 30, 1962, Stanley Brothers, Stanley Series, vol. 2, no. 4, Copper Creek CCSS-V2N4, 1987.

34. Dorothy Horstman, *Sing Your Heart Out, Country Boy*, rev. ed. (Nashville: Country Music Foundation Press, 1986), 48.

35. Ray Davis, *The Ray Davis Show*, WAMU-FM's BluegrassCountry.org, November 2, 2007.

36. Basic biographical information for Earl Taylor can be found in Tom Ewing, "Earl Taylor: One of the Bluegrass Greats," *Bluegrass Unlimited* 11 (September 1976): 10–14.

37. Ralph Stanley, interview with the author, December 18, 1993.

38. Blanton Owen, liner notes to *Virginia Traditions Ballads from British Tradition*, Blue Ridge Institute BRI-002, 1978, 11–12.

39. Rev. J. L. Sisk, et al, *Heartfelt Songs* (Toccoa, Georgia: Sisk Music Co., 1935), 98.

40. Dan Whittle, "Christmas Standard Birthed in Rutherford County Barn," *The Daily News Journal*, December 22, 1991, 1.

41. Mac Odell, telephone interview with the author, ca. January 1994.

42. J. Noble Moore, *Heaven's Song Parade No. 2* (Charleston, West Virginia: Moore's Publishing & Recording Company, 1954), 175.

43. PI is an abbreviation for "per inquiry," a type of advertising campaign in which a media outlet, in this case a radio station, receives a percentage of each sale of the merchandise that is being promoted, as opposed to a flat fee for a promotional campaign. In this instance, Paul Mullins assembled a various artists album that was sold on the radio on a "per inquiry" basis.

44. Paul Mullins, telephone interview with the author, January 24, 1994.

45. Bill Vernon, liner notes to Stanley Brothers, *The Stanley Brothers of Virginia*, vol. 1, *That Little Old Country Church House*, County 738, 1973.

46. Ray Davis, *The Ray Davis Show*, WAMU-FM's BluegrassCountry.org, September 3, 2008.

47. Ray Davis, *The Ray Davis Show*, WAMU-FM's BluegrassCountry.org, December 23, 2007.

48. In his notes to the County Records reissue of Wango 104, Bill Vernon indicates that the instrumentals appearing on the album were culled from radio shows that were made during the week in 1964 that this album was recorded. According to commentary by Ray Davis, at least one of the tunes, "Cluck Old Hen," was recorded at the sessions, specifically for the album. The other two instrumentals, "Wildwood Flower" and "Mountain Pickin'," were most likely pulled from the December 1963 radio shows.

49. Ray Davis, *The Ray Davis Show*, WAMU-FM's BluegrassCountry.org, December 23, 2007.

50. Ray Davis, *The Ray Davis Show*, WAMU-FM's BluegrassCountry.org, October 29, 2006.

51. Ray Davis, *The Ray Davis Show*, WAMU-FM's BluegrassCountry.org, December 9, 2009.

52. G. Malcolm Laws Jr., *Native American Balladry: A Descriptive Study and a Bibliographical Syllabus* (Philadelphia: The American Folklore Society, 1950), 217.

53. Ray Davis, *The Ray Davis Show*, WAMU-FM's BluegrassCountry.org, May 1, 2011.

54. Ray Davis, *The Ray Davis Show*, WAMU-FM's BluegrassCountry.org, July 9, 2008.

55. Carter Stanley, comments on transcribed radio program, Bristol, Va., ca. 1947, Stanley Brothers, *On WCYB Bristol*, Rebel REB-855, 1988.

56. Ray Davis, *The Ray Davis Show*, WAMU-FM's BluegrassCountry.org, November 29, 2009.

57. Ray Davis, *The Ray Davis Show*, WAMU-FM's BluegrassCountry.org, September 3, 2008.

58. Tracy Schwarz, "My Memories of the American Folk Festival," liner notes to *American Folk & Country Music Festival*, Bear Family BCD-16849, 2006, 24.

59. Charlie Monroe, as quoted in Charles Wolfe, liner notes to Bill Monroe, *Blue Moon of Kentucky, 1936–1949*, Bear Family BCD-16399, 2002, 11.

60. Ralph Stanley, interview with the author, December 18, 1993.

61. Ron Lenhoff, telephone interview with the author, December 3, 1979.

62. William Lynwood Montell, *Grassroots Music in the Upper Cumberland* (Knoxville: University of Tennessee Press, 2006), 205.

63. Barry Glickman, telephone interview with the author, August 19, 1977.

64. Ray Davis, *The Ray Davis Show*, WAMU-FM's BluegrassCountry.org, October 13, 2010.

65. Al Young, *Kinds of Blue: Musical Memoirs* (San Francisco: D. S. Ellis, 1984), 143.

66. Ralph Stanley, interview with Mike Seeger, Stockholm, Sweden, March 1966.

67. Ray Davis, *The Ray Davis Show*, WAMU-FM's BluegrassCountry.org, August 27, 2009.

68. Ralph Stanley, *Old Country Church*, Rebel SLP-1508, 1971.

69. Colin Escott, liner notes to *Best of Bluegrass: Preachin' Prayin' and Singin'*, Mercury 314-532 998-2, 1996.

70. Ray Davis, *The Ray Davis Show*, WAMU-FM's BluegrassCountry.org, December 2, 2009.

71. Ray Davis, *The Ray Davis Show*, WAMU-FM's BluegrassCountry.org, December 23, 2007.

72. Ibid.

73. Ray Davis, *The Ray Davis Show*, WAMU-FM's BluegrassCountry.org, February 15, 2009.

74. Ray Davis, *The Ray Davis Show*, WAMU-FM's BluegrassCountry.org, October 13, 2010.

75. Ray Davis, *The Ray Davis Show*, WAMU-FM's BluegrassCountry.org, December 2, 2009.

76. Ray Davis, *The Ray Davis Show*, WAMU-FM's BluegrassCountry.org, August 27, 2009.

77. "Arthur K. 'Sonny' Miller," *Bluegrass Unlimited* 16 (January 1982): 4.

78. Carter Stanley, interview with Mike Seeger, West Germany, March 1966.

79. Ralph Stanley, interview with the author, December 18, 1993.

80. Richard K. Spottswood, review of *Greatest Country and Western Show on Earth*, *Bluegrass Unlimited* 1 (August 1966): 5.

81. Carter Stanley, comments on live show, Brown County Jamboree, Bean Blossom, Indiana, October 16, 1966, Stanley Brothers, Stanley Series, vol. 1, no. 4, Copper Creek CCSS-V1N4, 1984.

82. George Pullen Jackson, *Spiritual Folk-Songs of Early America: Two Hundred and Fifty Tunes and Texts with an Introduction and Notes* (New York: J. J. Augustin, 1937), 219.

83. Ralph Stanley, interview with the author, December 18, 1993.

84. Ibid.

85. Because of the passing of Carter Stanley on December 1, 1966, the tour of Vietnam referenced here did not take place.

86. Carter Stanley, comments on live show, Brown County Jamboree, Bean Blossom, Indiana, October 16, 1966, Stanley Brothers, Stanley Series, vol. 1, no. 4, Copper Creek CCSS-V1N4, 1984.

87. Charles Wolfe, liner notes to *Kitty Wells: The Queen of Country Music*, Bear Family BCD-15638, 1993, 12.

88. Fay McGinnis, *Stanley Brothers Fan Club Newsletter*, November 1965, 1

89. Ralph Mayo, interview with Frankie Moore, March 4, 1981.

90. George Shuffler, interview with the author, Valdese, N.C., October 13, 1977.

91. Ray Davis, conversation with the author, Baltimore, Md., ca. summer 1977.

92. Loys Raney, letter to the author, November 23, 2009.

93. Ralph Stanley, liner notes to Stanley Brothers, *In Memory of Carter Stanley: "An Empty Mansion,"* Rimrock RLP 153, 1967.

94. Kim Field, "Wayne Raney," in *Encyclopedia of Country Music*, ed. Paul Kingsbury, 2nd ed. (New York: Oxford University Press, 2012), 429.

95. Bob Artis, *Bluegrass* (New York: Hawthorn Books, 1975), 38.

96. Basic biographical information for Melvin Goins can be found in Penny Parsons, "The Many Hats of Melvin Goins," *Bluegrass Unlimited* 43 (June 2009): 26–31.

97. Basic biographical information for Birch Monroe can be found in Neil V. Rosenberg, "A Front Porch Visit with Birch Monroe," *Bluegrass Unlimited* (September 1982): 58–63.

BIBLIOGRAPHY

Articles

"American Folk Tunes: Cowboy and Hillbilly Tunes and Tunesters." *Billboard*, October 4, 1947, 124.

"Arthur K. 'Sonny' Miller." *Bluegrass Unlimited* 16 (January 1982): 4.

Asbell, Bernie. "'D' Kilpatrick as C&W 'Man of Year.'" *Billboard*, November 17, 1958, 18, 22.

Bartenstein, Fred. "The Ralph Stanley Story: An Interview with Fred Bartenstein." *Muleskinner News* 2 (March 1972): 16.

Brower, Barry. "Making the Blend: The Jack Cooke Story." *Bluegrass Unlimited* 21 (January 1987): 55–57.

———. "Ralph Stanley: Keeping It Right Down and Simple." *Bluegrass Unlimited* 21 (February 1987): 13.

Cantwell, Bob. "The Lonesome Sound of Carter Stanley." *Bluegrass Unlimited* 10 (June 1976): 15.

Carlson, Norman. "Vernon Derrick." *Bluegrass Unlimited* 4 (December 1969): 10.

Cheatham, Russ. "Charlie & Lee Cline and the Lonesome Pine Fiddlers." *Bluegrass Unlimited* 14 (February 1980): 18–22.

Daniel, Wayne W. "Chick Stripling: Dancer, Comedian, and Old-Time Fiddler." *Bluegrass Unlimited* 28 (November 1993): 36–39.

"Don Pierce Named C&W Man of Year." *Billboard*, November 9, 1959, 22.

"Donald 'Chubby' Anthony." *Bluegrass Unlimited* 14 (March 1980).

Erbsen, Wayne. "Lester Woodie: Coming Up the Hard Road." *Bluegrass Unlimited* 14 (March 1980): 44–45.

———. "Wiley & Zeke: The Morris Brothers." *Bluegrass Unlimited* 15 (August 1980): 48–49.

Ewing, Tom. "Earl Taylor: One of the Bluegrass Greats." *Bluegrass Unlimited* 11 (September 1976): 10–14.

"General Store." *Bluegrass Unlimited* 14 (March 1980): 7.

"King A. & R. Men, Branch Mgrs. Confab." *Billboard*, July 18, 1960, 4.

McGinnis, Fay. Untitled Article. *Stanley Brothers Fan Club Newsletter*, November 1965, 1.

Mitchell, Larry. "Dr. Ralph Stanley!" *Pickin'* 4 (August 1977): 6.

Moore, David. "Vernon Derrick: Master Musician and Great Friend." *Arab Tribune*, January 9, 2008, 1 and 7.

Palmer, Jack. "'Grandpa' Jones." *In the Groove* (June 2000): 15.

Parsons, Penny. "Curly Seckler, Bluegrass Pioneer." *Bluegrass Unlimited* 38 (June 2004): 41.

———. "The Many Hats of Melvin Goins." *Bluegrass Unlimited* 43 (June 2009): 26–31.

Reid, Gary. "Mayo's the Name, Fiddlin's My Game: The Life and Times of Ralph Mayo." Unpublished manuscript, last modified July 17, 2012. Microsoft Word file.

Review of "Hard Times." *Billboard*, March 5, 1955, 34.

Review of "Hard Times." *Country & Western Jamboree* 1 (April 1955): 25.

Review of "Little Bessie." *Billboard*, May 15, 1961, 48.

Review of Mercury 71064. *Country & Western Jamboree* 3 (June 1957).

"Reviews of New C & W Records." *Billboard*, February 11, 1956, 43.

"Reviews of New C & W Records." *Billboard*, June 16, 1956, 45.

"Reviews of New C & W Records." *Billboard*, March 9, 1957, 59.

"Reviews of New Pop Records." *Billboard*, June 24, 1957, 56.

Rhodes, Don. "Make That Fiddle Sing! Chubby Anthony." *Bluegrass Unlimited* 13 (February 1979): 30–33.

Rinzler, Ralph. "Ralph Stanley: The Tradition from the Mountains." *Bluegrass Unlimited* 8 (March 1974): 8, 10–11.

Rosenberg, Neil V. "A Front Porch Visit with Birch Monroe." *Bluegrass Unlimited* 17 (September 1982): 58–63.

———. "From Sound to Style: The Emergence of Bluegrass." *Journal of American Folklore* 80 (April–June 1967): 146.

Saunders, Walter V. "Notes & Queries." *Bluegrass Unlimited* 43 (September 2008): 21–26.

———. "Notes & Queries." *Bluegrass Unlimited* 43 (November 2008): 14–16.

Sayers, Bob. "Leslie Keith: Black Mountain Odyssey." *Bluegrass Unlimited* 11 (December 1976): 16.

Sippel, Johnny. "Folk Talent and Tunes." *Billboard*, November 25, 1950, 29.

———. "Folk Talent and Tunes." *Billboard*, September 1, 1951, 30.

Spottswood, Dick. "Carl Sauceman: The Odyssey of a Bluegrass Pioneer." *Bluegrass Unlimited* 11 (August 1976): 15.

———. Review of *Greatest Country and Western Show on Earth*. *Bluegrass Unlimited* 1 (August 1966): 5.

Tribe, Ivan M. "Curley Lambert: Bluegrass Evergreen." *Bluegrass Unlimited* 10 (February 1976): 12–15.

———. "Joe Meadows: Mountain State Fiddler." *Bluegrass Unlimited* 13 (October 1978): 30–35.

———. "Sing Your Song: The Jimmy Williams Story." *Bluegrass Unlimited* 11 (June 1977): 28–32.

Whittle, Dan. "Christmas Standard Birthed in Rutherford County Barn." *The Daily News Journal*, December 22, 1991, 1.

Wiggins, Gene, and Tony Russell. "Hell Broke Loose in Gordon County, Georgia." *Old Time Music* (Summer 1977): 11.

Wilgus, D. K. "Record Reviews." *Journal of American Folklore* 72 (July–September 1959): 290.

Wolfe, Charles. "Bill Monroe." *Journal of the American Academy for the Preservation of Old-Time Country Music* 16 (August 1993): 8.

———. "The Odyssey of Arthur Smith." *Bluegrass Unlimited* 13 (August 1978): 53.

Zabelin, Leo. "Upsets Mark First Readers' Poll." *Country & Western Jamboree* (December 1955): 9.

Interviews

Clifton, Bill. Interview with the author. December 2, 2006.

Davis, Ray. Conversation with author. Baltimore, Md. ca. summer 1977.

Elliott, Al. Interview with Douglas Gordon and Roy Burke III. Coeburn, Va. May 28, 1977.

Glickman, Barry. Telephone interview with the author. August 19, 1977.

Hughes, Jay. Telephone interview with the author. Sept. 8, 1978.

Lambert, Curley. Interview with the author, Douglas Gordon, and Roy Burke III. Coeburn, Va. May 28, 1977.

Lenhoff, Ron. Telephone interview with the author. December 3, 1979.

Lowe, Bill. Interview with the author. Sykesville, Md. January 7, 1978.

Malone, Red. Telephone interview with the author. April 21, 1979.

Mayo, Ralph. Interview with Frankie Moore. March 4, 1981.

Meadows, Gene. Telephone interview with the author. September 16, 1978.

Meadows, Joe. Telephone interview with the author. ca. 1982.

Morris, Doug. Telephone interview with the author. July 22, 2009.

Mullins, Paul. Telephone interview with the author. January 24, 1994.

Napier, Bill. Interview with the author. Detroit, Mich. May 15, 1977.

Newsome, Cuddles. Telephone interview with the author. ca. January 1983.

Odell, Mac. Telephone interview with the author. ca. January 1994.

Osborne, Bobby. Telephone interview with the author. August 26, 1993.

Rose, Tom. Telephone interview with the author. October 10, 1981.

Savitz, Bill. Telephone interview with the author. January 22, 1985.

Schwarz, Tracy. Telephone interview with the author. ca. 2002.

Seeger, Mike. Telephone interview with the author. January 26, 1994.

Seitz, Chuck. Telephone interview with the author. December 3, 1979.

Shuffler, George. Interview with the author. Valdese, N.C. October 13, 1977.

———. Telephone interview with the author. January 16, 1985.

Shuffler, John. Telephone interview with the author. July 23, 2009.

Spencer, Lance. Telephone interview with the author. December 28, 1993.

Stamper, Art. Telephone interview with the author. February 4, 1982.

Stanley, Carter. Interview with Mike Seeger. West Germany. March 1966.

———. Interview with Pete Wernick. Fincastle, Va. Sept. 1965.

Stanley, Ralph. Interview with Charlie Sizemore. March 1981.

———. Interview with Fred Bartenstein. Camp Springs, N.C. Ralph Stanley Day, Labor Day Weekend, 1969.

———. Interview with Mike Seeger. Stockholm, Sweden. March 1966.

———. Interviews with the author. May 31, 1981; Glasgow, Del., September 6, 1981; ca. 1982; December 18, 1993; Troutville, Va., ca. 2007.

Stanton, Jim. Telephone interview with the author. ca. September 1978.

Starcher, Buddy. Interview with the author. Harrisonburg, Va. October 17, 1993.

Story, Carl. Radio interview with Gary Henderson. WAMU-FM, Washington, D.C. July 1, 1976.

Webb, Roy. Interview with the author. Bristol, Tenn. January 6, 2008.

White, Roland. Interview with the author. Owensboro, Ky. June 26, 2009.

Williams, Benny. Telephone interview with the author. February 26, 1992.

Woodie, Lester. Telephone interview with the author. March 26, 1981.

Albums / CDs / Liner Notes

American Folk and Country Music Festival. Bear Family BCD-16849 BK, 2007.

The Audience Pleased. Oberlin Folk Music Club OCF-42–756, 1975.

Blue Sky Boys. "Little Bessie." Bluebird B-8017, 1938.

Cain, Benny. Interview with Walt Saunders. Stanley Brothers, *Stanley Series*. Vol. 2, no. 1. Copper Creek CCSS-V2N1, 1984.

Escott, Colin. Liner notes to *Best of Bluegrass: Preachin' Prayin' and Singin'*. Mercury 314-532 998-2, 1996.

Folk Festival. StanleyTone ST 5003, 2001.

Foster, Alice, and Ralph Rinzler. Liner notes to Bill Monroe and His Blue Grass Boys, *A Voice from On High*. Decca-5135, 1969.

Gerrard, Alice. Liner notes to *Hazel Dickens & Alice Gerrard—Pioneering Women of Bluegrass*. Smithsonian Folkways SF CD 40065, 1996.

Green, Douglas B. Liner notes to Bill Monroe and His Blue Grass Boys, *The Classic Bluegrass Recordings*, Vol. 1. County CCS-104, 1980.

Janssen, Rienk. Liner notes to Bill Clifton, *Around the World to Poor Valley*. Bear Family BCD-16425 HK, 2001.

Kazee, Buell. "Little Bessie" and "My Mother." Brunswick BR-215, 1928.

Monroe, Charlie. *On the Noon-day Jamboree*. County-538, 1974.

Neely, Hal. Liner notes to Stanley Brothers, *Folk Concert*. King KLP-834, 1963.

Owen, Blanton. Liner notes to *Virginia Traditions Ballads from British Tradition*. Blue Ridge Institute BRI-002, 1978.

Reid, Gary. Liner notes to Stanley Brothers, *Old-Time Songs*. StanleyTone ST-5001, 1999.

———. Liner notes to Stanley Brothers, *Folk Festival*. StanleyTone ST 5003, 2001.

Samuelson, Dave. Liner notes to Stanley Brothers, *Stanley Series*. Vol. 4, no. 1. Copper Creek CCSS-5513, 1996.

Schwarz, Tracy. Liner notes to *American Folk & Country Music Festival*. Bear Family BCD-16849 BK, 2006.

Seeger, Mike. Liner notes to *Mountain Music, Bluegrass Style*. Folkways FA-2318, 1959.

Siegel, Peter. Liner notes to *FOTM Friends of Old Time Music*. Folkways FA-2390, 1964.

Skinker, Chris. Liner notes to Ralph Stanley and Friends, *Clinch Mountain Country*. Rebel REB-5001, 1998.

Stanley, Ralph. *Cry from the Cross*. Rebel SLP 1499, 1971.

———. "Hills of Home (A Tribute to Carter Stanley)." *Hills of Home*. King KSD-1069, 1969.

———. Liner notes to Stanley Brothers, *In Memory of Carter Stanley: An Empty Mansion*. Rimrock RLP 153, 1967.

———. *A Man and His Music*. Rebel SLP-1530, 1974.

———. *Old Country Church*. Rebel SLP-1508, 1971.

Stanley Brothers. *The Early Starday King Years 1958–1961*. Highland Music 7000, 2003.

———. *An Evening Long Ago*. Columbia/DMZ/Legacy CK-86747, 2004.

———. *Folk Festival*. StanleyTone ST-5003, 2001.

———. *The Legendary Stanley Brothers*. Vol. 2. Rebel SLP-1495, 1970.

———. *The Remarkable Stanley Brothers Play and Sing Bluegrass Songs for You*. Old Homestead OHCS-323, 1986.

———. *The Stanley Brothers and the Clinch Mountain Boys*. Vol. 1. Mercury FDX-9063–4, 1974.

———. *The Stanley Brothers and the Clinch Mountain Boys*. Vol. 2. CBS Sony 20AP 13, 1976.

———. *Stanley Series*. Vol. 1, no. 4. Copper Creek CCSS-V1N4, 1984.

———. *Stanley Series*. Vol. 2, no. 4. Copper Creek CCSS-V2N4, 1987.

———. *Stanley Series*. Vol. 3, no. 4. Copper Creek CCSS-V3N4, 1992.

Tottle, Jack. Liner notes to *Live Again! WCYB Bristol Farm and Fun Time*. Rebel REB-854, 1988.

———. Liner notes to Stanley Brothers, *The Stanley Brothers on WCYB Bristol*. Rebel REB-855, 1988.

Unsigned. Liner notes to Leslie Keith, *Black Mountain Blues*. Briar BF-4201, 1974.

———. Liner notes to *The Early Days of Bluegrass*. Vol. 1. Rounder ROU-1013, 1974.

———. Liner notes to *Live at Antioch College*. Vintage Collectors Club ZK-002, ca. 1981.

———. Liner notes to *The Rich-R-Tone Story: The Early Days of Bluegrass*. Vol. 5. Rounder ROU-1017, 1974.

———. Liner notes to Stanley Brothers, *Stanley Series*. Vol. 1, no. 1. Copper Creek CCSS-V1N1, 1982.

———. Liner notes to Stanley Brothers, *Stanley Series*. Vol. 1, no. 2. Copper Creek CCSS-V1N2, 1982.

———. Liner notes to Stanley Brothers, *Stanley Series*. Vol. 1, no. 3. Copper Creek CCSS-V1N3, 1982.

———. Liner notes to Stanley Brothers, *Stanley Series*. Vol. 2, no. 4. Copper Creek CCSS V2N4, 1987.

Vernon, Bill. Liner notes to Stanley Brothers, *The Stanley Brothers of Virginia*, Vol. 1, *That Little Old Country Church House*. County CO-738, 1973.

Wolfe, Charles. Liner notes to Bill Monroe, *Blue Moon of Kentucky, 1936–1949*. Bear Family BCD-16399, 2002.

———. Liner notes to Kitty Wells, *The Queen of Country Music*. Bear Family BCD-15638, 1993.

Wright Brothers. "I Just Came from Your Wedding." Gold Leaf 45–106, 1960.

Books

Artis, Bob. *Bluegrass*. New York: Hawthorn Books, 1975.

Broven, John. *Record Makers and Breakers: Voices of the Independent Rock 'n' Roll Pioneers*. Urbana: University of Illinois Press, 2009.

Coggin, John Nelson Clark. *Plantation Melodies and Spiritual Songs*. 3rd ed. Philadelphia: Hall Mack, 1927.

Davis, Kyle, Jr. *Folk-Songs of Virginia: A Descriptive Index and Classification*. Durham, N.C.: Duke University Press, 1949.

Delmore Brothers. *Songs We Sing*. 1937.

Erbsen, Wayne. *Rural Roots of Bluegrass*. Asheville, N.C.: Native Ground Music, 2003.

Favorite Songs and Picture Album. "As featured by the Stanley Brothers, your Radio Friends." ca. 1951.

Field, Kim. "Wayne Raney." In *Encyclopedia of Country Music*, 412. Edited by Paul Kingsbury. 2nd edition. New York: Oxford University Press, 2012.

Horstman, Dorothy. *Sing Your Heart Out, Country Boy*. Nashville: Country Music Foundation Press, 1986.

Jackson, George Pullen. *Spiritual Folk-Songs of Early America: Two Hundred and Fifty Tunes and Texts with an Introduction and Notes*. New York: J. J. Augustin, 1937.

———. *White and Negro Spirituals: Their Life Span and Kinship, Tracing 200 Years of Untrammeled Song Making and Singing Among Our Country Folk, with 116 Songs as Sung by Both Races*. New York: J. J. Augustin, 1944.

Johnson, David W. *Lonesome Melodies: The Lives and Music of the Stanley Brothers*. Jackson: University Press of Mississippi, 2013.

Kosser, Michael. *How Nashville Became Music City, U.S.A.: 50 Years of Music Row*. Milwaukee: Hal Leonard Corporation, 2006.

Larkin, Colin. *The Encyclopedia of Popular Music*. 3rd ed. London: MUZE UK Ltd, 1998.

Laws, G. Malcolm, Jr. *Native American Balladry: A Descriptive Study and a Bibliographical Syllabus*. Philadelphia: The American Folklore Society, 1950.

Lomax, Alan. *The Folk Songs of North America in the English Language*. Garden City, N.J.: Doubleday & Company, Inc., 1960.

Mable, Norman. *Popular Hymns and Their Writers*. Rev. ed. London: Independent Press, 1951.

Malone, Bill. *Country Music U. S. A.: A Fifty-Year History*. Austin: University of Texas Press, 1968.

Meade, Guthrie T., Jr., Dick Spottswood, and Douglas S. Meade. *Country Music Sources: A Biblio-Discography of Commercially Recorded Traditional Music*. Chapel Hill: University of North Carolina Press, 2002.

Montell, William Lynwood. *Grassroots Music in the Upper Cumberland*. Knoxville: University of Tennessee Press, 2006.

Moore, J. Noble. *Heaven's Song Parade No. 2*. Charleston, W. Va.: Moore's Publishing & Recording Company, 1954.

Pierce, Don. "A Biography on the Stanley Brothers." *The Stanley Brothers Clinch Mountain Song Review*. ca. 1957.

Puryear, Robert Barton III. *Border Forays and Adventures, From the Manuscripts of Lyman Copeland Draper and the Wisconsin Historical Society*. Westminster, Md.: Heritage Books, 2007.

Rosenberg, Neil V. *Bluegrass: A History*. Urbana: University of Illinois Press, 1985.

Rosenberg, Neil V., and Charles K. Wolfe. *The Music of Bill Monroe*. Urbana: University of Illinois Press, 2007.

Russell, Fran. *Stanley Brothers . . . and the Clinch Mountain Boys*. ca. 1955.

Scarborough, Dorothy. *A Song Catcher in the Southern Mountains: American Folk Songs of British Ancestry*. New York: Columbia University Press, 1937.

Sisk, Rev. J. L., et al. *Heartfelt Songs*. Toccoa, Ga.: Sisk Music, 1935.

Songs for Home Folks. "By the Stanley Brothers." ca. 1956.

Stanley, Ralph. *Man of Constant Sorrow: My Life and Times*. With Eddie Dean. New York: Gotham Books, 2009.

The Stanley Brothers and the Clinch Mountain Boys: Picture and Song Favorites. Folio No. 2. ca. 1949.

The Stanley Brothers Clinch Mountain Song Review. ca. 1957.

The Stanley Brothers: Your Favorite Songs. Folio No. 1. ca. 1947.

Thomas, Jean. *Ballad Makin' in the Mountains of Kentucky.* New York: Henry Holt and Company, 1939.

Vaughan, James D., et al, *Hallelujahs—For Sunday-Schools, Singing-Schools, Revivals, Conventions and General Use in Christian Work and Worship.* Lawrenceburg, Tenn.: James D. Vaughan, 1922.

Trott, Walt. "Ernie Newton." In *Encyclopedia of Country Music.* Edited by Paul Kingsbury. New York: Oxford University Press, 1998. 360.

———. "Lightnin' Chance." In *Encyclopedia of Country Music.* Edited by Paul Kingsbury. New York: Oxford University Press, 1998. 90.

Young, Al. *Kinds of Blue: Musical Memoirs.* San Francisco: D. S. Ellis, 1984.

Electronic Records

Army enlistment record for Carter G. Stanley. World War II Army Enlistment Records Data File, ca. 1938–1946, Record Group 64. College Park, Md.: National Archives and Records Administration. Accessed December 13, 2011, www.aad.archives.gov.

Gary Reid, "2005 Inductee—Benjamin Edward 'Benny' Martin." International Bluegrass Music Museum. Accessed June 11, 2014, http://bluegrassmuseum.org./hall-of-fame/2005-inductee-benjamin-edward-benny-martin.

"Howdy Forrester: Artist Biography." AllMusic.com. Accessed June 11, 2014, www.allmusic.com/artist/howdy-forrester-mn0000230143.

"James C. Petrillo." *WTTW.com.* Accessed July 4, 2014, http://www.wttw.com/main.taf?p=1,7,1,1,38.

Jere Hall and Robert L. Bailey. "The Killer Poet." Roane County Heritage Commission. Accessed December 31, 2011, http://www.roanetnheritage.com/research/m&m/05.htm.

Klaiber, Teresa Martin. "Come All You Tender Hearted." Eastern Kentucky Genealogy. Accessed July 10, 2014, http://easternkentuckygenealogy.blogspot.com/2010/12/come-all-you-tender-hearted.html.

"'Little' Roy Wiggins." Brad's Page of Steel. Accessed June 8, 2014, http://www.well.com/~wellvis/wiggins.html.

McCormack, Robert E. "The Fire Tragedy." Cherry Tree, WV. Accessed July 10, 2014, http://wp.cherrytreewv.com/2012/04/2891/?doing_wp_cron=1405010212.8246290683746337890625.

Monroe, Bill. "Out in the Cold World" [partial home recording]. 1944. Accessed July 4, 2014, http://www.youtube.com/watch?v=Qg62FL2ioFk.

"RCA Victor—1525 McGavock St." Scotty Moore: The Official Website. Accessed June 8, 2014, http://www.scottymoore.net/studio_mcgavock.html.

Newspapers

"At the 71 Drive-In Theatre," *Northwest Arkansas Times,* July 5, 1951, 11.

The Cecil Democrat, advertisement for concert at New River Ranch, July 5, 1951, 6.

The Cecil Democrat, advertisement for concert at New River Ranch, June 30, 1955, 7.

Charleston Daily Mail, radio listing, May 23, 1952, 8.

Danville Bee (Va.), advertisement, August 13, 1955, 10.

Danville Bee (Va.), advertisement, November 12, 1955, 13.

Huntington Herald-Dispatch, radio listing, July 3, 1950, 16.

"Man Killed in Crash on Shirley Hwy." *The Washington Post,* September 25, 1964, C1.

Nashville Tennessean, radio listing, July 07, 1951, 10.

The Lexington Herald, advertisement, October 28, 1950, 9.

The Lexington Herald, radio listing, April 5, 1952, 8.

"Nation's Worst School Bus Tragedy Kills 23 Children." *Lima News* (Lima, Ohio), March 1, 1958, 1.

"New Radio Station on Air Here Today." *Bristol Herald Courier*, December 13, 1946, 6.

The News and Observer, radio listing, July 5, 1948, 3.

The Pikeville Daily News, radio listing, April 15, 1952, 7.

The Pikeville Daily News, radio listing, April 30, 1952, 7.

Richmond Times-Dispatch, advertisement, March 9, 1955, 15.

Richmond Times-Dispatch, advertisement, April 9, 1955, 9.

Shreveport Times, radio listing, October 9, 1950, 8.

Shreveport Times, radio listing, October 25, 1950, 9.

"Songwriters to Appear at the Music Center." *Winter Haven Daily News-Chief*, October 21, 1964, 2.

Correspondence

Anthony, Chubby, undated letter to the author, postmarked October 25, 1977.

Carlson, Norm, correspondence to Fay McGinnis, Walter Saunders, R. J. Ronald, and Nick Barr, October 26, 1969.

Clifton, Bill, letter to the author, postmarked December 21, 2009.

Fore, Scott, e-mail to the author, March 20, 2013.

Leva, James, e-mail to the author, April 3, 2013.

Raney, Loys, letter to the author, November 23, 2009.

Rosenberg, Neil V., e-mail to the author, November 11, 2009.

Shelton, James Alan, e-mail to the author, May 9, 2010.

Spottswood, Dick, e-mail to the author, April 22, 2013.

Radio Broadcasts

Davis, Ray. *The Ray Davis Show*. WAMU-FM's BluegrassCountry.org, October 29, 2006; November 2, 2007; December 2, 2007; December 23, 2007; July 9, 2008; September 3, 2008; February 15, 2009; August 27, 2009; November 29, 2009; December 2, 2009; December 9, 2009; October 13, 2010; May 1, 2011.

Spottswood, Dick. *The Dick Spottswood Show*. WAMU-FM's BluegrassCountry.org, October 14, 2007.

"The Stanley Brothers." *Bluegrass Hornbook*. National Public Radio. WAMU-FM. July 1976.

GENERAL INDEX

Bristol, Va./Tenn., 6, 13, 16, 20, 21, 23, 33, 35, 46, 61, 63; Birthplace of Country Music Museum, 4; Bristol Sessions, 4, 33; *Farm & Fun Time*, 5, 11, 17, 22, 25, 232; Flatt & Scruggs, 23, 59; Leslie Keith, 9; Curly King, 68, 69; Red Malone, 63, 98; radio, 101, 135, 173; Rhythm and Roots festival, 4; Stanley Brothers headquarters, 10, 30, 40, 93; Willow Branch Quartet, 109, 110. *See also* WCYB; WOPI

Brown, Frankie, 167, 201

Brown, Hylo, 110

Brown, James, 90

Brown County, Ind., 52, 57

Brown County Jamboree: Marvin Hedrick, 53; Bill Monroe, 53, 57, 197, 199; recordings made at, 74, 222, 224, 233; Stanley Brothers performances at, 46, 50, 88, 197, 199

Brown County Jamboree, 233

Browns Ferry Four, 177, 179, 210

Brumley, Albert E., 113; "Campin' in Canaan Land," 124; "Hold Fast to the Right," 182; hymnal, 188, 189; "If We Never Meet Again," 133, 146, 162; "I'll Fly Away," 132, 161; "Nobody Answered Me," 188; "Rank Stranger," 109, 110, 214; Stamps-Baxter, 181; "When He Reached Down His Hand for Me," 160

Burke, Roy, III, 91, 95, 243n11

Busby, Buzz, 53

Bush, Roger, 134, 162, 163, 164

Cabin Creek, 190, 217, 218, 226

Cain, Benny, 59, 60

Callahan Brothers, 11, 88, 102

Campbell, Alex, 52, 173, 190, 191, 217

Candler Enterprises. *See* Samuel Candler Enterprises

Caney Ridge, Va., 103

Capitol Records, 40, 41, 56, 165, 176

Carlisle, Bill, 167

Carlisles, 41, 87

Carolina Buddies, 117

Carolina Jamboree, 50

Carson, Fiddlin' John, 4

Carter, A. P., 33, 38, 82, 83, 114, 124, 202

Carter, Mother Maybelle, 63, 169

Carter, Sara, 81

Carter County, Ky., 115

Carter Family, 167; border radio, 2; Bristol Sessions, 4; influence on Stanley Brothers, 7, 103 —songs: "Are You Tired of Me, Darling," 114; "Can the Circle Be Unbroken," 177; "East Virginia Blues," 181; "Happy in Prison," 186; "I Know What It Means to Be Lonesome," 121; "Just Another Broken Heart," 65, 68; "Let the Church Roll On," 110; "Let Us Be Lovers Again," 117; "Little Darlin', Pal of Mine," 169; "Little Joe," 119; "Meet Me by the Moonlight," 60, 99; "The Storms Are on the Ocean," 91; "Sweet Fern," 133; "Two More Years," 181; "The Wandering Boy," 33; "Weeping Willow," 103; "When I Lay My Burden Down," 186; "Where We'll Never Grow Old," 130; "Wildwood Flower," 114, 150; "Will the Circle Be Unbroken," 177; "Will You Miss Me," 176; "Working on a Building," 124

Carter Sisters, 63

Cartwright, Hoss, 134

Cartwright, Little Joe, 134

Cash, Johnny, 55

Cassady, Ed, 196

Castle Studio, 23, 27, 28, 36, 37, 38, 41

Chance, Floyd "Lightnin'," 45, 49, 71, 72

Chapman, Steve, 202

Charles, Ray, 124

Charleston, W.Va., 194

Charlie Monroe's Boys, 178

Charlotte, N.C., 41, 95

Charlottesville, Va., 129, 160

Chatzky, Carl, 89, 135, 158, 164

Checker, Chubby, 119

Chicago, Ill.: Larry Ehrlich, 58; Mercury Records, 40, 42; Monroe Brothers, 198; Stanley Brothers recordings made at, 152, 153, 216; Ray Tate, 189; WLS, 27. *See also* University of Chicago Folk Festival

Christian Choruses, 95

Christian Way, 103

Christmas Songs, 230

Church Brothers, 6, 98

Cincinnati, Ohio: Church of the Redeemer, 131; "Come All Ye Tenderhearted," 116; Emery Theater, 50; finger poppers, 114; "How Can We Thank Him for What He Has Done,"

95; King recording studio, 91; King Records; 90, 92, 166; Mount Storm Park, 94; Wayne Raney, 195; Stanley Brothers recording at, 93, 111, 170, 184, 191; Stanley Brothers sessions at, 139, 140, 142, 143, 150, 151, 154, 155, 158–162, 201–203, 210, 211, 213, 218, 219; Earl Taylor, 176; Temple of Love, 97; WCKY, 115, 189, 185

Clark, Johnny, 62

Classic Bluegrass Collection, 234

Clear, Lindy: Antioch College, 107, 146; bio, 57; live performances, 65; Melody Ranch, 81; New River Ranch, 56, 61, 73, 74, 78, 79, 147; Newport Folk Festival, 100, 142; Shipps Park, 60, 77; Silver Creek Ranch, 80; Valley View Park, 82

Clifton, Bill: Blue Ridge, 98; Bluegrass Day, 134; Charlottesville, Va., 129, 130, 160; Curley Lambert, 58; Mercury-Starday, 83, 86; Oak Leaf Park, 126, 127; Ralph Stanley, 62, 68; Starday, 61, 68, 81; "Thinking of the Old Days," 64, 68, 82

Clinch Mountain, 4

Clinch Mountain Bluegrass, 186, 234

Clinch Mountain Boys, 30, 31; American Folk & Country Music Festival, 197; Bear Family Records, 225; break-up of band, 40; Central Sun Video, 226; Charlie Cline, 46; Jack Cooke, 65; Henry Dockery, 170; King Records, 93, 230; Curley Lambert, 58; Pee Wee Lambert, 7; Bill Lowe, 46; naming of band 4; Bill Napier, 65; New River Ranch, 56; Reno & Smiley, 169; Curly Seckler, 32; Shenandoah Valley Bowl, 60; George Shuffler, 32; University of Chicago Folk Festival, 120; Frank Wakefield, 65; Lester Woodie, 104; "You Go to Your Church," 68

Clinch Mountain Gospel, 178

Clinch Mountain Quartet, 22, 68

Clinch Mountain Song Review, 88

Clinch Valley Insurance, 3

Cline, Charlie, 31, 46, 47, 48, 49, 72

Cline, Curly Ray, 46

Cline, Ezra, 46

Cline, Ned, 46

Clintwood, Va., 1, 27

Cohen, John, 172, 178, 197, 221

Cohen, Paul, 38

Collection of Orignal [sic] Gospel & Sacred Songs, A, 192, 230

Columbia Records, 1, 20, 40, 86; 1st session, 23, 25, 36; 2nd session, 26, 37; 3rd session, 28, 37; 4th session, 32, 38; Roy Acuff, 125, 128, 188; *An Evening Long Ago*, 59; Harold and Owen Bradley, 58; Wilma Lee & Stoney Cooper, 132; Flatt & Scruggs, 131; "Gathering Flowers for the Master's Bouquet," 111, 187; "Hey! Hey! Hey!" 117; "I'm a Man of Constant Sorrow," 29, 103; Pee Wee Lambert, 64; Don Law, 27; "Let Me Be Your Friend," 25; "Let's Part the Best of Friends," 33; "A Life of Sorrow," 32, 67, 68; listing of releases, 226; "The Little Glass of Wine," 24, 25, 34; "The Lonesome River," 29; Masters Family, 60; Bill Monroe, 12, 15, 47, 54, 95, 123, 175, 199; Molly O'Day, 119; "Pretty Polly," 180; Bill & Mary Reid, 58; Rounder Records, 232; Art Satherley, 20, 21, 27; George Shuffler, 28; Carter Stanley, 30; Stanley Brothers signed contract with, 21, 35; Carter Stanley's songs, 23; "Sweet Thing," 102; trio sound, 22, 24, 60, 32; "The White Dove," 24, 95

Columbia Sessions, 1949–'50, Vol. 1, 232

Columbia Sessions, Vol. 2, 232

Columbia/DMZ/Legacy, 59

Columbus, Ga., 106

Como, Miss., 45

Complete Columbia Stanley Brothers, The, 226

Complete Mercury Recordings, The, 231

Cooke, Jack: bio, 65; Cabin Creek Records, 190, 217, 218; "Cookie Bird," 189; "Farther Along," 189; Front Royal, 82; Barry Glickman, 186; "Little Old Country Church House," 188; live recordings, 65; Melody Ranch, 82; New River Ranch, 82, 126, 129, 155, 158, 159; "Shake Hands with Mother Again," 189; Sunset Park, 69, 83, 84; Wango Records, 175, 186, 210, 215, 216; Mac Wiseman, 186

Coon Creek Girls, 35

Cooper, Wilma Lee & Stoney, 6, 132

Copas, Cowboy, 66, 101, 102, 104

Copper Creek Records: Ash Grove, 135, 162, 163; Bean Blossom, 198, 224; Front Royal, Va., 82; Lamar Grier, 55; listing of releases, 226, 227; Melody Ranch, 81, 82; New River

Ranch, 61, 73, 78, 82, 89, 108, 126, 137, 147, 153; Oak Leaf Park, 127, 136; Oberlin College, 130, 160; Mike Seeger, 55; *Shadows of the Past*, 61, 130; Shenandoah Valley Bowl, 60, 87; Shipps Park, 60, 77; Silver Creek Ranch, 61, 80; Sunset Park, 83; Valley View Park, 82. *See also* Stanley Series

Country and Western Jamboree magazine, 48, 49, 56

Country Boys, 134

Country Folk Music Spotlight, 67, 133, 169, 170, 171, 230

Country Gentlemen, 65, 70, 89, 127, 130

Country Music Association, 41, 126

Country Music Foundation, 4, 197

Country Music Hall of Fame, 66

Country Music, U.S.A., 7

Country Pickin' and Singin', 58, 70, 231

County Records: "Big Tilda," 118; *Country Folk Music Spotlight*, 133; *Jim Walter Jamboree*, 144; listing of releases, 227; Stanley Brothers, 248n48

Cousin Emmy, 35, 172, 196, 221

Crockett, Davy, 56

Crosby, Bing, 52

Crosby, Fanny J., 104, 143, 182

Crosby, Stills, Nash, and Young, 124

Crudup, Arthur, 73

Curtis Artist Productions, 119

Cyp Landreneau's Cajun Band, 196

Daffan, Ted, 167

Daily, Harold W. "Pappy," 62, 81, 86

Davis, Gussie L., 97

Davis, Jimmie, 103, 143, 180, 181

Davis, Ray: Baltimore, 30; bio, 173; Christmas party, 174; *Good Old Camp Meeting Songs*, 134; Johnny's Used Cars, 134; King Records, 134; New River Ranch, 30; "Pig in the Pen," 168; radio shows, 173; Rimrock Records, 195; session #1, 173, 204–209; session #2, 174, 209; session #3, 174–176, 210; session #4, 180–183, 211–212, 248n48; session #5, 186–189, 215–216; "Sugar Coated Love," 30; Wango Records, 12, 173; WBMD, 56, 174

Davis, Smokey, 30, 42

Day, James W., 116

Dean, Eddie, 41

Dean, Jimmy, 55

Decca Records, 40; Owen Bradley, 41, Callahan Brothers, 11; Bill Carlisle, 167; Carter Family, 65; listing of Decca releases, 227; "The Little Girl and the Dreadful Snake," 34; Benny Martin, 66; Jimmy Martin, 176; Bill Monroe, 95, 124, 167, 170, 173, 185; Webb Pierce, 124; Shelton Brothers, 166; Carter Stanley sessions with Bill Monroe, 30–31, 38, 127, 167; "Sweet Thing," 102

Dee, Buddy, 51, 81, 83

Definitive Stanley Brothers, 1947–1966, The, 57, 127, 135, 234

Delmore Brothers, 2, 90, 128, 132, 166, 168, 170, 195

Delmore, Alton, 128, 179, 211

Delmore, Rabon, 179

Denny, Jim, 49

Department of Health, Education, and Welfare, 227

Derrick, Vernon: Ash Grove, 134–135, 162–164; bio, 111; "Come All Ye Tenderhearted," 116; *Folk Concert*, 167, 201; *In Person*, 111, 150; New York University, 135, 164; *Old Time Camp Meeting*, 122–123, 154–155; University of Chicago Folk Festival, 120–122, 152–154

Derricks, Cleavant, 50, 73, 77, 175

Dickens, Hazel, 53, 5

Dickens, Little Jimmy, 63

Dickenson County, Va.: "Dickenson County Breakdown," 44, 71, 73, 76, 77, 78, 80, 83, 84, 137, 138, 231; "The Drunkard's Hell," 27; Gene Duty, 193; Spencer Brothers, 123, 124; Stanley Brothers, 1, 4, 62; "Tragic Love," 51; "Train 45," 93; "Wild Bill Jones," 118

Disc Collector magazine, 89

Dixie Entertainers, 99

Dockery, Henry: *America's Finest 5-String Banjo Hootenanny*, 170, 202; bio, 170; *Country Folk Music Spotlight*, 170, 202, 203; Wango session #1, 174, 204–209; Wango session #2, 209; Wango session #3, 174–176, 210

Down from the Mountain (tour), 178

Dred, or the Dismal Swamp, 169

Duffey, John, 83

Duty, Gene, 193, 194, 219

Dylan, Bob, 98

Powhatan, Chief, 58
Presley, Elvis, 46, 47, 50, 66, 167
Price, Albert, 80, 163
Price, Melvin, 56
Price, Ray, 61
Primitive Baptist church, 2, 175
Primitive Baptist Hymnal, 125
Puckett, Riley, 99
Pure Country, 55

Quonset hut studio, 57, 66

Radio Series, Vols. 1–7, 174, 235
Rager, Lyman, 175
Rainbow Quest, 196, 225
Rakes, Ruby: pseudonym 91; songs credited
    to, 139–145, 147, 155–157, 162, 163, 202, 214;
    "Suwannee River Hoedown," 95
Raleigh, N.C., 20, 21, 35, 59
Raney, Loys, 195
Raney, Wayne, 115, 116, 150, 189, 194, 195, 219,
    220
Rank Strangers, 234
RCA Records, 40; Shannon Grayson, 244n44;
    Lonesome Pine Fiddlers, 198; Benny Martin,
    66; Ray Pennington, 165; Jim Reeves, 112;
    Carl Sauceman, 16; Stanley Brothers, 16, 20;
    Porter Wagoner, 198
RCA Studio: Chet Atkins, 50; Bill Clifton,
    62, 68, 81, 83; Mercury session #6, 50, 72;
    Mercury session #10, 64, 81; Mercury session
    #11, 66, 82, 83; Bob Moore, 50; Steve Shoals,
    50
Rebel Records: Ash Grove, 164; Brown County
    Jamboree, 222; Cabin Creek, 190; Char-
    lottesville, Va., 160; "Cluck Old Hen," 181;
    "The Cry from the Cross," 60; *Farm & Fun
    Time*, 10, 11, 17, 36; "Give Me the Roses,"
    187; *The Legendary Stanley Brothers*, 60, 89,
    107, 108, 127, 130, 135, 199; listing of releases,
    232; *Live Again!*, 25, 26, 232; "Oh Death,"
    178; *On WCYB Bristol*, 11, 17; "Shout Little
    Lulie," 170; *Together for the Last Time*, 60, 115,
    197; "Village Church Yard," 125; Watermelon
    Park, 157; "Will He Wait a Little Longer," 58
Recorded Live at Vanderbilt University, 131
Red River School, 199

Redd, Gene, 114, 166, 201
Redding, Otis, 119
Reed, Ola Belle, 190, 191
Reed's Record Store, 30
Reedy, John, 124, 125, 178, 211
Reeves, Jim, 112, 113
Reid, Bill & Mary, 26, 45, 58, 88
*Remarkable Stanley Brothers Play and Sing Blue-
    grass Songs for You, The*, 128, 183, 230
Renfro Valley Barn Dance, 129
Reno, Don, 32, 66, 169, 190, 202
Reno, Ronnie, 169, 202
Reno & Smiley, 53, 128, 129, 165, 169, 172, 184,
    186
Revenant Records, 232
Rice, Tony, 134
Rich, Fred, 104
Richmond, Va., 49, 58, 126
Rich-R-Tone Records, 6, 40; "Are You Waiting
    Just for Me," 60; "The Jealous Lover," 12;
    "Little Birdie," 168; listing of releases, 232;
    "The Little Glass of Wine," 24, 25; "Our
    Darling's Gone," 11, 184; Rounder Records,
    232; Carl Sauceman, 16; session #1, 7–10, 17;
    session #2, 13–14, 18; session #3, 14, 16, 18,
    19; session #4, 33–35, 38, 39; Stanley Brothers,
    6; Jim Stanton, 6; transition to bluegrass, 7, 16
Riddle, Leslie, 121
Riding That New River Train, 129, 233
Rimrock Records, 194, 195, 196, 219, 220, 232
Rinzler, Ralph, 6, 172, 185; Friends of Old Time
    Music, 172; Newport Folk Festival, 185;
    Ralph Stanley, 6
Rising Sun, Md., 30, 46, 50, 147, 155, 158
Ritchie, Jean, 118
Ritter Lumber Company, 13
Roane County, Tenn., 168
Roanoke, Va., 30, 133, 169, 202
Robinson, Russ, 7
Rodgers, Jimmie, 4
Rogers, Fey, 5
Roll, Larry, 68
Rome, Ga., 43
Roosevelt, Franklin D., 12
Rose, Enoch, 103
Rose, Fred, 76
Rose, Tom, 108

Rose, Wesley, 62

Rosenberg, Neil V., 15, 48

Rosine, Ky., 198

Rounder Records, 21, 232

Rouse, Ervin T., 73, 76, 80, 143, 145

Rouse, Gordon, 73, 76, 80, 143

Rowe, James, 182, 187

Rural Rhythm Records, 169, 232

Russell, Roy, 46

Ryman Auditorium, 67

Sacramento, Calif., 134

Sacred Songs from the Hills, 110, 234

Samuel Candler Enterprises, 106, 144

San Jose, Calif., 134

Satherley, Arthur "Uncle Art," 20, 21, 27, 36

Sauceman, Carl, 16, 43

Sauceman Brothers, 5

Saunders, Walter V., 98, 199

Savitz, Bill, 96, 97, 98

Scarborough, Estel Lee, 46, 97, 141, 145

Schwarz, Tracy: American Folk & Country Music Festival, 197; Bear Family Records, 221; Melody Mountain Boys, 53; "Pretty Little Miss in the Garden," 171, 172; "Sunny Side of Life," 182

Scott, Jim, 128, 158

Scriven, Joseph, 111

Scruggs, Earl, 1, 6, 12, 15, 16, 127, 134, 175

Scruggs, Louise, 127

Seckler, Curly, 32

Seeger, Charles, 52

Seeger, Mike: American Folk & Country Music Festival, 222; Antioch College, 107, 146; bio, 52; Larry Ehrlich, 121; Jeremy Foster, 53; Friends of Old Time Music, 120; Lamar Grier, 54; "Little Willie," 118; *Mountain Music Bluegrass Style*, 118; New River Ranch, 56, 61, 73; Newport Folk Festival, 185; Oak Leaf Park, 127, 157; "Pretty Little Miss," 172; interviews with Carter and Ralph Stanley, 5; Chick Stripling, 121, 122; "Sunny Side of Life," 182; taping in 1957, 64; University of Chicago Folk Festival, 120, 152, 153

Seeger, Pete, 100, 127, 196, 221, 226

Seitz, Charles L. "Chuck": *Folk Concert*, 152; *Folk Song Festival*, 158, 159; *Good Old Camp Meeting Songs*, 160–162; "He Went to Sleep and the Hogs Ate Him," 166; "I Don't Want Your Rambling Letters," 166; *In Person*, 150; *Sing the Songs They Like Best*, 151

Seldom Scene, 127

Selph, Jimmy, 68, 83

Setters, Jilson, 116

Shadows of the Past, 53, 61, 64, 130, 226

Shanachie, 220, 221, 233

Sharp, Cecil, 118

Shelton, B. F., 37

Shelton, Bob, 166, 201

Shelton, James Alan, 134

Shelton, Joe, 166, 201

Shelton Brothers, 166, 167

Shenandoah Valley Bowl, 59, 60

Shipps Park, 60

Shoals, Steve, 50

Shouns, Tenn., 110

Shreveport, La., 28, 33, 35, 43

Shuffler, George: Bean Blossom, 57, 74, 197, 198, 222–224; bio, 32; Castle Studio, 28; Charlottesville, Va., 129, 130, 160; Bill Clifton, 62, 81, 129, 130, 160; Columbia session #4, 32, 38; German television, 221; Idaho Falls, Idaho, 61; Lexington, Ky., 32; Mercury session #1, 41, 42, 71; Mercury session #10, 64, 81; New River Ranch, 126, 129, 155, 156, 158, 159; Newport Folk Festival, 184, 185, 213, 214; Oak Leaf Park, 127, 156, 157; Oberlin College, 160; Rich-R-Tone session #4, 33; Rimrock Records, 195, 219, 220; Wango session #1, 174, 204–209; Wango session #2, 174, 209; Wango session #3, 174–176, 210; Wango session #4, 180, 181, 183, 211, 212; Wango session #5, 187; Watermelon Park, 127, 157

—songs and recordings: *American Folk & Country Music Festival*, 221, 222; *America's Finest 5-String Banjo Hootenanny*, 170, 172, 202, 203; *A Collection of Orignal [sic] Gospel & Sacred Songs*, 191, 192, 218, 219; "Come All Ye Tenderhearted," 116, 150; *Country Folk Music Spotlight*, 170, 172, 202, 203; *Everybody's Country Favorites*, 101, 142, 143; "The Flood," 63, 81; *Folk Song Festival*, 116, 117, 128, 129, 152, 159, 160; *For the Good People*, 143, 144; *Good Old Camp Meeting Songs*, 130, 160–162;

Webster Brothers, 43, 108

Wells, Kitty, 66, 117

Westendorf, Thomas P., 133

Westmoreland, Paul, 152

Wheeling, W.Va., 88, 102, 132, 190, 191

When the Saints Go Marching In, 131

White, Clarence, 134

Whitley, Keith, 178

Whitman, Slim, 28

Whitter, Henry, 13, 25, 110, 119, 135

Wiggins, Little Roy, 66, 67, 82–83

Wilbanks, John, 173, 174

Wilder Lounge, 160

Wilkins, Marijohn, 155

Williams, Benny, 88, 172, 173, 185, 203

Williams, E. P., 68, 83

Williams, Hank, 110, 127, 157, 187

Williams, Hank, Jr., 112

Williams, Hank, III, 112

Williams, Jim: "Big Tilda," 58; bio, 33; Bill Lowe, 46; Mercury session #1, 41, 42, 71; Mercury session #2, 43, 71; Mercury session #3, 45, 71, 72; Mercury session #6, 50, 72, 73; Bill Napier, 65; New River Ranch, 56, 73, 74; Rich-R-Tone session #4, 33, 39

Williams, Paul, 33

Williams, Tex, 30

Williamson, Dixie Lee, 168

Willis Brothers, 67

Willow Branch Quartet, 109, 110

Wilmington, Del., 217

Wiltshire, Bill, 62, 81

Winsett, R. E., 132, 182

Winston-Salem, N.C., 26, 28, 35

Wise, Chubby, 54, 101, 142, 145, 156, 186

Wise, Va., 65

Wise County, Va., 61

Wiseman, Mac: Blue Grass Day at Oak Leaf Park, 127; Brown County Jamboree, 53; Jack Cooke, 186; Vernon Derrick, 111; *Farm & Fun Time*, 5; Barry Glickman, 186; Marvin Hedrick, 53; Ralph Mayo, 43; Bill Monroe, 12; "Shackles and Chains," 103; Red Stanley, 185; "Two More Years and I'll Be Free," 181; Benny Williams, 172; Jim Williams, 33

Wiseman, Scott, 142, 147, 157

WJHL, 3

WJXT, 96, 112

WKGW, 130

WKDE, 26

WKOY, 198

WLAC, 45

WLBC, 185

WLEX, 28

WLS, 27

WLSI, 7, 33, 34, 38–39, 198

WNER, 93, 96, 99, 105, 106, 111, 141, 144, 150

WNJU-TV, 220

WNOX, 8, 194

WNVA, 3

WOAY, 33, 40

Wolfe, Charles, 168

Woodie, Lester: background info, 26; Castle Studio, 27; Columbia session #2, 26, 27, 37; Columbia session #3, 29, 30, 37; "Hard Times," 48, 49; "Over in the Glory Land," 104; George Shuffler, 32; John Shuffler, 32, 43; Bobby Sumner, 26; Slim Whitman, 28; WTOB, 28

Wooten, Art, 21; bio, 14, 15; Columbia session #4, 32, 38; Bill Lowe, 46; Rich-R-Tone session #3, 15, 16, 18; Carter Stanley, trio sound, 23

WOPI, 7, 17, 69

WORK, 56

World of Folk Music Starring Oscar Brand, The, 190, 227

World War II: Bailes Brothers, 194; Bristol, 4; "Lightnin'" Chance, 45; "Filipino Baby," 93; Howdy Forrester, 66; Leslie Keith, 9; D. Kilpatrick, 41; Pee Wee Lambert, 7; Red Malone, 63; Jack Mullin, 52; "Searching for a Soldier's Grave," 194; Red Stanley, 184; Stanley Brothers, 3; Art Wooten, 15

WPTF, 20

Wright, Johnnie, 125, 151, 194

Wright, Len, 97, 141, 145

Wright, Tommy, 97

Wright Brothers, 97, 133

WRVA, 49

WSAZ, 28, 30

WSB, 112, 120

WSM, 2, 28, 41, 45, 62, 115, 189, 195

WTCR, 179

WTOB, 26, 28
WVLK, 32
WWVA *Jamboree*, 88, 102, 132, 190, 191, 195

XEPN, 195

Y'All Come, Have a Country Christmas, 111
Yates, Bill, 196
Yates, Wayne, 196
Yellow Springs, Ohio, 53, 57, 107, 146

York, William: "Beneath the Maple," 141; "Choo Choo Coming," 142; "Come All Ye Tender-hearted," 150; "Corey," 83; "Don't Go Out Tonight," 149; "Gathering Flowers for the Master's Bouquet," 149; "I Saw the Light," 149; "I'm Ready to Go," 149; "In Heaven We'll Never Grow Old," 144; "Let the Church Roll On" 149; "Little Maggie," 149, 214; Don Pierce, 106; "Rank Stranger," 149; "Rock of Ages," 149; "What a Friend," 149

SONG INDEX

"Gathering Flowers for the Master's Bouquet," 24, 36, 111, 149, 182, 215, 226, 233

"Gathering Flowers from the Hillside," 62, 81, 142, 174, 204, 206, 233

"Get Down on Your Knees and Pray," 31, 38, 227

"Girl Behind the Bar, The," 9, 10, 17, 232

"Give Me the Roses While I Live," 187, 215

"Give Me Your Hand," 189, 215

"Glory Land Way, The," 218

"God Gave You to Me," 108, 109, 148, 149, 158, 204, 207, 233

"God's Highway," 192, 193, 218, 229

"Going to Georgia," 61, 80, 207

"Going to the Races," 64, 65, 70, 82, 84, 88

"Gonna Paint the Town," 65, 88, 89, 94, 121, 137, 140, 147, 152, 233

"Good Ole Mountain Dew." *See* "Mountain Dew"

"Goodbye Old Pal," 12, 18

"Ground Hog," 203

"Hallelujah, We Shall Rise," 132, 161

"Hand in Hand with Jesus," 134, 162, 220

"Handsome Molly," 75, 119, 139, 152

"Happy Birthday," 159

"Happy in Prison," 186

"Happy, Sunny Side of Life," 182

"Harbor of Love," 48, 72, 132, 161, 231

"Hard Times," 48, 49, 72, 74, 76, 78, 79, 84, 136, 163, 164, 185, 213, 214, 231

"Have You Someone (in Heaven Awaiting)," 36, 226

"He Said If I Be Lifted Up," 94, 95, 140, 230

"He Went to Sleep and the Hogs Ate Him," 166, 167, 201, 205, 229

"Heaven," 107, 145

"Heaven Bells Are Ringing," 132

"Heaven Seemed So Near," 91, 139, 228, 229

"Heavenly Light Is Shining On Me," 132, 209

"Heaven's Light Is Shining On Me," 132, 161, 218

"He'll Save Your Soul Yet," 192, 218

"He'll Set Your Fields on Fire," 70, 85, 108, 145, 148

"Here Today and Gone Tomorrow," 64, 82

"He's Passing Along This Way," 179

"He's Passing This Way," 179, 211, 229

"Hey! Hey! Hey!" 29, 37, 117, 151, 226

"Hide You in the Blood," 189, 215

"Highway Ambush," 229

"Highway of Regret," 98, 141, 233

"Hills of Roan County, The," 70, 84, 168, 201, 229

"Hold Fast to the Right," 181, 182, 212, 218, 234

"Hold to God's Unchanging Hand," 186, 215, 220

"Holiday Pickin'," 88, 137, 233

"Home Sweet Home," 147, 156, 169, 202

"How About You," 218

"How Bad I Do Feel," 184, 213, 229

"How Beautiful Heaven Must Be," 179, 211, 219

"How Can We Thank Him for What He Has Done," 95, 140, 228, 229

"How Far to Little Rock," 104, 105, 121, 122, 144, 145, 147, 148, 152, 154, 159, 163, 206, 223, 228

"How Mountain Girls Can Love," 86, 89, 90, 91, 107, 111, 126, 130, 135, 138, 139, 142, 144, 146, 155, 159, 160, 162, 185, 190, 197, 209, 214, 216, 217, 221, 228, 229

"How You've Tortured My Mind," 184, 213, 229

"Husband's Dream, The," 133

"I Am a Pilgrim," 175, 210

"I Believed in You, Darling," 60, 76

"I Can Tell You the Time," 9, 17, 232

"I Cried Again," 207

"I Don't Want Your Rambling Letters," 166, 201, 229

"I Feel Like Going Home," 192, 194, 218, 229

"I Feel Like Traveling On," 217

"I Hear a Voice Callin'." *See* "Voice from on High, A"

"I Hear My Savior Calling," 50, 72, 231

"I Heard My Mother Call My Name in Prayer," 124, 188, 215

"I Hope You Have Learned," 64, 82

"I Just Came from Your Wedding," 133, 161, 228

"I Just Dropped By," 178, 211

"I Just Got Wise," 60, 72, 77, 79, 84, 231

"I Just Stood There," 169, 173, 204, 229

"I Know What It Means to be Lonesome," 121, 152, 198, 206, 224

"I Long to See the Old Folks," 44, 71, 137, 231

"I Love No One but You," 27, 37, 226

"I Need the Prayers," 217

Gary Reid is the founder and head of Copper Creek Records, a label specializing in bluegrass and old-time music, and is a three-time winner of the International Bluegrass Music Award for best liner notes.

MUSIC IN AMERICAN LIFE

The University of Illinois Press
is a founding member of the
Association of American University Presses.

———————————————————————

Designed by Dustin J. Hubbart
Composed in 10.5/14 Bembo
with LHF Country Road display
by Jim Proefrock
at the University of Illinois Press
Manufactured by Sheridan Books, Inc.

University of Illinois Press
1325 South Oak Street
Champaign, IL 61820-6903
www.press.uillinois.edu